Worldwide Acclaim for Sudoku

"Diabolically addictive."
  —*New York Post*

"A puzzling global phenomenon."
  —*The Economist*

"The biggest craze to hit *The Times* since the first crossword puzzle was published in 1935."
  —*The Times* of London

"The latest craze in games."
  —BBC News

"Sudoku is dangerous stuff. Forget work and family—think papers hurled across the room and industrial-sized blobs of correction fluid. I love it!"
  —*The Times* of London

"Sudoku are to the first decade of the twenty-first century what Rubik's Cube was to the 1970s."
  —*The Daily Telegraph*

"Britain has a new addiction. Hunched over newspapers on crowded subway trains, sneaking secret peeks in the office, a puzzle-crazy nation is trying to slot numbers into small checkerboard grids."
  —Associated Press

"Forget crosswords."
  —*The Christian Science Monitor*

Will Shortz Presents
The Super-Colossal
SUDOKU CHALLENGE

Also Available

Sudoku Easy Presented by Will Shortz, Volume 1

Sudoku Easy to Hard Presented by Will Shortz, Volume 2

Sudoku Easy to Hard Presented by Will Shortz, Volume 3

The Ultimate Sudoku Challenge Presented by Will Shortz

Sudoku for Your Coffee Break Presented by Will Shortz

Sudoku to Boost Your Brainpower Presented by Will Shortz

Will Shortz Presents Sun, Sand, and Sudoku

Will Shortz's Favorite Sudoku Variations

Will Shortz Presents Simple Sudoku, Volume 1

Will Shortz Presents Sudoku for Stress Relief

Will Shortz Presents Sudoku for Your Bedside

Will Shortz Presents Quick Sudoku, Volume 1

Will Shortz Presents Easiest Sudoku

Will Shortz Presents Fitness for the Mind Sudoku

Will Shortz Presents Sudoku for a Sunday Morning

Will Shortz Presents Sudoku for a Lazy Afternoon

Will Shortz Presents the First World Sudoku Championships

Will Shortz Presents Simply Sudoku, Volume 2

Will Shortz Presents the Monster Book of Sudoku for Kids

Will Shortz Presents Stress-Buster Sudoku

Will Shortz Presents Sudoku for Your Vacation

Will Shortz Presents Ultra Easy Sudoku

Will Shortz Presents Ready, Set, Sudoku

Will Shortz Presents Sudoku for Dads

Will Shortz Presents Sudoku for Your Lunch Hour

Will Shortz Presents Sudoku by the Sea

Will Shortz Presents Coffee, Tea or Sudoku

Will Shortz Presents Starter Sudoku

Will Shortz Presents Jungle Book of Sudoku for Kids

Will Shortz Presents the Joy of Sudoku

Will Shortz Presents Rise and Shine Sudoku

Will Shortz Presents Seduced by Sudoku

Will Shortz Presents Let's Play Sudoku: Take it Easy

Will Shortz Presents Let's Play Sudoku: Middle of the Road

Will Shortz Presents Let's Play Sudoku: Over the Edge

Will Shortz Presents The Little Flip Book of Sudoku

Will Shortz Presents Puzzles from the World Sudoku Championship

Will Shortz Presents Sudoku for 365 Days

Will Shortz Presents Sleepless with Sudoku

Will Shortz Presents Easy Afternoon Sudoku

Will Shortz Presents Sudoku to Soothe Your Soul

Will Shortz Presents Beyond Sudoku

Will Shortz Presents Tame Sudoku

Will Shortz Presents Wild Sudoku

Will Shortz Presents Ferocious Sudoku

Will Shortz Presents Sun, Surf and Sudoku

Will Shortz Presents 1,001 Sudoku Puzzles To Do Right Now

Will Shortz Presents Every Day Sudoku

Will Shortz Presents Stress-Free Sudoku

Will Shortz Presents Single Scoop Sudoku

Will Shortz Presents Double Dip Sudoku

Will Shortz Presents Triple Threat Sudoku

Will Shortz Presents The Little Luxe Book of Sudoku

Will Shortz Presents Life Lessons From Sudoku

Will Shortz Presents the Double Flip Book of New York Times Crosswords and Sudoku

Will Shortz Presents To Do Sudoku

Will Shortz Presents Simply Sneaky Sudoku

Will Shortz Presents Simply Scary Sudoku

Will Shortz Presents Simply Sinister Sudoku

Will Shortz Presents The Dangerous Book of Sudoku

Will Shortz Presents Coffee Break Sudoku

Will Shortz Presents Sudoku to Exercise Your Brain

Will Shortz Presents Sudoku for the Weekend

Will Shortz Presents Quick Sudoku Volume 1

Will Shortz Presents Tough Sudoku

Will Shortz Presents Treacherous Sudoku

Will Shortz Presents Terrifying Sudoku

Will Shortz Presents Cup o'Joe Sudoku

Will Shortz Presents
The Super-Colossal
SUDOKU CHALLENGE

300 WORDLESS CROSSWORD PUZZLES

EDITED BY
WILL SHORTZ

PUZZLES BY
PZZL.COM

ST. MARTIN'S GRIFFIN
NEW YORK

Some of the puzzles in this volume have previously appeared in *Will Shortz Presents Coffee and Sudoku* and *Will Shortz Presents Sudoku for a Brain Workout*.

WILL SHORTZ PRESENTS THE SUPER-COLOSSAL SUDOKU CHALLENGE. Copyright © 2010 by Will Shortz. All rights reserved. Printed in the United States of America. For information, address St. Martin's Press, 175 Fifth Avenue, New York, N.Y. 10010.

www.stmartins.com

ISBN 978-0-312-60793-7

First Edition: April 2010

10   9   8   7   6   5   4   3   2   1

Introduction

Throughout the history of puzzles and games, many of the biggest successes have come as complete surprises, because they've broken all the "rules."

Parker Bros. Famously turned down the rights to the game Monopoly in 1934, because it had "52 design errors." It was too complicated, they said, it had too many pieces, and it took too long to play. So the inventor, Charles B. Darrow, produced and sold 5,000 handmade copies of Monopoly, they quickly sold out, and—once Parker Bros. finally bought the rights—it became the biggest game hit of 1935.

Similarly, the "experts" initially pooh-poohed Scrabble, Trivial Pursuit, crossword puzzles, and many other game and puzzle successes over the years.

Hardly anyone thought sudoku would be popular when it was introduced in Britain in late 2004 and the U.S. in 2005. The public was not interested in number puzzles, according to conventional wisdom. Yet we all know what happened. In less than a year sudoku has become one of the most popular puzzles in history. Virtually every newspaper has made room for a daily sudoku, sudoku books have been bestsellers for six straight months, and sudoku tournaments have been held across the country and around the world. Language Report named "sudoku" the Word of the Year for 2005.

The craze goes on, and, to everyone's surprise, shows little sign of abating.

What's So Great About Sudoku?

The appeal of sudoku comes partly from the simplicity of the rules, which can be stated in a single sentence, and the compactness of the grid, just 9×9 squares—combined with some unexpectedly subtle logic. Even long-time enthusiasts may not understand all the techniques needed to work it. Sudoku packs a lot of punch for so small a feature.

Sudoku is a flexible puzzle. It can be easy, medium, or hard, which you can select according to your skills and mood. And the amount of time needed to solve one—generally between 10 and 30 minutes, for most people for most puzzles—is about perfect in order to feed a daily addiction. If sudoku took less time, it wouldn't pose enough challenge, and if it took more, you might lose interest or simply not be able to fit sudoku into your schedule.

Like crosswords, sudoku puzzles have blank squares that are inviting to fill in. It's said nature abhors a vacuum. We as human beings seem to have a natural compulsion to fill up empty spaces. A sudoku addict has difficulty turning a page that has empty puzzle squares begging to be completed.

Sudoku also provides an appealing rhythm of solving. Generally the first few numbers are easy to enter. Then, in the harder examples at least, you can get stymied and maybe a bit frustrated. Once you make the critical breakthrough (or breakthroughs), though, the final numbers can come quickly, giving you a rush and a heady sense of achievement—often tempting you to start another sudoku immediately. Hence the addictiveness of sudoku, which is the "crack cocaine" of puzzles.

New Challenges

On the following pages are 300 absolutely top quality sudoku puzzles rated Light and Easy (#1-50); Moderate (#51-100); Demanding (#101-175); and Beware! Very Challenging (#176-300). Every one has been checked, rechecked, and then re-rechecked to ensure that it has a unique solution, and that it can be solved using step-by-step logic. You never have to guess here.

As usual, all the puzzles in this book were created by my colleague Peter Ritmeester and the staff of PZZL.com.

Try them. And as one correspondent wrote me recently, you, too, will go "sudoku kuku."

—Will Shortz

How to Solve Sudoku

A sudoku puzzle consists of a 9 × 9-square grid subdivided into nine 3 × 3 boxes. Some of the squares contain numbers. The object is to fill in the remaining squares so that every row, every column, and every 3 × 3 box contains each of the numbers from 1 to 9 exactly once.

Solving a sudoku puzzle involves pure logic. No guesswork is needed—or even desirable. Getting started involves mastering just a few simple techniques.

Take the example on this page (in which we've labeled the nine 3 × 3 boxes A to I as shown). Note that the boxes H and I already have 8's filled in, but box G does not. Can you determine where the 8 goes here?

5	8	6					1	2
			5	2	8	6		
2	4		8	1				3
			5		3		9	
			8	1	2	4		
4		5	6			7	3	8
	5		2	3			8	1
7				8				
3	6			5				

A	B	C
D	E	F
G	H	I

The 8 can't appear in the top row of squares in box G, because an 8 already appears in the top row of I—and no number can be repeated in a row. Similarly, it can't appear in the middle row of G, because an 8 already appears in the middle row of H. So, by process of elimination, an 8 must appear in the bottom row of G. Since only one square in this row is empty—next to the 3 and 6—you have your first answer. Fill in an 8 to the right of the 6.

Next, look in the three left-hand boxes of the grid, A, D, and G. An 8 appears in both A and G (the latter being the one you just entered). In box A, the 8 appears in the middle column, while in G the 8 appears on the right. By elimination, in box D, an 8 must go in the leftmost column. But which square? The column here has two squares open.

The answer is forced by box E. Here an 8 appears in the middle row. This means an 8 cannot appear in the middle row of D. Therefore, it must appear in the top row of the leftmost column of D. You have your second answer.

In solving a sudoku, build on the answers you've filled in as far as possible—left, right, up, and down—before moving on.

For a different kind of logic, consider the sixth row of numbers—4, ?, 5, 6, ?, ?, 7, 3, 8. The missing numbers must be 1, 2, and 9, in some order. The sixth square can't be a 1, because box E already has a 1. And it can't be a 2, because a 2 already appears in the sixth column in box B. So the sixth square in the sixth row has to be a 9. Fill this in.

Now you're left with just 1 and 2 for the empty squares of this row. The fifth square can't be a 1, because box E already has a 1. So the fifth square must be a 2. The second square, by elimination, has a 1. Voilà! Your first complete row is filled in.

Box E now has only two empty squares, so this is a good spot to consider next. Only the 4 and 7 remain to be filled in. The leftmost square of the middle row can't be a 4, because a 4 already appears in this row in box F. So it must be 7. The remaining square must be 4. Your first complete box is done.

One more tip, and then you're on your own.

Consider 3's in the boxes A, B, and C. Only one 3 is filled in—in the ninth row, in box C. In box A you don't have enough information to fill in a 3 yet. However, you know the 3 can't appear in A's bottom row, because 3 appears in the bottom row of C. And it can't appear in the top row, because that row is already done. Therefore, it must appear in the middle row. Which square you don't know yet. But now, by elimination, you do know that in box B a 3 must appear in the top row. Specifically, it must appear in the fourth column, because 3's already appear in the fifth and sixth columns of E and H. Fill this in.

Following logic, using these and other techniques left for you to discover, you can work your way around the grid, filling in the rest of the missing numbers. The complete solution is shown below.

5	8	6	3	7	4	9	1	2
1	3	7	9	5	2	8	6	4
2	4	9	8	1	6	5	7	3
8	7	2	5	4	3	1	9	6
6	9	3	7	8	1	2	4	5
4	1	5	6	2	9	7	3	8
9	5	4	2	3	7	6	8	1
7	2	1	4	6	8	3	5	9
3	6	8	1	9	5	4	2	7

Remember, don't guess. Be careful not to repeat a number where you shouldn't, because a wrong answer may force you to start over. And don't give up. Soon you'll be a sudoku master!

Like Sudoku?
You'll Love KenKen!™

"The most addictive puzzle since sudoku." —Will Shortz

How to Solve:

1. Fill in #s so that each # appears once and only once in each row and column.
2. In each thickly lined block, the target #, shown in the top left corner, must be calculated from all #s in the block using the symbols shown (+/−/÷/×).

Example:

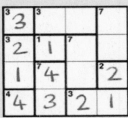

Try KenKen!

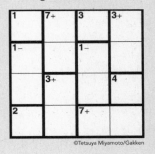

©Tetsuya Miyamoto/Gakken

Will Shortz Presents
KenKen

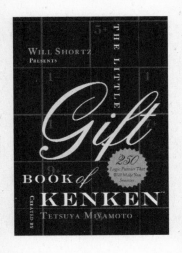

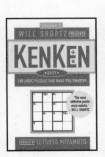

7	2	3	1				9	
5	6	9	2		7		8	
				3	9			5
			7		4			3
3		1	8					9
4	8				2			
	9	5						8
	3				1	9	7	4
1			9	6			3	

4			8		9			2
2	8	9	1				4	
	1					8		9
				1	8		3	
1	3		4	9				5
		4		2			8	
8					4	1	5	
	2				1		6	3
6			5		7		9	8

	1					2		9
	4	5			9	3		
6		7		1	2	8	5	
	6	1				4		
	3			2		9		
7		9		4		6	3	1
		6	2		7		4	8
1				5			9	3
4		3	8				6	2

4 Light and Easy

				5			9	8
7			3	9	1			4
9			4		8			5
8	5	7	2	3	4			
	2				9		5	
	1	9			7	3	4	2
		3	1		2	4	8	
2	9							
	4		9				2	

	2	8	9				7	
1	5		6				8	
7				5				2
2			7	3	6	8		9
4	7					5	1	
			4	1		2		
3		1	5		7			
5					4			
9	8		3	2		4	5	

Light and Easy

2	4			5	9		1	
	7		1	2	3	4	5	6
	6		8					
8	1					3	7	
						6		2
	2				5		4	
4	9			3	6	5		
	3		5		8		6	
		6	9		7	1		

				3			2	
	3				9	8		6
2	4	8	6	7		5		
				6				
	9	4						1
8		6	4			7		
	8		3	9		1		
4							7	5
9	7	2		5		6		

						5		6
9			8				3	1
		1	3		7		9	
				2			6	
	8		1			4	2	5
			6			9		
		6		3	1		5	8
1	3	8		5		6		9
	2	9			6	3		4

8	3	1	7	5				
4				8		3		9
6	9		3					7
			2	3	6	4		
5			9			2	7	3
3				4			9	6
	1	6			5			
7	4	3	1				6	
	5	8		6		7		

		7		1	4	8		
						3	7	4
4				3	7	1	2	
		9		2	1	4	6	8
7	6				3			5
	4				9	2		
	1		3		5			
5							8	3
	7		6	4		5	9	1

	7	1			6			8
5	3		2	7	1	4		
9		6					1	
				8	5			
1			7	3				4
3	4			6	2		7	
		3	8	2			9	
7		4	6					2
			9	1		3	4	6

3			6		5	9		
1	6			3	4		7	
		4			8			1
	4	8		9			6	2
					3		9	
6				4			5	
4		9		5	1			
2		6	7	8	9			3
				2	6	7		

2	1		9				7	
9		5	6			2		
8		7	3		4	9		
		8	1		6	3		2
1	2	4			3	7	6	
			2					
7	5		8	6				1
					9		2	7
4			7		5		9	

Light and Easy

8	1			9			7	
9					1			
5		2				1		8
7		4						1
1	5				8	7	3	6
	3	6						4
	7	5	4	8		2		
	9		7	5				
				6			5	

		7	2		1	6		
6	1				5		2	
				4	6			
	7	6		5	2			
2		1			4		3	
	4		7	9			6	
9	2		5	1		4	7	6
		8	4	3			5	9
	5	4	6	2			8	

16   Light and Easy

1	4	8	5			2		
6	2		4	1		5	8	
		5	8	3		4		
5	6				7		1	4
				4	1	7		9
7			9					6
4			2	6				
3						9	7	
		1	7	9	3			8

	5	8		6	3			
		2				5	6	
					9			
		5			6		1	
	4	7		8				2
	6		3					5
	8			1	2	9		7
	1	9	5		7	4		
		6				3	2	1

18   Light and Easy

6				5	4			
	3			8	2		7	
			3	1	6			
8			1		5			6
	1		6		3	5		9
	5					2	1	
	7			6	9		2	8
2			4				6	
	6			7		9	5	3

4		6				3	1	8
		1	9					
	5			1	3			
5		2				1		
6	7	9	4		1			3
				5		6		
8	6			2		4		
				3			5	6
2					4		7	9

6					1	4		
					8		5	
	4		5			8	9	
				5		9	2	
2		5		7	9		3	
7	1		8				6	
	2				5	3		9
		4			3			5
5	3			9		7		2

9				7		8		6
	6				8		4	5
1					4	7	2	
			8	4				
	3		5			1	8	
8		4	1	3	6			
5		1		8		4		
	7			9				
4	8	6	7			9	3	1

22   Light and Easy

	8		3			1		2
5	1		8	6	2	9		
							6	
8		7						5
2				1	8			
3	5			7	9	4		
			6	2			3	
4	3	5					2	7
1		6				8		

		1	9		7	4	8	
3	7		8			2	6	
	4			3	5	1		
						6		9
4					3			
			2		6	5		
2	3		7		9	8	5	1
		7				3		4
1	5	8						6

24 Light and Easy

	6					9		1
1		4						2
2	5	7	4			8		3
				8		3	1	9
9	1			6	5			8
3					7			6
				4	3			
4		5	9	2			3	7
			5		8	2	9	

	8	9				7	4	6
				6	4	5	8	1
6			7	1			9	
				3	6		5	7
	7	2				1		4
9	5							8
	6		3		2	8	1	
						4		
		3		5				

			2	7				
3		9			6	7		5
7	4				8	6		2
				2			4	
	3		4		7	5		9
2					9			1
				6				
	6						5	3
	9	5	3	8		4		

2	1	8	3					
		5	7	8				
	7		5	2		8		
	8	2	1					4
7			4				2	
1	3		2	6		7		
8			6		3	4	5	2
6	4			5	2	9		1
	2					6	3	

Light and Easy

9	8		3		6			7
5		2		1		8	6	
			8					
	9		5				4	8
8	3		7			6		
				8			9	1
	2		4	9				
		9		3				
1			6		8	9		2

3								
5	7	8	2			1		6
	2		6	4			8	3
4		1					6	
				6				2
		2	4	3	1			8
9	1			5	8	6		
8	3				6		5	9
2			9	7		8		

3								1
		7	4	3				
	5			7	8			6
	7			2	9			
	9	5	8	6	4			
8		2						9
7		6	3		1	8		
			2			1	3	7
2		1	9				6	

2		3	9	5	1	6		4
			7	8	3	2	1	
7					2		4	3
	1	2				5		6
3		5			9	1	2	
	2	1				9	5	8
	3			9	5			1
9	5	7		6				2

32 Light and Easy

	9	1	8			3		
7			1	3			9	
	8		9	6		2	1	5
		7		2			8	4
6		2	5				7	
	3	8			1	9		6
8			2					
	7					6		
3	2			5	9	8	4	1

8								
	3	5	4					
6	7					8		
	6	1	5		2			3
	5					6		
3				6			1	4
		8	1	2	6		3	
	9			4				
				9	3		5	2

34   Light and Easy

7	3	2				5		6
4	9	8		6	7			
							7	
	8		4		3	7	6	
3				2	6	8	4	5
6					5	1		
		3		4		9		2
8		7		9			5	
		4			2	3	8	

1	7	3				8	9	4
6		2		1				
	4				7			
	5	1		2	4		7	
3	2						1	
					5	9	3	2
	1			8		5	4	
7					9	3		1
		9	5	6		2		

36　Light and Easy

						8		
			1			7		4
6		7		2	4	3	5	
1		3			5	2	4	
5				7	1		3	6
		4		3				1
2	5	6			3	4	8	
	4	9		8			2	3
	8				2		9	

5		8			2	7		
	1		4					3
	2	3		1				9
	5		1		8		2	6
8						5	1	7
3	6	1					9	
6		5		3		1	8	2
2		9	5		1		3	4
1				2	6	9		

38 Light and Easy

		7	9	5	2		1	6
		3			4		5	
6		9				4		
7				1		6	2	8
5			2	6				
1						5	7	
				7				
	7						6	3
9		6	1	2				

3	5		4	2				
		9	8	5				
	2	4	9			3		5
	6	2	1	8			7	
9	4		5					6
	8							
						5	9	7
4		8	6		5			2
7		5						

40   Light and Easy

1			7					
			6	4	9			5
						3	4	
5	6	3	4		8		7	
				9	1		5	
		9	5			2	3	
6	4	7		8			9	2
9		1				7		6
		5			6			

9			5					
6		7			2			
						6		
7			2	8	3			
8	3	9			5			
2	5			9				4
3			6	4	7	8		
5		4	8				6	
						7		

6		1	3					
		5		9		3		
	3	4	2					8
				4			9	
4		3					6	1
					6		4	
		9	8				5	
		6			1			7
1	2						8	6

	2	5						
3	4				6		9	
		7	9			1	4	5
					9	8	1	4
4	1			2		3	5	
	5				1	2		
5							6	
	3					4		
			6		7			8

							5	
5			9			1	6	8
6	8				5	7	3	
1		7	5					
	2			7				
				6		9		
		8	2					
3	6					2		5
	4		6	9	8			7

	5				4	8		
	6				5		9	7
	3	9	7					4
						9	8	1
	2		9	1	6			
		1						
		4		8				6
		2	5				1	
	8	3		7				

	4		8			1		
		3	5	9			4	
		2			4		6	5
9	5			6				
	3		9	5	8		7	6
		8		2		9		
3			7			6	1	
5	2	7		1		8		4
	1	6			3		9	

6	3	9		1	4			
8						3	9	
			3	7	9			4
5			6		1		8	3
		4			3			7
9			5			4		
					8		3	
7		3	4		2		5	

48 Light and Easy

		1		8	9			
	6		5			9		
	9	8		1		7		5
3	4			9			1	
8			3	2	5		4	7
5	2			4				8
			4					3
						8		4
6				3	7			9

		1			4	9	5	
		8	5			6	7	
5			9	6		2		8
	6	4		5				
			8	7			6	
7					2		3	
	1	6			8			5
	5				6			9
	9	2	7		5	1	4	6

	7			5	3			
	6	1						
4			2		6		7	8
		3			9			5
	9		3	8		4		
	8	2			4			9
					2			
		9	1	7				3
	1			3	5			6

8	9			7				
						5	7	1
6					3			
		3	4		6	1		
				8	2	4		
	8	2		5	7			6
7			9					
	4	8	6			7		9
	2			1		6	4	

52 Moderate

				3	9	2		
	9	7	2		5	8		
6	5			4		9		
4				2	8	5		1
			6					
		8			4			
		9				1	4	3
2	1			9		7	8	
8				1			2	

		3	9	2	6		4	1
		9		3		5	6	2
						8		7
			6	9	5			
	9						3	5
9	2	6		1		4		
	5	4				1		3
	7		2	8				

54 Moderate

				3			9	
9		1	4					
5	6		9	8	7		3	
	5				4			2
8				7		5		3
2					3	8		
6	4		5		2			
3			7					1
		7	3				6	

7		6						
	8	1	2					
	5				8		7	6
3				4		7		9
	6						2	3
5						1		8
		2	1	8			3	
					4			
		7	3		6	8	5	

56 Moderate

2			3			6		8
		5	6		4		9	
			2					1
9	5				7			3
				2				
7	2						6	9
5	8	7					1	
							7	
1	3	6		9				2

2				3				
				6				9
4	3		5		2	6		7
				4				2
			6				7	
5	9				7			
		8		7	4	2	3	
1		2		8		5		
3	4			5				

58 Moderate

5		6						9
	9					1		2
		4		2	3			
		5	6					7
3		1	7			9		4
		7		5	1			3
	1	2	3		5		8	
				1				
4			8		6			

	3		4			2	5	
				7				
	1	2	5	6			9	8
		9			7			
	8	5	1			7		9
4		6				1	8	
				1				5
	9	3				8		
5				8		9	3	

60 Moderate

8					5		9	
9		6	7	2		1	8	
	1			8			2	3
		5		7				8
3			5					
7	6						3	
				9	1			
	9							4
4		7		3	6	9		

					5	2		4
9			4			3		8
			8		7			
			1	5		4	2	
				4	3			
6					8		9	
3		9				5		
	8		5	6	1			7
1			9		4		6	

62 Moderate

9		2				1		7
	3	1			8			
		5					4	
			9	8			1	
		3	6					2
8			5			6	9	3
5					6	3	7	
1				4			2	5
3							6	8

	9	6						
	7	5		3			4	
	4					3	9	
	1				8		2	
4		3	6					
7					1			
6	2			5	9		1	
		8	1	7		5	6	
	5			6		4		

4		2	6					9
	6				7	3		
		3		5			4	7
		9	7			5		
	3		9					1
		4				9	2	6
	8	1	3	7	6	4		
		6			9		7	
	5					2		

		2		5			3	
1			8	3			6	4
	6		2	7			9	
					6			
					2			6
8			3		5	4		
3	2						1	
6	9		5			3	4	2
	1							5

66 Moderate

	1							
3	6	8	1					
	2			7		1	6	4
5							3	
1	7				3		4	8
						7	1	6
	3	1	5		6			2
				1				7
			9	3				

8			5	7			4	
6								
	7					5		8
		7		8	9			
	4	1		2				
	6			5	1			3
3				4	8		5	1
	2			9	5	8		
				6		7		

68 Moderate

						1		
		2	3				5	4
4			2		1			6
	2	6	4				8	9
7						3		2
8							4	
		1		3				
		5	9	2		8	6	
		4			8		7	

5					3	1		
		1		6			5	9
		8		9		4		7
				4	6	5		3
							4	
4	9			7	8			
8								
9	6	5	7	1			8	
	3						6	

70   Moderate

				2				
1		9			8		4	3
			3		1	9	7	
			4	8		6		
		4					2	8
9								
			8	6		2	5	4
6	7							
		8	2		3		6	7

6	5		1				8	
7	3	8	9					1
			4		2	1	3	
	6					5		2
			3				4	9
		9		8	6	2		3
8		1	2		3	6	5	
					1			8

	7	8			4		6	
1			9			8		
	2					3	1	
				7				
		3	1			4	7	5
	5	1		2			9	8
	1	2	3			7		
			2	4	8			
5		4				9		

	8	3			6			
		4	3				8	1
1	2			4		7		6
4		2				1	5	
		7			3	6		
3			1	9		8	7	
2				6	5			
					8		6	
				2		3	9	

					5	9		8
6	8				9	5	7	
	5		2			4	6	
1				2				
	7	4						
2		3	8			6	1	
5			7		1			
		9	4	8		3		
				6				

	1	3	2	9				
7		6		8			3	
				4				5
2	5	7						9
	3							8
		4	3		2			1
	7	2	8	6	9		5	
					1			7
		5			7		2	

1	5	9						
		2	8			9		
			3	1				
							9	
			4		6		1	2
	6			7	2			
4	3			2	1			
		1		3		7		8
7								3

5			2			1		7
		9				6		
				3				
3					8		7	1
	9		1		3		8	
	5	8		4				
		3	7		2	5		
6						2	1	8

78 Moderate

7		9			6			
			2	7		1		
	8			1		9		
	9	8		5	2		1	
3					8	7		
	5		3				9	
				8			7	
		2						3
5	3			2				

		5	9	8	4			2
				7				
1		8						
	1			3	9	2		
				4	1			5
9		7			5		8	
	2							
			6				4	3
	9		5			6		

8		5			9			
			7	4	1			
	2			5				
	3					9		
	6	7	1	9				
		1	6			4	5	
		8				2		1
	4				3			
	5				8	3		

1	9				7		6	
7	6		2			8		
		5	6					7
9	7					6		
5							8	
8			5	7			1	4
		3				5		
4								3
	1						9	

Moderate

9	7						3	
		4	8	7	9	6		
		1	3					
			9				1	8
3	6	8	1			2	5	
				6				4
7	4	6						
	2	5				7		

				3			5	
8		1		9			7	
				8	7			
	2					9		
6	4		3	2				
		5						7
	5	4			6	8		
					4			
	8						9	

84 Moderate

	8		9				5	
		3			7			4
						9		
					9			6
		2			8	1		7
6				4				9
			1			3	7	
4	3				2			
		6				2		1

		1		2			6	
4			6			1		
	6		3	8				
	1		5	7	9		8	
			1			2		9
7	8				2			6
	5		8			6	4	7
							2	

86   Moderate

	7							3
3		5					2	7
			1		9	4		
		8		7		9		
6			5					
	3	6	7					
2				8	1			
	9				4		3	

			2	6	4			
		7		9		2	3	6
2	4	8			6	7	5	
			8			6	2	
		3						
9								
	1					9		4
				7	5	8		

88 Moderate

6	8	2					5	
				8				2
7	5			1				
						3	4	
5				7	6			
9		1						
		6	7			4		
				6			1	
4	3				2		9	

			8				6	
					4	9		
5					7		4	3
			7				8	
9			5	8		3		
	3			2			5	9
				4	8	5	1	
	2							
7	4			9		2		

	4				6			
	2	7	9					
		9		8				5
9		1		2	7			
	7		3	4	9			
						2		
		2				6	7	
			1		4		2	
7		8	2		5			

1	9		2				7	
		3		9	6		2	
6	8						9	
			4	1	5			8
					2			3
					3			
	7		8		4	5		9
	6						1	

92   Moderate

							5	
	9			3		1		
	3				9		2	
				8	6		4	
2							1	
	5		3				9	2
		1			5			
		3		7		2		
	2		4					8

2				3		8		1
				6	2			
9				8			2	
	2		8				9	3
		9			7		5	
	1	8						
	6			2			8	
			6		4	5		
	4					2		

94　Moderate

			7			2		
	2	4		5			3	
		8	4					1
6	4				8		5	9
						3		
							7	
3	9		5				6	
	8	2	6				1	
					3	5		

			3	2				8
	7		1					5
	3				9			
9	8	6					7	
		4				5		
			2	6				
1		7		8				
	2					3	5	
							8	6

96 Moderate

	2			5			8	
	3				2		4	
4	1		3				5	
				6				
7		4		2				9
			7	9				
6			5	1	8	2		
						5		
8			6			7		1

	6					4	1	2
	2	1				5		
		9	8				6	
						8	3	
				4				
					9	2		4
5				6			2	
9			1			7		
	1	8		2	4			

Moderate

	4							2
	2	8						7
	1			9	8			
					6			4
				7			9	
	7		1	5				
3							1	8
	5							
9								3

8								2
4					6			
	7					6		
	4				7	8	9	
	1						6	
	3	8				4		1
2					4	1		9
9			6		8		7	
		4	9			2		

100 Moderate

		4	9					8
		9			6	3	4	
				1	7		6	9
	9				5	4	7	
		3					8	
7		8						
4							3	
					3	5		
			7					1

7	6			5		3		
								2
9	3		8			1	6	
1				7				4
					4	9	1	
								6
				4		5		
5					9			7
	4	6					9	

102 Demanding

					7		9	
4		2				7		
	9		2					6
			4			6		5
				9	5			
	6			3				
	5		9		8			
7	3							
		6			4	9		

	4	2						
	1							
			1			7	8	
6	7		5		4			
3					9			
		4			2			
						5	3	4
				7		1		
8						6		

104 Demanding

7					8		4	
			2		4			8
	1					5		
				1				6
1							5	
	2	8	6					
		6		7		3	1	
				4				5
	3			6				

			9				4	
				1		7		
					5	8	6	
	2			5				1
7	3							
4		9			8			
	1	4						9
5								
			7				5	

106　Demanding

		9			1	3		
3		4						2
				5				
			7					
6			5				4	
	1		2				5	
		8			9	1		3
					7			4
5			6					8

4	7		6			5		
							9	
	5		3					2
		2	7			6		4
				1				
7						8		
		6		8				
5	3						6	
8					9	1		

108 Demanding

		7		1				
	8		3				6	
2		4	6				3	
		6			8			1
			2	3				4
9								
				5	4	1	8	
		1		6	5	9		

4		6		5				
				4			5	
	2	3	7					
	7					8		1
		9		2				6
2			5					
	3				1			
	8						6	
		2	9			4	8	

110 Demanding

1	6				7	9		
5		8					1	
							6	
3	8						2	
		2		4	1			
		5						
			6	7				8
			3					
7	1	3	8		4			

2				3	4		9	
		8			5		2	
								8
		6	3				1	5
5					6			
							8	
4				9				
						9	7	4
	7	2	1					

112 Demanding

	2					1	4	
	4	3			1			5
			3	5				
	9						5	
			8					
1			2		9		7	
			5					
7	6				8			
		1		4	6		3	

		9					8	
				2	3			
		5					1	6
5	3							
					6		3	1
		1	4			2	9	
	6		1			7	2	
	9			4				
			9					

114 Demanding

	6		9				5	
			2	3				
		4				6		
7	4	5						
			3		4			
				8	2			1
			1		8			
1	5			9			4	
2							9	

1			6	9		7		
3	6				2			
		4	1			2		
					6		1	
2			3					8
9							7	2
	2	1		8			4	
	5			6	9			

116 Demanding

	6				2	5		4
			1	5				
			3					6
		7	9				5	
		6				7		
9				4		8		1
	7							
	4	3						
	9		8			2		

					5	9		
	9			1	7			5
4	3							
9				4	1			
	7							
				2		6	8	
			5					7
		2		3			4	9
						2	5	

118 Demanding

		2			9	3		
3			5			8		
9	7		6					
			4			6	3	5
				3				
	9				1			
		5		4				
		7						2
6			2					7

	4	3					2	
			3					
7				8				5
	6		7	2	3		5	
	3		5				1	
			6	9				
	5							
9							4	
	2	1				9	6	3

120 Demanding

		2		5	8	9	3	
			6		3			
	1		2					
8			4	3		6	2	
					2		1	
	2							
		8						
				4	6		5	7
	9	5		8				

9	6					7		
		3					2	8
						3		
4		9						7
					8		1	
5					7			2
6					2			
	4		8	1				
	8		9			5	4	

122   Demanding

	5			2				3
						2	8	
6								
						9	4	7
	3		6					
9		4			2			
					9		7	5
					1			4
	1	7	2		5			

		8		2				
		5			7	6	1	
7	1				6			
		3		9		5		
	4		1	5				8
		6		3		9		
3							4	
	6	2						
								3

124 Demanding

	6	8	7					
2					3			
		1						3
	5				1	3		8
			6	7		4		
				9		7		2
							5	6
8	7		1					
		5	4	8				

			4					9
					1	5		6
				8	9			
7	9	6						
	5				3			
					2		8	
						4		
		5		7		2	3	
9		8		4				

126 Demanding

8			5					2
	6		2			9		
1	7			4				
			6			3	2	
			8	5		4		
4		1	3		2			9
			1	3			9	8
						5		
3	8						4	

			6	1		9	7	
			9				2	8
		8						
	2	9					1	
		1						5
7	8					3		
1	9		4					6
		7	5	6				
		6	1		9	5		7

128 Demanding

	1		5		6	3		
			3					4
9		6	2				8	
		7	9					2
	2				4		1	
8								5
			8		5	4	2	6
							7	3
7			4			8		

3			4		5		6	
	6	5		1	2	7	4	
	7							
		9	7	2		4		
	8			9		2		1
2			8		3			
				4				
8							2	5
	3		2	6				

130 Demanding

		3		1	5	2		
	7			2		1		
				3				
	4	1	3			9		
6							4	
	3	8			2	6	5	
1		5						9
	2	9						3
			7				2	6

	7						5	
4	6			8	7	2		9
8	1				3	5		
		9				7		
6		7		1				
		1	5	7	8	6		
				6		8	4	
5			4			3	7	

132 Demanding

			9		1			7
		9						
1	7		6	8		2		3
7	4		3			5		6
2				4		1		9
	3	5						
	8							5
		7			2			
				5	6			

8	4						7	
	3	5						
				6	3			8
	9				7	1		
		7			2		6	3
	5					7	8	
	6	4						
			6	1				2
		8	5	2			9	

134 Demanding

	5			1				
					8			
1	4			9	5			6
	8			2		7		4
9		6	1	8				3
2								
			5		9	4	3	8
	3		2					1
	9	5						

		3	5	7			6	8
			6			7		
7	1				9			
6	8		7					
	2							
				9	8		5	
3	7	1		6				
		2	8			3		9
		5	4					1

136 Demanding

6	2				4	8		
	1		8			6		3
					1		4	2
			4			5		
			9		3	2		1
1	8		5	2				
	3							
4		9					5	
						7		6

1				8			4	
				3	7		5	
	7		5			6		8
	2	9		5	1			
7		6		4		8		
8	4					1		
			2					7
	8	2				9	1	
4								

138 Demanding

		6			8			2
1								9
		8		9				
				3			7	6
9				4	7			
	5			2		4	8	
	7	1	5	8	6			
4	2							
		9		7	4	3		5

			9	2		3	1	
4							6	
		9		8		4		
2								6
	1	6			8	5	4	
				9	7			
7			1		5	2	3	
						6		
3								5

140 Demanding

4					6	9	7		
3						2		1	
	6			7				8	
5		4	8						6
							8	4	
		3	5				9		
7			9						1
								9	
				3	5			6	7

								8
7		8				4		3
1	5	9						
6				5		2		
	4		3		7			
	7			9		3		4
		1			2			7
		6	9			1		
	2			3	8			

142 Demanding

		5		2	3	4		
	8			1				
	7	2		6	8			
	2	1		5	6	9		
	6			3		5		
								2
3			5					
8	4				2			1
						7	6	

	7	4			9			
5					7	2		1
3			6				5	
2					5	6		8
	9			7				
8	4		1					
							8	3
		2					4	7
				5	8			

144 Demanding

			7		3	2	4	6
		9	4			5		
2	4					3		
				7		9	6	
	2	8			9			7
6								
						1	8	3
9				1	6			2
7	3							

8					5			7
	6						9	
4								
	7			1	6	4	3	
							2	1
		9	2		7			
5		4			8			
9		8				6	1	
	1		9			3		5

146　Demanding

	8			6	9			
		1			4			6
	3	4		5			1	
3				9			8	
	4			8	7			
		9						5
1			6		8		4	
4	9		7					
5						1	7	

	8						7	
1		7			9	3	2	
9		6	7	8			4	
	2		8					5
	6						3	
			1	3	5	8		
					7	2		
2	4		9	1	3			
5								

148 Demanding

							3	1
		8		1				
7			2		4			9
4			1				8	
	8			9	3			7
				6	5		2	
	3	9				1		
8	7					6	4	
6						3		5

6						9		8
	5		7		8	6		
			9		3	1		
			1		4			2
		2						5
9	3					7		
	4	8						
3				8		2		
5	9						1	7

150 Demanding

				8	1			5
1		3	2					
6		2					3	
			9	2				
		4		3				
			6			7		1
5				7		6		
4								2
9		7		1		3	8	

						9		3
					3	5		
	8		7		6			
5	2			6				
	1		2		8			
6						4		
4				5				
			8		1			2
			3					1

152 Demanding

			6		4			
		8			5		6	2
						3	7	
9		1	7					
		3				5		
			8					6
					6		1	5
	7	2		1				4
	6							

		1			3			
				7	2			6
		8						9
		2	1	3			5	
						3		
	9							
6	2						1	4
9				8			6	
	1							7

154 Demanding

8	3			7				
	9		6					
	5				2		4	
1	4					3		
				9			2	6
		4		3				
				8			9	
	2		9				6	5

3	7		2			1		
					9	8		
5					6		4	
6			9				3	1
	2	1	4			9		
4	5							6
			1		5	2		3

156 Demanding

5	4				6			
1	7					2		
				8		3		
6						8	9	
							6	
	8			9				7
		1	2			4	8	
							1	
2				5				

					4	7		1
	1	4			8		5	
5								
7	5				9			
						8		
	9		6	7				
					1			4
	7		3	2				
2				5			3	

158 Demanding

8						2		
	4		7			6		
		5	9					
1	3	9						
						7		6
		2	3			1		
7								
				4	2			
2				8		9		

6		3	1	4				
				9	2			
							5	3
			6					7
	1						2	
9	4	5						
						4		
5				7	8			
	9	4		2		8		

160 Demanding

	8	1					9	
			6					7
		6		5				1
	5	8	1	7				
							2	8
7				6				
						8	3	
				2	7		4	
	9		3		8			2

7		1					6	
			6					
				3	4	5		7
6			2		1			
		8		6				
		5			9			1
							9	
3				9	7		5	4
1		7						3

162 Demanding

			5		6		4	
						7		
2				1		9		
	8							
		5	3					
6	2					8		
3			4			6		5
4				3	2			8
		8	7		1			4

8						1		
		3						
4			8		6	7		
7	8			1	9			
	6			5	4			
		2		8				4
		6		9			2	
	9			2	7			
			5					

164 Demanding

4			1					
7				6				
					3	5	4	8
				2			3	
		5						
					4			9
8				1			6	7
3			6			8		
	2		9					

					3			
		2		7	9	1	4	
								2
	4							
			6	8	1			
9	6	8			2	5		
	2					9	6	
	3	7		4				1
	8					4		

166 Demanding

		6	2			8		5
		9			3			
8		3		6	5	2		
				2				
			4					3
7						1		
		4			9		8	
			3			4		
9			8		6			7

	4	9						
				6		7		
			5			6	2	
	8					1		
	6				7			4
5				3	4			
1						8	3	
7		3			5			
	9							1

		3		2	8		6	
			6			8		
	9				1			
4					6		1	9
			5	9		4		
		1		3	7			8
		9					7	1
3			2					

							2	3
	5			7	2			4
6			4	3		5		
			8	5				
	7	9				6		
				2				
8				1		4		7
		5	2		8			
1								

				1	4			
		5			8			
9								2
1	9		8	2			7	
						5	2	
	3				6	1		
						3		
	8			3			1	
	2						4	9

7		3						
		1		2				3
4	6	8						
6		4		7		8		
	7		5					6
							9	
				9			8	2
		9					1	
			2	3	6			

172 Demanding

				9				7
	1						5	
5		2						
3		4				1		5
8			9			3		
		7		6				
		9			2			4
					3			
		3	1	8				

								5
						6		
	4	7		5	8			2
				8				7
		6	9	7				
	3	8				4	6	
	9	2					7	
			1		3	2		
	1			2				4

174 Demanding

					7			9
		1	9	3				
	6	2					8	
					3	5		
	7							1
			8		5			
	4	3						
			3	1			6	
	5	6			9		2	

				5			6	3
		3	8		9			2
		5						
					2		7	
8	7					4		6
3	4			9				
	6				7			1
9								
		8			3		9	

176 Beware! Very Challenging!

9					1			4
		3	2					9
	6						3	
		8					7	
6	4		3				1	
		5		4				
1						8		
			5			7	4	
		2	1					

			9		7	1		
	7		4	3			5	
3		1						
	1	4	7					
							7	
	9	6						
				8				7
2					3			4
	5						3	9

178 Beware! Very Challenging!

4		6	1				8	
				5				2
1		9						
7				4				
		2	3					5
	6			9		4		7
					5	8		
			8					3
				7			6	

			5		7			6
								2
					4	3	7	
1	4			2				
			6	1				
3		2	4		5			
9	8					2		1
2								9
	5					6	4	

180 Beware! Very Challenging!

7	1		8	6				
	6	8		7	4			2
		1					3	
6	5							
	9	2					8	
5			7					9
			6				1	
			3				2	8

6						7		
		9			3			
3	4			8			9	
7		4				5		8
	6		9	5				
		2	1			6		
								7
4			5			3		
	1	7					8	5

182 Beware! Very Challenging!

				3		7	5	
	9							6
9			4	7	8	3		
		5	2					
6			3				7	
		4		5				3
7				1				
			8		2			

	7	2		4				
	1				6		4	
						8	1	
9			2		3			6
								3
		8		7		4		2
2								
	4			3	8			
		1			5	6	3	

184 Beware! Very Challenging!

				9			1	
4			8	7				2
		7		2		3		
			3				2	
	4	3			2		9	
2				5				
					6			
	6					8		4
	7	2				5		

2					5		6	
		4	6			8		
	3		7					
				9	8		2	
9					1			
	7	8						4
	8			4				
						6	5	
1								3

Beware! Very Challenging!

9		4	2		8			1
	2							
	6		1		3	5		
	8			9				6
7		3					4	
6				7				
4	1			8		6		
					6		5	7

			4	9		8	6	
	1					5		
5								
1		9	8		7			4
				4		6		
		5		1	2			
	2						9	
9		6				2		
							8	3

Beware! Very Challenging!

	4	9	2					
			8				1	
								3
2		3		5	6			
4								
9				4			5	1
	8				2			
			5			8		
		7	3			9		

	6			7	8	5		
9					5		4	
						9		
						4		
	5	1			6		8	
		6	5					9
2	8							
				4			3	
4			7	1				

		5	4		3			6
				1				
		1	8		5	7		
7		9			6			
8				9		2		
				4				
	2		3			6	1	
3							8	
	7						4	

	5			9			4	
				6				
			8				6	9
4			2					
2			7		8			
	9	8		4				
		2	1		3	5		
		4					3	
1				2				

192   Beware! Very Challenging!

		4				5		
8	1						6	4
9			1		5		8	2
	2							
		7						1
2				8		3		
	4	5			3			
6					9	4		

	1			8				
8		3	9	2	5		4	
5		6			4			
6						3		7
	9						2	
		4					1	
			2	9				
		1	3					
			8			9	3	

194 Beware! Very Challenging!

8						2	4	5
	2				7	9		
9	8			2				
				8				1
			3					6
			5				3	
		4	6					
		3		9	4	5		7

		8			7			
9						1		
	5				2		9	
						2	5	
	3			4				
1			7			6		
		5						8
		2	4					
4		6	8			9	7	

196 Beware! Very Challenging!

						6	9	
	7	2						
3		1	6	2		8		
1					9		7	
	4							
		3	7		8		6	
			5					
						4		9
4				6	1		8	

				9		6		
		8	1	2				
							5	
		7				5		3
	4				1		6	
	8		4	6				1
	6			5				
1		2				7		
	9					8		

198 Beware! Very Challenging!

7								
		9				8		3
					8	6		1
			7				4	
		6		1	3	7		2
	1							
				8	6			
	2	5						
					2		5	9

		2			6			
	5			2		7	1	
			4	9				
					1	3		
3					8			7
								6
	8				7	6	5	
	7						4	
5	6	9						

	1			5				7
				2		4		5
4	3							
						9	5	4
			9			2		
		3	1					
	5			9			7	
3						8	4	
9			8		6			3

		5				4		6
				2	5		1	
		9						
		6						1
1				9		2		4
8					1			
	5	7		4				
						8	6	2
					2	5		

Beware! Very Challenging!

3		4				1		
				5	2	8		
		7					9	
				3	6		2	
	8		4					
	4						3	5
4		6			1	9		
1			6		7			

				6				2
3					8			
	9					1	4	
			6					9
8		1				3		
	4			3		2		7
					3			
9				2				8
		2	1		9			

4	3					1		
						2		4
9					6			
		7			4			
	1		5		7		8	6
			6			4		5
				3				
	2							1
				8	9			

		6		7	8	9		
			4				2	
1	2		7					
								3
8		9			3			4
		1	8				3	
	7			1	9			
		5			4			6

206 Beware! Very Challenging!

		1						7
3		9						
						6	4	5
	8	7			6	9	1	
				7				
	1			5				8
					7			
		4	2					
6			3					2

	6						9	
		5						
3	4			6		2		5
9				5				3
	3		7				2	1
1					9		6	
	2		1	4				
	5			9	3	4		
		3				1		

208 Beware! Very Challenging!

	3	4						
2	9	8		6	5			
					8			
			9			4	3	
	6				1			
5								2
1			7					
						8		3
9	5	6		1				

			7		1	8		
9				6				
	7				3			
3							2	9
	5		8	7			6	4
4			5	2			1	
	3				9			
			1				5	

210 Beware! Very Challenging!

		3		8			2	
1						6		
			5					1
	3	7		4	8			
	4		6					5
	2						3	
					2	8		
	9	6	7	5			4	

Beware! Very Challenging! 211

								6
		6		2		7	8	
3		5			1			
				7		5		
7		3	2					
4			3					9
							6	
	7	1			3	2		
	9		5					

212 Beware! Very Challenging!

2			1		6	9		
	5		3					
							4	
		6				3		
				7			8	
7					4	2		5
		7						
6		9	5				1	4
1							6	

1			9	7				
				3			2	
9		7						6
		8						
		2			3	8		
			6				4	
			1	4	8		9	
5	6						7	
						1		

		3		9	4	7		8
	1	4			2			
			1			6		
					3			
	8							
5			2		6			
				1				9
		6	7					2
		9					8	

	7							
			2	1	3			
	6		9				8	
		4	8			1		
					2			5
5								9
						9		
1	4							
	2		6	8	9		7	

Beware! Very Challenging!

			8		9			
	4		7			1	3	
			6					7
3	7							4
						2		1
		8			7			9
	9					4		
	8	5			4			
				3			5	

		5						
	8			6				5
			2				8	4
		1	3	2				
			1	8	7			
		6			4			7
	7				1		2	
9							1	
			5	4				3

5				7				
	2	4		1		8		
7	9		5		6			
					5			6
							3	
8		9	4		3			
	1							
	4			2		6		
					7		2	

			7				8	
		1					2	
	7							3
	2			6		5		
	6	4			8			1
	3		1		4			2
9	4							
			6			4	9	5
				5				

	1							
8				2				9
		7	4		8			
9		1				7		
	8			3				
				8	6	4		
			6		9			2
							1	
4	2					3	9	

			1					4
					6			3
	8			9	7			
2		9		1	8		3	
8				4		5		
6			2				7	
	6	3						
				2				
		2					9	1

222 Beware! Very Challenging!

1								
8	3	2	4					
						6		9
		3	1	5		7		
			3					
	5				4	8		
			9		6	3	2	
		5		7			1	8

			7	6				
2		4			3			
	5			4				
			8				1	
	8	5			6		3	
		1				9		4
7	2							
			1					6
		3		8	7			

	5	9	1				8	
1			4					
								9
			6			7		
4	6			3	1			
3								
2			7			6		
	3			2				
				1	5	2	3	

	7							
		6	3	5	9	2		
5			6			1		
			7					1
					6			2
			4			9		
6		9	5					
	8				1			7
				6			3	

226 Beware! Very Challenging!

5	2	4						
			3					
	1				5		6	4
6					2			
				3		1		5
2		8						9
9				6		7		
						4		
			5	1			9	3

	5		3				1	2
								8
4	9					5	3	
2			6					
				5	3			
8							4	7
				2				
	4							
6		2	1		8			

Beware! Very Challenging!

3					9	1		8
		6				9		
				2				
		5					7	6
	4			5				
9		7	2					
		2	1					7
8				9	4	2		
				8				3

		6	3				9	1
				2			3	
					7		4	8
					9			
			6			8		
2	4	3				5		
6	2		7	8				
					4			
5	9							

Beware! Very Challenging!

		5			8		9	7
9				6		1		8
8								
		2			5			6
	9	4				2		
				7				3
5					7			
			4					
			3	9			4	

	9	3	2		8		4	
		2				8		
				6				
					1		8	
	8		4			3		
	6				3	7		5
		6				5	2	9
					7			
		1						

Beware! Very Challenging!

	9			4	5			1
8				3			5	
	1							3
	8		2		9			
5			1					4
						6		
		3	4	7				8
							3	
					2			

		9	5	3			6	8
								9
						3	7	
3				8	1			
4								
8	9			7	6			
						6		1
	3	5	2					
		8				4		3

234   Beware! Very Challenging!

	6			3				
4	8				7	9	3	
			4		2			
						5		7
	5		6		8			
							9	
		9						4
8	7							6
3		2	1					

				6	2	1		9
4			7			3		
	3			1				
						4		
		6		7				1
	8					6	3	
	9							
2			5		8			
6	7			9			5	

236 Beware! Very Challenging!

		4				8		
8				5				1
9		7						
		3	4					9
		6			7		8	
					2	1		
		9				7		
	6	5	7			9		
				9	3		5	

		2			9		6	
9					7			
						3		5
		5		7			2	1
6								
3			1			6		7
		4			1		7	
7				4	3		5	
1				5				

238 Beware! Very Challenging!

	1	9			4		2	
4			7	3			5	
			8		2			
		3						
				6	5		1	
6	2				1	9		
9			1	7		2		
	7					3		
							9	

		9			8			
	1		2				8	
	2			3				4
							9	
			3	5	2			
7	6							
		8					6	2
5			9		7			
				6	4	5	7	

Beware! Very Challenging!

			8			2		
	1			9				
						5	1	6
8		7						
5							3	
	6					8		7
2		3		6		4	9	
					9			1
4			5		8			

			7			9		3
		1						
3						8	5	
	9		2	7				
		3	1		8	6		9
8		7		6				
			4		3			
9								8
	2					4		

242   Beware! Very Challenging!

		1	4	2				
8								
		4		1			5	
		2			4			3
	1	7		3				9
9	8				2		4	
					9		8	
				7				2
3						1		

		7					5	1
8					4			
				8				9
					6			
9	7			1				8
					2		3	
7	9					4		
4	8	1		6				
	6	3		2			8	

Beware! Very Challenging!

4				9		2	1	
								4
		7	2	6			9	
9		2						
				3	2	9		8
		1		7		4		
8					9		7	
		4						
	1				3	6		

			3		6			
			7	8		1		
		6				9		2
		7						
8		2		5	9			7
		1					8	
	9					6		8
			2	6	3			
								1

246　Beware! Very Challenging!

7								3
		4		2	1			
5			9		4			
		1	2					
	7				6	9		5
	5					8		
4					8	7		
								8
			3				5	4

		4		3			2	
	8							
			7		9	5		
	1		6	5			7	
	3	7						8
9								2
7				4	8			
			5				6	
					2			3

Beware! Very Challenging!

5		7			1			4
	9							8
	1		8		9			
7						2		
				3			6	
						5		9
6				5		3	4	
		9						
			2		7	6		

					3		7	
	6		7				1	
	4					5	3	2
				4			5	
	9		3				6	
	6		9		2			
			1	6				
	7		8					5
	5		7		3			

250 Beware! Very Challenging!

			1		3	6		
	8			6				
		7	9		5		3	
		5		4				9
	3				6			
	2	8	5				7	
		1		2	8	9		
				9		7		
		2						4

9	1	8				4		
			4					2
	3				7			
		7		2	3	5		
	8							
			7	9			3	
	6	4	9					8
					2	1		
	5				6	2		

7								6
				8		5		
3	2			4		7		
	6	9				4	7	
		6	6					1
2		1		7				
			4					
	4		2	5	3		1	
		6					9	

		3						
		1	9					
			7				2	
7			4	8	9			
			9		1			
4		5		6				
9	4					7	8	
2		1			6			
			4					

254 Beware! Very Challenging!

6		5				7		
	4	3				2		
	1		7					
			9	7		4		
5		8		1				
			6					
		7	2				1	8
		4			5		3	
3						6		

		4						8
5	2	8		4		7		
	1			7	3			
	7	3				2		
					9			
					2	5	3	4
	8		9	6				7
		2		5				
	9					6		

Beware! Very Challenging!

	2	3						
					1			5
		9		6	2			
8		7						
				5	8			
		1				5		6
		2		9	5			4
9			6				1	
				3				8

5			9					
			7					4
	2	4			1		3	
						8	4	
9					5	6		
		1						
		9		8	7			
7	8					5		
	5		6					9

258 Beware! Very Challenging!

	6							
		2			8		9	
		3		4				
2			4		7			
9							1	7
8		1		6		5		
			6			1		3
			8					6
			7					4

				5				
						7	9	2
		7	8				3	
				9				
			7		1		8	4
					2			3
7		4				5		
		8					1	
9			5	3	8		4	

Beware! Very Challenging!

	6			3		1		
					4	7		5
								8
	3	9				6		
		1		6			2	
6	5				9	3		4
1	7				8			
		2					8	
		4	9		5			

	9					2		
				6				
4				5		8		
					8	1	4	
		6			7			
		7	9					2
	1					6		
6				1			5	
	8	2					9	

262 Beware! Very Challenging!

	2	6		4				
			8		2			
8		7	3					
	5			1		9		
								6
	4	3		9		5		
	9							7
1				8		2	6	
		4	7				3	

2		7						
							8	3
	1			8		4	6	
					5			
	7					3		9
		9	2		4	1		8
			5		3			
								2
3		5		6				1

264 Beware! Very Challenging!

	2			7				
	3		4	1				
						2	5	3
			9		6	4		
		8	2				3	
7								
	1	4		5	9			
		2				7		4
			1					9

	7		5				9	
5					2	8		
	6					3	2	
3	2		1					
						9		4
6			7			5		
2								
7	9			3				
	1			5				

266 Beware! Very Challenging!

			5			6		
7			4			2		
	6	9			8			
				9				8
	4							
		5				1	3	
8		4	1					
3								4
9	1			6			2	

7				8				
	1			7		5		9
6	8		9		1	4		
				1	2	8	3	
8	2			9			1	
			8				2	
9		4	7					
					3			

268 Beware! Very Challenging!

			6		2	3		7
	7							8
				8	5	1		
8								
1		2		4	3	5		
6						4		
		6			4			
4			3		9			
		1		2				

					3		5	
4								
		5	2			9		
	7				6		8	
6					8			4
					7	5		
8	4					2	1	
7		2					9	
							3	
1			6			4		

				4				6
		4		5		9		2
7					3	5		
	7						8	
							5	
	8		1			3		
		3				2		
1	9		6					8
			8					

2	1							5
				1				
			6	7	8			
9						2	8	
			5			6	1	
	4	8						
1	3							
	2	6	9					
5			3		2			6

272 Beware! Very Challenging!

			8		9	5		
	4							
				1	6	7		
6			4		8	2		
					7	1		
	5	9						
4						9		3
			6					
		6		5	1			

		7		8		4		
	8					6	1	
		4	1	9				2
			5	7		8	6	
5		6						
	1							
					6			4
6				2	5	7		
		9			3			

274 Beware! Very Challenging!

4				9	6	8		
								3
3			1		4			
	2	9		6				
						2	1	
		8				9		
	6	2				7		
			8			3		1
		5						

						1		3
2					1	6	5	
		3			9	2		8
4				1		5		
				3				
	9	8					4	2
	7	1			4			
		6	7	5		9		
	5							

276 Beware! Very Challenging!

		2	5			6		
		4		9	3			
1								4
	5		1					
8								
7					6		3	
	3				7		2	1
	9			5				8
			8				6	

	7					2		
		8						
2					4		5	
4		7						
	6						3	1
5			9		6		4	
				8		6		
				4				
		3			7	8		9

278 Beware! Very Challenging!

			7			8	9	
5				1	9			3
	1			3		5		
	5	4						
						9		8
	3	6						
				9	1		2	
		3			2			
				8		3		7

		2				8	5	
	8			3				
	6	7		1				3
		4					1	
	5	1					8	
9					8	7		
			6					
5		3					4	
	1				9			

280 Beware! Very Challenging!

5		7			1		8	
				6				3
1		3	9		4	2		
			6		8		3	
		4						
6								8
2				1				
	4	8	2				5	9
	5							

6					9	3		
								2
		7		3				
	1	9			4			
					5	8		
			3			4		
7			6					1
3		1						7
		4				9	2	

282 Beware! Very Challenging!

		5	8					4
		9	6				8	
4				5				
	9					1		2
				1	3			7
			7				6	
6	7		3				4	
2				6				
	3		2					

		1			8		4	
		8		5				
			7			6		
4	9			6			5	
							1	
								9
		5			4	3		
	2				3			6
					1	2	7	

284 Beware! Very Challenging!

	2			5				
4		1	9					
	3						9	
		8	2					1
	7	6				2		
					3			7
2							6	4
					8			
				1	9		5	

				2	9			
			7		6			
	5						7	1
		7		3				2
							1	
3						4		7
8	2		5					
		6		1				3
				4	8		9	

286 Beware! Very Challenging!

6			2			9		
	4		3				8	
								1
		8						
		2		3	5			
			4		2		5	7
				1	7			4
				5		1		2
8								

	6		8	7			2	
4					2	7		
						1		
5						6	8	4
	9							
	1				3			
6				9	5			
	7							
2	8				7	5		6

288 Beware! Very Challenging!

6	4		9		3			
8	5							
							9	6
			1		2			
	6						7	
				7	8	3		9
				8		1		
5						7	2	
	1		4		9			

						5		
3		2					1	
	8	4			9			
				7	8	3		
1								5
	2	8	6					
		9		2		7		6
4	6			5			3	
			3					

290 Beware! Very Challenging!

7		5	9					8
			7	6		5		1
								5
1			2	4			3	
	2	8		3		1		9
9								
				5	2	3		
			4		6			

							9	7
	7	8						
1					5			
		4		2		1	3	
		1			7		2	4
	3							
			6					2
	8				3	5		
9			2			8		1

					5			
	5						4	1
							2	3
7				4		6		
1					8			
		8	9					7
2			8		6	1		
		7						
	9	5			4		7	2

	5				6		2	8
	3	9					4	
			3		5			
				4	2			
	4				3	1		
			8				9	
		7						
						2		3
3	6	8			1			

294 Beware! Very Challenging!

		6		9			1	
			2				3	4	
	7			5				2
		7			2			
	8	9		1	6	5		
4	1				8			
					5	1		
						7		
		8	6					

	7		5		4	6		
				6			5	
2								8
		1			7			
				3	1	4		
		6		8				
		9	8				7	
3					5		9	
	5							2

Beware! Very Challenging!

					7		4	9
	2			3				1
7					9			5
	3		4					
		1				5		
				7		2		
							6	
	1	9		8			3	
			6	2				

		8						
		9		7			1	3
	5	6					9	
	2	7			4			
8						5		2
			6			1		
					8			9
6			5	4				
	3					4		

			4					2
1		6		9				8
					1		7	5
	3						9	
				6				
8	6		5	3	4			
					3	8		
4				2		1		
5	7							

	9	8			5	3	2	
		2	6					
		3	4					
		7					5	
	3				8	6		
	2			1				
						4		1
					4	7		
6						9		

300 Beware! Very Challenging!

	1							5
8	3	9				4		
		4						
	9			1			3	2
		6						
					7	1		8
			1	9		7		
	2			8				
				6		3		

ANSWERS

1

7	2	3	1	8	5	4	9	6
5	6	9	2	4	7	3	8	1
8	1	4	6	3	9	7	2	5
9	5	2	7	1	4	8	6	3
3	7	1	8	5	6	2	4	9
4	8	6	3	9	2	1	5	7
2	9	5	4	7	3	6	1	8
6	3	8	5	2	1	9	7	4
1	4	7	9	6	8	5	3	2

2

4	7	6	8	5	9	3	1	2
2	8	9	1	7	3	5	4	6
3	1	5	6	4	2	8	7	9
9	5	2	7	1	8	6	3	4
1	3	8	4	9	6	7	2	5
7	6	4	3	2	5	9	8	1
8	9	3	2	6	4	1	5	7
5	2	7	9	8	1	4	6	3
6	4	1	5	3	7	2	9	8

3

3	1	8	4	6	5	2	7	9
2	4	5	7	8	9	3	1	6
6	9	7	3	1	2	8	5	4
8	6	1	9	7	3	4	2	5
5	3	4	1	2	6	9	8	7
7	2	9	5	4	8	6	3	1
9	5	6	2	3	7	1	4	8
1	8	2	6	5	4	7	9	3
4	7	3	8	9	1	5	6	2

4

4	3	2	7	5	6	1	9	8
7	8	5	3	9	1	2	6	4
9	6	1	4	2	8	7	3	5
8	5	7	2	3	4	9	1	6
3	2	4	6	1	9	8	5	7
6	1	9	5	8	7	3	4	2
5	7	3	1	6	2	4	8	9
2	9	6	8	4	3	5	7	1
1	4	8	9	7	5	6	2	3

5

6	2	8	9	4	3	1	7	5
1	5	9	6	7	2	3	8	4
7	3	4	1	5	8	6	9	2
2	1	5	7	3	6	8	4	9
4	7	6	2	8	9	5	1	3
8	9	3	4	1	5	2	6	7
3	4	1	5	6	7	9	2	8
5	6	2	8	9	4	7	3	1
9	8	7	3	2	1	4	5	6

6

2	4	3	6	5	9	7	1	8
9	7	8	1	2	3	4	5	6
1	6	5	8	7	4	2	3	9
8	1	9	4	6	2	3	7	5
3	5	4	7	8	1	6	9	2
6	2	7	3	9	5	8	4	1
4	9	1	2	3	6	5	8	7
7	3	2	5	1	8	9	6	4
5	8	6	9	4	7	1	2	3

7

1	6	9	5	3	8	4	2	7
5	3	7	2	4	9	8	1	6
2	4	8	6	7	1	5	9	3
7	5	1	9	6	2	3	8	4
3	9	4	7	8	5	2	6	1
8	2	6	4	1	3	7	5	9
6	8	5	3	9	7	1	4	2
4	1	3	8	2	6	9	7	5
9	7	2	1	5	4	6	3	8

8

8	7	3	2	1	9	5	4	6
9	6	2	8	4	5	7	3	1
4	5	1	3	6	7	8	9	2
3	9	4	5	2	8	1	6	7
6	8	7	1	9	3	4	2	5
2	1	5	6	7	4	9	8	3
7	4	6	9	3	1	2	5	8
1	3	8	4	5	2	6	7	9
5	2	9	7	8	6	3	1	4

9

8	3	1	7	5	9	6	4	2
4	2	7	6	8	1	3	5	9
6	9	5	3	2	4	8	1	7
1	7	9	2	3	6	4	8	5
5	6	4	9	1	8	2	7	3
3	8	2	5	4	7	1	9	6
2	1	6	8	7	5	9	3	4
7	4	3	1	9	2	5	6	8
9	5	8	4	6	3	7	2	1

10

6	3	7	2	1	4	8	5	9
9	2	1	8	5	6	3	7	4
4	8	5	9	3	7	1	2	6
3	5	9	7	2	1	4	6	8
7	6	2	4	8	3	9	1	5
1	4	8	5	6	9	2	3	7
8	1	6	3	9	5	7	4	2
5	9	4	1	7	2	6	8	3
2	7	3	6	4	8	5	9	1

11

4	7	1	3	9	6	2	5	8
5	3	8	2	7	1	4	6	9
9	2	6	5	4	8	7	1	3
2	6	7	4	8	5	9	3	1
1	8	5	7	3	9	6	2	4
3	4	9	1	6	2	8	7	5
6	1	3	8	2	4	5	9	7
7	9	4	6	5	3	1	8	2
8	5	2	9	1	7	3	4	6

12

3	8	7	6	1	5	9	2	4
1	6	2	9	3	4	8	7	5
9	5	4	2	7	8	6	3	1
5	4	8	1	9	7	3	6	2
7	2	1	5	6	3	4	9	8
6	9	3	8	4	2	1	5	7
4	7	9	3	5	1	2	8	6
2	1	6	7	8	9	5	4	3
8	3	5	4	2	6	7	1	9

13

2	1	3	9	5	8	6	7	4
9	4	5	6	7	1	2	8	3
8	6	7	3	2	4	9	1	5
5	7	8	1	9	6	3	4	2
1	2	4	5	8	3	7	6	9
3	9	6	2	4	7	1	5	8
7	5	9	8	6	2	4	3	1
6	8	1	4	3	9	5	2	7
4	3	2	7	1	5	8	9	6

14

8	1	3	5	9	4	6	7	2
9	6	7	8	2	1	3	4	5
5	4	2	3	7	6	1	9	8
7	8	4	6	3	5	9	2	1
1	5	9	2	4	8	7	3	6
2	3	6	9	1	7	5	8	4
6	7	5	4	8	3	2	1	9
4	9	1	7	5	2	8	6	3
3	2	8	1	6	9	4	5	7

15

4	3	7	2	8	1	6	9	5
6	1	9	3	7	5	8	2	4
5	8	2	9	4	6	7	1	3
3	7	6	1	5	2	9	4	8
2	9	1	8	6	4	5	3	7
8	4	5	7	9	3	1	6	2
9	2	3	5	1	8	4	7	6
1	6	8	4	3	7	2	5	9
7	5	4	6	2	9	3	8	1

16

1	4	8	5	7	6	2	9	3
6	2	3	4	1	9	5	8	7
9	7	5	8	3	2	4	6	1
5	6	9	3	2	7	8	1	4
8	3	2	6	4	1	7	5	9
7	1	4	9	8	5	3	2	6
4	9	7	2	6	8	1	3	5
3	8	6	1	5	4	9	7	2
2	5	1	7	9	3	6	4	8

17

1	5	8	7	6	3	2	4	9
7	9	2	8	4	1	5	6	3
6	3	4	2	5	9	1	7	8
3	2	5	9	7	6	8	1	4
9	4	7	1	8	5	6	3	2
8	6	1	3	2	4	7	9	5
4	8	3	6	1	2	9	5	7
2	1	9	5	3	7	4	8	6
5	7	6	4	9	8	3	2	1

18

6	8	1	7	5	4	3	9	2
5	3	4	9	8	2	6	7	1
9	2	7	3	1	6	8	4	5
8	4	9	1	2	5	7	3	6
7	1	2	6	4	3	5	8	9
3	5	6	8	9	7	2	1	4
1	7	3	5	6	9	4	2	8
2	9	5	4	3	8	1	6	7
4	6	8	2	7	1	9	5	3

19

4	9	6	2	7	5	3	1	8
3	2	1	9	4	8	7	6	5
7	5	8	6	1	3	9	4	2
5	4	2	3	9	6	1	8	7
6	7	9	4	8	1	5	2	3
1	8	3	7	5	2	6	9	4
8	6	7	5	2	9	4	3	1
9	1	4	8	3	7	2	5	6
2	3	5	1	6	4	8	7	9

20

6	5	8	9	2	1	4	7	3
1	9	7	3	4	8	2	5	6
3	4	2	5	6	7	8	9	1
4	8	3	1	5	6	9	2	7
2	6	5	4	7	9	1	3	8
7	1	9	8	3	2	5	6	4
8	2	6	7	1	5	3	4	9
9	7	4	2	8	3	6	1	5
5	3	1	6	9	4	7	8	2

21

9	4	3	2	7	5	8	1	6
2	6	7	9	1	8	3	4	5
1	5	8	3	6	4	7	2	9
7	1	5	8	4	9	2	6	3
6	3	9	5	2	7	1	8	4
8	2	4	1	3	6	5	9	7
5	9	1	6	8	3	4	7	2
3	7	2	4	9	1	6	5	8
4	8	6	7	5	2	9	3	1

22

6	8	9	3	4	7	1	5	2
5	1	3	8	6	2	9	7	4
7	4	2	1	9	5	3	6	8
8	9	7	4	3	6	2	1	5
2	6	4	5	1	8	7	9	3
3	5	1	2	7	9	4	8	6
9	7	8	6	2	4	5	3	1
4	3	5	9	8	1	6	2	7
1	2	6	7	5	3	8	4	9

23

5	6	1	9	2	7	4	8	3
3	7	9	8	1	4	2	6	5
8	4	2	6	3	5	1	9	7
7	2	5	4	8	1	6	3	9
4	8	6	5	9	3	7	1	2
9	1	3	2	7	6	5	4	8
2	3	4	7	6	9	8	5	1
6	9	7	1	5	8	3	2	4
1	5	8	3	4	2	9	7	6

24

8	6	3	7	5	2	9	4	1
1	9	4	8	3	6	7	5	2
2	5	7	4	1	9	8	6	3
5	7	6	2	8	4	3	1	9
9	1	2	3	6	5	4	7	8
3	4	8	1	9	7	5	2	6
7	2	9	6	4	3	1	8	5
4	8	5	9	2	1	6	3	7
6	3	1	5	7	8	2	9	4

25

1	8	9	5	2	3	7	4	6
2	3	7	9	6	4	5	8	1
6	4	5	7	1	8	2	9	3
4	1	8	2	3	6	9	5	7
3	7	2	8	9	5	1	6	4
9	5	6	1	4	7	3	2	8
5	6	4	3	7	2	8	1	9
7	2	1	6	8	9	4	3	5
8	9	3	4	5	1	6	7	2

26

5	8	6	2	7	3	9	1	4
3	2	9	1	4	6	7	8	5
7	4	1	9	5	8	6	3	2
9	1	7	8	2	5	3	4	6
6	3	8	4	1	7	5	2	9
2	5	4	6	3	9	8	7	1
4	7	3	5	6	1	2	9	8
8	6	2	7	9	4	1	5	3
1	9	5	3	8	2	4	6	7

27

2	1	8	3	9	6	5	4	7
4	6	5	7	8	1	2	9	3
3	7	9	5	2	4	8	1	6
9	8	2	1	7	5	3	6	4
7	5	6	4	3	8	1	2	9
1	3	4	2	6	9	7	8	5
8	9	7	6	1	3	4	5	2
6	4	3	8	5	2	9	7	1
5	2	1	9	4	7	6	3	8

28

9	8	4	3	5	6	2	1	7
5	7	2	9	1	4	8	6	3
6	1	3	8	2	7	4	5	9
2	9	7	5	6	1	3	4	8
8	3	1	7	4	9	6	2	5
4	5	6	2	8	3	7	9	1
3	2	8	4	9	5	1	7	6
7	6	9	1	3	2	5	8	4
1	4	5	6	7	8	9	3	2

29

3	4	6	8	1	5	2	9	7
5	7	8	2	9	3	1	4	6
1	2	9	6	4	7	5	8	3
4	9	1	7	8	2	3	6	5
7	8	3	5	6	9	4	1	2
6	5	2	4	3	1	9	7	8
9	1	7	3	5	8	6	2	4
8	3	4	1	2	6	7	5	9
2	6	5	9	7	4	8	3	1

30

3	2	8	6	9	5	7	4	1
6	1	7	4	3	2	9	8	5
9	5	4	1	7	8	3	2	6
4	7	3	5	2	9	6	1	8
1	9	5	8	6	4	2	7	3
8	6	2	7	1	3	4	5	9
7	4	6	3	5	1	8	9	2
5	8	9	2	4	6	1	3	7
2	3	1	9	8	7	5	6	4

31

2	7	3	9	5	1	6	8	4
1	9	8	4	2	6	3	7	5
5	4	6	7	8	3	2	1	9
7	6	9	5	1	2	8	4	3
4	1	2	8	3	7	5	9	6
3	8	5	6	4	9	1	2	7
6	2	1	3	7	4	9	5	8
8	3	4	2	9	5	7	6	1
9	5	7	1	6	8	4	3	2

32

2	9	1	8	4	5	3	6	7
7	6	5	1	3	2	4	9	8
4	8	3	9	6	7	2	1	5
9	1	7	6	2	3	5	8	4
6	4	2	5	9	8	1	7	3
5	3	8	4	7	1	9	2	6
8	5	4	2	1	6	7	3	9
1	7	9	3	8	4	6	5	2
3	2	6	7	5	9	8	4	1

33

8	2	4	6	5	9	3	7	1
1	3	5	4	7	8	2	6	9
6	7	9	2	3	1	8	4	5
4	6	1	5	8	2	7	9	3
9	5	7	3	1	4	6	2	8
3	8	2	9	6	7	5	1	4
5	4	8	1	2	6	9	3	7
2	9	3	7	4	5	1	8	6
7	1	6	8	9	3	4	5	2

34

7	3	2	1	8	4	5	9	6
4	9	8	5	6	7	2	3	1
1	5	6	2	3	9	4	7	8
2	8	5	4	1	3	7	6	9
3	7	1	9	2	6	8	4	5
6	4	9	8	7	5	1	2	3
5	6	3	7	4	8	9	1	2
8	2	7	3	9	1	6	5	4
9	1	4	6	5	2	3	8	7

35

1	7	3	6	5	2	8	9	4
6	9	2	4	1	8	7	5	3
5	4	8	9	3	7	1	2	6
9	5	1	3	2	4	6	7	8
3	2	7	8	9	6	4	1	5
8	6	4	1	7	5	9	3	2
2	1	6	7	8	3	5	4	9
7	8	5	2	4	9	3	6	1
4	3	9	5	6	1	2	8	7

36

4	9	5	3	6	7	8	1	2
8	3	2	1	5	9	7	6	4
6	1	7	8	2	4	3	5	9
1	7	3	6	9	5	2	4	8
5	2	8	4	7	1	9	3	6
9	6	4	2	3	8	5	7	1
2	5	6	9	1	3	4	8	7
7	4	9	5	8	6	1	2	3
3	8	1	7	4	2	6	9	5

37

5	9	8	3	6	2	7	4	1
7	1	6	4	8	9	2	5	3
4	2	3	7	1	5	8	6	9
9	5	7	1	4	8	3	2	6
8	4	2	6	9	3	5	1	7
3	6	1	2	5	7	4	9	8
6	7	5	9	3	4	1	8	2
2	8	9	5	7	1	6	3	4
1	3	4	8	2	6	9	7	5

38

8	4	7	9	5	2	3	1	6
2	1	3	6	8	4	9	5	7
6	5	9	7	3	1	4	8	2
7	3	4	5	1	9	6	2	8
5	9	8	2	6	7	1	3	4
1	6	2	3	4	8	5	7	9
3	2	5	4	7	6	8	9	1
4	7	1	8	9	5	2	6	3
9	8	6	1	2	3	7	4	5

39

3	5	1	4	2	6	7	8	9
6	7	9	8	5	3	4	2	1
8	2	4	9	1	7	3	6	5
5	6	2	1	8	4	9	7	3
9	4	7	5	3	2	8	1	6
1	8	3	7	6	9	2	5	4
2	1	6	3	4	8	5	9	7
4	9	8	6	7	5	1	3	2
7	3	5	2	9	1	6	4	8

40

1	5	4	7	3	2	8	6	9
3	7	8	6	4	9	1	2	5
2	9	6	8	1	5	3	4	7
5	6	3	4	2	8	9	7	1
7	8	2	3	9	1	6	5	4
4	1	9	5	6	7	2	3	8
6	4	7	1	8	3	5	9	2
9	3	1	2	5	4	7	8	6
8	2	5	9	7	6	4	1	3

41

9	8	3	5	6	4	1	2	7
6	1	7	9	3	2	4	5	8
4	2	5	1	7	8	6	3	9
7	4	6	2	8	3	5	9	1
8	3	9	4	1	5	2	7	6
2	5	1	7	9	6	3	8	4
3	9	2	6	4	7	8	1	5
5	7	4	8	2	1	9	6	3
1	6	8	3	5	9	7	4	2

42

6	8	1	3	7	4	5	2	9
2	7	5	6	9	8	3	1	4
9	3	4	2	1	5	6	7	8
7	6	8	1	4	3	2	9	5
4	9	3	7	5	2	8	6	1
5	1	2	9	8	6	7	4	3
3	4	9	8	6	7	1	5	2
8	5	6	4	2	1	9	3	7
1	2	7	5	3	9	4	8	6

43

9	2	5	1	7	4	6	8	3
3	4	1	5	8	6	7	9	2
6	8	7	9	3	2	1	4	5
7	6	2	3	5	9	8	1	4
4	1	9	7	2	8	3	5	6
8	5	3	4	6	1	2	7	9
5	7	8	2	4	3	9	6	1
1	3	6	8	9	5	4	2	7
2	9	4	6	1	7	5	3	8

44

9	7	1	3	8	6	4	5	2
5	3	4	9	2	7	1	6	8
6	8	2	4	1	5	7	3	9
1	9	7	5	3	4	8	2	6
8	2	6	1	7	9	5	4	3
4	5	3	8	6	2	9	7	1
7	1	8	2	5	3	6	9	4
3	6	9	7	4	1	2	8	5
2	4	5	6	9	8	3	1	7

45

1	5	7	3	9	4	8	6	2
4	6	8	1	2	5	3	9	7
2	3	9	7	6	8	1	5	4
3	7	6	4	5	2	9	8	1
8	2	5	9	1	6	4	7	3
9	4	1	8	3	7	6	2	5
7	1	4	2	8	9	5	3	6
6	9	2	5	4	3	7	1	8
5	8	3	6	7	1	2	4	9

46

7	4	5	8	3	6	1	2	9
1	6	3	5	9	2	7	4	8
8	9	2	1	7	4	3	6	5
9	5	4	3	6	7	2	8	1
2	3	1	9	5	8	4	7	6
6	7	8	4	2	1	9	5	3
3	8	9	7	4	5	6	1	2
5	2	7	6	1	9	8	3	4
4	1	6	2	8	3	5	9	7

47

6	3	9	8	1	4	2	7	5
8	4	7	2	5	6	3	9	1
2	5	1	3	7	9	8	6	4
5	7	2	6	4	1	9	8	3
3	9	8	7	2	5	1	4	6
1	6	4	9	8	3	5	2	7
9	8	6	5	3	7	4	1	2
4	2	5	1	6	8	7	3	9
7	1	3	4	9	2	6	5	8

48

7	5	1	2	8	9	4	3	6
2	6	3	5	7	4	9	8	1
4	9	8	6	1	3	7	2	5
3	4	7	8	9	6	5	1	2
8	1	9	3	2	5	6	4	7
5	2	6	7	4	1	3	9	8
9	7	2	4	5	8	1	6	3
1	3	5	9	6	2	8	7	4
6	8	4	1	3	7	2	5	9

49

6	7	1	2	8	4	9	5	3
9	2	8	5	1	3	6	7	4
5	4	3	9	6	7	2	1	8
2	6	4	3	5	1	8	9	7
1	3	5	8	7	9	4	6	2
7	8	9	6	4	2	5	3	1
3	1	6	4	9	8	7	2	5
4	5	7	1	2	6	3	8	9
8	9	2	7	3	5	1	4	6

50

2	7	8	9	5	3	6	1	4
9	6	1	8	4	7	3	5	2
4	3	5	2	1	6	9	7	8
1	4	3	7	2	9	8	6	5
5	9	6	3	8	1	4	2	7
7	8	2	5	6	4	1	3	9
3	5	4	6	9	2	7	8	1
6	2	9	1	7	8	5	4	3
8	1	7	4	3	5	2	9	6

51

8	9	5	2	7	1	3	6	4
2	3	4	8	6	9	5	7	1
6	1	7	5	4	3	2	9	8
5	7	3	4	9	6	1	8	2
9	6	1	3	8	2	4	5	7
4	8	2	1	5	7	9	3	6
7	5	6	9	2	4	8	1	3
1	4	8	6	3	5	7	2	9
3	2	9	7	1	8	6	4	5

52

1	8	4	7	3	9	2	5	6
3	9	7	2	6	5	8	1	4
6	5	2	8	4	1	9	3	7
4	3	6	9	2	8	5	7	1
5	2	1	6	7	3	4	9	8
9	7	8	1	5	4	3	6	2
7	6	9	5	8	2	1	4	3
2	1	3	4	9	6	7	8	5
8	4	5	3	1	7	6	2	9

53

5	8	3	9	2	6	7	4	1
1	4	9	8	3	7	5	6	2
2	6	7	4	5	1	3	8	9
6	1	5	3	4	2	8	9	7
7	3	8	6	9	5	2	1	4
4	9	2	1	7	8	6	3	5
9	2	6	5	1	3	4	7	8
8	5	4	7	6	9	1	2	3
3	7	1	2	8	4	9	5	6

54

4	7	8	1	3	5	2	9	6
9	3	1	4	2	6	7	5	8
5	6	2	9	8	7	1	3	4
7	5	3	8	9	4	6	1	2
8	9	6	2	7	1	5	4	3
2	1	4	6	5	3	8	7	9
6	4	9	5	1	2	3	8	7
3	8	5	7	6	9	4	2	1
1	2	7	3	4	8	9	6	5

55

7	9	6	4	5	3	2	8	1
4	8	1	2	6	7	3	9	5
2	5	3	9	1	8	4	7	6
3	2	8	5	4	1	7	6	9
1	6	4	8	7	9	5	2	3
5	7	9	6	3	2	1	4	8
6	4	2	1	8	5	9	3	7
8	3	5	7	9	4	6	1	2
9	1	7	3	2	6	8	5	4

56

2	7	9	3	5	1	6	4	8
3	1	5	6	8	4	2	9	7
6	4	8	2	7	9	5	3	1
9	5	4	1	6	7	8	2	3
8	6	1	9	2	3	7	5	4
7	2	3	5	4	8	1	6	9
5	8	7	4	3	2	9	1	6
4	9	2	8	1	6	3	7	5
1	3	6	7	9	5	4	8	2

57

2	6	9	7	3	8	1	4	5
7	8	5	4	6	1	3	2	9
4	3	1	5	9	2	6	8	7
6	1	7	9	4	3	8	5	2
8	2	4	6	1	5	9	7	3
5	9	3	8	2	7	4	6	1
9	5	8	1	7	4	2	3	6
1	7	2	3	8	6	5	9	4
3	4	6	2	5	9	7	1	8

58

5	2	6	1	4	8	3	7	9
8	9	3	5	6	7	1	4	2
1	7	4	9	2	3	5	6	8
2	4	5	6	3	9	8	1	7
3	6	1	7	8	2	9	5	4
9	8	7	4	5	1	6	2	3
7	1	2	3	9	5	4	8	6
6	3	8	2	1	4	7	9	5
4	5	9	8	7	6	2	3	1

59

6	3	8	4	9	1	2	5	7
9	5	4	2	7	8	3	1	6
7	1	2	5	6	3	4	9	8
1	2	9	8	4	7	5	6	3
3	8	5	1	2	6	7	4	9
4	7	6	9	3	5	1	8	2
8	4	7	3	1	9	6	2	5
2	9	3	6	5	4	8	7	1
5	6	1	7	8	2	9	3	4

60

8	7	2	3	1	5	4	9	6
9	3	6	7	2	4	1	8	5
5	1	4	6	8	9	7	2	3
1	2	5	9	7	3	6	4	8
3	4	9	5	6	8	2	1	7
7	6	8	1	4	2	5	3	9
6	5	3	4	9	1	8	7	2
2	9	1	8	5	7	3	6	4
4	8	7	2	3	6	9	5	1

61

8	1	6	3	9	5	2	7	4
9	2	7	4	1	6	3	5	8
5	4	3	8	2	7	6	1	9
7	3	8	1	5	9	4	2	6
2	9	1	6	4	3	7	8	5
6	5	4	2	7	8	1	9	3
3	6	9	7	8	2	5	4	1
4	8	2	5	6	1	9	3	7
1	7	5	9	3	4	8	6	2

62

9	8	2	4	6	5	1	3	7
4	3	1	7	9	8	2	5	6
6	7	5	2	3	1	8	4	9
2	5	6	9	8	3	7	1	4
7	9	3	6	1	4	5	8	2
8	1	4	5	7	2	6	9	3
5	4	9	8	2	6	3	7	1
1	6	8	3	4	7	9	2	5
3	2	7	1	5	9	4	6	8

63

3	9	6	4	1	5	2	7	8
8	7	5	9	3	2	1	4	6
2	4	1	7	8	6	3	9	5
5	1	9	3	4	8	6	2	7
4	8	3	6	2	7	9	5	1
7	6	2	5	9	1	8	3	4
6	2	4	8	5	9	7	1	3
9	3	8	1	7	4	5	6	2
1	5	7	2	6	3	4	8	9

64

4	7	2	6	1	3	8	5	9
5	6	8	4	9	7	3	1	2
1	9	3	2	5	8	6	4	7
8	2	9	7	6	1	5	3	4
6	3	5	9	4	2	7	8	1
7	1	4	8	3	5	9	2	6
2	8	1	3	7	6	4	9	5
3	4	6	5	2	9	1	7	8
9	5	7	1	8	4	2	6	3

65

9	8	2	6	5	4	1	3	7
1	5	7	8	3	9	2	6	4
4	6	3	2	7	1	5	9	8
2	4	1	7	8	6	9	5	3
5	3	9	1	4	2	8	7	6
8	7	6	3	9	5	4	2	1
3	2	5	4	6	8	7	1	9
6	9	8	5	1	7	3	4	2
7	1	4	9	2	3	6	8	5

66

4	1	7	6	5	9	8	2	3
3	6	8	1	2	4	9	7	5
9	2	5	3	7	8	1	6	4
5	8	4	7	6	1	2	3	9
1	7	6	2	9	3	5	4	8
2	9	3	8	4	5	7	1	6
7	3	1	5	8	6	4	9	2
6	5	9	4	1	2	3	8	7
8	4	2	9	3	7	6	5	1

67

8	1	2	5	7	6	3	4	9
6	5	9	8	3	4	1	2	7
4	7	3	9	1	2	5	6	8
5	3	7	6	8	9	4	1	2
9	4	1	3	2	7	6	8	5
2	6	8	4	5	1	9	7	3
3	9	6	7	4	8	2	5	1
7	2	4	1	9	5	8	3	6
1	8	5	2	6	3	7	9	4

68

5	3	7	6	4	9	1	2	8
6	1	2	3	8	7	9	5	4
4	9	8	2	5	1	7	3	6
1	2	6	4	7	3	5	8	9
7	4	9	8	6	5	3	1	2
8	5	3	1	9	2	6	4	7
2	8	1	7	3	6	4	9	5
3	7	5	9	2	4	8	6	1
9	6	4	5	1	8	2	7	3

69

5	7	9	4	8	3	1	2	6
3	4	1	2	6	7	8	5	9
6	2	8	1	9	5	4	3	7
1	8	2	9	4	6	5	7	3
7	5	6	3	2	1	9	4	8
4	9	3	5	7	8	6	1	2
8	1	7	6	3	4	2	9	5
9	6	5	7	1	2	3	8	4
2	3	4	8	5	9	7	6	1

70

7	4	3	5	2	9	8	1	6
1	2	9	6	7	8	5	4	3
8	6	5	3	4	1	9	7	2
2	3	7	4	8	5	6	9	1
5	1	4	9	3	6	7	2	8
9	8	6	7	1	2	4	3	5
3	9	1	8	6	7	2	5	4
6	7	2	1	5	4	3	8	9
4	5	8	2	9	3	1	6	7

71

6	5	2	1	3	4	9	8	7
7	3	8	9	2	5	4	6	1
1	9	4	6	7	8	3	2	5
9	8	7	4	5	2	1	3	6
4	6	3	8	1	9	5	7	2
2	1	5	3	6	7	8	4	9
5	4	9	7	8	6	2	1	3
8	7	1	2	9	3	6	5	4
3	2	6	5	4	1	7	9	8

72

3	7	8	5	1	4	2	6	9
1	4	6	9	3	2	8	5	7
9	2	5	6	8	7	3	1	4
4	6	9	8	7	5	1	2	3
2	8	3	1	9	6	4	7	5
7	5	1	4	2	3	6	9	8
8	1	2	3	5	9	7	4	6
6	9	7	2	4	8	5	3	1
5	3	4	7	6	1	9	8	2

73

7	8	3	5	1	6	9	2	4
9	6	4	3	7	2	5	8	1
1	2	5	8	4	9	7	3	6
4	9	2	6	8	7	1	5	3
8	1	7	2	5	3	6	4	9
3	5	6	1	9	4	8	7	2
2	3	9	7	6	5	4	1	8
5	4	1	9	3	8	2	6	7
6	7	8	4	2	1	3	9	5

74

3	4	1	6	7	5	9	2	8
6	8	2	1	4	9	5	7	3
9	5	7	2	3	8	4	6	1
1	6	5	3	2	4	7	8	9
8	7	4	9	1	6	2	3	5
2	9	3	8	5	7	6	1	4
5	3	6	7	9	1	8	4	2
7	1	9	4	8	2	3	5	6
4	2	8	5	6	3	1	9	7

75

5	1	3	2	9	6	7	8	4
7	4	6	1	8	5	9	3	2
8	2	9	7	4	3	6	1	5
2	5	7	6	1	8	3	4	9
6	3	1	9	5	4	2	7	8
9	8	4	3	7	2	5	6	1
4	7	2	8	6	9	1	5	3
3	6	8	5	2	1	4	9	7
1	9	5	4	3	7	8	2	6

76

1	5	9	2	4	7	8	3	6
3	4	2	8	6	5	9	7	1
6	8	7	3	1	9	2	5	4
2	1	4	5	8	3	6	9	7
8	7	5	4	9	6	3	1	2
9	6	3	1	7	2	4	8	5
4	3	8	7	2	1	5	6	9
5	9	1	6	3	4	7	2	8
7	2	6	9	5	8	1	4	3

77

5	8	6	2	9	4	1	3	7
4	3	9	8	1	7	6	5	2
1	2	7	5	3	6	8	4	9
3	6	5	4	2	8	9	7	1
8	4	1	9	7	5	3	2	6
7	9	2	1	6	3	4	8	5
2	5	8	6	4	1	7	9	3
9	1	3	7	8	2	5	6	4
6	7	4	3	5	9	2	1	8

78

7	1	9	8	3	6	5	2	4
6	4	5	2	7	9	1	3	8
2	8	3	4	1	5	9	6	7
4	9	8	7	5	2	3	1	6
3	2	6	1	9	8	7	4	5
1	5	7	3	6	4	8	9	2
9	6	4	5	8	3	2	7	1
8	7	2	9	4	1	6	5	3
5	3	1	6	2	7	4	8	9

79

3	6	5	9	8	4	7	1	2
2	4	9	1	7	6	5	3	8
1	7	8	3	5	2	4	6	9
5	1	4	8	3	9	2	7	6
6	8	2	7	4	1	3	9	5
9	3	7	2	6	5	1	8	4
7	2	6	4	9	3	8	5	1
8	5	1	6	2	7	9	4	3
4	9	3	5	1	8	6	2	7

80

8	1	5	3	2	9	7	6	4
6	9	3	7	4	1	5	2	8
7	2	4	8	5	6	1	9	3
4	3	2	5	8	7	9	1	6
5	6	7	1	9	4	8	3	2
9	8	1	6	3	2	4	5	7
3	7	8	9	6	5	2	4	1
1	4	9	2	7	3	6	8	5
2	5	6	4	1	8	3	7	9

81

1	9	8	4	5	7	3	6	2
7	6	4	2	9	3	8	5	1
3	2	5	6	8	1	9	4	7
9	7	1	8	4	2	6	3	5
5	4	2	1	3	6	7	8	9
8	3	6	5	7	9	2	1	4
2	8	3	9	1	4	5	7	6
4	5	9	7	6	8	1	2	3
6	1	7	3	2	5	4	9	8

82

9	7	2	6	1	4	8	3	5
5	3	4	8	7	9	6	2	1
6	8	1	3	2	5	9	4	7
2	5	7	9	3	6	4	1	8
3	6	8	1	4	7	2	5	9
4	1	9	2	5	8	3	7	6
1	9	3	7	6	2	5	8	4
7	4	6	5	8	3	1	9	2
8	2	5	4	9	1	7	6	3

83

4	7	9	6	3	1	2	5	8
8	3	1	5	9	2	4	7	6
5	6	2	4	8	7	3	1	9
1	2	8	7	6	5	9	4	3
6	4	7	3	2	9	1	8	5
3	9	5	1	4	8	6	2	7
2	5	4	9	7	6	8	3	1
9	1	3	8	5	4	7	6	2
7	8	6	2	1	3	5	9	4

84

1	8	4	9	3	6	7	5	2
5	9	3	2	1	7	8	6	4
2	6	7	4	8	5	9	1	3
3	1	5	7	2	9	4	8	6
9	4	2	6	5	8	1	3	7
6	7	8	3	4	1	5	2	9
8	2	9	1	6	4	3	7	5
4	3	1	5	7	2	6	9	8
7	5	6	8	9	3	2	4	1

85

5	3	1	9	2	4	7	6	8
4	2	8	6	5	7	1	9	3
9	6	7	3	8	1	4	5	2
2	1	6	5	7	9	3	8	4
3	4	5	1	6	8	2	7	9
7	8	9	4	3	2	5	1	6
8	7	4	2	1	6	9	3	5
1	5	2	8	9	3	6	4	7
6	9	3	7	4	5	8	2	1

86

9	7	2	8	1	5	6	4	3
3	8	5	9	4	6	1	2	7
4	6	1	2	3	7	8	5	9
7	2	3	1	6	9	4	8	5
5	1	8	4	7	3	9	6	2
6	4	9	5	2	8	3	7	1
8	3	6	7	9	2	5	1	4
2	5	4	3	8	1	7	9	6
1	9	7	6	5	4	2	3	8

87

1	3	9	2	6	4	5	8	7
5	2	6	3	8	7	4	9	1
4	8	7	5	9	1	2	3	6
2	4	8	1	3	6	7	5	9
7	5	1	8	4	9	6	2	3
6	9	3	7	5	2	1	4	8
9	7	2	4	1	8	3	6	5
8	1	5	6	2	3	9	7	4
3	6	4	9	7	5	8	1	2

88

6	8	2	3	9	7	1	5	4
3	1	4	6	8	5	9	7	2
7	5	9	2	1	4	6	3	8
8	6	7	5	2	1	3	4	9
5	4	3	9	7	6	2	8	1
9	2	1	8	4	3	5	6	7
1	9	6	7	3	8	4	2	5
2	7	5	4	6	9	8	1	3
4	3	8	1	5	2	7	9	6

89

4	9	3	8	1	2	7	6	5
6	7	1	3	5	4	9	2	8
5	8	2	9	6	7	1	4	3
2	5	6	7	3	9	4	8	1
9	1	4	5	8	6	3	7	2
8	3	7	4	2	1	6	5	9
3	6	9	2	4	8	5	1	7
1	2	5	6	7	3	8	9	4
7	4	8	1	9	5	2	3	6

90

8	4	3	7	5	6	9	1	2
5	2	7	9	3	1	8	6	4
1	6	9	4	8	2	7	3	5
9	8	1	6	2	7	4	5	3
2	7	5	3	4	9	1	8	6
6	3	4	5	1	8	2	9	7
4	5	2	8	9	3	6	7	1
3	9	6	1	7	4	5	2	8
7	1	8	2	6	5	3	4	9

91

1	9	5	2	3	8	6	7	4
7	4	3	5	9	6	8	2	1
6	8	2	7	4	1	3	9	5
5	2	6	3	8	9	1	4	7
9	3	7	4	1	5	2	6	8
8	1	4	6	7	2	9	5	3
4	5	9	1	2	3	7	8	6
2	7	1	8	6	4	5	3	9
3	6	8	9	5	7	4	1	2

92

1	7	2	8	6	4	3	5	9
4	9	5	7	3	2	1	8	6
6	3	8	1	5	9	4	2	7
3	1	9	2	8	6	7	4	5
2	6	4	5	9	7	8	1	3
8	5	7	3	4	1	6	9	2
7	8	1	6	2	5	9	3	4
5	4	3	9	7	8	2	6	1
9	2	6	4	1	3	5	7	8

93

2	5	4	7	3	9	8	6	1
1	8	3	4	6	2	9	7	5
9	7	6	1	8	5	3	2	4
4	2	7	8	5	1	6	9	3
6	3	9	2	4	7	1	5	8
5	1	8	3	9	6	7	4	2
7	6	1	5	2	3	4	8	9
8	9	2	6	1	4	5	3	7
3	4	5	9	7	8	2	1	6

94

1	3	6	7	8	9	2	4	5
9	2	4	1	5	6	7	3	8
7	5	8	4	3	2	6	9	1
6	4	3	2	7	8	1	5	9
2	7	5	9	1	4	3	8	6
8	1	9	3	6	5	4	7	2
3	9	7	5	2	1	8	6	4
5	8	2	6	4	7	9	1	3
4	6	1	8	9	3	5	2	7

95

5	9	1	3	2	6	7	4	8
6	7	2	1	4	8	9	3	5
4	3	8	7	5	9	6	1	2
9	8	6	4	3	5	2	7	1
2	1	4	8	9	7	5	6	3
7	5	3	2	6	1	8	9	4
1	6	7	5	8	3	4	2	9
8	2	9	6	1	4	3	5	7
3	4	5	9	7	2	1	8	6

96

9	2	7	1	5	4	6	8	3
5	3	6	9	8	2	1	4	7
4	1	8	3	7	6	9	5	2
2	9	1	4	6	3	8	7	5
7	6	4	8	2	5	3	1	9
3	8	5	7	9	1	4	2	6
6	7	3	5	1	8	2	9	4
1	4	9	2	3	7	5	6	8
8	5	2	6	4	9	7	3	1

97

8	6	3	5	9	7	4	1	2
7	2	1	4	3	6	5	8	9
4	5	9	8	1	2	3	6	7
2	9	4	6	7	1	8	3	5
3	7	5	2	4	8	6	9	1
1	8	6	3	5	9	2	7	4
5	4	7	9	6	3	1	2	8
9	3	2	1	8	5	7	4	6
6	1	8	7	2	4	9	5	3

98

6	4	9	5	3	7	1	8	2
5	2	8	4	6	1	9	3	7
7	1	3	2	9	8	6	4	5
1	9	5	3	2	6	8	7	4
2	3	6	8	7	4	5	9	1
8	7	4	1	5	9	3	2	6
3	6	2	9	4	5	7	1	8
4	5	1	7	8	3	2	6	9
9	8	7	6	1	2	4	5	3

99

8	9	6	7	4	3	5	1	2
4	2	5	8	1	6	9	3	7
1	7	3	2	9	5	6	4	8
6	4	2	1	3	7	8	9	5
5	1	9	4	8	2	7	6	3
7	3	8	5	6	9	4	2	1
2	6	7	3	5	4	1	8	9
9	5	1	6	2	8	3	7	4
3	8	4	9	7	1	2	5	6

100

6	7	4	9	3	2	1	5	8
2	1	9	5	8	6	3	4	7
8	3	5	4	1	7	2	6	9
1	9	6	8	2	5	4	7	3
5	4	3	6	7	1	9	8	2
7	2	8	3	4	9	6	1	5
4	5	1	2	9	8	7	3	6
9	8	7	1	6	3	5	2	4
3	6	2	7	5	4	8	9	1

101

7	6	2	4	5	1	3	8	9
8	5	1	9	6	3	4	7	2
9	3	4	8	2	7	1	6	5
1	9	5	3	7	6	8	2	4
6	2	7	5	8	4	9	1	3
4	8	3	1	9	2	7	5	6
2	7	9	6	4	8	5	3	1
5	1	8	2	3	9	6	4	7
3	4	6	7	1	5	2	9	8

102

6	8	3	5	1	7	2	9	4
4	1	2	8	6	9	7	5	3
5	9	7	2	4	3	8	1	6
9	7	1	4	8	2	6	3	5
3	4	8	6	9	5	1	2	7
2	6	5	7	3	1	4	8	9
1	5	4	9	7	8	3	6	2
7	3	9	1	2	6	5	4	8
8	2	6	3	5	4	9	7	1

103

7	4	2	9	6	8	3	5	1
5	1	8	3	2	7	4	6	9
9	3	6	1	4	5	7	8	2
6	7	9	5	8	4	2	1	3
3	2	5	7	1	9	8	4	6
1	8	4	6	3	2	9	7	5
2	6	7	8	9	1	5	3	4
4	5	3	2	7	6	1	9	8
8	9	1	4	5	3	6	2	7

104

7	5	2	1	3	8	6	4	9
6	9	3	2	5	4	1	7	8
8	1	4	9	6	7	5	2	3
3	7	5	4	1	2	8	9	6
1	6	9	7	8	3	2	5	4
4	2	8	6	9	5	7	3	1
5	4	6	8	7	9	3	1	2
2	8	7	3	4	1	9	6	5
9	3	1	5	2	6	4	8	7

105

3	6	8	9	7	2	1	4	5
2	4	5	8	1	6	7	9	3
1	9	7	3	4	5	8	6	2
8	2	6	4	5	7	9	3	1
7	3	1	2	6	9	5	8	4
4	5	9	1	3	8	6	2	7
6	1	4	5	8	3	2	7	9
5	7	2	6	9	4	3	1	8
9	8	3	7	2	1	4	5	6

106

2	6	9	7	4	1	3	8	5
3	5	4	9	6	8	7	1	2
1	8	7	3	2	5	4	9	6
4	9	5	8	7	6	2	3	1
6	7	2	5	1	3	8	4	9
8	1	3	2	9	4	6	5	7
7	2	8	4	5	9	1	6	3
9	3	6	1	8	7	5	2	4
5	4	1	6	3	2	9	7	8

107

4	7	3	6	9	2	5	8	1
1	2	8	4	5	7	3	9	6
6	5	9	3	1	8	7	4	2
9	8	2	7	3	5	6	1	4
3	6	5	8	4	1	2	7	9
7	1	4	9	2	6	8	3	5
2	9	6	1	8	3	4	5	7
5	3	1	2	7	4	9	6	8
8	4	7	5	6	9	1	2	3

108

3	6	7	9	1	2	8	4	5
1	8	9	3	5	4	7	6	2
2	5	4	6	8	7	1	3	9
5	3	6	4	7	8	9	2	1
7	1	8	2	3	9	6	5	4
9	4	2	5	6	1	3	8	7
6	2	3	7	9	5	4	1	8
4	7	1	8	2	6	5	9	3
8	9	5	1	4	3	2	7	6

109

4	9	6	8	5	2	3	1	7
7	1	8	3	4	6	2	5	9
5	2	3	7	1	9	6	4	8
3	7	5	6	9	4	8	2	1
8	4	9	1	2	3	5	7	6
2	6	1	5	7	8	9	3	4
6	3	4	2	8	1	7	9	5
9	8	7	4	3	5	1	6	2
1	5	2	9	6	7	4	8	3

110

1	6	4	5	3	7	9	8	2
5	9	8	4	2	6	3	1	7
2	3	7	1	9	8	5	6	4
3	8	1	7	6	5	4	2	9
6	7	2	9	4	1	8	5	3
9	4	5	2	8	3	6	7	1
4	5	9	6	7	2	1	3	8
8	2	6	3	1	9	7	4	5
7	1	3	8	5	4	2	9	6

111

2	6	7	8	3	4	5	9	1
1	9	8	7	6	5	4	2	3
3	5	4	9	1	2	7	6	8
8	4	6	3	7	9	2	1	5
5	1	9	2	8	6	3	4	7
7	2	3	4	5	1	6	8	9
4	8	5	6	9	7	1	3	2
6	3	1	5	2	8	9	7	4
9	7	2	1	4	3	8	5	6

112

5	2	6	9	8	7	1	4	3
9	4	3	6	2	1	7	8	5
8	1	7	3	5	4	9	6	2
6	9	8	4	7	3	2	5	1
4	7	2	8	1	5	3	9	6
1	3	5	2	6	9	4	7	8
3	8	4	5	9	2	6	1	7
7	6	9	1	3	8	5	2	4
2	5	1	7	4	6	8	3	9

113

3	4	9	6	7	1	5	8	2
8	1	6	5	2	3	9	7	4
7	2	5	8	9	4	3	1	6
5	3	4	2	1	9	8	6	7
9	8	2	7	5	6	4	3	1
6	7	1	4	3	8	2	9	5
4	6	3	1	8	5	7	2	9
1	9	7	3	4	2	6	5	8
2	5	8	9	6	7	1	4	3

114

3	6	2	9	4	1	8	5	7
5	8	7	2	3	6	9	1	4
9	1	4	8	5	7	6	2	3
7	4	5	6	1	9	3	8	2
8	2	1	3	7	4	5	6	9
6	3	9	5	8	2	4	7	1
4	9	6	1	2	8	7	3	5
1	5	8	7	9	3	2	4	6
2	7	3	4	6	5	1	9	8

115

5	7	2	4	3	1	8	6	9
1	4	8	6	9	5	7	2	3
3	6	9	8	7	2	1	5	4
7	9	4	1	5	8	2	3	6
8	3	5	9	2	6	4	1	7
2	1	6	3	4	7	5	9	8
9	8	3	5	1	4	6	7	2
6	2	1	7	8	3	9	4	5
4	5	7	2	6	9	3	8	1

116

3	6	1	7	9	2	5	8	4
7	8	4	1	5	6	3	2	9
5	2	9	3	8	4	1	7	6
8	1	7	9	6	3	4	5	2
4	5	6	2	1	8	7	9	3
9	3	2	5	4	7	8	6	1
1	7	8	4	2	9	6	3	5
2	4	3	6	7	5	9	1	8
6	9	5	8	3	1	2	4	7

117

1	2	7	4	6	5	9	3	8
8	9	6	3	1	7	4	2	5
4	3	5	2	9	8	7	6	1
9	6	3	8	4	1	5	7	2
2	7	8	6	5	3	1	9	4
5	1	4	7	2	9	6	8	3
6	4	9	5	8	2	3	1	7
7	5	2	1	3	6	8	4	9
3	8	1	9	7	4	2	5	6

118

4	5	2	1	8	9	3	7	6
3	1	6	5	7	4	8	2	9
9	7	8	6	2	3	5	1	4
7	8	1	4	9	2	6	3	5
2	6	4	8	3	5	7	9	1
5	9	3	7	6	1	2	4	8
8	2	5	9	4	7	1	6	3
1	4	7	3	5	6	9	8	2
6	3	9	2	1	8	4	5	7

119

8	4	3	9	6	5	1	2	7
6	1	5	3	7	2	8	9	4
7	9	2	1	8	4	6	3	5
1	6	8	7	2	3	4	5	9
2	3	9	5	4	8	7	1	6
5	7	4	6	9	1	3	8	2
3	5	6	4	1	9	2	7	8
9	8	7	2	3	6	5	4	1
4	2	1	8	5	7	9	6	3

120

6	4	2	7	5	8	9	3	1
9	8	7	6	1	3	5	4	2
5	1	3	2	9	4	7	8	6
8	7	9	4	3	1	6	2	5
3	5	6	8	7	2	4	1	9
1	2	4	5	6	9	3	7	8
7	6	8	3	2	5	1	9	4
2	3	1	9	4	6	8	5	7
4	9	5	1	8	7	2	6	3

121

9	6	2	3	8	1	7	5	4
1	7	3	6	5	4	9	2	8
8	5	4	7	2	9	3	6	1
4	2	9	1	6	5	8	3	7
7	3	6	2	9	8	4	1	5
5	1	8	4	3	7	6	9	2
6	9	7	5	4	2	1	8	3
3	4	5	8	1	6	2	7	9
2	8	1	9	7	3	5	4	6

122

4	5	9	1	2	8	7	6	3
7	3	1	4	5	6	2	8	9
6	2	8	3	9	7	4	5	1
1	6	2	5	8	3	9	4	7
5	7	3	9	6	4	8	1	2
9	8	4	7	1	2	5	3	6
2	4	6	8	3	9	1	7	5
8	9	5	6	7	1	3	2	4
3	1	7	2	4	5	6	9	8

123

6	3	8	9	2	1	4	5	7
4	2	5	3	8	7	6	1	9
7	1	9	5	4	6	8	3	2
2	8	3	6	9	4	5	7	1
9	4	7	1	5	2	3	6	8
1	5	6	7	3	8	9	2	4
3	9	1	8	7	5	2	4	6
8	6	2	4	1	3	7	9	5
5	7	4	2	6	9	1	8	3

124

3	6	8	7	2	9	5	4	1
2	4	7	5	1	3	6	8	9
5	9	1	8	6	4	2	7	3
7	5	9	2	4	1	3	6	8
1	2	3	6	7	8	4	9	5
6	8	4	3	9	5	7	1	2
4	1	2	9	3	7	8	5	6
8	7	6	1	5	2	9	3	4
9	3	5	4	8	6	1	2	7

125

5	3	1	4	6	7	8	2	9
4	8	9	2	3	1	5	7	6
2	6	7	5	8	9	1	4	3
7	9	6	8	1	4	3	5	2
8	5	2	7	9	3	6	1	4
3	1	4	6	5	2	9	8	7
6	7	3	1	2	8	4	9	5
1	4	5	9	7	6	2	3	8
9	2	8	3	4	5	7	6	1

126

8	4	9	5	6	7	1	3	2
5	6	3	2	8	1	9	7	4
1	7	2	9	4	3	8	5	6
7	9	8	6	1	4	3	2	5
2	3	6	8	5	9	4	1	7
4	5	1	3	7	2	6	8	9
6	2	4	1	3	5	7	9	8
9	1	7	4	2	8	5	6	3
3	8	5	7	9	6	2	4	1

127

4	5	2	6	1	8	9	7	3
6	1	3	9	7	5	4	2	8
9	7	8	3	4	2	6	5	1
5	2	9	8	3	6	7	1	4
3	6	1	7	9	4	2	8	5
7	8	4	2	5	1	3	6	9
1	9	5	4	2	7	8	3	6
8	4	7	5	6	3	1	9	2
2	3	6	1	8	9	5	4	7

128

2	1	4	5	8	6	3	9	7
5	7	8	3	9	1	2	6	4
9	3	6	2	4	7	5	8	1
1	5	7	9	3	8	6	4	2
6	2	3	7	5	4	9	1	8
8	4	9	1	6	2	7	3	5
3	9	1	8	7	5	4	2	6
4	8	5	6	2	9	1	7	3
7	6	2	4	1	3	8	5	9

129

3	2	8	4	7	5	1	6	9
9	6	5	3	1	2	7	4	8
4	7	1	9	8	6	5	3	2
6	5	9	7	2	1	4	8	3
7	8	3	6	9	4	2	5	1
2	1	4	8	5	3	6	9	7
1	9	2	5	4	8	3	7	6
8	4	6	1	3	7	9	2	5
5	3	7	2	6	9	8	1	4

130

4	9	3	8	1	5	2	6	7
8	7	6	9	2	4	1	3	5
5	1	2	6	3	7	8	9	4
2	4	1	3	5	6	9	7	8
6	5	7	1	8	9	3	4	2
9	3	8	4	7	2	6	5	1
1	6	5	2	4	3	7	8	9
7	2	9	5	6	8	4	1	3
3	8	4	7	9	1	5	2	6

131

9	7	3	6	4	2	1	5	8
1	2	8	9	3	5	4	6	7
4	6	5	1	8	7	2	3	9
8	1	4	7	9	3	5	2	6
2	3	9	8	5	6	7	1	4
6	5	7	2	1	4	9	8	3
3	4	1	5	7	8	6	9	2
7	9	2	3	6	1	8	4	5
5	8	6	4	2	9	3	7	1

132

8	2	6	9	3	1	4	5	7
3	5	9	2	7	4	6	1	8
1	7	4	6	8	5	2	9	3
7	4	1	3	2	9	5	8	6
2	6	8	5	4	7	1	3	9
9	3	5	1	6	8	7	4	2
6	8	2	4	1	3	9	7	5
5	1	7	8	9	2	3	6	4
4	9	3	7	5	6	8	2	1

133

8	4	6	2	9	5	3	7	1
9	3	5	7	8	1	2	4	6
7	2	1	4	6	3	9	5	8
6	9	3	8	5	7	1	2	4
1	8	7	9	4	2	5	6	3
4	5	2	1	3	6	7	8	9
2	6	4	3	7	9	8	1	5
5	7	9	6	1	8	4	3	2
3	1	8	5	2	4	6	9	7

134

8	5	9	6	1	2	3	4	7
3	6	2	4	7	8	1	9	5
1	4	7	3	9	5	2	8	6
5	8	3	9	2	6	7	1	4
9	7	6	1	8	4	5	2	3
2	1	4	7	5	3	8	6	9
7	2	1	5	6	9	4	3	8
6	3	8	2	4	7	9	5	1
4	9	5	8	3	1	6	7	2

135

2	4	3	5	7	1	9	6	8
9	5	8	6	2	4	7	1	3
7	1	6	3	8	9	2	4	5
6	8	4	7	5	3	1	9	2
5	2	9	1	4	6	8	3	7
1	3	7	2	9	8	4	5	6
3	7	1	9	6	2	5	8	4
4	6	2	8	1	5	3	7	9
8	9	5	4	3	7	6	2	1

136

6	2	3	7	9	4	8	1	5
9	1	4	8	5	2	6	7	3
8	7	5	3	6	1	9	4	2
3	9	2	4	1	8	5	6	7
5	4	6	9	7	3	2	8	1
1	8	7	5	2	6	3	9	4
7	3	1	6	8	5	4	2	9
4	6	9	2	3	7	1	5	8
2	5	8	1	4	9	7	3	6

137

1	5	3	6	8	2	7	4	9
9	6	8	4	3	7	2	5	1
2	7	4	5	1	9	6	3	8
3	2	9	8	5	1	4	7	6
7	1	6	9	4	3	8	2	5
8	4	5	7	2	6	1	9	3
5	9	1	2	6	4	3	8	7
6	8	2	3	7	5	9	1	4
4	3	7	1	9	8	5	6	2

138

7	9	6	4	5	8	1	3	2
1	4	2	7	6	3	8	5	9
5	3	8	1	9	2	6	4	7
2	1	4	8	3	5	9	7	6
9	8	3	6	4	7	5	2	1
6	5	7	9	2	1	4	8	3
3	7	1	5	8	6	2	9	4
4	2	5	3	1	9	7	6	8
8	6	9	2	7	4	3	1	5

139

6	5	7	9	2	4	3	1	8
4	8	2	5	1	3	7	6	9
1	3	9	7	8	6	4	5	2
2	7	3	4	5	1	8	9	6
9	1	6	2	3	8	5	4	7
8	4	5	6	9	7	1	2	3
7	9	8	1	6	5	2	3	4
5	2	4	3	7	9	6	8	1
3	6	1	8	4	2	9	7	5

140

4	2	8	1	6	9	7	5	3
3	5	7	4	8	2	6	1	9
9	6	1	7	5	3	2	8	4
5	9	4	8	2	7	1	3	6
1	7	2	3	9	6	8	4	5
6	8	3	5	1	4	9	7	2
7	3	6	9	4	8	5	2	1
2	4	5	6	7	1	3	9	8
8	1	9	2	3	5	4	6	7

141

2	3	4	7	1	6	9	5	8
7	6	8	5	2	9	4	1	3
1	5	9	4	8	3	7	2	6
6	1	3	8	5	4	2	7	9
9	4	2	3	6	7	5	8	1
8	7	5	2	9	1	3	6	4
5	9	1	6	4	2	8	3	7
3	8	6	9	7	5	1	4	2
4	2	7	1	3	8	6	9	5

142

1	9	5	7	2	3	4	8	6
6	8	3	4	1	5	2	9	7
4	7	2	9	6	8	1	3	5
7	2	1	8	5	6	9	4	3
9	6	4	2	3	7	5	1	8
5	3	8	1	4	9	6	7	2
3	1	6	5	7	4	8	2	9
8	4	7	6	9	2	3	5	1
2	5	9	3	8	1	7	6	4

143

1	7	4	5	2	9	8	3	6
5	6	8	4	3	7	2	9	1
3	2	9	6	8	1	7	5	4
2	3	7	9	4	5	6	1	8
6	9	1	8	7	3	4	2	5
8	4	5	1	6	2	3	7	9
7	5	6	2	9	4	1	8	3
9	8	2	3	1	6	5	4	7
4	1	3	7	5	8	9	6	2

144

8	1	5	7	9	3	2	4	6
3	7	9	4	6	2	5	1	8
2	4	6	5	8	1	3	7	9
4	5	3	2	7	8	9	6	1
1	2	8	6	5	9	4	3	7
6	9	7	1	3	4	8	2	5
5	6	2	9	4	7	1	8	3
9	8	4	3	1	6	7	5	2
7	3	1	8	2	5	6	9	4

145

8	9	3	6	2	5	1	4	7
7	6	2	4	8	1	5	9	3
4	5	1	3	7	9	2	6	8
2	7	5	8	1	6	4	3	9
3	8	6	5	9	4	7	2	1
1	4	9	2	3	7	8	5	6
5	3	4	1	6	8	9	7	2
9	2	8	7	5	3	6	1	4
6	1	7	9	4	2	3	8	5

146

7	8	5	1	6	9	4	3	2
9	2	1	3	7	4	8	5	6
6	3	4	8	5	2	9	1	7
3	5	7	2	9	1	6	8	4
2	4	6	5	8	7	3	9	1
8	1	9	4	3	6	7	2	5
1	7	3	6	2	8	5	4	9
4	9	8	7	1	5	2	6	3
5	6	2	9	4	3	1	7	8

147

4	8	2	3	5	1	6	7	9
1	5	7	4	6	9	3	2	8
9	3	6	7	8	2	5	4	1
3	2	1	8	7	6	4	9	5
8	6	5	2	9	4	1	3	7
7	9	4	1	3	5	8	6	2
6	1	9	5	4	7	2	8	3
2	4	8	9	1	3	7	5	6
5	7	3	6	2	8	9	1	4

148

9	6	4	5	7	8	2	3	1
3	2	8	9	1	6	7	5	4
7	1	5	2	3	4	8	6	9
4	5	3	1	2	7	9	8	6
2	8	6	4	9	3	5	1	7
1	9	7	8	6	5	4	2	3
5	3	9	6	4	2	1	7	8
8	7	1	3	5	9	6	4	2
6	4	2	7	8	1	3	9	5

149

6	1	3	4	2	5	9	7	8
4	5	9	7	1	8	6	2	3
8	2	7	9	6	3	1	5	4
7	8	5	1	9	4	3	6	2
1	6	2	8	3	7	4	9	5
9	3	4	2	5	6	7	8	1
2	4	8	6	7	1	5	3	9
3	7	1	5	8	9	2	4	6
5	9	6	3	4	2	8	1	7

150

7	4	9	3	8	1	2	6	5
1	8	3	2	5	6	9	4	7
6	5	2	7	9	4	1	3	8
8	1	6	9	2	7	4	5	3
2	7	4	1	3	5	8	9	6
3	9	5	6	4	8	7	2	1
5	2	8	4	7	3	6	1	9
4	3	1	8	6	9	5	7	2
9	6	7	5	1	2	3	8	4

151

1	6	7	5	2	4	9	8	3
2	4	9	1	8	3	5	7	6
3	8	5	7	9	6	2	1	4
5	2	8	4	6	7	1	3	9
9	1	4	2	3	8	7	6	5
6	7	3	9	1	5	4	2	8
4	3	1	6	5	2	8	9	7
7	9	6	8	4	1	3	5	2
8	5	2	3	7	9	6	4	1

152

2	1	7	6	3	4	9	5	8
3	9	8	1	7	5	4	6	2
5	4	6	9	2	8	3	7	1
9	5	1	7	6	2	8	4	3
6	8	3	4	9	1	5	2	7
7	2	4	8	5	3	1	9	6
4	3	9	2	8	6	7	1	5
8	7	2	5	1	9	6	3	4
1	6	5	3	4	7	2	8	9

153

2	6	1	9	4	3	7	8	5
5	4	9	8	7	2	1	3	6
7	3	8	6	1	5	4	2	9
4	7	2	1	3	6	9	5	8
1	8	6	5	9	7	3	4	2
3	9	5	4	2	8	6	7	1
6	2	7	3	5	9	8	1	4
9	5	4	7	8	1	2	6	3
8	1	3	2	6	4	5	9	7

154

2	7	6	1	5	8	9	3	4
8	3	5	4	7	9	6	1	2
4	9	1	6	2	3	5	7	8
6	5	9	3	1	2	8	4	7
1	4	2	8	6	7	3	5	9
7	8	3	5	9	4	1	2	6
9	6	4	7	3	5	2	8	1
5	1	7	2	8	6	4	9	3
3	2	8	9	4	1	7	6	5

155

3	7	8	2	5	4	1	6	9
1	4	6	7	3	9	8	2	5
5	9	2	8	1	6	3	4	7
9	3	4	5	8	1	6	7	2
6	8	5	9	7	2	4	3	1
7	2	1	4	6	3	9	5	8
4	5	9	3	2	8	7	1	6
2	1	3	6	9	7	5	8	4
8	6	7	1	4	5	2	9	3

156

5	4	3	1	2	6	9	7	8
1	7	8	9	3	5	2	4	6
9	2	6	4	8	7	3	5	1
6	1	7	5	4	2	8	9	3
3	9	2	7	1	8	5	6	4
4	8	5	6	9	3	1	2	7
7	3	1	2	6	9	4	8	5
8	5	9	3	7	4	6	1	2
2	6	4	8	5	1	7	3	9

157

8	2	3	5	9	4	7	6	1
9	1	4	7	6	8	3	5	2
5	6	7	1	3	2	9	4	8
7	5	2	8	4	9	6	1	3
3	4	6	2	1	5	8	9	7
1	9	8	6	7	3	4	2	5
6	3	5	9	8	1	2	7	4
4	7	1	3	2	6	5	8	9
2	8	9	4	5	7	1	3	6

158

8	6	7	4	3	5	2	9	1
9	4	1	7	2	8	6	5	3
3	2	5	9	6	1	8	4	7
1	3	9	8	7	6	4	2	5
4	5	8	2	1	9	7	3	6
6	7	2	3	5	4	1	8	9
7	8	4	6	9	3	5	1	2
5	9	6	1	4	2	3	7	8
2	1	3	5	8	7	9	6	4

159

6	7	3	1	4	5	2	9	8
1	5	8	3	9	2	7	6	4
4	2	9	7	8	6	1	5	3
8	3	2	6	1	9	5	4	7
7	1	6	8	5	4	3	2	9
9	4	5	2	3	7	6	8	1
2	8	7	9	6	3	4	1	5
5	6	1	4	7	8	9	3	2
3	9	4	5	2	1	8	7	6

160

5	8	1	7	4	3	2	9	6
9	4	2	6	8	1	3	5	7
3	7	6	2	5	9	4	8	1
2	5	8	1	7	4	9	6	3
6	1	4	9	3	5	7	2	8
7	3	9	8	6	2	5	1	4
1	2	7	4	9	6	8	3	5
8	6	3	5	2	7	1	4	9
4	9	5	3	1	8	6	7	2

161

7	4	1	9	2	5	3	6	8
5	2	3	6	7	8	4	1	9
9	8	6	1	3	4	5	2	7
6	7	9	2	4	1	8	3	5
4	1	8	5	6	3	9	7	2
2	3	5	7	8	9	6	4	1
8	5	4	3	1	2	7	9	6
3	6	2	8	9	7	1	5	4
1	9	7	4	5	6	2	8	3

162

8	3	9	5	7	6	2	4	1
5	4	1	9	2	3	7	8	6
2	7	6	8	1	4	9	5	3
1	8	3	2	4	7	5	6	9
7	9	5	3	6	8	4	1	2
6	2	4	1	9	5	8	3	7
3	1	2	4	8	9	6	7	5
4	5	7	6	3	2	1	9	8
9	6	8	7	5	1	3	2	4

163

8	7	5	9	4	2	1	6	3
6	2	3	1	7	5	4	8	9
4	1	9	8	3	6	7	5	2
7	8	4	6	1	9	2	3	5
3	6	1	2	5	4	9	7	8
9	5	2	7	8	3	6	1	4
5	3	6	4	9	1	8	2	7
1	9	8	3	2	7	5	4	6
2	4	7	5	6	8	3	9	1

164

4	8	2	1	5	9	6	7	3
7	5	3	4	6	8	9	2	1
6	1	9	2	7	3	5	4	8
9	4	8	5	2	1	7	3	6
1	3	5	7	9	6	4	8	2
2	6	7	8	3	4	1	5	9
8	9	4	3	1	5	2	6	7
3	7	1	6	4	2	8	9	5
5	2	6	9	8	7	3	1	4

165

8	1	4	2	6	3	7	5	9
3	5	2	8	7	9	1	4	6
7	9	6	1	5	4	3	8	2
2	4	1	5	9	7	6	3	8
5	7	3	6	8	1	2	9	4
9	6	8	4	3	2	5	1	7
4	2	5	7	1	8	9	6	3
6	3	7	9	4	5	8	2	1
1	8	9	3	2	6	4	7	5

166

1	7	6	2	9	4	8	3	5
5	2	9	1	8	3	7	4	6
8	4	3	7	6	5	2	9	1
4	3	1	9	2	7	5	6	8
2	6	8	4	5	1	9	7	3
7	9	5	6	3	8	1	2	4
3	1	4	5	7	9	6	8	2
6	8	7	3	1	2	4	5	9
9	5	2	8	4	6	3	1	7

167

6	4	9	7	2	8	3	1	5
2	1	5	3	6	9	7	4	8
8	3	7	5	4	1	6	2	9
9	8	4	2	5	6	1	7	3
3	6	2	9	1	7	5	8	4
5	7	1	8	3	4	9	6	2
1	5	6	4	9	2	8	3	7
7	2	3	1	8	5	4	9	6
4	9	8	6	7	3	2	5	1

168

7	5	3	9	2	8	1	6	4
1	2	4	6	5	3	8	9	7
8	9	6	7	4	1	5	3	2
9	3	2	1	8	4	7	5	6
4	8	5	3	7	6	2	1	9
6	1	7	5	9	2	4	8	3
5	6	1	4	3	7	9	2	8
2	4	9	8	6	5	3	7	1
3	7	8	2	1	9	6	4	5

169

9	1	4	6	8	5	7	2	3
3	5	8	1	7	2	9	6	4
6	2	7	4	3	9	5	1	8
4	3	1	8	5	6	2	7	9
2	7	9	3	4	1	6	8	5
5	8	6	9	2	7	3	4	1
8	6	2	5	1	3	4	9	7
7	4	5	2	9	8	1	3	6
1	9	3	7	6	4	8	5	2

170

8	7	3	2	1	4	9	5	6
2	4	5	9	6	8	7	3	1
9	1	6	5	7	3	4	8	2
1	9	4	8	2	5	6	7	3
7	6	8	3	9	1	5	2	4
5	3	2	7	4	6	1	9	8
4	5	9	1	8	2	3	6	7
6	8	7	4	3	9	2	1	5
3	2	1	6	5	7	8	4	9

171

7	2	3	6	1	4	9	5	8
9	5	1	7	2	8	4	6	3
4	6	8	9	5	3	2	7	1
6	9	4	3	7	1	8	2	5
8	7	2	5	4	9	1	3	6
3	1	5	8	6	2	7	9	4
5	4	6	1	9	7	3	8	2
2	3	9	4	8	5	6	1	7
1	8	7	2	3	6	5	4	9

172

4	3	8	5	9	6	2	1	7
9	1	6	2	3	7	4	5	8
5	7	2	8	1	4	6	9	3
3	9	4	7	2	8	1	6	5
8	6	1	9	4	5	3	7	2
2	5	7	3	6	1	8	4	9
1	8	9	6	5	2	7	3	4
6	2	5	4	7	3	9	8	1
7	4	3	1	8	9	5	2	6

173

2	6	9	4	3	1	7	8	5
5	8	1	2	9	7	6	4	3
3	4	7	6	5	8	9	1	2
9	5	4	3	8	6	1	2	7
1	2	6	9	7	4	5	3	8
7	3	8	5	1	2	4	6	9
4	9	2	8	6	5	3	7	1
8	7	5	1	4	3	2	9	6
6	1	3	7	2	9	8	5	4

174

5	3	4	6	8	7	2	1	9
7	8	1	9	3	2	6	5	4
9	6	2	4	5	1	3	8	7
4	2	8	1	7	3	5	9	6
6	7	5	2	9	4	8	3	1
3	1	9	8	6	5	7	4	2
1	4	3	5	2	6	9	7	8
2	9	7	3	1	8	4	6	5
8	5	6	7	4	9	1	2	3

175

4	8	7	2	5	1	9	6	3
6	1	3	8	7	9	5	4	2
2	9	5	3	6	4	7	1	8
1	5	6	4	8	2	3	7	9
8	7	9	1	3	5	4	2	6
3	4	2	7	9	6	1	8	5
5	6	4	9	2	7	8	3	1
9	3	1	6	4	8	2	5	7
7	2	8	5	1	3	6	9	4

176

9	2	7	8	3	1	6	5	4
4	5	3	2	7	6	1	8	9
8	6	1	4	5	9	2	3	7
2	3	8	9	1	5	4	7	6
6	4	9	3	2	7	5	1	8
7	1	5	6	4	8	3	9	2
1	9	4	7	6	3	8	2	5
3	8	6	5	9	2	7	4	1
5	7	2	1	8	4	9	6	3

177

6	8	5	9	2	7	1	4	3
9	7	2	4	3	1	6	5	8
3	4	1	8	6	5	7	9	2
8	1	4	7	5	9	3	2	6
5	2	3	6	4	8	9	7	1
7	9	6	3	1	2	4	8	5
1	3	9	2	8	4	5	6	7
2	6	7	5	9	3	8	1	4
4	5	8	1	7	6	2	3	9

178

4	5	6	1	3	2	7	8	9
3	7	8	9	5	6	1	4	2
1	2	9	7	8	4	3	5	6
7	9	3	5	4	1	6	2	8
8	4	2	3	6	7	9	1	5
5	6	1	2	9	8	4	3	7
2	3	7	6	1	5	8	9	4
6	1	4	8	2	9	5	7	3
9	8	5	4	7	3	2	6	1

179

4	2	9	5	3	7	8	1	6
5	3	7	1	6	8	4	9	2
6	1	8	2	9	4	3	7	5
1	4	6	8	2	9	5	3	7
8	7	5	6	1	3	9	2	4
3	9	2	4	7	5	1	6	8
9	8	3	7	4	6	2	5	1
2	6	4	3	5	1	7	8	9
7	5	1	9	8	2	6	4	3

180

7	1	5	8	6	2	4	9	3
3	6	8	9	7	4	1	5	2
9	2	4	5	1	3	8	6	7
8	7	1	2	5	6	9	3	4
6	5	3	4	8	9	2	7	1
4	9	2	1	3	7	5	8	6
5	8	6	7	2	1	3	4	9
2	3	9	6	4	8	7	1	5
1	4	7	3	9	5	6	2	8

181

6	8	1	4	9	5	7	2	3
2	7	9	6	1	3	8	5	4
3	4	5	7	8	2	1	9	6
7	9	4	2	3	6	5	1	8
1	6	3	9	5	8	4	7	2
8	5	2	1	4	7	6	3	9
5	3	6	8	2	1	9	4	7
4	2	8	5	7	9	3	6	1
9	1	7	3	6	4	2	8	5

182

4	5	7	8	2	6	9	3	1
2	8	6	1	3	9	7	5	4
1	9	3	5	4	7	8	2	6
9	2	1	4	7	8	3	6	5
3	7	5	2	6	1	4	8	9
6	4	8	3	9	5	1	7	2
8	1	4	7	5	2	6	9	3
7	6	2	9	1	3	5	4	8
5	3	9	6	8	4	2	1	7

183

5	7	2	8	4	1	3	6	9
8	1	9	3	5	6	2	4	7
4	3	6	7	9	2	8	1	5
9	5	4	2	8	3	1	7	6
1	2	7	5	6	4	9	8	3
3	6	8	1	7	9	4	5	2
2	8	3	6	1	7	5	9	4
6	4	5	9	3	8	7	2	1
7	9	1	4	2	5	6	3	8

184

5	2	8	6	9	3	4	1	7
4	3	6	8	7	1	9	5	2
1	9	7	4	2	5	3	8	6
7	5	9	3	6	4	1	2	8
6	4	3	1	8	2	7	9	5
2	8	1	7	5	9	6	4	3
8	1	4	5	3	6	2	7	9
9	6	5	2	1	7	8	3	4
3	7	2	9	4	8	5	6	1

185

2	9	1	3	8	5	4	6	7
7	5	4	6	1	9	8	3	2
8	3	6	7	2	4	5	1	9
6	1	3	4	9	8	7	2	5
9	4	2	5	7	1	3	8	6
5	7	8	2	6	3	1	9	4
3	8	5	9	4	6	2	7	1
4	2	9	1	3	7	6	5	8
1	6	7	8	5	2	9	4	3

186

9	5	4	2	6	8	7	3	1
3	2	1	7	5	9	4	6	8
8	6	7	1	4	3	5	9	2
1	8	5	3	9	4	2	7	6
7	9	3	6	2	1	8	4	5
6	4	2	8	7	5	3	1	9
5	7	6	9	3	2	1	8	4
4	1	9	5	8	7	6	2	3
2	3	8	4	1	6	9	5	7

187

3	7	2	4	9	5	8	6	1
6	1	4	7	2	8	5	3	9
5	9	8	1	3	6	7	4	2
1	6	9	8	5	7	3	2	4
2	8	7	9	4	3	6	1	5
4	3	5	6	1	2	9	7	8
8	2	3	5	7	4	1	9	6
9	4	6	3	8	1	2	5	7
7	5	1	2	6	9	4	8	3

188

6	4	9	2	3	1	5	7	8
7	3	2	8	6	5	4	1	9
8	5	1	4	7	9	6	2	3
2	1	3	9	5	6	7	8	4
4	7	5	1	2	8	3	9	6
9	6	8	7	4	3	2	5	1
5	8	4	6	9	2	1	3	7
3	9	6	5	1	7	8	4	2
1	2	7	3	8	4	9	6	5

189

1	6	4	9	7	8	5	2	3
9	2	8	1	3	5	6	4	7
5	7	3	2	6	4	9	1	8
7	9	2	3	8	1	4	5	6
3	5	1	4	9	6	7	8	2
8	4	6	5	2	7	3	9	1
2	8	9	6	5	3	1	7	4
6	1	7	8	4	9	2	3	5
4	3	5	7	1	2	8	6	9

190

2	8	5	4	7	3	1	9	6
4	3	7	6	1	9	8	2	5
6	9	1	8	2	5	7	3	4
7	1	9	2	3	6	4	5	8
8	4	3	5	9	7	2	6	1
5	6	2	1	4	8	3	7	9
9	2	8	3	5	4	6	1	7
3	5	4	7	6	1	9	8	2
1	7	6	9	8	2	5	4	3

191

6	5	1	3	9	2	8	4	7
8	2	9	4	6	7	3	5	1
7	4	3	8	1	5	2	6	9
4	7	5	2	3	9	6	1	8
2	1	6	7	5	8	4	9	3
3	9	8	6	4	1	7	2	5
9	6	2	1	8	3	5	7	4
5	8	4	9	7	6	1	3	2
1	3	7	5	2	4	9	8	6

192

3	6	4	9	2	1	5	7	8
5	7	2	4	6	8	1	9	3
8	1	9	5	3	7	2	6	4
9	3	6	1	4	5	7	8	2
1	2	8	3	7	6	9	4	5
4	5	7	8	9	2	6	3	1
2	9	1	7	8	4	3	5	6
7	4	5	6	1	3	8	2	9
6	8	3	2	5	9	4	1	7

193

4	1	9	6	8	3	7	5	2
8	7	3	9	2	5	1	4	6
5	2	6	1	7	4	8	9	3
6	5	2	4	1	9	3	8	7
1	9	7	5	3	8	6	2	4
3	8	4	7	6	2	5	1	9
7	3	8	2	9	1	4	6	5
9	4	1	3	5	6	2	7	8
2	6	5	8	4	7	9	3	1

194

8	6	7	1	3	9	2	4	5
1	4	9	2	5	8	6	7	3
3	2	5	4	6	7	9	1	8
9	8	1	7	2	6	3	5	4
4	3	6	9	8	5	7	2	1
7	5	2	3	4	1	8	9	6
6	7	8	5	1	2	4	3	9
5	9	4	6	7	3	1	8	2
2	1	3	8	9	4	5	6	7

195

2	4	8	9	1	7	5	3	6
9	7	3	5	6	4	1	8	2
6	5	1	3	8	2	7	9	4
8	6	4	1	3	9	2	5	7
5	3	7	2	4	6	8	1	9
1	2	9	7	5	8	6	4	3
3	9	5	6	7	1	4	2	8
7	8	2	4	9	5	3	6	1
4	1	6	8	2	3	9	7	5

196

5	8	4	1	7	3	6	9	2
6	7	2	8	9	4	5	3	1
3	9	1	6	2	5	8	4	7
1	6	8	4	3	9	2	7	5
9	4	7	2	5	6	3	1	8
2	5	3	7	1	8	9	6	4
8	3	9	5	4	7	1	2	6
7	1	6	3	8	2	4	5	9
4	2	5	9	6	1	7	8	3

197

4	3	1	5	9	7	6	8	2
5	7	8	1	2	6	3	9	4
9	2	6	8	3	4	1	5	7
6	1	7	2	8	9	5	4	3
2	4	5	3	7	1	9	6	8
3	8	9	4	6	5	2	7	1
8	6	3	7	5	2	4	1	9
1	5	2	9	4	8	7	3	6
7	9	4	6	1	3	8	2	5

198

7	8	1	6	3	9	5	2	4
4	6	9	2	5	1	8	7	3
3	5	2	4	7	8	6	9	1
8	9	3	7	2	5	1	4	6
5	4	6	9	1	3	7	8	2
2	1	7	8	6	4	9	3	5
9	3	4	5	8	6	2	1	7
1	2	5	3	9	7	4	6	8
6	7	8	1	4	2	3	5	9

199

8	4	2	1	7	6	5	3	9
9	5	6	8	2	3	7	1	4
7	3	1	4	9	5	8	6	2
6	9	8	7	4	1	3	2	5
3	1	5	2	6	8	4	9	7
4	2	7	5	3	9	1	8	6
2	8	4	9	1	7	6	5	3
1	7	3	6	5	2	9	4	8
5	6	9	3	8	4	2	7	1

200

8	1	2	6	5	4	3	9	7
7	6	9	3	2	1	4	8	5
4	3	5	7	8	9	1	2	6
6	8	1	2	3	7	9	5	4
5	4	7	9	6	8	2	3	1
2	9	3	1	4	5	7	6	8
1	5	8	4	9	3	6	7	2
3	7	6	5	1	2	8	4	9
9	2	4	8	7	6	5	1	3

201

7	1	5	8	3	9	4	2	6
6	8	4	7	2	5	3	1	9
3	2	9	1	6	4	7	5	8
5	4	6	2	8	3	9	7	1
1	7	3	5	9	6	2	8	4
8	9	2	4	7	1	6	3	5
2	5	7	6	4	8	1	9	3
4	3	1	9	5	7	8	6	2
9	6	8	3	1	2	5	4	7

202

3	5	4	8	6	9	1	7	2
9	6	1	7	5	2	8	4	3
8	2	7	1	4	3	5	9	6
7	1	5	9	3	6	4	2	8
2	8	3	4	7	5	6	1	9
6	4	9	2	1	8	7	3	5
5	7	8	3	9	4	2	6	1
4	3	6	5	2	1	9	8	7
1	9	2	6	8	7	3	5	4

203

1	7	4	9	6	5	8	3	2
3	2	6	4	1	8	7	9	5
5	9	8	3	7	2	1	4	6
2	3	7	6	8	4	5	1	9
8	5	1	2	9	7	3	6	4
6	4	9	5	3	1	2	8	7
7	6	5	8	4	3	9	2	1
9	1	3	7	2	6	4	5	8
4	8	2	1	5	9	6	7	3

204

4	3	5	9	7	2	1	6	8
6	7	1	3	5	8	2	9	4
9	8	2	1	4	6	7	5	3
5	6	7	8	9	4	3	1	2
3	1	4	5	2	7	9	8	6
2	9	8	6	1	3	4	7	5
8	4	6	7	3	1	5	2	9
7	2	9	4	6	5	8	3	1
1	5	3	2	8	9	6	4	7

205

4	9	2	5	3	1	8	6	7
5	3	6	2	7	8	9	4	1
7	1	8	4	9	6	3	2	5
1	2	3	7	4	5	6	9	8
6	4	7	9	8	2	1	5	3
8	5	9	1	6	3	2	7	4
2	6	1	8	5	7	4	3	9
3	7	4	6	1	9	5	8	2
9	8	5	3	2	4	7	1	6

206

4	5	1	6	8	2	3	9	7
3	6	9	7	4	5	8	2	1
7	2	8	1	3	9	6	4	5
5	8	7	4	2	6	9	1	3
9	4	3	8	7	1	2	5	6
2	1	6	9	5	3	4	7	8
8	3	2	5	9	7	1	6	4
1	7	4	2	6	8	5	3	9
6	9	5	3	1	4	7	8	2

207

2	6	8	3	1	5	7	9	4
7	1	5	9	2	4	6	3	8
3	4	9	8	6	7	2	1	5
9	7	6	2	5	1	8	4	3
5	3	4	7	8	6	9	2	1
1	8	2	4	3	9	5	6	7
6	2	7	1	4	8	3	5	9
8	5	1	6	9	3	4	7	2
4	9	3	5	7	2	1	8	6

208

6	3	4	1	7	9	5	2	8
2	9	8	3	6	5	7	4	1
7	1	5	2	4	8	3	6	9
8	7	1	9	5	2	4	3	6
3	6	2	4	8	1	9	5	7
5	4	9	6	3	7	1	8	2
1	8	3	7	2	4	6	9	5
4	2	7	5	9	6	8	1	3
9	5	6	8	1	3	2	7	4

209

6	4	3	7	5	1	8	9	2
9	1	8	2	6	4	5	3	7
2	7	5	9	8	3	6	4	1
7	2	4	3	9	6	1	8	5
3	8	6	4	1	5	7	2	9
1	5	9	8	7	2	3	6	4
4	6	7	5	2	8	9	1	3
5	3	1	6	4	9	2	7	8
8	9	2	1	3	7	4	5	6

210

6	5	3	9	8	1	7	2	4
4	7	2	3	6	5	9	1	8
1	8	9	2	7	4	6	5	3
2	6	8	5	3	9	4	7	1
5	3	7	1	4	8	2	9	6
9	4	1	6	2	7	3	8	5
7	2	4	8	1	6	5	3	9
3	1	5	4	9	2	8	6	7
8	9	6	7	5	3	1	4	2

211

9	2	7	8	3	4	1	5	6
1	4	6	9	2	5	7	8	3
3	8	5	7	6	1	9	2	4
8	1	9	4	7	6	5	3	2
7	6	3	2	5	9	8	4	1
4	5	2	3	1	8	6	7	9
2	3	8	1	9	7	4	6	5
5	7	1	6	4	3	2	9	8
6	9	4	5	8	2	3	1	7

212

2	7	4	1	8	6	9	5	3
9	5	1	3	4	7	6	2	8
3	6	8	2	9	5	1	4	7
4	9	6	8	5	2	3	7	1
5	1	2	9	7	3	4	8	6
7	8	3	6	1	4	2	9	5
8	2	7	4	6	1	5	3	9
6	3	9	5	2	8	7	1	4
1	4	5	7	3	9	8	6	2

213

1	2	5	9	7	6	3	8	4
4	8	6	5	3	1	9	2	7
9	3	7	8	2	4	5	1	6
6	4	8	2	1	9	7	5	3
7	1	2	4	5	3	8	6	9
3	5	9	6	8	7	2	4	1
2	7	3	1	4	8	6	9	5
5	6	1	3	9	2	4	7	8
8	9	4	7	6	5	1	3	2

214

6	2	3	5	9	4	7	1	8
7	1	4	8	6	2	9	3	5
9	5	8	1	3	7	6	2	4
4	6	2	9	8	3	5	7	1
3	8	7	4	5	1	2	9	6
5	9	1	2	7	6	8	4	3
2	7	5	3	1	8	4	6	9
8	3	6	7	4	9	1	5	2
1	4	9	6	2	5	3	8	7

215

9	7	3	5	6	8	2	1	4
4	5	8	2	1	3	7	9	6
2	6	1	9	7	4	5	8	3
6	3	4	8	9	5	1	2	7
8	9	7	1	4	2	3	6	5
5	1	2	7	3	6	8	4	9
7	8	6	4	5	1	9	3	2
1	4	9	3	2	7	6	5	8
3	2	5	6	8	9	4	7	1

216

2	3	7	8	1	9	6	4	5
9	4	6	7	5	2	1	3	8
8	5	1	6	4	3	9	2	7
3	7	2	1	9	6	5	8	4
4	6	9	3	8	5	2	7	1
5	1	8	4	2	7	3	6	9
6	9	3	5	7	8	4	1	2
1	8	5	2	6	4	7	9	3
7	2	4	9	3	1	8	5	6

217

2	4	5	7	9	8	3	6	1
1	8	7	4	6	3	2	9	5
3	6	9	2	1	5	7	8	4
7	5	1	3	2	6	9	4	8
4	9	3	1	8	7	6	5	2
8	2	6	9	5	4	1	3	7
5	7	8	6	3	1	4	2	9
9	3	4	8	7	2	5	1	6
6	1	2	5	4	9	8	7	3

218

5	3	1	8	7	2	4	6	9
6	2	4	3	1	9	8	5	7
7	9	8	5	4	6	3	1	2
1	7	3	2	8	5	9	4	6
4	6	2	7	9	1	5	3	8
8	5	9	4	6	3	2	7	1
2	1	6	9	5	4	7	8	3
3	4	7	1	2	8	6	9	5
9	8	5	6	3	7	1	2	4

219

3	9	2	7	1	5	6	8	4
8	5	1	3	4	6	7	2	9
4	7	6	8	9	2	1	5	3
1	2	8	9	6	3	5	4	7
7	6	4	5	2	8	9	3	1
5	3	9	1	7	4	8	6	2
9	4	5	2	8	7	3	1	6
2	8	7	6	3	1	4	9	5
6	1	3	4	5	9	2	7	8

220

3	1	9	5	6	7	2	8	4
8	4	5	1	2	3	6	7	9
2	6	7	4	9	8	1	5	3
9	3	1	2	5	4	7	6	8
6	8	4	7	3	1	9	2	5
5	7	2	9	8	6	4	3	1
1	5	3	6	7	9	8	4	2
7	9	8	3	4	2	5	1	6
4	2	6	8	1	5	3	9	7

221

3	9	5	1	8	2	7	6	4
7	2	1	4	5	6	9	8	3
4	8	6	3	9	7	1	2	5
2	5	9	7	1	8	4	3	6
8	3	7	6	4	9	5	1	2
6	1	4	2	3	5	8	7	9
9	6	3	5	7	1	2	4	8
1	4	8	9	2	3	6	5	7
5	7	2	8	6	4	3	9	1

222

1	6	9	7	3	5	2	8	4
8	3	2	4	6	9	1	5	7
5	7	4	8	1	2	6	3	9
9	4	3	1	5	8	7	6	2
2	8	6	3	9	7	5	4	1
7	5	1	6	2	4	8	9	3
3	2	8	5	4	1	9	7	6
4	1	7	9	8	6	3	2	5
6	9	5	2	7	3	4	1	8

223

8	3	9	7	6	1	4	5	2
2	1	4	9	5	3	7	6	8
6	5	7	2	4	8	1	9	3
4	7	2	8	3	9	6	1	5
9	8	5	4	1	6	2	3	7
3	6	1	5	7	2	9	8	4
7	2	6	3	9	5	8	4	1
5	9	8	1	2	4	3	7	6
1	4	3	6	8	7	5	2	9

224

7	5	9	1	6	2	3	8	4
1	2	3	4	9	8	5	7	6
8	4	6	3	5	7	1	2	9
9	1	2	6	8	4	7	5	3
4	6	7	5	3	1	8	9	2
3	8	5	2	7	9	4	6	1
2	9	8	7	4	3	6	1	5
5	3	1	8	2	6	9	4	7
6	7	4	9	1	5	2	3	8

225

9	7	3	2	1	8	4	6	5
1	4	6	3	5	9	2	7	8
5	2	8	6	4	7	1	9	3
8	6	2	7	9	5	3	4	1
3	9	4	1	8	6	7	5	2
7	5	1	4	2	3	9	8	6
6	3	9	5	7	2	8	1	4
4	8	5	9	3	1	6	2	7
2	1	7	8	6	4	5	3	9

226

5	2	4	1	7	6	9	3	8
8	9	6	3	2	4	5	7	1
3	1	7	8	9	5	2	6	4
6	5	1	9	4	2	3	8	7
7	4	9	6	3	8	1	2	5
2	3	8	7	5	1	6	4	9
9	8	5	4	6	3	7	1	2
1	7	3	2	8	9	4	5	6
4	6	2	5	1	7	8	9	3

227

7	5	6	3	8	9	4	1	2
3	2	1	4	6	5	9	7	8
4	9	8	2	7	1	5	3	6
2	1	3	6	4	7	8	9	5
9	7	4	8	5	3	6	2	1
8	6	5	9	1	2	3	4	7
5	8	9	7	2	4	1	6	3
1	4	7	5	3	6	2	8	9
6	3	2	1	9	8	7	5	4

228

3	2	4	6	7	9	1	5	8
5	7	6	4	1	8	9	3	2
1	9	8	3	2	5	7	6	4
2	8	5	9	3	1	4	7	6
6	4	1	8	5	7	3	2	9
9	3	7	2	4	6	5	8	1
4	5	2	1	6	3	8	9	7
8	6	3	7	9	4	2	1	5
7	1	9	5	8	2	6	4	3

229

7	8	6	3	4	5	2	9	1
4	1	9	8	2	6	7	3	5
3	5	2	9	1	7	6	4	8
1	6	8	4	5	9	3	7	2
9	7	5	6	3	2	8	1	4
2	4	3	1	7	8	5	6	9
6	2	4	7	8	1	9	5	3
8	3	7	5	9	4	1	2	6
5	9	1	2	6	3	4	8	7

230

4	6	5	2	1	8	3	9	7
9	3	7	5	6	4	1	2	8
8	2	1	7	3	9	5	6	4
3	8	2	1	4	5	9	7	6
7	9	4	6	8	3	2	5	1
1	5	6	9	7	2	4	8	3
5	4	3	8	2	7	6	1	9
6	7	9	4	5	1	8	3	2
2	1	8	3	9	6	7	4	5

231

5	9	3	2	1	8	6	4	7
6	7	2	3	4	9	8	5	1
4	1	8	7	6	5	9	3	2
3	5	9	6	7	1	2	8	4
1	8	7	4	5	2	3	9	6
2	6	4	8	9	3	7	1	5
7	3	6	1	8	4	5	2	9
8	4	5	9	2	7	1	6	3
9	2	1	5	3	6	4	7	8

232

3	9	2	6	4	5	8	7	1
8	7	6	9	3	1	4	5	2
4	1	5	8	2	7	9	6	3
7	8	4	2	6	9	3	1	5
5	6	9	1	8	3	7	2	4
2	3	1	7	5	4	6	8	9
1	2	3	4	7	6	5	9	8
6	4	8	5	9	2	1	3	7
9	5	7	3	1	8	2	4	6

233

7	4	9	5	3	2	1	6	8
5	6	3	7	1	8	2	4	9
2	8	1	6	4	9	3	7	5
3	5	6	4	8	1	7	9	2
4	1	7	9	2	5	8	3	6
8	9	2	3	7	6	5	1	4
9	7	4	8	5	3	6	2	1
1	3	5	2	6	4	9	8	7
6	2	8	1	9	7	4	5	3

234

2	6	7	9	3	1	8	4	5
4	8	1	5	6	7	9	3	2
5	9	3	4	8	2	6	7	1
9	2	8	3	1	4	5	6	7
7	5	4	6	9	8	1	2	3
1	3	6	7	2	5	4	9	8
6	1	9	8	7	3	2	5	4
8	7	5	2	4	9	3	1	6
3	4	2	1	5	6	7	8	9

235

8	5	7	3	6	2	1	4	9
4	6	1	7	5	9	3	2	8
9	3	2	8	1	4	5	6	7
1	2	3	9	8	6	4	7	5
5	4	6	2	7	3	9	8	1
7	8	9	1	4	5	6	3	2
3	9	5	6	2	7	8	1	4
2	1	4	5	3	8	7	9	6
6	7	8	4	9	1	2	5	3

236

6	5	4	3	7	1	8	9	2
8	3	2	6	5	9	4	7	1
9	1	7	2	4	8	6	3	5
1	7	3	4	8	6	5	2	9
5	2	6	9	1	7	3	8	4
4	9	8	5	3	2	1	6	7
2	8	9	1	6	5	7	4	3
3	6	5	7	2	4	9	1	8
7	4	1	8	9	3	2	5	6

237

5	1	2	8	3	9	7	6	4
9	4	3	5	6	7	2	1	8
8	6	7	2	1	4	3	9	5
4	9	5	3	7	6	8	2	1
6	7	1	4	2	8	5	3	9
3	2	8	1	9	5	6	4	7
2	5	4	6	8	1	9	7	3
7	8	6	9	4	3	1	5	2
1	3	9	7	5	2	4	8	6

238

7	1	9	6	5	4	8	2	3
4	8	2	7	3	9	1	5	6
5	3	6	8	1	2	4	7	9
1	5	3	9	2	7	6	8	4
8	9	4	3	6	5	7	1	2
6	2	7	4	8	1	9	3	5
9	4	5	1	7	3	2	6	8
2	7	8	5	9	6	3	4	1
3	6	1	2	4	8	5	9	7

239

6	5	9	1	4	8	2	3	7
3	1	4	2	7	5	6	8	9
8	2	7	6	3	9	1	5	4
2	4	5	7	8	6	3	9	1
9	8	1	3	5	2	7	4	6
7	6	3	4	9	1	8	2	5
4	7	8	5	1	3	9	6	2
5	3	6	9	2	7	4	1	8
1	9	2	8	6	4	5	7	3

240

3	7	5	8	1	6	2	4	9
6	1	2	4	9	5	7	8	3
9	4	8	3	7	2	5	1	6
8	3	7	1	2	4	9	6	5
5	2	9	6	8	7	1	3	4
1	6	4	9	5	3	8	2	7
2	5	3	7	6	1	4	9	8
7	8	6	2	4	9	3	5	1
4	9	1	5	3	8	6	7	2

241

4	6	2	7	8	5	9	1	3
5	8	1	9	3	2	7	4	6
3	7	9	6	4	1	8	5	2
1	9	6	2	7	4	3	8	5
2	4	3	1	5	8	6	7	9
8	5	7	3	6	9	1	2	4
6	1	8	4	2	3	5	9	7
9	3	4	5	1	7	2	6	8
7	2	5	8	9	6	4	3	1

242

7	5	1	4	2	6	9	3	8
8	3	6	9	5	7	4	2	1
2	9	4	8	1	3	6	5	7
5	6	2	7	9	4	8	1	3
4	1	7	5	3	8	2	6	9
9	8	3	1	6	2	7	4	5
1	7	5	2	4	9	3	8	6
6	4	8	3	7	1	5	9	2
3	2	9	6	8	5	1	7	4

243

2	4	7	6	9	3	8	5	1
8	3	9	1	5	4	6	7	2
1	5	6	2	8	7	3	4	9
3	2	5	8	7	6	1	9	4
9	7	4	3	1	5	2	6	8
6	1	8	9	4	2	7	3	5
7	9	2	5	3	8	4	1	6
4	8	1	7	6	9	5	2	3
5	6	3	4	2	1	9	8	7

244

4	6	5	8	9	7	2	1	3
2	9	8	3	1	5	7	6	4
1	3	7	2	6	4	8	9	5
9	8	2	4	5	6	1	3	7
7	4	6	1	3	2	9	5	8
3	5	1	9	7	8	4	2	6
8	2	3	6	4	9	5	7	1
6	7	4	5	2	1	3	8	9
5	1	9	7	8	3	6	4	2

245

1	2	4	3	9	6	8	7	5
3	5	9	7	8	2	1	6	4
7	8	6	5	1	4	9	3	2
5	4	7	8	3	1	2	9	6
8	3	2	6	5	9	4	1	7
9	6	1	4	2	7	5	8	3
2	9	3	1	7	5	6	4	8
4	1	8	2	6	3	7	5	9
6	7	5	9	4	8	3	2	1

246

7	1	9	8	6	5	4	2	3
6	8	4	3	2	1	5	7	9
5	3	2	9	7	4	6	8	1
8	4	1	2	5	9	3	6	7
2	7	3	4	8	6	9	1	5
9	5	6	7	1	3	8	4	2
4	2	5	1	9	8	7	3	6
3	6	7	5	4	2	1	9	8
1	9	8	6	3	7	2	5	4

247

1	7	4	8	3	5	9	2	6
5	8	9	4	2	6	1	3	7
3	2	6	7	1	9	5	8	4
2	1	8	6	5	4	3	7	9
6	3	7	2	9	1	4	5	8
9	4	5	3	8	7	6	1	2
7	6	3	1	4	8	2	9	5
4	9	2	5	7	3	8	6	1
8	5	1	9	6	2	7	4	3

248

5	8	7	6	2	1	9	3	4
4	9	6	5	7	3	1	2	8
3	1	2	8	4	9	7	5	6
7	4	5	1	9	6	2	8	3
9	2	8	7	3	5	4	6	1
1	6	3	4	8	2	5	7	9
6	7	1	9	5	8	3	4	2
2	5	9	3	6	4	8	1	7
8	3	4	2	1	7	6	9	5

249

9	1	5	2	4	3	6	7	8
3	6	2	7	5	8	9	1	4
7	4	8	9	6	1	5	3	2
1	8	3	6	2	4	7	5	9
5	2	9	8	3	7	4	6	1
4	7	6	1	9	5	2	8	3
2	3	4	5	1	6	8	9	7
6	9	7	3	8	2	1	4	5
8	5	1	4	7	9	3	2	6

250

9	5	4	1	7	3	6	2	8
1	8	3	2	6	4	5	9	7
2	6	7	9	8	5	4	3	1
6	1	5	7	4	2	3	8	9
7	3	9	8	1	6	2	4	5
4	2	8	5	3	9	1	7	6
5	7	1	4	2	8	9	6	3
8	4	6	3	9	1	7	5	2
3	9	2	6	5	7	8	1	4

251

9	1	8	2	6	5	4	7	3
5	7	6	4	3	9	8	1	2
4	3	2	8	1	7	9	6	5
6	4	7	1	2	3	5	8	9
3	8	9	6	5	4	7	2	1
1	2	5	7	9	8	6	3	4
2	6	4	9	7	1	3	5	8
7	9	3	5	8	2	1	4	6
8	5	1	3	4	6	2	9	7

252

7	9	8	5	3	2	1	4	6
6	1	4	9	8	7	5	3	2
3	2	5	1	4	6	7	8	9
8	6	9	3	2	1	4	7	5
4	7	3	6	9	5	8	2	1
2	5	1	8	7	4	9	6	3
1	8	2	4	6	9	3	5	7
9	4	7	2	5	3	6	1	8
5	3	6	7	1	8	2	9	4

253

5	7	3	4	6	2	8	1	9
8	2	1	9	3	5	4	7	6
6	9	4	8	7	1	5	2	3
7	1	2	3	4	8	9	6	5
3	5	6	2	9	7	1	4	8
4	8	9	5	1	6	2	3	7
9	4	5	6	2	3	7	8	1
2	3	7	1	8	9	6	5	4
1	6	8	7	5	4	3	9	2

254

6	8	5	3	2	1	7	9	4
7	4	3	5	8	9	2	6	1
2	1	9	7	4	6	8	5	3
1	3	6	9	7	8	4	2	5
5	9	8	4	1	2	3	7	6
4	7	2	6	5	3	1	8	9
9	6	7	2	3	4	5	1	8
8	2	4	1	6	5	9	3	7
3	5	1	8	9	7	6	4	2

255

7	3	4	2	9	5	1	6	8
5	2	8	6	4	1	7	9	3
9	1	6	8	7	3	4	5	2
4	7	3	5	8	6	2	1	9
2	5	1	4	3	9	8	7	6
8	6	9	7	1	2	5	3	4
1	8	5	9	6	4	3	2	7
6	4	2	3	5	7	9	8	1
3	9	7	1	2	8	6	4	5

256

5	2	3	8	7	9	6	4	1
7	6	8	3	4	1	2	9	5
1	4	9	5	6	2	8	3	7
8	5	7	9	1	6	4	2	3
2	3	6	4	5	8	1	7	9
4	9	1	7	2	3	5	8	6
3	8	2	1	9	5	7	6	4
9	7	5	6	8	4	3	1	2
6	1	4	2	3	7	9	5	8

257

5	1	7	9	3	4	2	6	8
8	9	3	7	6	2	1	5	4
6	2	4	8	5	1	9	3	7
3	7	5	1	9	6	8	4	2
9	4	8	3	2	5	6	7	1
2	6	1	4	7	8	3	9	5
1	3	9	5	8	7	4	2	6
7	8	6	2	4	9	5	1	3
4	5	2	6	1	3	7	8	9

258

7	6	8	1	2	9	4	3	5
4	5	2	3	7	8	6	9	1
1	9	3	5	4	6	7	2	8
2	3	5	4	1	7	8	6	9
9	4	6	2	8	5	3	1	7
8	7	1	9	6	3	5	4	2
5	2	7	6	9	4	1	8	3
3	1	4	8	5	2	9	7	6
6	8	9	7	3	1	2	5	4

259

2	4	3	9	5	7	8	6	1
8	5	6	1	4	3	7	9	2
1	9	7	8	2	6	4	3	5
4	8	1	3	9	5	2	7	6
3	2	5	7	6	1	9	8	4
6	7	9	4	8	2	1	5	3
7	3	4	6	1	9	5	2	8
5	6	8	2	7	4	3	1	9
9	1	2	5	3	8	6	4	7

260

9	6	5	8	3	7	1	4	2
8	2	3	1	9	4	7	6	5
4	1	7	6	5	2	9	3	8
2	3	9	4	8	1	6	5	7
7	4	1	5	6	3	8	2	9
6	5	8	7	2	9	3	1	4
1	7	6	2	4	8	5	9	3
5	9	2	3	7	6	4	8	1
3	8	4	9	1	5	2	7	6

261

3	9	5	7	8	4	2	1	6
2	7	8	1	6	9	4	3	5
4	6	1	2	5	3	8	7	9
9	5	3	6	2	8	1	4	7
1	2	6	5	4	7	9	8	3
8	4	7	9	3	1	5	6	2
7	1	4	3	9	5	6	2	8
6	3	9	8	1	2	7	5	4
5	8	2	4	7	6	3	9	1

262

5	2	6	1	4	9	3	7	8
4	3	9	8	7	2	6	1	5
8	1	7	3	6	5	4	9	2
7	5	2	6	1	8	9	4	3
9	8	1	5	3	4	7	2	6
6	4	3	2	9	7	5	8	1
3	9	8	4	2	6	1	5	7
1	7	5	9	8	3	2	6	4
2	6	4	7	5	1	8	3	9

263

2	8	7	3	4	6	9	1	5
9	6	4	1	5	7	2	8	3
5	1	3	9	8	2	4	6	7
1	3	8	7	9	5	6	2	4
4	7	2	6	1	8	3	5	9
6	5	9	2	3	4	1	7	8
7	4	1	5	2	3	8	9	6
8	9	6	4	7	1	5	3	2
3	2	5	8	6	9	7	4	1

264

9	2	6	3	7	5	1	4	8
8	3	5	4	1	2	6	9	7
4	7	1	6	9	8	2	5	3
2	5	3	9	8	6	4	7	1
1	6	8	2	4	7	9	3	5
7	4	9	5	3	1	8	2	6
6	1	4	7	5	9	3	8	2
5	9	2	8	6	3	7	1	4
3	8	7	1	2	4	5	6	9

265

1	7	2	5	8	3	4	9	6
5	3	4	9	6	2	8	7	1
9	6	8	4	7	1	3	2	5
3	2	9	1	4	5	6	8	7
8	5	7	3	2	6	9	1	4
6	4	1	7	9	8	5	3	2
2	8	5	6	1	9	7	4	3
7	9	6	2	3	4	1	5	8
4	1	3	8	5	7	2	6	9

266

4	3	2	5	7	9	6	8	1
7	8	1	4	3	6	2	5	9
5	6	9	2	1	8	4	7	3
2	7	3	6	9	1	5	4	8
1	4	8	7	5	3	9	6	2
6	9	5	8	4	2	1	3	7
8	5	4	1	2	7	3	9	6
3	2	6	9	8	5	7	1	4
9	1	7	3	6	4	8	2	5

267

7	4	9	2	8	5	3	6	1
3	1	2	6	7	4	5	8	9
6	8	5	9	3	1	4	7	2
4	9	6	5	1	2	8	3	7
8	2	3	4	9	7	6	1	5
1	5	7	3	6	8	2	9	4
5	6	1	8	4	9	7	2	3
9	3	4	7	2	6	1	5	8
2	7	8	1	5	3	9	4	6

268

5	1	8	6	9	2	3	4	7
2	7	9	4	3	1	6	5	8
3	6	4	7	8	5	1	9	2
8	4	7	9	5	6	2	1	3
1	9	2	8	4	3	5	7	6
6	5	3	2	1	7	4	8	9
9	2	6	1	7	4	8	3	5
4	8	5	3	6	9	7	2	1
7	3	1	5	2	8	9	6	4

269

4	1	6	8	9	3	7	5	2
3	8	5	2	7	1	9	4	6
2	7	9	5	4	6	1	8	3
6	5	1	9	2	8	3	7	4
9	2	3	4	1	7	5	6	8
8	4	7	3	6	5	2	1	9
7	6	2	1	3	4	8	9	5
5	9	4	7	8	2	6	3	1
1	3	8	6	5	9	4	2	7

270

9	3	5	2	4	1	8	7	6
6	1	4	7	5	8	9	3	2
7	2	8	9	6	3	5	1	4
3	7	9	5	2	6	4	8	1
2	4	1	3	8	9	6	5	7
5	8	6	1	7	4	3	2	9
8	6	3	4	1	7	2	9	5
1	9	2	6	3	5	7	4	8
4	5	7	8	9	2	1	6	3

271

2	1	7	4	9	3	8	6	5
8	6	3	2	1	5	9	4	7
4	9	5	6	7	8	3	2	1
9	5	1	7	3	6	2	8	4
3	7	2	5	8	4	6	1	9
6	4	8	1	2	9	7	5	3
1	3	4	8	6	7	5	9	2
7	2	6	9	5	1	4	3	8
5	8	9	3	4	2	1	7	6

272

7	6	3	8	4	9	5	1	2
1	4	8	2	7	5	3	9	6
5	9	2	3	1	6	7	4	8
6	7	1	4	9	8	2	3	5
2	3	4	5	6	7	1	8	9
8	5	9	1	2	3	6	7	4
4	1	5	7	8	2	9	6	3
9	2	7	6	3	4	8	5	1
3	8	6	9	5	1	4	2	7

273

1	5	7	6	8	2	4	9	3
9	8	2	3	5	4	6	1	7
3	6	4	1	9	7	5	8	2
4	2	3	5	7	1	8	6	9
5	9	6	4	3	8	2	7	1
7	1	8	2	6	9	3	4	5
8	3	5	7	1	6	9	2	4
6	4	1	9	2	5	7	3	8
2	7	9	8	4	3	1	5	6

274

4	5	1	3	9	6	8	2	7
2	9	6	5	7	8	1	4	3
3	8	7	1	2	4	6	5	9
7	2	9	4	6	1	5	3	8
5	4	3	7	8	9	2	1	6
6	1	8	2	3	5	9	7	4
1	6	2	9	4	3	7	8	5
9	7	4	8	5	2	3	6	1
8	3	5	6	1	7	4	9	2

275

7	6	4	8	2	5	1	9	3
2	8	9	3	7	1	6	5	4
5	1	3	6	4	9	2	7	8
4	3	7	9	1	2	5	8	6
6	2	5	4	3	8	7	1	9
1	9	8	5	6	7	3	4	2
3	7	1	2	9	4	8	6	5
8	4	6	7	5	3	9	2	1
9	5	2	1	8	6	4	3	7

276

9	8	2	5	1	4	6	7	3
5	6	4	7	9	3	8	1	2
1	7	3	2	6	8	9	5	4
3	5	6	1	2	9	4	8	7
8	4	1	3	7	5	2	9	6
7	2	9	4	8	6	1	3	5
6	3	8	9	4	7	5	2	1
2	9	7	6	5	1	3	4	8
4	1	5	8	3	2	7	6	9

277

3	7	4	1	9	5	2	8	6
1	5	8	7	6	2	4	9	3
2	9	6	8	3	4	1	5	7
4	8	7	5	1	3	9	6	2
9	6	2	4	7	8	5	3	1
5	3	1	9	2	6	7	4	8
7	1	5	3	8	9	6	2	4
8	2	9	6	4	1	3	7	5
6	4	3	2	5	7	8	1	9

278

3	4	2	7	6	5	8	9	1
5	7	8	2	1	9	4	6	3
6	1	9	8	3	4	5	7	2
9	5	4	1	2	8	7	3	6
1	2	7	6	5	3	9	4	8
8	3	6	9	4	7	2	1	5
7	8	5	3	9	1	6	2	4
4	6	3	5	7	2	1	8	9
2	9	1	4	8	6	3	5	7

279

3	9	2	7	6	4	8	5	1
1	8	5	9	3	2	4	6	7
4	6	7	8	1	5	2	9	3
8	2	4	5	9	7	3	1	6
7	5	1	3	2	6	9	8	4
9	3	6	1	4	8	7	2	5
2	4	9	6	5	3	1	7	8
5	7	3	2	8	1	6	4	9
6	1	8	4	7	9	5	3	2

280

5	6	7	3	2	1	9	8	4
4	2	9	8	6	7	5	1	3
1	8	3	9	5	4	2	7	6
9	1	2	6	4	8	7	3	5
8	3	4	7	9	5	6	2	1
6	7	5	1	3	2	4	9	8
2	9	6	5	1	3	8	4	7
3	4	8	2	7	6	1	5	9
7	5	1	4	8	9	3	6	2

281

6	2	8	7	1	9	3	5	4
1	3	5	4	8	6	7	9	2
9	4	7	5	3	2	1	6	8
5	1	9	8	7	4	2	3	6
4	7	3	2	6	5	8	1	9
2	8	6	3	9	1	4	7	5
7	9	2	6	4	3	5	8	1
3	5	1	9	2	8	6	4	7
8	6	4	1	5	7	9	2	3

282

7	6	5	8	3	1	9	2	4
3	1	9	6	4	2	7	8	5
4	8	2	9	5	7	6	1	3
5	9	7	4	8	6	1	3	2
8	2	6	5	1	3	4	9	7
1	4	3	7	2	9	5	6	8
6	7	8	3	9	5	2	4	1
2	5	4	1	6	8	3	7	9
9	3	1	2	7	4	8	5	6

283

6	7	1	2	3	8	9	4	5
9	3	8	4	5	6	1	2	7
5	4	2	7	1	9	6	3	8
4	9	7	1	6	2	8	5	3
8	5	6	3	9	7	4	1	2
2	1	3	8	4	5	7	6	9
7	8	5	6	2	4	3	9	1
1	2	4	9	7	3	5	8	6
3	6	9	5	8	1	2	7	4

284

9	2	7	3	5	6	4	1	8
4	6	1	9	8	7	5	2	3
8	3	5	1	4	2	7	9	6
5	9	8	2	7	4	6	3	1
3	7	6	8	9	1	2	4	5
1	4	2	5	6	3	9	8	7
2	1	9	7	3	5	8	6	4
6	5	3	4	2	8	1	7	9
7	8	4	6	1	9	3	5	2

285

6	7	8	1	2	9	5	3	4
1	3	4	7	5	6	8	2	9
9	5	2	3	8	4	6	7	1
4	6	7	8	3	1	9	5	2
2	9	5	4	6	7	3	1	8
3	8	1	2	9	5	4	6	7
8	2	9	5	7	3	1	4	6
5	4	6	9	1	2	7	8	3
7	1	3	6	4	8	2	9	5

286

6	3	1	2	7	8	9	4	5
2	4	5	3	9	1	7	8	6
9	8	7	5	4	6	3	2	1
4	5	8	7	6	9	2	1	3
7	6	2	1	3	5	4	9	8
1	9	3	4	8	2	6	5	7
5	2	6	9	1	7	8	3	4
3	7	9	8	5	4	1	6	2
8	1	4	6	2	3	5	7	9

287

1	6	9	8	7	4	3	2	5
4	5	8	1	3	2	7	6	9
3	2	7	9	5	6	1	4	8
5	3	2	7	1	9	6	8	4
7	9	4	5	6	8	2	1	3
8	1	6	4	2	3	9	5	7
6	4	3	2	9	5	8	7	1
9	7	5	6	8	1	4	3	2
2	8	1	3	4	7	5	9	6

288

6	4	1	9	5	3	2	8	7
8	5	9	2	6	7	4	3	1
3	7	2	8	4	1	9	6	5
9	8	7	1	3	2	5	4	6
1	6	3	5	9	4	8	7	2
4	2	5	6	7	8	3	1	9
2	3	6	7	8	5	1	9	4
5	9	4	3	1	6	7	2	8
7	1	8	4	2	9	6	5	3

289

7	1	6	2	8	3	5	9	4
3	9	2	5	6	4	8	1	7
5	8	4	7	1	9	2	6	3
6	4	5	1	7	8	3	2	9
1	7	3	9	4	2	6	8	5
9	2	8	6	3	5	4	7	1
8	3	9	4	2	1	7	5	6
4	6	1	8	5	7	9	3	2
2	5	7	3	9	6	1	4	8

290

2	4	6	1	8	5	9	7	3
7	1	5	9	2	3	4	6	8
8	9	3	7	6	4	5	2	1
3	7	4	6	1	9	2	8	5
1	5	9	2	4	8	7	3	6
6	2	8	5	3	7	1	4	9
9	8	2	3	7	1	6	5	4
4	6	1	8	5	2	3	9	7
5	3	7	4	9	6	8	1	2

291

3	4	5	8	1	6	2	9	7
6	7	8	9	3	2	4	1	5
1	2	9	7	4	5	6	8	3
7	9	4	5	2	8	1	3	6
8	5	1	3	6	7	9	2	4
2	3	6	4	9	1	7	5	8
5	1	7	6	8	9	3	4	2
4	8	2	1	7	3	5	6	9
9	6	3	2	5	4	8	7	1

292

4	8	1	3	2	5	7	9	6
3	5	2	6	9	7	4	8	1
9	7	6	4	8	1	5	2	3
7	3	9	5	4	2	6	1	8
1	2	4	7	6	8	9	3	5
5	6	8	9	1	3	2	4	7
2	4	3	8	7	6	1	5	9
8	1	7	2	5	9	3	6	4
6	9	5	1	3	4	8	7	2

293

7	5	1	4	9	6	3	2	8
2	3	9	7	1	8	5	4	6
6	8	4	3	2	5	7	1	9
9	7	6	1	4	2	8	3	5
8	4	2	9	5	3	1	6	7
5	1	3	8	6	7	4	9	2
4	2	7	5	3	9	6	8	1
1	9	5	6	8	4	2	7	3
3	6	8	2	7	1	9	5	4

294

5	2	6	4	9	3	8	1	7
8	9	1	2	6	7	3	4	5
3	7	4	8	5	1	6	9	2
6	3	7	5	4	2	9	8	1
2	8	9	7	1	6	5	3	4
4	1	5	9	3	8	2	7	6
7	4	2	3	8	5	1	6	9
9	6	3	1	2	4	7	5	8
1	5	8	6	7	9	4	2	3

295

9	7	8	5	1	4	6	2	3
1	4	3	2	6	8	9	5	7
2	6	5	3	7	9	1	4	8
4	3	1	6	5	7	2	8	9
7	8	2	9	3	1	4	6	5
5	9	6	4	8	2	7	3	1
6	1	9	8	2	3	5	7	4
3	2	7	1	4	5	8	9	6
8	5	4	7	9	6	3	1	2

296

1	6	3	2	5	7	8	4	9
9	2	5	8	3	4	6	7	1
7	8	4	1	6	9	3	2	5
5	3	8	4	1	2	7	9	6
2	7	1	3	9	6	5	8	4
4	9	6	5	7	8	2	1	3
8	5	2	9	4	3	1	6	7
6	1	9	7	8	5	4	3	2
3	4	7	6	2	1	9	5	8

297

3	1	8	4	9	6	7	2	5
2	4	9	8	7	5	6	1	3
7	5	6	2	1	3	8	9	4
5	2	7	1	8	4	9	3	6
8	6	1	9	3	7	5	4	2
4	9	3	6	5	2	1	8	7
1	7	4	3	6	8	2	5	9
6	8	2	5	4	9	3	7	1
9	3	5	7	2	1	4	6	8

298

3	8	7	4	6	5	9	1	2
1	5	6	2	9	7	4	3	8
9	4	2	3	8	1	6	7	5
7	3	4	8	1	2	5	9	6
2	1	5	9	7	6	3	8	4
8	6	9	5	3	4	7	2	1
6	2	1	7	5	3	8	4	9
4	9	3	6	2	8	1	5	7
5	7	8	1	4	9	2	6	3

299

4	9	8	1	7	5	3	2	6
7	5	2	6	8	3	1	9	4
1	6	3	4	2	9	5	7	8
8	1	7	3	4	6	2	5	9
5	3	4	2	9	8	6	1	7
9	2	6	5	1	7	8	4	3
3	7	9	8	5	2	4	6	1
2	8	1	9	6	4	7	3	5
6	4	5	7	3	1	9	8	2

300

2	1	7	3	4	6	8	9	5
8	3	9	5	2	1	4	7	6
5	6	4	8	7	9	2	1	3
7	9	8	6	1	4	5	3	2
1	5	6	2	3	8	9	4	7
3	4	2	9	5	7	1	6	8
6	8	3	1	9	5	7	2	4
4	2	1	7	8	3	6	5	9
9	7	5	4	6	2	3	8	1

"The Christian faith made a difference. The resurrection of Christ from the dead revealed that human life was ultimately and with finality the will of God. Human life had a value that was transcendent. Such a faith postured the Christian attitude as distinctly counter to many of the cultural and social habits of the Roman Empire. And nowhere was this more the case than in the church's attitude toward killing. In a most helpful way and with an evident knowledge of the primary sources, Ronald Sider presents in translation a comprehensive sourcebook of early Christian statements on the issues of abortion, capital punishment, and military service. While not hiding his own ethical stance and at times responding to opinion he regards as mistaken, Sider confronts the reader with the relevant texts themselves and so allows us to make our own independent judgment on the important question of the early church's position on these difficult and yet highly relevant themes. The sourcebook will be an asset in the libraries of pastors and laypeople alike and a welcome text in college and seminary classrooms."

—**William C. Weinrich**, Concordia Theological Seminary,
Fort Wayne, Indiana

"The composite portrait that these texts create is one of a radical Christian ethic and of a church that struggled to live into it. Even in the midst of this complexity, one can still see the outlines of a 'consistent ethic of life' in which aversion to the shedding of blood is paired with a willingness to lay down one's life in witness to the Prince of Peace. Should today's Christian communities have ears to hear this message, then the death-dealing powers that organize our world might have a genuine revolution on their hands."

—**Christian Collins Winn**, Bethel University

The Early Church on Killing

A COMPREHENSIVE SOURCEBOOK ON
WAR, ABORTION, AND CAPITAL PUNISHMENT

EDITED BY

Ronald J. Sider

Baker Academic
a division of Baker Publishing Group
Grand Rapids, Michigan

Published by Baker Academic
a division of Baker Publishing Group
P.O. Box 6287, Grand Rapids, MI 49516-6287
www.bakeracademic.com

Printed in the United States of America

Library of Congress Cataloging-in-Publication Data
Sider, Ronald J.
    The early church on killing : a comprehensive sourcebook on war, abortion, and capital punishment / Ronald J. Sider.
        p.   cm.
    Includes bibliographical references (p.   ) and indexes.
    ISBN 978-0-8010-3630-9 (pbk.)
    1. Death—Religious aspects—Christianity—History of doctrines—Early church, ca. 30–600. 2. Murder—Religious aspects—Christianity. 3. War—Religious aspects—Christianity. 4. Abortion—Religious aspects—Christianity. 5. Capital punishment—Religious aspects—Christianity. I. Title.
BT825.S56 2012
241′.697—dc23   2012002598

12   13   14   15   16   17   18   7   6   5   4   3   2   1

To Naomi Miller,
gifted administrative assistant for
twenty-eight years

Contents

Acknowledgments   9
Abbreviations   11
Introduction   13

Part 1   Christian Writers before Constantine

Didache   19
The Epistle of Barnabas   20
First Clement   20
Second Clement   21
Apocalypse of Peter   22
Justin Martyr   23
Tatian   26
Irenaeus   27
Athenagoras   30
Clement of Alexandria   32
Tertullian   42
Minucius Felix   63
Didascalia apostolorum   64
Julius Africanus   65
Origen   67
Cyprian   83
Gregory Thaumaturgus   90
Dionysius of Alexandria   91
Archelaus   92
Adamantius, *Dialogue on the True Faith*   93
Arnobius of Sicca   101
Lactantius   103

Part 2 Church Orders and Synods

Apostolic Tradition   119
Three Later Church Orders   122
Synod of Arles   124

Part 3 Miscellaneous Items

The Infancy Gospel of Thomas   129
Paul of Samosata   131
The Acts of Xanthippe and Polyxena   132

Part 4 Other Evidence of Christian Soldiers before Constantine

"The Thundering Legion"   137
A Third-Century Christian Prayer Hall Near a Military
    Camp   144
Epitaphs   145
Military Martyrs   151
Eusebius's *Ecclesiastical History*   159
An Early Christian Kingdom?   161

Afterword   163
Bibliography   197
Scripture Index   203
Index of Ancient Sources and Early Christian
Writings   205
Author Index   209
Subject Index   211

Acknowledgments

I want to thank the many people who have helped make this book possible.

A number of gifted graduate students (Ayres, Wilberforce, and Sider Scholars) at Palmer Seminary provided excellent research assistance. Peter Sensenig, Regina Downing, Anya Eckelbarger, and Lori Baynard read through the fathers helping to locate relevant texts and identify material for introductions. Heather Biscoe tracked down innumerable books I needed. Stephanie Israel typed most of the manuscript.

Many scholars answered questions: Harold Attridge, Alan Kreider, Michael Gorman, Robert Sider, and Glen Stassen. Rob Arner, Robb Davis, and John Stoner commented on parts of the manuscript. Owen Ewald provided translations of almost all the inscriptions used here. John Helgeland graciously helped with my work on the inscriptions.

Colleagues at Palmer Seminary provided invaluable help. Our librarian, Melody Mazuk, spent hours tracking down obscure texts. Her colleague, Jeron Frame, procured a long stream of needed books on inter-library loan. Chris Hall (Eastern University chancellor, Palmer Seminary dean, and patristics scholar) helped at several stages. Craig Keener and Deborah Watson answered queries.

My two administrative assistants helped in various ways even as they effectively kept the rest of my complicated life on track: Naomi Miller, my wonderful, efficient secretary, colleague, and friend for twenty-eight years, retired in the midst of this project, but Joshua Cradic has effectively taken her place. Finally, thanks to my long-time editor at Baker, Bob Hosack.

None of these friends and colleagues are responsible for weaknesses or mistakes that remain in this book, but without them it would not have been possible.

Abbreviations

ACW	Ancient Christian Writers: The Works of the Fathers in Translation. Johannes Quasten, Joseph C. Plumpe, and Dennis D. McManus, eds. 61 vols. (Westminster, MD, and New York: Newman Press, 1946–2008).
ANF	*Ante-Nicene Fathers: The Writings of the Fathers Down to A.D. 325.* Alexander Roberts and James Donaldson, eds. 9 vols. (1885; repr., Peabody, MA: Hendrickson, 2004).
ANRW	Aufstieg und Niedergang der römischen Welt
AJP	*American Journal of Philology*
CC	*Cross Currents*
CEHCP	Collection d'études d'histoire, de critique et de philologie
CH	*Church History*
CSS	Cistercian Studies Series
DACL	*Dictionnaire d'Archéologie Chrétienne et de Liturgie.* Fernand Cabrol and Henri Leclercq, eds. (Paris: Letouzey et Ané, 1933).
ESH	Ecumenical Studies in History
EQ	*Evangelical Quarterly*
Exp.	*Expositor*
FC	Fathers of the Church
HTR	*Harvard Theological Review*
HUS	*Harvard Ukrainian Studies*
ITQ	*Irish Theological Quarterly*
JEH	*Journal of Ecclesiastical History*
JRE	*Journal of Religious Ethics*
JRS	*Journal of Roman Studies*
JTS	*Journal of Theological Studies*
LCC	Library of Christian Classics
LCL	Loeb Classical Library

NPNF	*Nicene and Post-Nicene Fathers, First Series.* Philip Schaff and Henry Wace, eds. 14 vols. (1886; repr., Peabody, MA: Hendrickson, 1994).
*NPNF*²	*Nicene and Post-Nicene Fathers, Second Series.* Philip Schaff and Henry Wace, eds. 14 vols. (1890; repr., Peabody, MA: Hendrickson, 1994).
SC	Sources chrétiennes
SCES	Sixteenth Century Essays and Studies
SP	Studia Patristica
RSR	*Religious Studies Review*
TS	*Theological Studies*
TTH	Translated Texts for Historians

Introduction

The literature on our topic is vast.[1] Among the hundreds of books and articles, a few stand out as especially important because of their scholarship and influence.[2] But even the best of these publications reflect major disagreement about the witness of the early church on killing and war. Some scholars have argued that the early church up until Constantine was largely pacifist. Other scholars have vigorously rejected that view.[3] And there is still no scholarly consensus.

Further study is important for at least three reasons. It is important to know as much as we can about the witness of the early church on killing simply in order to have a more complete, more accurate historical understanding.[4] Further, what the earliest Christians in the first three centuries understood to be the teaching of Jesus on killing surely has some relevance for our understanding of what Jesus taught. We cannot simply assume that the early Christians accurately understood Jesus's teaching. But it seems plausible to suppose that Christians much closer to the time of Jesus, who lived in a (pre-Constantinian) sociopolitical setting more similar to that of Jesus than Christians living after the reign of Constantine, would be more likely to understand Jesus's teaching on loving enemies than those who lived centuries later. Finally, in a world where devastating violence has wreaked terrible havoc over the centuries—and

1. See Peter Brock's lengthy bibliography covering the years 1888–1987 ("Selected Bibliography").

2. *Militia Christi*, published by the great German church historian Adolf Harnack in 1905; *The Early Christian Attitude to War*, published by C. J. Cadoux in 1919; *Christian Attitudes Toward War and Peace* by Yale historian Roland H. Bainton, published in 1960; and two well-researched scholarly articles by John Helgeland published in 1974 ("Christians") and 1979 ("Roman Army"). In 1992, David G. Hunter wrote a careful survey of the previous decade's further research ("Decade of Research").

3. See p. 163 below for more detailed discussion of the various interpretations.

4. It is astounding that George Weigel begins his commentary on the heritage of Catholic thought on war and peace with St. Augustine—thus ignoring the first three centuries (*Tranquilitas Ordinis*, 23).

continues to do so in the present—the witness of the Christians in the first three centuries provides one source of ethical guidance on a topic of current significance.

Unfortunately no one has published a comprehensive book that includes all the relevant existing data on our topic. Many authors have included (often in translation) some of the most important texts. But no one has sought to compile all the relevant material in one place. That is the task of this volume.

In this book I have sought to provide in English translation all extant data directly relevant to the witness of the early church on killing. The largest amount of data comes from the writings of the early church. A few epitaphs from Christian "tombstones" are also relevant, as are a few statements by pagan Roman historians and recent archaeological discoveries. Doubtless there are relevant data that I have inadvertently missed. And ongoing archeological and other research will discover new data. But I have tried to include everything currently known that is directly relevant to our topic.[5]

Since I hope this volume will be useful not only to scholars but also to the general Christian community, I provide brief introductions to every Christian writer cited and explanatory notes on many specific texts. In every case, I have tried to be as objective as possible and avoid mere speculation. This book is intended to be a careful historical presentation because I believe strongly that the historian must seek vigorously to avoid inserting his or her own biases into the historical task.

That does not mean that I think it is possible entirely to escape one's own personal bias. Every historian starts at a particular location in history. I do not conceal the fact that I grew up in the Anabaptist tradition, which is pacifist. As a Christian, ethicist, and theologian, I remain committed to that tradition. But I think it would be fundamentally immoral to choose to slant the historical data to support my ethics and theology. I also believe not only that the historian has a moral imperative to strive vigorously for objectivity but also that it is possible to make great progress in moving toward that goal, even though it is never fully reached. Therefore I invite and welcome others to point out places where my personal views rather than the historical data have shaped my conclusions.

The vast majority of the translations here come from the volumes of the *Ante-Nicene Fathers*. I have slightly modernized the text, primarily to substitute male terms when the reference was clearly about both genders.

The excerpt from *Dio's Roman History* is reprinted by permission of the publishers and the Trustees of the Loeb Classical Library from *Dio Cassius: Roman History, Volume 9*, Loeb Classical Library vol. 177, trans. Earnest

---

5. I say "directly" relevant because there is a sense in which a vast body of literature and data, both Christian and Greco-Roman, is relevant in a broad sense to our topic. That would include, for example, voluminous material on the Roman emperors and the Roman army in the first three centuries. But to include that kind of "indirectly" relevant material would require many volumes.

Cary (Cambridge, MA: Harvard University Press, 1927), 27–33. The excerpt from Adamantius's *Dialogue on the True Faith* is reprinted by permission of the publisher from *Adamantius: Dialogue on the True Faith in God*, ed. and trans. Robert A. Pretty and Garry W. Trompf (Leuven: Peeters, 1997). The excerpt from *The Infancy Gospel of Thomas* is reprinted by permission of the publisher from Tony Chartrand-Burke, *De infantia Iesu euangelium Thomae graece*, Corpus Christianorum Series Apocraphorum 17 (Turnhout: Brepols, 2011), 3.2–8.2. The excerpts from *The Acts of Maximilian*, *The Acts of Marcellus*, and *The Martyrdom of Julius the Veteran* is reprinted by permission of the publisher from Herbert Musurillo, *The Acts of the Christian Martyrs* (New York: Oxford University Press, 1972).

One final comment about the larger society in which this Christian material on killing emerged. Killing was widespread and acceptable in the world where the early Christians lived. Roman culture of course accepted and glorified killing by the Roman army. Capital punishment via the sword and crucifixion was also the norm. In addition, Greco-Roman culture in the first three centuries justified and accepted widespread abortion, infanticide, and suicide.[6] And one of the most popular "sports" events of the time was the gladiatorial contests, where trained gladiators fought to the death, cheered on by thousands of spectators.[7] That was the context in which the early Christians developed their own witness on killing.

---

6. See Gorman, *Abortion*, and Arner, *Pro-Life*. Only a relatively small number of the texts cited here relate specifically to the topics of abortion and capital punishment. The index will enable the reader to quickly locate those passages.

7. Kyle, *Spectacles*.

Christian Writers before Constantine

Didache (c. AD 80–120)

The *Didache* ("the Teaching") is an anonymous early Christian document. No author, time, or location of writing is mentioned. Contemporary scholars date it anywhere from AD 50 to 180; many consider the period between AD 80 and 120 to be a good estimate (Jefford, *Apostolic Fathers*, 19–22; Grant, *Apostolic Fathers*, 71–76; *Fathers*, 1.167–70; Holmes, *Apostolic Fathers*, 334–43).

The first few chapters contrast the two ways: the way of life and the way of death. Central to the way of life is loving your neighbor, even your enemy. Chapter 2 lists a number of things that should not be done, including murder, adultery, abortion, and infanticide. Both abortion and infanticide were widespread in first-century Roman life (Gorman, *Abortion*, 24–32).

1. There are two ways, one of life and one of death. . . . The way of life, then, is this: First, you shall love God who made you; second, your neighbor as yourself. And whatever you would not want to happen to you, you should not do to another. And of these sayings the teaching is this: Bless them that curse you, and pray for your enemies, and fast for them that persecute you. For what thanks is there, if you love them that love you? Do not also the Gentiles do the same? But you should love them that hate you, and you shall not have an enemy. . . . If one gives you a blow upon your right cheek, turn the other also; and you shall be perfect [cf. Matt. 5:39–48].[1]

2. And the second commandment . . . ; you shall not commit murder, you shall not commit adultery, . . . you shall not murder a child by abortion nor commit infanticide.[2]

1. *ANF* 7:377.
2. Ibid.

The Epistle of Barnabas (c. AD 70–135)

This is an anonymous letter, written perhaps in Alexandria, Egypt, sometime between AD 70 and 135. Much of the document is an argument for Christian faith. In chapters 18–20, the author contrasts the "Two Ways" of light and darkness in a way similar to the *Didache*, but scholars do not think the one is directly dependent on the other. Clement of Alexandria assigned it the same authority as the Catholic Epistles, and it appears in the famous fourth-century biblical manuscript Codex Sinaiticus.

See the introduction and large secondary literature cited in Holmes, *Apostolic Fathers*, 370–79.

19. You shall not abort a child nor, again, commit infanticide.[3]

First Clement (c. AD 80–100)

One of the earliest extant Christian documents outside of the New Testament, *First Clement* is a letter, as its salutation declares, from "the church of God that sojourns in Rome to the church of God that sojourns in Corinth" (Holmes, *Apostolic Fathers*, 45). It was written to help resolve a serious schism in the Corinthian church.

Contemporary scholars generally agree that the author was Clement, a prominent leader in Rome at the end of the first century. Both strong ancient tradition and most extant manuscripts say Clement is the author. We cannot date the letter precisely, but most scholars believe it was written in the last couple decades of the first century.

Later tradition (e.g., Irenaeus, one hundred years later) considered Clement the third successor of St. Peter as bishop of Rome (Glimm et al., *Apostolic Fathers*, 3). Protestant scholars, who think there was probably a group of bishops in Rome at this time, consider Clement to have been a prominent member of such a group (Holmes, *Apostolic Fathers*, 34–35).

The text says nothing explicit about killing. Rather it uses military imagery to describe the desired unity of the Christian church. Christ is the "emperor" and church leaders "the governors" of the church, which Clement calls "our government troops."

3. Holmes, *Apostolic Fathers*, 435.

What implications this use of military imagery has for Clement's attitude toward killing and the military is disputed. Swift argues that although the letter does not endorse Christian engagement in war, "one would nevertheless have difficulty in reconciling it with a pacifist stance" (Swift, *Military*, 33). Such a conclusion, however, goes well beyond the evidence. Many Christians in the first few centuries used military imagery (Helgeland et al., *Military*, 18–19; Harnack, *Militia*, 37–62; Cadoux, *War*, 161–70)—including those who explicitly argue that Christians dare never kill (see the section on "Use of Military Language" below).

For additional introductory material and a large bibliography, see Ehrman, *Fathers*, 1:18–33.

37. With all zeal, then, brethren, let us serve as good soldiers under his [i.e., Christ's] irreproachable command. Let us remember the discipline, obedience and submission that our government troops exhibit when they carry out orders. It is not everyone's job to lead a thousand men, or a hundred, or fifty or some such number. Each one carries out the orders of the emperor and the governors according to his own rank. Those with great responsibility cannot do without those who have less and vice-versa. Together they form a kind of whole, and therein lies the benefit.[4]

Second Clement

Nothing is known about the author, date, or occasion of this sermon (the oldest surviving Christian sermon outside the New Testament). In the manuscripts, it appears immediately after *First Clement* and probably dates from the first part of the second century. See Holmes, *Apostolic Fathers*, 132–37 and the literature cited there.

13. Therefore, brothers and sisters, let us repent immediately. . . . For when they hear from us that God says, "It is no credit to you if you love those who love you, but it is a credit to you if you love your enemies and those who hate you," when they hear these things, they marvel at such extraordinary goodness. But when they see that we not only do not love those who hate us but do not even love those who love us, they scornfully laugh at us, and the Name is blasphemed.[5]

4. Swift, *Military*, 33.
5. Holmes, *Apostolic Fathers*, 155.

Apocalypse of Peter (c. AD 100–150)

Some unknown author, not Jesus's disciple Peter, wrote the *Apocalypse*. Scholars agree that it was written sometime in the first half of the second century. Several early Christian writers cite the *Apocalypse* starting as early as AD 180. It circulated widely in the West and the East, and for a time some even considered it part of the church's inspired writings.

We have two major manuscripts: a shorter Greek text and a longer Ethiopian translation. Here I use the latter, which many scholars think better presents the original.

Section 8 (section 26 in the Greek) is part of a longer description of hell where many different kinds of sinners suffer excruciating torment. This selection speaks of those who committed abortion—especially those who aborted babies conceived by fornication.

For background, see Hennecke, *Apocrypha*, 2:663–68, and Bremmer and Czachesz, *Apocalypse*.

8. And near this flame there is a great and very deep pit and into it there flow all kinds of . . . horrifying things and excretions. And the women are swallowed up by this up to their necks and are punished with great pain. These are they who have procured abortions and have ruined the work of God which he has created. Opposite them is another place where the children sit, but both alive, and they cry to God. And lightnings go forth from those children which pierce the eyes of those who, by fornication, have brought about their destruction.[6] Other men and women stand above them naked. And their children stand opposite to them in a place of delight. And they sigh and cry to God because of their parents, "These are they who neglected and cursed and transgressed thy commandment. They killed us and cursed the angel who created us and hung us up. And they withheld from us the light which thou hast appointed for all." And the milk of the mothers flows from their breasts and congeals and smells foul, and from it come forth beasts that devour flesh, which turn and torture them forever with their husbands, because they forsook the commandment of God and killed their children. And the children shall be given to the angel Temlakos. And those who slew them will be tortured forever, for God wills it to be so.[7]

---

6. The Greek text reads: "And these are those who produced children outside marriage and who procured abortions."

7. Hennecke, *Apocrypha*, 2:674–75.

Justin Martyr (c. AD 100–167)

Justin Martyr is one of the earliest Christian apologists, writing at least two defenses of Christianity in the middle of the second century. Born in Samaria into a gentile family in approximately AD 100, Justin received a Greek education, came to admire Plato, and later became convinced that Christianity was the only true philosophy. He taught for some time in Rome where he was martyred (beaten and beheaded) after refusing to sacrifice to the Roman gods sometime between AD 162 and 167.

Justin's *First Apology*, addressed to Emperor Antoninus Pius, must have been written sometime between AD 137 and 161. Other evidence (see Barnard, *St. Justin*, 11) suggests that Justin probably wrote it sometime between AD 151 and 155. His purpose was to correct the widespread slander and misunderstanding of Christians and portray Christian faith as the true philosophy. He denies that Christians are guilty of atheism, immorality, and disloyalty. In chapters 14–20 (including 14–17, quoted here), he describes the moral power of Christian truth.

Justin's central argument appears in sections 30–53, where he argues at great length that the Old Testament contains numerous predictions that were fulfilled in Christ. The selection from chapter 39 is just one example. The prophets predicted that in the time of the Messiah, people would beat their swords into ploughshares (Isa. 2:2–4; Mic. 4:1–4). Christians represent the fulfillment of that prophecy because they have turned away from murder and refuse to make war upon their enemies.

The *Dialogue with Trypho* takes the form of a discussion with a Jew named Trypho (otherwise unknown) soon after Trypho had fled Judea after the last Jewish revolt against Rome (AD 132–35). It is thought that Justin Martyr may have written our present document much later at Rome, perhaps sometime between AD 155 and 161. The *Dialogue* is a lengthy argument that Jews should accept the truth of Christianity if they understand their own scriptures.

In this *Dialogue*, as in the *First Apology*, Justin Martyr cites Micah 4:1–4 (Isa. 2:2–4) and then argues that Jesus and the church are the fulfillment of this messianic prophecy. In section 109, Justin Martyr cites all of Micah 4:1–7. Then in section 110, quoted here, he argues that because Christians, who were formerly filled with war, have through Christ changed their swords into ploughshares, they represent the fulfillment of the ancient prophecy.

Some authors argue that Justin Martyr had no position on whether Christians should be in the army (see Cadoux, *War*, 102–3) because none of these texts explicitly state that Christians dare never kill or serve in the Roman army. But they clearly say that Christians have turned away from violence and murder, and now love their enemies, thus fulfilling the prophetic prediction that in the messianic time, people would abandon war.

For introductory material, see Barnard, *St. Justin*, 3–21; Swift, *Military*, 34–35; ANF 1:159–61; Falls, *Justin Martyr*, 9–18, 23–27, 139–40.

First Apology

14. We who hated and destroyed one another, and on account of their different manners would not live with people of a different tribe, now, since the coming of Christ, live familiarly with them, and pray for our enemies,[8] and endeavor to persuade those who hate us unjustly to live according to the good precepts of Christ, to the end that they may become partakers with us of the same joyful hope of a reward from God the ruler of all.

15. For Christ . . . taught thus: "If you love them that love you, what new thing do you do? For even fornicators do this. But I say unto you, Pray for your enemies, and love them that hate you, and bless them that curse you, and pray for them that despitefully use you" [cf. Matt. 5:44; Rom. 12:14].

16. And concerning our being patient of injuries, and ready to serve all, and free from anger, this is what He said: "To him that smiteth thee on the one cheek, offer also the other; and him that taketh away thy cloak or coat, forbid not. And whosoever shall be angry, is in danger of fire. And every one that compelleth thee to go with him a mile, follow him two" [cf. Matt. 5:22, 39–41]. For we ought not to strive; neither has He desired us to be imitators of wicked people, but He has exhorted us to lead all people, by patience and gentleness, from shame and the love of evil. And this indeed is proved in the case of many who once were of your way of thinking, but have changed their violent and tyrannical disposition.

17. And everywhere we, more readily than all people, endeavor to pay to those appointed by you the taxes both ordinary and extraordinary, as we have been taught by Him; for at that time some came to Him and asked Him, if one ought to pay tribute to Caesar; and He answered, "Tell Me, whose image does the coin bear?" And they said, "Caesar's." And again He answered them, "Render therefore to Caesar the things that are Caesar's, and to God the things that are God's" [cf. Matt. 22:17–21]. Whence to God alone we render worship, but in other things we gladly serve you, acknowledging you as kings and rulers of people, and praying that with your kingly power you be found to possess also sound judgment.[9]

---

8. Cf. also *Dialogue with Trypho* 85: "Jesus commanded to love even enemies" (ANF 1:242).
9. ANF 1:167–68.

39. And when the Spirit of prophecy speaks as predicting things that are to come to pass, He speaks in this way: "For out of Zion shall go forth the law, and the word of the Lord from Jerusalem. And He shall judge among the nations, and shall rebuke many people; and they shall beat their swords into ploughshares, and their spears into pruning-hooks: nation shall not lift up sword against nation, neither shall they learn war any more" [Isa. 2:3–4; Mic. 4:1–4]. And that it did so come to pass, we can convince you. For from Jerusalem there went out into the world, men, twelve in number, and these illiterate, of no ability in speaking: but by the power of God they proclaimed to every race of people that they were sent by Christ to teach to all the word of God; and we who formerly used to murder one another do not only now refrain from making war upon our enemies, but also, that we may not lie or deceive our examiners, willingly die confessing Christ.[10]

Second Apology

4. But lest someone say to us, "Go then all of you and kill yourselves, and pass even now to God, and do not trouble us," I will tell you why we do not so, but why, when examined, we fearlessly confess. We have been taught that God did not make the world aimlessly, but for the sake of the human race; and we have before stated that He takes pleasure in those who imitate His properties, and is displeased with those that embrace what is worthless either in word or deed. If, then, we all kill ourselves, we shall become the cause, as far as in us lies, why no one should be born, or instructed in the divine doctrines, or even why the human race should not exist; and we shall, if we so act, be ourselves acting in opposition to the will of God. But when we are examined, we make no denial.[11]

Dialogue with Trypho

85. And I said, "Listen, my friends, to the Scripture which induces me to act thus. Jesus commanded [us] to love even [our] enemies, as was predicted by Isaiah in many passages."[12]

96. And in addition to all this we pray for you [Jews and pagans who oppose Christians], that Christ may have mercy upon you. For He taught us to pray

10. *ANF* 1:175–76.
11. *ANF* 1:189.
12. *ANF* 1:242.

for our enemies also, saying, "Love your enemies; be kind and merciful, as your heavenly Father is" [cf. Luke 6:35–36].[13]

110. And when I had finished these words [quoting Mic. 4:1–7], I continued: "Now I am aware that your teachers, sirs, admit the whole of the words of this passage to refer to Christ; and I am likewise aware that they maintain He has not yet come . . . just as if there was no fruit as yet from the words of the prophecy. O unreasoning people! . . . [We] Christians, . . . having learned the true worship of God from the law, and the word which went forth from Jerusalem by means of the apostles of Jesus, have fled for safety to the God of Jacob and God of Israel; and we who were filled with war, and mutual slaughter, and every wickedness, have each through the whole earth changed our warlike weapons,—our swords into ploughshares, and our spears into implements of tillage,—and we cultivate piety, righteousness, philanthropy, faith, and hope, which we have from the Father Himself through Him who was crucified. Now it is evident that no one can terrify or subdue us who have believed in Jesus all over the world. For it is plain that, though beheaded, and crucified, and thrown to wild beasts, and chains, and fire, and all other kinds of torture, we do not give up our confession; but the more such things happen, the more do others in larger numbers become faithful, and worshipers of God through the name of Jesus."[14]

Tatian (c. AD 110–70)

A native of Mesopotamia and a student of philosophy, Tatian became a Christian and was instructed by Justin Martyr in Rome. He compiled the first harmony of the four Gospels, but his only extant book is his *Address to the Greeks* (written about AD 167). See Goodspeed, *History*, 106–9.

Address to the Greeks

11. I do not wish to be a king; I am not anxious to be rich; I decline military command; I detest fornication; I am not impelled by an insatiable love of gain to go to sea; I do not contend for chaplets.[15]

13. *ANF* 1:247. So too chap. 133.
14. *ANF* 1:253–54.
15. *ANF* 2:69.

Irenaeus (c. AD 130–202)

Irenaeus, the bishop of Lyons, France, from about AD 177 to 202, is widely regarded as the most significant theologian of the second century. Born in Syria or Asia Minor sometime between AD 120 and 140, Irenaeus studied under the great bishop Polycarp of Smyrna, who sent him to Gaul to help evangelize what is now southern France.

When he visited Rome in 177, he was horrified to discover that the bishop of Rome and others had embraced heretical beliefs. That visit helped move Irenaeus toward his lifelong task of combating Christian heresies, especially gnosticism. He wrote the five books of *Adversus Haereses* (*Against Heresies*) over the course of fifteen or more years between 177 and 202. Written in Greek, *Against Heresies*'s primary audience may have been Christians in Rome, but it was read widely and was often quoted by Christian writers from the third century on. As Irenaeus refuted the heretics, he explained Christian faith so well that he is sometimes considered the founder of Christian theology.

There are three different places in *Against Heresies* where Irenaeus writes of things directly related to our topic. In 2.32, he refers to Jesus's command to love enemies. In 4.34, he claims that Christians' turning away from war to peace is the fulfillment of the prophecy in Isaiah (2:3) and Micah (4:2).

In 5.24, he quotes Romans 13 to say that God has ordained human government. He understands Romans 13:4 (government "beareth not the sword in vain") to show that God wants government to restrain evil. But neither here nor in a similar passage in 4.36 is there any suggestion (contrary to Hornus, *Not Lawful*, 65) that Christians should use the sword.

The final selections from Irenaeus come from his *Proof of the Apostolic Preaching*. Eusebius of Caesarea mentions this writing, but it was presumed lost until an Armenian translation was found in 1904. Written while Irenaeus was bishop of Lyons, *Proof* is a letter written to a brother (probably another church leader) to provide a summary of Christian teaching. In chapters 86–100, Irenaeus argues that Christ enables believers to live the law of charity which replaces the Old Testament law (Smith, *Proof*, 3–44).

For introductory information, see Unger, *Irenaeus*, 1; *ANF* 1:309–13; Smith, *Proof*, 3–44; Goodspeed and Grant, *History*, 119–23.

Against Heresies

2.32. Moreover, this impious opinion of theirs with respect to actions—namely, that it is incumbent on them to have experience of all kinds of deeds, even the most abominable—is refuted by the teaching of the Lord, with whom not only is the adulterer rejected, but also the person who desires to commit adultery; and not only is the actual murderer held guilty of having killed another to his own damnation, but the person also who is angry with his brother without a cause: [Christ] commanded His disciples not only not to hate people, but also to love their enemies;[16] and enjoined them not only not to swear falsely, but not even to swear at all; . . . and not only not to strike, but even, when themselves struck, to present the other cheek to those that maltreated them; and not only not to refuse to give up the property of others, but even if their own were taken away, not to demand it back again from those that took it; and not only not to injure their neighbors, nor to do them any evil, but also, when themselves wickedly dealt with, to be long-suffering, and to show kindness towards those that injured them, and to pray for them [cf. Matt. 5:21–48], that by means of repentance they might be saved—so that we should in no respect imitate the arrogance, lust, and pride of others.[17]

4.34. The Jews used the Mosaic law until the coming of the Lord; but from the Lord's advent, the new covenant which brings back peace, and the law which gives life, has gone forth over the whole earth, as the prophets said: "For out of Zion shall go forth the law, and the word of the Lord from Jerusalem; and He shall rebuke many people; and they shall break down their swords into ploughshares, and their spears into pruning-hooks, and they shall no longer fight" [Isa. 2:3–4; Mic. 4:2–3]. If therefore another law and word, going forth from Jerusalem, brought in such a reign of peace among the Gentiles which received it [the word], and convinced, through them, many a nation of its folly, then only it appears that the prophets spake of some other person. But if the law of liberty, that is, the word of God, preached by the apostles (who went forth from Jerusalem) throughout all the earth, caused such a change in the state of things, that these nations did form the swords and war-lances into ploughshares, and changed them into pruning-hooks for reaping the corn, that is, into instruments used for peaceful purposes, and that they are now unaccustomed to fighting, but when smitten, offer also the other cheek, then the prophets have not spoken these things of any other person, but of Him who effected them. This person is our Lord.[18]

5.24. As therefore the devil lied at the beginning, so did he also in the end, when he said, "All these are delivered unto me, and to whomsoever I will I give them" [Matt. 4:9]. For it is not he who has appointed the kingdoms of this world, but God; for "the heart of the king is in the hand of God" [Prov. 21:1]. Paul the apostle also says upon this same subject: "Be ye subject to all

16. Cf. also 4.13, where he says the Lord taught us "not to love our neighbors only, but even our enemies" (*ANF* 1:477; see also 3.18).

17. *ANF* 1:408.

18. *ANF* 1:512.

the higher powers; for there is no power but of God: now those which are have been ordained of God" [Rom. 13:1]. And again, in reference to them he says, "For he beareth not the sword in vain; for he is the minister of God, the avenger for wrath to him who does evil" [Rom. 3:4].

For since humanity, by departing from God, reached such a pitch of fury even to look upon his brother as his enemy, and engaged without fear in every kind of restless conduct, and murder, and avarice; God imposed upon humanity the fear of people, as they did not acknowledge the fear of God, in order that, being subjected to human authority, and kept under restraint by their laws, they might attain to some degree of justice, and exercise mutual forbearance through dread of the sword suspended full in their view, as the apostle says: "For he beareth not the sword in vain; for he is the minister of God, the avenger for wrath upon him who does evil." And for this reason too, magistrates themselves, having laws as a clothing of righteousness whenever they act in a just and legitimate manner, shall not be called into question for their conduct, nor be liable to punishment. But whatsoever they do to the subversion of justice, iniquitously, and impiously, and illegally, and tyranni-cally, in these things shall they also perish; for the just judgment of God comes equally upon all, and in no case is defective. Earthly rule, therefore, has been appointed by God for the benefit of nations, and not by the devil.[19]

Proof of the Apostolic Preaching

61. [Here he expounds Isa. 11:6–7, which he quoted earlier in chap. 59.] Those who formerly acted like animals and waged war on other people have now been transformed by faith in Christ. For he now tells in parable the gathering together in peaceful concord, through the name of Christ, of people of different nations and like character; for the assembly of the just, who are likened to calves and lambs and kids and children, will not be hurt at all by those, both men and women, who at an earlier time had become brutal and beast-like because of selfish pride, till some of them took on the likeness of wolves and lions, ravaging the weaker, and waged war on their like, . . . these gathered together in one name will be possessed by the grace of God in justice of conduct, changing their wild and untamed nature. And this has already come to pass, for those who were before most perverse, to the extent of omitting no work of ungodliness, coming to know Christ, and believing Him, no sooner believed than they were changed.[20]

96. Therefore also we have no need of the law as pedagogue. . . . For no more shall the law say: . . . *thou shalt not kill*, to him who has put away from himself

19. *ANF* 1:552.
20. Smith, *Proof*, 88.

all anger and enmity. . . . Nor *an eye for an eye and a tooth for a tooth*, to him who counts no man his enemy, but all his neighbors, and therefore cannot even put forth his hand to revenge.[21]

Athenagoras (d. c. AD 180)

Athenagoras was probably a fairly prominent leader in Alexandria's Platonic school. After his conversion, he became one of the most learned Christian apologists of the second century. Internal evidence shows that his *Plea for the Christians* was written sometime between AD 177 and 180. Here Athenagoras refutes the widespread charges that Christians were guilty of atheism, cannibalism, and incest.

Athenagoras does not explicitly state that Christians do not go to war and kill as soldiers. But he refers to and quotes from Matthew 5:38, including Jesus's command to love enemies, and claims that even uneducated Christians do that (chaps. 1, 11).

In chapter 35, he argues not only that Christians do not kill but also that they even refuse to attend the enormously popular contests of gladiators. Christians also condemn abortion and infanticide as murder. By opposing killing everywhere, he claims, Christians consistently follow their rule.

For introductory material, see Crehan, *Athenagoras*, 3–27; Gorman, *Abortion*, 53–54; ANF 2:127; Goodspeed and Grant, *History*, 115–16; Rankin, *Athenagoras*.

A Plea for the Christians

To the Emperors Marcus Aurelius Antoninus and Lucius Aurelius Commodus, conquerors of Armenia and Sarmatia, and more than all, philosophers.

1. In your empire, greatest of sovereigns, different nations have different customs and laws; and no one is hindered by law or fear of punishment from following his ancestral usages. . . . In short, among every nation and people, people offer sacrifices and celebrate whatever mysteries they please. . . . But for us who are called Christians you have not in like manner cared; but although we commit

---

21. See also chaps. 59–61, where Irenaeus quotes from Isa. 11:1–9 and then explains (chap. 61) that formerly vicious people who waged war had come to know Christ and changed their "wild and untamed nature." The text here is from Smith, *Proof*, 106.

no wrong—nay, as will appear in the sequel of this discourse, are of all people most piously and righteously disposed towards the Deity and towards your government—you allow us to be harassed, plundered, and persecuted, the multitude making war upon us for our name alone. . . . You will learn from this discourse that we suffer unjustly. . . . For we have learned, not only not to return blow for blow, nor to go to law with those who plunder and rob us, but to those who smite us on one side of the face to offer the other side also, and to those who take away our coat to give likewise our cloak.[22]

11. If I go minutely into the particulars of our doctrine, let it not surprise you. . . . What, then, are those teachings in which we are brought up? "I say unto you, Love your enemies; bless them that curse you; pray for them that persecute you; that ye may be the sons of your Father who is in heaven, who causes His sun to rise on the evil and the good, and sends rain on the just and the unjust" [cf. Matt. 5:44–45]. . . . Who of those . . . who teach homonyms and synonyms, and categories and axioms, and what is the subject and what the predicate, and who promise their disciples by these and such like instructions to make them happy: who of them have so purged their souls as, instead of hating their enemies, to love them; and, instead of speaking ill of those who have reviled them (to abstain from which is of itself an evidence of no mean forbearance), to bless them; and to pray for those who plot against their lives? On the contrary, they . . . are ever bent on working some ill, making the art of words and not the exhibition of deeds their business and profession. But among us you will find uneducated persons, and artisans, and old women, who, if they are unable in words to prove the benefit of our doctrine, yet by their deeds exhibit the benefit arising from their persuasion of its truth: they do not rehearse speeches, but exhibit good works; when struck, they do not strike again; when robbed, they do not go to law; they give to those that ask of them, and love their neighbors as themselves.[23]

35. What person of sound mind, therefore, will affirm . . . that we are murderers? For we cannot eat human flesh till we have killed someone. . . . If anyone should ask them . . . whether they have seen what they assert, not one of them would be so barefaced as to say that he had. And yet we have slaves, some more and some fewer, by whom we could not help being seen; but even of these, not one has been found to invent even such things against us. For when they know that we cannot endure even to see a person put to death, though justly; who of them can accuse us of murder or cannibalism? Who does not reckon among the things of greatest interest the contests of gladiators and wild beasts, especially those which are given by you? But we, deeming that to

22. *ANF* 2:129.
23. *ANF* 2:134.

see a person put to death is much the same as killing him, have abjured such spectacles. How, then, when we do not even look on, lest we should contract guilt and pollution, can we put people to death? And when we say that those women who use drugs to bring on abortion commit murder, and will have to give an account to God for the abortion, on what principle should we commit murder? For it does not belong to the same person to regard the very fetus in the womb as a created being, and therefore an object of God's care, and when it has passed into life, to kill it; and not to expose an infant, because those who expose them are chargeable with child-murder, and on the other hand, when it has been reared to destroy it. But we are in all things always alike and the same, obedient to our rule, and not ruling over it.[24]

Clement of Alexandria (c. AD 150–215)

Well educated in Greek philosophy and poetry before his conversion, Clement became a sophisticated proponent of Christianity and a prominent teacher and eventually leader of a famous Christian school in Alexandria led by Pantaenus. A Greek city, Alexandria was the second largest city in the Roman Empire with a vibrant intellectual community and superb libraries with vast holdings. Perhaps born in Athens, Clement traveled widely before he settled in Alexandria about 180. He taught there for more than twenty years, and Origen was his most famous student. During the intense persecution of 202–3 that killed thousands of Christians, Clement fled from Alexandria. He died about AD 215.

In his many writings, Clement sought to combine the best of Greek and Christian thought, trying to show that Christianity was intellectually respectable. He clearly loved the Greek classics and his works contain over seven hundred quotations from about three hundred pagan authors. We have no exact information on the dates of his major writings, but many of them were probably written in the second half of his time in Alexandria.

His *Exhortation* (*Protreptikos*) *to the Greeks* attempts to demonstrate that Christianity is the fulfillment of the best of Greek poetry and philosophy. The *Educator* (*Paedagogus*) is a lengthy treatise (three books) on what the Christian life should be, showing how Christ the Educator molds Christian character. And *Miscellanies* (*Stromata*) is a vast writing (eight books) covering a wide range of topics that seeks to explain the knowledge that will lead a Christian

24. *ANF* 2:147. In the last sentence, I follow the translation of Crehan, *Athenagoras*, 76, and Barnard, *Athenagoras*, 173.

toward perfection. It is frequently difficult to follow Clement's meandering thought in *Miscellanies*.

I include several sections from each of these major works plus one from fragments of other lost books and one from *Prophetic Eclogues*.

In spite of the large size of Clement's extant writings, there is very little about war and abortion. In the two passages on abortion, it is quite clear that Clement is totally opposed to it. But the nine brief passages related to enemies, war, and the military are less clear. One scholar observes that in Clement "there is to be no compromise with the world . . . in military service" (Chadwick, *Early Christian Thought*, 62). Another argues that Clement considers military service one acceptable occupation for Christians. In fact, this author suggests that one can see in Clement the general idea of the Just War tradition (Johnson, *Peace*, 20–22, 50). Even Cadoux says that some of Clement's statements "concede the compatibility of military service with the Christian faith" (*War*, 232).

While not explicitly prohibiting Christian participation in the army, a number of passages stress the peaceful nature of Christians. Clement says that Christians employ the Word ("the one instrument of peace") rather than the trumpets used by experts in war (*Exhortation* 4). Christ gathers his "bloodless host" of "soldiers of peace" rather than blowing the trumpet that collects "soldiers and proclaims war" (*Exhortation* 11). He cites Jesus's call to turn the other cheek (*Educator* 2.12; *Miscellanies* 4.8). He notes that Christians not only do not train women to be warriors but also "wish the men even to be peaceable" (*Miscellanies* 4.8), and he quotes Jesus's call to love enemies (*Miscellanies* 4.14; *Educator* 3.12).

In a few passages, Clement refers to military service without any indication whether he thinks Christians should be soldiers (*Educator* 2.12–13). He notes John the Baptist's advice to soldiers to be content with their wages without any comment on what that means for Christians and the army (*Educator* 3.12). The same is true of his brief reference to the Deuteronomic teaching that the man who is betrothed but not yet married should be free of military service (*Miscellanies* 2.18).

There is one passage (*Exhortation* 10) that some claim clearly shows that Clement considers military service acceptable for Christians.[25] But as I show in a note on that passage (see pp. 34–35), that interpretation goes well beyond what the text says.

It is surprising that an author who wrote so much, especially on how Christians should live, said so little on war and the military. But we dare not read our own preferences into Clement's relative silence.

For introductory material, see Ferguson, *Clement*, 3–19; Chadwick, *Early Christian Thought*, 31–65; Oulton and Chadwick, *Alexandrian Christianity*,

25. Johnson, *Peace*, 20–22, 50, and Helgeland, "Christians," 154.

15–39; Wood, *Clement*, vii–xviii; Butterworth, *Clement*, xiii–xx; Johnson, *Peace*, 20–22, 50–53.

Exhortation to the Greeks

3. Well, now, let us say in addition, what inhuman demons, and hostile to the human race, your gods were, not only delighting in the insanity of people, but gloating over human slaughter,—now in the armed contests for superiority in the stadia, and now in the numberless contests for renown in the wars providing for themselves the means of pleasure, that they might be able abundantly to satiate themselves with the murder of human beings.[26]

The meaning of the following passage is disputed. Johnson (*Peace*, 20–21) cites this passage as evidence that Clement "accepted military service [for Christians] as one possible occupation alongside others (he mentions farmers, sailors and merchants)" (so too Helgeland, "Christians," 154; Swift, *Military*, 52; and Harnack, *Militia Christi*, 75). But two things make that interpretation questionable. First, in the case of farming and sailing, the text explicitly urges Christians to participate in that activity, albeit in knowledge and dependence on God. But the wording in the third case is quite different. He does not say, "Be a soldier." Rather he says that if one became a Christian while one was a soldier, then one should do what the commander says. The second consideration relates to the question: Who is the commander? If it is a military leader, then Johnson is probably right. But if it is Christ, then the text only says that soldiers who become Christians must obey Christ. It says nothing about what Christ wants a soldier who converts to do. That the commander to be obeyed is Christ is rather likely in light of another statement by Clement where he explicitly speaks of Christ the Instructor (or Teacher), using the image of a military leader and seafaring pilot: "As therefore the general directs the phalanx, consulting the safety of his soldiers, and the pilot steers the vessel, desiring to save the passengers, so also the Instructor [i.e., Christ] guides the children to a saving course of conduct. . . . Whatever we ask in accordance with reason from God to be done to us, will happen to those who believe in the Instructor" (*The Educator* 1.7; ANF 2:223). And in another place (*The Educator* 1.8), he refers to "our great General, the Word, the Commander-in-Chief of the universe" (see Bainton, "Early Church," 199). Furthermore, as Bainton points out, in the case of farming and sailing Clement refers to God in the second part of the sentence. Therefore it is likely that he does the same in the case of the third example. It is also relevant that later in the same chapter, Clement says that those who become Christians should follow God's laws not to kill and rather

26. *ANF* 2:183.

to turn the other cheek. To assert that in this statement Clement says that military service is as acceptable for Christians as farming or seafaring is to go well beyond what the text says. Rather than seeing this text as an endorsement of Christians serving in the military, it is more likely that we should understand the text in light of the *Apostolic Tradition* (see below, pp. 119–21). In that case, Clement would think that if a soldier becomes a Christian, he dare not kill.

10. Persons have been otherwise constituted by nature, so as to have fellowship with God. As, then, we do not compel the horse to plough, or the bull to hunt, but set each animal to that for which it is by nature fitted; so, placing our finger on what is a person's peculiar and distinguishing characteristic above other creatures, we invite him—born, as he is, for the contemplation of heaven, and being, as he is, a truly heavenly plant—to the knowledge of God, counseling him to furnish himself with what is his sufficient provision for eternity, namely, piety. Practice farming, we say, if you are a farmer; but while you till your fields, know God. Sail the sea, you who are devoted to navigation, yet call the whilst on the heavenly Pilot. Has knowledge taken hold of you while engaged in military service? Listen to the commander, who orders what is right. . . . If thou enroll thyself as one of God's people, heaven is thy country, God thy lawgiver. And what are the laws? "Thou shalt not kill; thou shalt not commit adultery; thou shalt not seduce boys; thou shalt not steal; thou shalt not bear false witness; thou shalt love the Lord thy God." And the complements of these are those laws of reason and words of sanctity which are inscribed on people's hearts: "Thou shalt love thy neighbor as thyself; to him who strikes thee on the cheek, present also the other."[27]

11. But it has been God's fixed and constant purpose to save the flock of people: for this end the good God sent the good Shepherd. And the Word, having unfolded the truth, showed to people the height of salvation, that either repenting they might be saved, or refusing to obey, they might be judged. This is the proclamation of righteousness: to those that obey, glad tidings; to those that disobey, judgment. The loud trumpet, when sounded, collects the soldiers, and proclaims war. And shall not Christ, breathing a strain of peace to the ends of the earth, gather together His own soldiers, the soldiers of peace? Well, by His blood, and by the word, He has gathered the bloodless host of peace, and assigned to them the kingdom of heaven. The trumpet of Christ is His Gospel. He hath blown it, and we have heard. "Let us array ourselves in the armor of peace, putting on the breastplate of righteousness, and taking the shield of faith, and binding our brows with the helmet of salvation; and let us sharpen the sword of the Spirit, which is the word of God" [cf. Eph. 6:14–17]. So the apostle in the spirit of peace commands. These are our invulnerable

27. *ANF* 2:200, 202.

weapons: armed with these, let us face the evil one. Let us quench "the fiery darts of the evil one" with the sword-points dipped in water that have been baptized by the Word. . . . O this holy and blessed power, by which God has fellowship with people! Better far, then, is it to become at once the imitator and the servant of the best of all beings; for only by holy service will anyone be able to imitate God, and to serve and worship Him only by imitating Him.[28]

The Educator

1.7. It is time for us in due course to say who our Instructor is.

He is called Jesus. Sometimes he calls himself a shepherd. . . .

As therefore the general directs the phalanx, consulting the safety of his soldiers, and the pilot steers the vessel, desiring to save the passengers; so also the Instructor guides the children to a saving course of conduct, through solicitude for us; and, in general, whatever we ask in accordance with reason from God to be done for us, will happen to those who believe in the Instructor. And just as the helmsman does not always yield to the winds, but sometimes, turning the prow towards them, opposes the whole force of hurricanes; so the Instructor never yields to the blasts that blow in this world, nor commits the child to them like a vessel to make shipwreck on a wild and licentious course of life.[29]

1.12. But let us, O children of the good Father—nurslings of the good Instructor—fulfill the Father's will, listen to the Word, and take on the mold of the true saving life of our Savior. . . . He makes preparation for a self-sufficing mode of life, for simplicity. . . . For He says, "Take no anxious thought for tomorrow" [Matt. 6:34], meaning that the person who has devoted himself to Christ ought to be sufficient to himself, and servant to himself, and moreover lead a life which provides for each day by itself. For it is not in war, but in peace, that we are trained. War needs great preparation, and luxury craves abundance, but peace and love, simple and quiet sisters, require no arms nor excessive supplies. The Word is their sustenance.[30]

2.4. For a person is truly a pacific instrument while other instruments, if you investigate, you will find to be warlike, inflaming to lusts, or kindling up illicit love affairs, or rousing wrath.

In their wars, therefore, the Etruscans use the trumpet, the Arcadians the pipe, the Sicilians the pectides, the Cretans the lyre, the Lacedaemonians the

28. ANF 2:204; cf. the translation in Merton, *Clement*, 27.
29. ANF 2:222–23.
30. ANF 2:234–35.

flute, the Thracians the horn, the Egyptians the drum, and the Arabians the cymbal. The one instrument of peace, the Word alone by which we honor God, is what we employ. We no longer employ the ancient psaltery, and trumpet, and timbrel, and flute, which those expert in war and despisers of the fear of God were wont to make use of also in the choruses at their festive assemblies.[31]

2.10. Our whole life can go on in observation of the laws of nature, if we gain dominion over our desires from the beginning and if we do not kill, by various means of a perverse art, the human offspring, born according to the designs of divine providence; for these women who, in order to hide their immorality, use abortive drugs which expel the matter completely dead, abort at the same time their human feelings.[32]

> The following passage comes at the end of a rather extended section on the importance of modest shoes for women. Women should not expose their feet, but going barefoot is quite acceptable for men—when they are in military service. The text does not give any clear indication whether Clement is speaking of military men in general or Christians in the military. However, given the fact that Clement's whole book is devoted to describing how Christians should live, we should probably assume that Clement is thinking of Christians in the army. But it goes beyond what the text says to claim (as does Helgeland, "Christians," 154n44) that this text is "another example of his neutral feelings about the military." At most, it shows that Clement knows of Christians in the army without telling us anything about what he thought about that.

2.12. Women are to be allowed a white shoe, except when on a journey, and then a greased shoe must be used. When on a journey, they require nailed shoes. Further, they ought for the most part to wear shoes; for it is not suitable for the foot to be shown naked: besides, woman is a tender thing, easily hurt. But for a man bare feet are quite in keeping, except when he is on military service. "For being shod is neighbor to being bound."

To go with bare feet is most suitable for exercise, and best adapted for health and ease, unless where necessity prevents.[33]

2.13. How much wiser to spend money on human beings, than on jewels and gold! . . . The excellence of man is righteousness, and temperance, and manliness, and godliness. The beautiful man is, then, he who is just, temperate,

31. *ANF* 2:248–49.
32. Gorman, *Abortion*, 52–53.
33. *ANF* 2:267.

and in a word, good, not he who is rich. But now even the soldiers wish to be decked with gold, not having read that poetical saying:

> With childish folly to the war he came,
> Laden with store of gold. [*Iliad* 2.872]

But the love of ornament, which is far from caring for virtue, but claims the body for itself when the love of the beautiful has changed to empty show, is to be utterly expelled.[34]

3.3. If only wild beasts were destroyed who wait to prey upon blood! Yet, it is not right for a person to touch blood, either, for his own body is nothing less than flesh quickened by blood. Human blood has its portion of reason, and its share in grace, along with the spirit. If anyone injures it, he will not escape punishment.[35]

3.12. Further, in respect to forbearance. "If thy brother," it is said, "sin against thee, rebuke him; and if he repent, forgive him. If he sin against thee seven times in a day, and turn to thee the seventh time, and say, I repent, forgive him" [Luke 17:3–4]. Also to the soldiers, by John, He commands, "to be content with their wages only" [Luke 3:14], and to the tax-collectors, "to exact no more than is appointed." To the judges He says, "Thou shalt not show partiality in judgment."

And of civil government: "Render to Caesar the things which are Caesar's; and unto God the things which are God's" [Matt. 22:21].

Wisdom pronounces anger a wretched thing, because "it will destroy the wise." And now He bids us "love our enemies, bless them that curse us, and pray for them that despitefully use us." And He says: "If any one strike thee on the one cheek, turn to him the other also; and if anyone take away thy coat, hinder him not from taking thy cloak also" [Matt. 5:40].[36]

Miscellanies

> Here Clement writes of the treasure the children of Israel took from the Egyptians as they fled Egypt.

1.23. Whether, then, as may be alleged is done in war, they thought it proper, in the exercise of the rights of conquerors, to take away the property of their

---

34. *ANF* 2:268.
35. Wood, *Clement*, 220.
36. *ANF* 2:293.

enemies, as those who have gained the day do from those who are defeated (and there was just cause of hostilities. The Hebrews came as suppliants to the Egyptians on account of famine; and they, reducing their guests to slavery, compelled them to serve them after the manner of captives, giving them no recompense); or as in peace, took the spoil as wages against the will of those who for a long period had given them no recompense, but rather had robbed them, it is all one.[37]

1.24. Our Moses then is a prophet, a legislator, skilled in military tactics and strategy, a politician, a philosopher. And in what sense he was a prophet, shall be by and by told, when we come to treat of prophecy. Tactics belong to military command, and the ability to command an army is among the attributes of kingly rule. Legislation, again, is also one of the functions of the kingly office, as also judicial authority.

Now, the Greeks had the advantage of receiving from Moses all these, and the knowledge of how to make use of each of them. And, for the sake of example, I shall cite one or two instances of leadership. . . . Furthermore, he put to flight and slew the hostile occupants of the land, falling upon them from a desert and rugged line of march (such was the excellence of his generalship). For the taking of the land of those hostile tribes was a work of skill and strategy.[38]

2.18. Again, it is said, "If anyone who has newly built a house, and has not previously inhabited it; or cultivated a newly-planted vine, and not yet partaken of the fruit; or betrothed a virgin, and not yet married her" [Deut. 20:5–7]. Such the humane law orders to be relieved from military service: from military reasons in the first place, lest, bent on their desires, they turn out sluggish in war; for it is those who are untrammeled by passion that boldly encounter perils; and from motives of humanity, since in view of the uncertainties of war, the law reckoned it not right that one should not enjoy his own labors, and another should, without bestowing pains, receive what belonged to those who had labored. The law seems also to point out manliness of soul, by enacting that he who had planted should reap the fruit, and he that built should inhabit, and he that had betrothed should marry.

Now love is conceived in many ways, in the form of meekness, of mildness, of patience, of liberty, of freedom from envy, of absence of hatred, of forgetfulness of injuries. . . . Does it not command us "to love strangers not only as friends and relatives, but as ourselves, both in body and soul?" . . . Accordingly it is expressly said, "You shall not abhor an Egyptian, for you were a sojourner in Egypt" [Deut. 23:7]; designating by the term Egyptian

37. *ANF* 2:336.
38. *ANF* 2:336–37.

either one of that race, or any one in the world. And enemies, although drawn up before the walls attempting to take the city, are not to be regarded as enemies until they are by the voice of the herald summoned to peace [cf. Deut. 20:10].[39]

4.8. Further, manliness is to be assumed in order to produce confidence and forbearance, so as "to him that strikes on the one cheek, to give to him the other; and to him that takes away the cloak, to yield to him the coat also" [cf. Matt. 5:39–40], strongly restraining anger. For we do not train our women like Amazons to manliness in war; since we wish the men even to be peaceable. I hear that the Sarmatian women practice war no less than the men; and the women of the Sacae besides, who shoot backwards, feigning flight as well as the men.[40]

> The following passage is especially difficult to understand. Much of it is a long, complex sentence. Clement seems to want to say that among the "things present" that cannot separate us from the love of Christ are "the hope entertained by the solider and the merchant's gain." Does that mean that Clement thought that there was no activity that soldiers or merchants could do that would separate them from the love of Christ? Probably not. Since this passage says nothing about activity Christian soldiers or merchants should not do, the passage probably tells us no more than that for Clement simply being in the army did not preclude one from being a Christian.

4.14. How great also is kindness? "Love your enemies," it is said, "bless them who curse you, and pray for them who despitefully use you" [Matt. 5:44–45], and the like; to which it is added, "that you may be the children of your Father who is in heaven," in allusion to resemblance to God. . . . "For I am persuaded that neither death," through the assault of persecutors, "nor life" in this world, "nor angels" (the apostate ones), "nor powers" (and Satan's power is the life which he chose, for such are the powers and principalities of darkness belonging to him), "nor things present," amid which we exist during the time of life, as the hope entertained by the soldier, and the merchant's gain, "nor height, nor depth, nor any other creature," in consequence of the energy proper to a man,—opposes the faith of him who acts according to free choice. "Creature" is synonymous with activity, being our work, and such activity "shall not be able to separate us from the love of God, which is in Christ Jesus our Lord" [Rom. 8:38–39].[41]

---

39. *ANF* 2:365–67.
40. *ANF* 2:420.
41. *ANF* 2:426.

Prophetic Eclogues

48. For example Peter in the Apocalypse says "that the children born abortively" receive the better part. These "are delivered to a care-taking (*temelouchos*) angel," so that after they have reached knowledge they may obtain the better abode, as if they had suffered what they would have suffered, had they attained to bodily life. But the others shall obtain salvation only as people who have suffered wrong and experienced mercy, and shall exist without torment, having received this as their reward.

49. "But the milk of the mothers which flows from their breasts and congeals," says Peter in the Apocalypse, "shall beget tiny flesh-eating beasts and they shall run over them and devour them"—which teaches that the punishments will come to pass by reason of the sins.[42]

50. An ancient said that the embryo is a living thing; for that the soul entering into the womb after it has been by cleansing prepared for conception, and introduced by one of the angels who preside over generation, and who knows the time for conception, moves the woman to intercourse; and that, on the seed being deposited, the spirit, which is in the seed, is, so to speak, appropriated, and is thus assumed into conjunction in the process of formation. He cited as a proof to all, how, when the angels give glad tidings to the barren, they introduce souls before conception. And in the Gospel "the babe leapt" as a living thing. And the barren are barren for this reason, that the soul, which unites for the deposit of the seed, is not introduced so as to secure conception and generation.[43]

Who Is the Rich Man That Shall Be Saved?

34. But be not deceived, thou who hast tasted of the truth, and been reckoned worthy of the great redemption. But contrary to what is the case with the rest of people, collect for thyself an unarmed, an unwarlike, a bloodless, a passionless, a stainless host, pious old men, orphans dear to God, widows armed with meekness, people adorned with love. Obtain with thy money such guards, for body and for soul, for whose sake a sinking ship is made buoyant, when steered by the prayers of saints alone; and disease at its height subdued, put to flight by the laying on of hands; and the attack of robbers is disarmed,

---

42. Hennecke, *Apocrypha* 2:675.

43. Available online at www.earlychristianwritings.com/text/theodotus.html. For a recent argument that Clement wrote *Prophetic Eclogues*, see Buell, "Producing Descent/Dissent," 91–92n7. I thank Michael Gorman for help on this text (personal correspondence, May 3, 2010).

spoiled by pious prayers; and the might of demons is crushed, put to shame in its operations by strenuous commands.[44]

Tertullian (c. AD 160–225)

Tertullian was the most important Christian author to write in Latin until the great theologian St. Augustine. Born into a pagan family in the city of Carthage (near the present-day Tunis in Tunisia) in North Africa about AD 160, Tertullian received a good education in rhetoric, philosophy, law, and medicine. After working for a time in Rome as a jurist, he returned to Carthage, one of the four largest cities of the Roman Empire.

We know very little about his conversion to Christianity, but in 197, he burst on the literary scene with his *Apology*. A large number of writings, many still extant, followed in the next couple decades. Modern scholars place his death around AD 225.

In his *Apology* (AD 197), Tertullian used every rhetorical device he could muster to refute the common charges against Christians. It is clear from the *Apology* (chaps. 37 and 42) that Tertullian knew of Christians serving in the military.[45] But he also said Christians count it better to be killed than to kill.

Some have questioned whether Tertullian wrote *Against the Jews*, but recent scholarship largely accepts it as a work of Tertullian's and suggests an early date of 197 (Dunn, *Tertullian*, 64–65; Barnes, *Tertullian*, 55). Apparently a public dispute between a Jew and a Christian prompted Tertullian to write this vigorous work, arguing that Christians had replaced Jews as God's faithful people. Helgeland ("Roman Army," 737) says that early in his career Tertullian portrayed the Christian "as an ideal citizen of the empire, enjoying its benefits and shouldering its responsibilities—including military service." But here in this early treatise Tertullian quotes Isaiah's prophecy about beating swords into ploughshares and says that Christians have turned away from the use of the sword and now engage instead in peaceful practices.

On the Spectacles and *On Patience* are also probably early writings. Barnes (*Tertullian*, 55) dates *On the Spectacles* in 196 or early 197 and *On Patience* between 198 and 203. In *On Patience*, Tertullian says Christ "cursed for the time to

---

44. *ANF* 2:601. The date of this sermon is not certain.

45. Helgeland ("Roman Army," 738) sees another possible reference in chap. 7. Tertullian speaks of soldiers telling lies about Christians "out of a desire to extort money." Helgeland speculates that this might mean that pagan soldiers were trying to extort money from Christian colleagues in the military. But there is nothing in the text to support that speculation.

come the works of the sword" (chap. 4). In fact, love of enemies is "the principal command" (chap. 6). *On Idolatry* may date from 203 to 206 (Waszink and van Winden, *Tertullian*, 13). In *On Idolatry*, Tertullian says that Christians cannot even serve in the lower military ranks, where there is no need to participate in pagan sacrifices, because Christ "by disarming Peter unbelted every soldier" (chap. 19).[46]

Tertullian's *Against Marcion* was written to refute the heresy of Marcion, who may have come to Rome as early as AD 130. Marcion rejected the Old Testament as well as the parts of the New Testament that speak of God the Creator. Tertullian may have written the first edition of *Against Marcion* as early as 198 but the edition used here was probably completed in AD 207 or 208 (Evans, *Tertullianus*, ix–xviii). He may also have written *On the Resurrection of the Dead* about 206–207.

Later in life, Tertullian at least partially embraced Montanism, a movement (eventually declared heretical) that claimed new revelations from the Holy Spirit and practiced a rigid asceticism. Tertullian's *On the Soul* (about 206–207), *The Crown* (perhaps from 211), *Flight in Time of Persecution* (perhaps 212), and *On Modesty* (about 210–211) reflect Montanist convictions.

It is clear that Tertullian was very concerned with idolatry. Some think that is the only or primary reason he condemned Christian participation in the army: "Tertullian's problem with Christian military service was idolatry, not bloodshed" (Helgeland, "Christians," 152). Others disagree (cf. Gero, *Military Service*, 294–95). Chapter 11 of *The Crown* is especially relevant to this debate and shows that Tertullian's opposition to Christians in the military went well beyond the issue of idolatry.

A number of authors draw a rather sharp contrast between Tertullian's views on warfare during his "orthodox" (pre-Montanist period) and his later views as a Montanist (e.g., Bethune-Baker, *Influence*, 23). The documents quoted here, however, demonstrate that already in his earlier, pre-Montanist writings, Tertullian said that Christians have turned away from the use of the sword and Christ "unbelted every soldier."

For further information on Tertullian, see also Sider, ed., *Tertullian*, xi–xvii; Sider, *Ancient Rhetoric*; Barnes, *Tertullian*; Dunn, *Tertullian*, 3–68; Swift, *Military*, 38–46; Arbesmann, Daly, and Quain, *Tertullian*, vii–xix; and the literature cited in these works, especially in Sider, Barnes, and Dunn.

Apology

9. That I may refute more thoroughly the charges, I will show that in part openly, part secretly, practices prevail among you which have led you perhaps

---

46. It is, in light of the evidence, surprising to have Robert J. Daly say, "Was Tertullian a pacifist? The evidence suggests not" ("Military Service," 3).

to credit similar things about us. Children were openly sacrificed in Africa to Saturn as lately as the pro-consulship of Tiberius. . . . In regard to child murder, it does not matter whether it is committed for a sacred object, or merely at one's own self-impulse. . . . How many, think you, of those crowding around and gaping for Christian blood,—how many even of your rulers, notable for their justice to you and for their severe measures against us, may I charge in their own consciences with the sin of putting their offspring to death? As to any difference in the kind of murder, it is certainly the more cruel way to kill by drowning, or by exposure to cold and hunger and dogs. A maturer age has always preferred death by the sword. In our case, murder being once for all forbidden, we may not destroy even the fetus in the womb, while as yet the human being derives blood from the other parts of the body for its sustenance. To hinder a birth is merely a speedier killing of a human being; nor does it matter whether you take away a life that is born, or destroy one that is coming to the birth. That is a human being which is going to be one; you have the fruit already in its seed.[47]

> In chapter 16, Tertullian tries to refute the charge that Christians worship the cross by arguing that Roman deities and the standards of the army are also in the shape of the cross. The standards of a military unit were considered sacred, partaking of "numen, the power communicated from the gods to the emperor and to the armies" (Helgeland, "Christians," 151). Tertullian believes the military standards do have an idolatrous character.

16. The camp religion of the Romans is all through a worship of the standards, as setting the standards above all gods. Well, as those images decking out the standards are ornaments of crosses. All of those hangings of your standards and banners are robes of crosses.[48]

> Helgeland cites the following passage to show that "Tertullian recognized the necessity of war, but qualified his approval of it" ("Roman Army," 735). Actually the passage says neither that Tertullian thought war was a necessity nor that he approved of it. It merely makes a factual point that empires are acquired by war.

25. Has its religion been the source of the prosperity in Rome? . . . Their greatness was not the result of their religion. Indeed, how could religion make a people great who have owed their greatness to their irreligion? For, if I am not mistaken, kingdoms and empires are acquired by wars, and are extended by victories. More than that, you cannot have wars and victories without the

47. *ANF* 3:24–25.
48. *ANF* 3:31.

taking, and often the destruction, of cities. That is a thing in which the gods have their share of calamity. Houses and temples suffer alike.[49]

30. Without ceasing, for all our emperors we offer prayer. We pray for life prolonged; for security to the empire; for protection to the imperial house; for brave armies, a faithful senate, a virtuous people, the world at rest, whatever, as man or Caesar, an emperor would wish.[50]

31. Learn from them [our sacred books] that a large benevolence is enjoined upon us, even so far as to pray to God for our enemies, and to beseech blessings on our persecutors.[51]

37. If we are enjoined, then, to love our enemies, as I have remarked above,[52] whom have we to hate? If injured, we are forbidden to retaliate, lest we become as bad ourselves: who can suffer injury at our hands? In regard to this, recall your own experiences. How often you inflict gross cruelties on Christians. . . . Yet, banded together as we are, ever so ready to sacrifice our lives, what single case of revenge for injury are you able to point to, though, if it were held right among us to repay evil by evil, a single night with a torch or two could achieve an ample vengeance? But away with the idea of a divine religion avenging itself by human fires, or shrinking from the sufferings in which it is tried. If we desired, indeed, to act the part of open enemies, not merely of secret avengers, would there be any lacking in strength, whether of numbers or resources? . . . [We are] spread over all the world! We are but of yesterday, and we have filled every place among you—cities, islands, fortresses, towns, market-places, the [military] camp itself, tribes, companies, palace, senate, forum,—we have left nothing to you but the temples of your gods. For what wars should we not be fit, and ready even with unequal forces, we who so willingly yield ourselves to the sword, if in our religion it were not counted better to be slain than to slay?[53]

42. But we are called to account as harm-doers on another ground, and are accused of being useless in the affairs of life. How in all the world can that be the case with people who are living among you, eating the same food, wearing

49. *ANF* 3:40.

50. *ANF* 3:42.

51. Ibid.

52. "A large benevolence is enjoined upon us, even so far as to supplicate God for our enemies and to beseech blessings on our persecutors" (*Apology* 31; cf. Matt. 5:44).

53. *ANF* 3:45, with small changes. For another translation, see Arbesmann, Daly, and Quain, *Tertullian*, 94–96. Bainton ("Early Church," 202) cites the last sentence of chap. 37 as evidence that Tertullian was a pacifist all his life. Helgeland ("Roman Army," 741) says that Tertullian was merely trying to reassure Romans that Christians would not revolt. "As such, this statement has no bearing on the subject of military service."

the same attire, having the same habits, under the same necessities of existence? . . . So we sojourn with you in the world, abjuring neither forum, nor
shambles, nor bath, nor booth, nor workshop, nor inn, nor weekly market,
nor any other places of commerce. We sail with you, and fight with you, and
till the ground with you.[54]

46. The Christian is noted for his fidelity even among those who are not of his
religion. If the matter of sincerity is to be brought to trial, Aristotle basely
thrust his friend Hermias from his place: the Christian does no harm even
to his foe.[55]

Against the Jews

3. We understand that the coming end of the former circumcision then given,
and the coming procession of a new law (not such as He had already given
to the fathers), are announced: just as Isaiah foretold, saying that in the last
days the mount of the Lord and the house of God were to be manifest above
the tops of the mounts: "And it shall be exalted," he says, "above the hills;
and there shall come over it all nations; and many shall walk, and say, Come,
ascend we unto the mount of the Lord, and unto the house of the God of
Jacob," not of Esau, the former son, but of Jacob, the second; that is, of our
"people," whose "mount" is Christ. . . . In short, the coming procession of a
new law out of this "house of the God of Jacob" Isaiah in the ensuing words
announces, saying, "For from Zion shall go out a law, and the word of the
Lord out of Jerusalem, and shall judge among the nations,"—that is, among
us, who have been called out of the nations,—"and they shall join to beat their
swords into ploughs, and their lances into sickles; and nations shall not take
up sword against nation, and they shall no more learn to fight" [Isa. 2:3–4].
Who else, therefore, are understood but we, who, fully taught by the new law,
observe these practices,—the old law being obliterated, the coming of whose
abolition the action itself demonstrates? For the practice of the old law was
to avenge itself by the vengeance of the sword, and to pluck out "eye for eye,"
and to inflict retaliatory revenge for injury. But the new law's practice was to
point to clemency, and to convert to tranquility the pristine ferocity of "swords"
and "lances," and to remodel the pristine execution of "war" upon the rivals
and foes of the law into the pacific actions of "ploughing" and "tilling" the
land. Therefore, as we have shown above that the coming end of the old law
and of the carnal circumcision was declared, so, too, the observance of the
new law and the spiritual circumcision has shone out in voluntary peaceful

54. ANF 3:49.
55. ANF 3:51.

obedience. . . . And accordingly we, who "were not the people of God" in days bygone, have been made His people, by accepting the new law above mentioned, and the new circumcision before foretold.[56]

On the Spectacles

The spectacles—gladiatorial contests, animals fighting animals or people, etc.—were a central and highly popular aspect of Roman life. The Romans captured wild animals (lions, tigers, etc.) and brought them to Rome to attack and kill people in the "games." In AD 107, the emperor Trajan held twenty-three days of games in which 11,000 animals were killed and 10,000 gladiators fought (Kyle, *Spectacles*, 3, 35, 52, 78–79, and elsewhere).

2. We must not, then, consider merely by whom all things were made, but by whom they have been perverted. . . . There is a vast difference between the corrupted state and that of primal purity, just because there is a vast difference between the Creator and the corrupter. Why, all sorts of evils, which as indubitably evils even the heathen prohibit, and against which they guard themselves, come from the works of God. Take, for instance, murder, whether committed by iron, by poison, or by magical enchantments. Iron and herbs and demons are all equally creatures of God. Has the Creator, withal, provided these things for people's destruction? No, He puts His prohibition on every sort of man-killing by that one summary precept, "Thou shalt not kill."[57]

16. God certainly forbids us to hate even with a reason for our hating; for he commands us to love our enemies.[58]

On Patience

3. God suffers Himself to be conceived in a mother's womb, and awaits the time for birth; and, when born, bears the delay of growing up; and, when grown up, is not eager to be recognized. . . . Not with that city even which had refused to receive Him was He angry [cf. Luke 9:51–56], when even the disciples had wished that the celestial fires should be forthwith hurled on so insolent a town. . . . Moreover, while He is being betrayed, while He is being led up "as a sheep for a victim," (for "so He no more opens His mouth than

56. *ANF* 3:154–55.
57. *ANF* 3:80.
58. *ANF* 3:86. For other statements on loving enemies, see *Against Marcion* 1:23 (*ANF* 3:288); *On the Soul* 35 (*ANF* 3:216); *On Prayer* 3 (*ANF* 3:682).

a lamb under the power of the shearer" [cf. Isa. 53:7]), He to whom, had He willed it, legions of angels would at one word have presented themselves from the heavens, approved not the avenging sword of even one disciple. The patience of the Lord was wounded in (the wound of) Malchus [cf. John 18:10–11; Luke 22:49–51]: And so, too, He cursed for ever after the works of the sword; and, by the restoration of health, He made satisfaction to him whom He had not hurt, through patience, the mother of mercy.[59]

6. For people were of old accustomed to require "eye for eye, and tooth for tooth" and to repay with usury "evil with evil;" for, as yet, patience was not on earth, because faith was not either. Of course, meantime, impatience used to enjoy the opportunities which the law gave. That was easy, while the Lord and Master of patience was absent. But after He has supervened, and has united the grace of faith with patience, now it is no longer lawful to attack even with word, nor to say "fool" even, without "danger of the judgment." Anger has been prohibited, our spirits restrained, the petulance of the hand checked, the poison of the tongue extracted. The law has found more than it has lost, while Christ says, "Love your personal enemies, and bless your cursers, and pray for your persecutors, that ye may be sons of your heavenly Father." Do you see whom patience gains for us as a Father? In this principal command the universal discipline of patience is succinctly comprised, since evil-doing is not conceded even when it is deserved.[60]

8. If one attempt to provoke you by manual violence, the admonition of the Lord is at hand: "To him," He saith, "who smiteth thee on the face, turn the other cheek likewise" [Matt. 5:39]. Let outrageousness grow weary from your patience. Whatever that blow may be, conjoined with pain and contumely, it shall receive a heavier one from the Lord.[61]

10. There is, too, another chief spur of impatience, the lust of revenge. . . . Revenge, in the estimation of error, seems a solace of pain; in the estimation of truth, on the contrary, it is convicted of malice. For what difference is there between provoker and provoked, except that the former is detected as prior in evil-doing, but the latter as posterior? Yet each stands impeached of hurting a person in the eye of the Lord, who both prohibits and condemns every wickedness. In evil doing there is no account taken of order, nor does place separate what similarity conjoins. And the precept is absolute, that evil is not to be repaid with evil [cf. Rom. 12:17]. . . . How many misfortunes has impatience of this kind been accustomed to run into! How often has it

59. *ANF* 3:708.
60. *ANF* 3:711.
61. *ANF* 3:712.

repented of its revenge! How often has its vehemence been found worse than the causes which led to it!—inasmuch as nothing undertaken with impatience can be effected without violence: nothing done with violence fails either to stumble, or else to fall altogether.[62]

On Idolatry

In earlier chapters, Tertullian discussed a wide variety of contexts that a Christian must avoid to escape idolatry. In chapter 17, he asks whether a Christian could exercise the "dignity and power" of a government official. After all, Old Testament figures served idolatrous kings without falling into idolatry. Tertullian answers by enumerating a long list of things (including imprisoning, torturing, or sitting in judgment on someone's life—and thus by implication participating in capital punishment) that such a person must avoid. The last sentence of the chapter shows that Tertullian doubts it is possible to be a magistrate and avoid these things.

17. Hence arose, very lately, a dispute whether a servant of God should take the administration of any dignity or power, if he be able, whether by some special grace, or by adroitness, to keep himself intact from every species of idolatry; after the example that both Joseph and Daniel, clean from idolatry, administered both dignity and power in the livery and purple of the prefecture of entire Egypt or Babylonia. And so let us grant that it is possible for anyone to succeed in moving, in whatsoever office, under the mere *name* of office, neither sacrificing nor lending his authority to sacrifices; not farming out victims; not assigning to others the care of temples; not looking after their tributes; not giving spectacles at his own or the public charge, or presiding over the giving them; making proclamation or edict for no solemnity; not even taking oaths: moreover (what comes under the head of power), neither sitting in judgment on any one's life or character, for you might bear with his judging about money; neither condemning nor fore-condemning; binding no one, imprisoning or torturing no one—if it is credible that all this is possible.[63]

In chapter 18 Tertullian argues both that the dress of government officials was connected with idolatry and also that Christ rejected the dress, dignity, and power of government office.

18. If, also, He exercised no right of power even over His own followers, to whom He discharged menial ministry; if, in short, though conscious of His

---

62. *ANF* 3:713. The word translated as "violence" here is *impetus*. I follow the translation of Arbesmann, Daly, and Quain, *Tertullian*, 211.
63. *ANF* 3:72.

own kingdom, He shrank back from being made a king, He in the fullest manner gave His own an example for turning coldly from all the pride and garb, as well of dignity as of power. For if they were to be used, who would rather have used them than the Son of God? . . . What kind of purple would bloom from His shoulders? What kind of gold would beam from His head, had He not judged the glory of the world to be alien both to Himself and to His? Therefore what He was unwilling to accept, He has rejected; what He rejected, He has condemned; what He condemned, He has counted as part of the devil's pomp. . . . Let even this fact help to remind you that all the powers and dignities of this world are not only alien to, but enemies of, God.[64]

> Now (chap. 19) Tertullian asks whether a Christian can be in the military even at the lower levels where he would not of necessity participate in either idolatrous activity or capital punishment. Helgeland ("Roman Army," 739–40) argues that the reason Tertullian says no is because of all the idolatrous aspects of military life. There is no doubt that army life involved many idolatrous practices. The chief standard of every legion was the eagle, which symbolized the god Jupiter. The military oath (sacramentum) was an oath to the emperor who was Pontifex Maximus (high priest). A calendar of army events for AD 226 reveals religious festivals about every ten days (see Helgeland et al., Military, 48–55). Clearly, Tertullian is concerned with the idolatrous practices of the Roman army. But here he asks whether one could be a solider even if one avoided pagan sacrifices. He argues that (1) one cannot commit ultimate loyalty to both God and Caesar; and (2) since Jesus "unbelted every soldier," the Christian cannot serve in the army even during a time of peace. Tertullian is clearly concerned with more than the idolatry of military life.

19. In that last section, decision may seem to have been given likewise concerning military service, which is between dignity and power. But now inquiry is made about this point, whether a believer may turn himself unto military service, and whether the military [man] may be admitted unto the faith, even the rank and file, or each inferior grade, to whom there is no necessity for taking part in sacrifices or capital punishments. There is no agreement between the divine and the human sacrament,[65] the standard of Christ and the standard of the devil, the camp of light and the camp of darkness. One soul cannot be due to two masters—God and Caesar. And yet Moses carried a rod,[66] and

---

64. *ANF* 3:73.

65. The same Latin word *sacramentum* was used by Christians to refer to the Eucharist, and by soldiers to refer to the oath of unconditional allegiance sworn to the emperor at enlistment every January and on the anniversary of the emperor's coming to power (Helgeland, "Roman Army," 739).

66. *Virgam*—the Roman centurion carried this rod.

Aaron wore a buckle,[67] and John (Baptist) is girt with leather, and Joshua the son of Nun leads a line of march; and the people warred: if it pleases you to sport with the subject.[68] But how will a Christian man war, nay, how will he serve even in peace, without a sword, which the Lord has taken away? For albeit soldiers had come unto John, and had received the formula of their rule; albeit, likewise, a centurion had believed; still the Lord afterward, in disarming Peter, unbelted every soldier. No dress is lawful among us, if assigned to any unlawful action.[69]

On the Resurrection of the Dead

In this section, Tertullian tries to show how the body is intimately connected with the soul even though the soul (not the body) is responsible for the actions of a person. Using an analogy with tools like a cup or sword, he argues that there is some connection even between inanimate objects and the people who use them. In this connection, he distinguishes between a sword used by a robber to murder someone and a sword used in war that has "honorable stains" because engaged in "better manslaughter." Swift (*Military*, 40) says this passage shows that Tertullian can distinguish "between murder and killing in war." But it is highly doubtful, in light of other things Tertullian writes, that the passage is meant to imply that a Christian may kill.

16. The soul alone, therefore, will have to be judged (at the last day) pre-eminently as to how it has employed the vessel of the flesh; the vessel itself, of course, not being amenable to a judicial award: for who condemns the cup if anyone has mixed poison in it? Or who sentences the sword to beasts, if someone has perpetrated with it the atrocities of a brigand? . . . As for the sword, which is drunk with the blood of the brigand's victims, who would not banish it entirely from the house, much more from his bedroom, or from his pillow, from the presumption that he would be sure to dream of nothing but the apparitions of the souls which were pursuing and disquieting him for lying down with the blade which shed their own blood? Take, however, the cup which has no reproach on it, and which deserves the credit of a faithful ministration, it will be adorned by its drinking-master with chaplets, or be honored with a handful of flowers. The sword also which has received honorable stains in war, and has been thus engaged in a better manslaughter, will secure its own praise by consecration. It is quite possible, then, to pass decisive sentences even on

---

67. Roman soldiers wore a buckle that was sometimes given as a military reward.

68. Waszink and van Winden (*Tertullian*, 269) think the best reading is: "and Peter [i.e., Simon Peter, who drew a sword at Jesus's arrest] waged war, if I may permit myself a joke."

69. ANF 3:73.

vessels and on instruments, that so they too may participate in the merits of their proprietors and employers. . . . And although the apostle is well aware that the flesh does nothing of itself which is not also imputed to the soul, he yet deems the flesh to be "sinful;" lest it should be supposed to be free from all responsibility by the mere fact of its seeming to be impelled by the soul.[70]

Against Marcion

3.14. This interpretation of ours will derive confirmation, when, on your supposing that Christ is in any passage called a warrior, from the mention of certain arms and expressions of that sort, you weigh well the analogy of their other meanings, and draw your conclusions accordingly. "Gird on Thy sword," says David, "upon Thy thigh" [Ps. 45:3]. But what do you read about Christ just before? "Thou art fairer than the children of men; grace is poured forth upon Thy lips" [Ps. 45:2]. It amuses me to imagine that blandishments of fair beauty and graceful lips are ascribed to one who had to gird on His sword for war! So likewise, when it is added, "Ride on prosperously in Thy majesty," the reason is subjoined: "Because of truth, and meekness, and righteousness" [Ps. 45:4]. But who shall produce these results with the sword, and not their opposites rather—deceit, and harshness, and injury—which, it must be confessed, are the proper business of battles? Let us see, therefore, whether that is not some other sword, which has so different an action. Now the Apostle John, in the Apocalypse, describes a sword which proceeded from the mouth of God as "a doubly sharp, two-edged one" [Rev. 1:16]. This may be understood to be the Divine Word, who is doubly edged with the two testaments of the law and the gospel—sharpened with wisdom, hostile to the devil, arming us against the spiritual enemies of all wickedness and concupiscence. . . . Our common master Paul, who "girds our loins about with truth, and puts on us the breastplate of righteousness, and shoes us with the preparation of the gospel of peace, not of war; who bids us take the shield of faith, wherewith we may be able to quench all the fiery darts of the devil, and the helmet of salvation, and the sword of the Spirit, which (he says) is the word of God" [cf. Eph. 6:14–17]. . . . If . . . the sword he brandishes is an allegorical one, then the Creator's Christ in the Psalm too may have been girded with the figurative sword of the Word, without any martial gear. . . . Thus is the Creator's Christ mighty in war, and a bearer of arms; thus also does He now take the spoils, not of Samaria alone, but of all nations. Acknowledge, then, that His spoils are figurative, since you have learned that His arms are allegorical.[71]

70. ANF 3:556.
71. ANF 3:332–33.

3.21. In these very words Isaiah says: "And it shall come to pass in the last days, that the mount of the Lord," that is, God's eminence, "and the house of God," that is, Christ, the Catholic temple of God, in which God is worshiped, "shall be established upon the mountains," over all the eminences of virtues and powers; "and all nations shall come unto it; and many people shall go and say, Come ye, and let us go up to the mountain of the Lord, and to the house of the God of Jacob; and He will teach us His way, and we will walk in it: for out of Zion shall go forth the law, and the word of the Lord from Jerusalem" [cf. Isa. 2:2–3]. The gospel will be this "way," of the new law and the new word in Christ, no longer in Moses. "And He shall judge among the nations," even concerning their error. "And these shall rebuke a large nation," that of the Jews themselves and their proselytes. "And they shall beat their swords into ploughshares, and their spears into pruning hooks;" in other words, they shall change the dispositions of injurious minds, and hostile tongues, and all kinds of evil, and blasphemy into pursuits of moderation and peace. "Nation shall not lift up sword against nation,"—shall not stir up discord. "Neither shall they learn war anymore" [cf. Isa. 2:4], that is, the provocation of hostilities; so that you here learn that Christ is promised not as powerful in war, but pursuing peace.[72]

3.22. You have the work of the apostles also predicted: "How beautiful are the feet of them which preach the gospel of peace, which bring good tidings of good" [cf. Isa. 52:7; Rom. 10:15], not of war nor evil tidings.[73]

> Tertullian argues in chapter 4 against Marcion's gnostic view that the Creator God of the Old Testament is a different God from the God revealed in Christ. In this passage, Tertullian rejects Marcion's claim that Christ's command to turn the other cheek points to a different God than the one who said: "an eye for an eye." Tertullian seems to argue both that the implications of Old Testament teaching imply Jesus's teaching and also that there is some progression in God's revelation.

4.16. "Love your enemies, and bless those which hate you, and pray for them which calumniate you." These commands the Creator included in one precept by His prophet Isaiah: "Say, you are our brethren, to those who hate you" [cf. Isa. 66:5]. For if they who are our enemies and hate us, and speak evil of us, and slander us, are to be called our brethren, surely He did in effect bid us bless them that hate us, and pray for them who slander us, when He instructed us to reckon them as brethren. Well, [Marcion says] but Christ plainly teaches a new kind of patience, when he actually prohibits the reprisals which the

72. *ANF* 3:339–40.
73. *ANF* 3:340.

Creator permitted in requiring "an eye for an eye, and a tooth for a tooth,"
and bids us, on the contrary, "to him who smiteth us on the one cheek, to offer
the other also, and to give up our coat to him that taketh away our cloak." No
doubt [Tertullian responds] these are supplementary additions by Christ, but
they are quite in keeping with the teaching of the Creator. And therefore this
question must at once be determined, Whether the discipline of patience be
enjoined by the Creator? When by Zechariah He commanded, "Let none of
you imagine evil against his brother" [cf. Zech. 7:10], He did not expressly
include his neighbor; but then in another passage He says, "Let none of you
imagine evil in your hearts against his neighbor" [cf. Zech. 8:17]. He who
counseled that an injury should be forgotten was still more likely to counsel
the patient endurance of it. But then, when He said, "Vengeance is mine, and
I will repay" [cf. Deut. 32:35], He thereby teaches that patience calmly waits
for the infliction of vengeance. Therefore, inasmuch as it is incredible that the
same God should seem to require "a tooth for a tooth and an eye for an eye,"
in return for an injury, who forbids not only all reprisals, but even a revenge-
ful thought or recollection of an injury, in so far does it become plain to us
in what sense He required "an eye for an eye and a tooth for a tooth,"—not,
indeed, for the purpose of permitting the repetition of the injury by retaliating
it, which it virtually prohibited when it forbade vengeance; but for the purpose
of restraining the injury in the first instance, which it had forbidden on pain
of retaliation or reciprocity; so that every person, in view of the permission
to inflict a second (or retaliatory) injury, might abstain from the commission
of the first (or provocative) wrong. For He knows how much more easy it is to
repress violence by the prospect of retaliation, than by the promise of indefinite
vengeance. Both results, however, it was necessary to provide, in consideration
of the nature and the faith of people, that the one who believed in God might
expect vengeance from God, while he who had no faith (to restrain him) might
fear the laws which prescribed retaliation. This purpose of the law, which it
was difficult to understand, Christ, as the Lord of the Sabbath and of the
law, and of all the dispensations of the Father, both revealed and made intelligible, when He commanded that "the other cheek should be offered (to the
smiter)," in order that He might the more effectually extinguish all reprisals
of an injury, which the law had wished to prevent by the method of retaliation, and which most certainly revelation had manifestly restricted, both by
prohibiting the memory of the wrong, and referring the vengeance thereof to
God. Thus, whatever new provision Christ introduced, He did it not in opposition to the law, but rather in furtherance of it, without at all impairing
the prescription of the Creator. If, therefore, one looks carefully into the very
grounds for which patience is enjoined (and that to such a full and complete
extent), one finds that it cannot stand if it is not the precept of the Creator,
who promises vengeance, who presents Himself as the judge (in the case).
If it were not so,—if so vast a weight of patience—which is to refrain from

giving blow for blow; which is to offer the other cheek; which is not only not to return railing for railing, but contrariwise blessing; and which, so far from keeping the coat, is to give up the cloak also—is laid upon me by one who means not to help me,—then all I can say is, he has taught me patience to no purpose, because he shows me no reward to his precept—I mean no fruit of such patience. There is revenge which he ought to have permitted me to take, if he meant not to inflict it himself; if he did not give me that permission, then he should himself have inflicted it; since it is for the interest of discipline itself that an injury should be avenged. For by the fear of vengeance all iniquity is curbed. . . . Now, should anyone wish to argue that the Creator's precepts extended only to a person's brethren, but Christ's to all that ask, so as to make the latter a new and different precept, I have to reply that one rule only can be made out of those principles, which show the law of the Creator to be repeated in Christ. For that is not a different thing which Christ enjoined to be done towards all people, from that which the Creator prescribed in favor of a person's brethren. For although that is a greater charity, which is shown to strangers, it is yet not preferable to that which was previously due to one's neighbors. . . . Since, however, the second step in charity is towards strangers, while the first is towards one's neighbors, the second step will belong to him to whom the first also belongs, more fitly than the second will belong to him who owned no first. Accordingly, the Creator, when following the course of nature, taught in the first instance kindness to neighbors, intending afterwards to enjoin it towards strangers; and when following the method of His dispensation, He limited charity first to the Jews, but afterwards extended it to the whole race of humanity. So long, therefore, as the mystery of His government was confined to Israel, He properly commanded that pity should be shown only to a person's brethren; but when Christ had given to Him "the Gentiles for His heritage, and the ends of the earth for His possession," then . . . Christ extended to all people the law of His Father's compassion, excepting none from His mercy, as He omitted none in His invitation. So that, whatever was the ampler scope of His teaching, He received it all in His heritage of the nations. "And as you would that people should do to you, do you also to them likewise" [cf. Luke 6:31].[74]

5.18. I, on my part, now wish to engage with you in a discussion on the allegorical expressions of the apostle. . . . "He led captivity captive" [cf. Eph. 4:8], says the apostle. With what arms? In what conflicts? From the devastation of what country? From the overthrow of what city? What women, what children, what princes did the Conqueror throw into chains? For when by David Christ is sung as "girded with His sword upon His thigh" [cf. Ps. 45:3], or by Isaiah as "taking away the spoils of Samaria and the power of Damascus" [cf. Isa.

---

74. *ANF* 3:370–72.

8:4], you make Him out to be visibly and truly a warrior. Learn then now that
His is a spiritual armor and warfare.[75]

On the Soul

> In this treatise, Tertullian argues at great length that the soul and body come
> together at the moment of conception. Unlike Roman law, which said the fetus
> is never a person, Tertullian insists that God knows the unborn "in his entire
> nature" (26). He is the first extant Christian writer to connect the biblical
> passages about Jeremiah (1:5) and John the Baptist (Luke 1:41–45) with the
> question of abortion. See Gorman, *Abortion*, 56–58.

26. These [Jesus and John] have life, each of them in his mother's womb.
Elizabeth exults with joy, for John had leaped in her womb [cf. Luke 1:41–45];
Mary magnifies the Lord, for Christ had inspired her within. The mothers
recognize each their own offspring, being moreover each recognized by their
infants, which were therefore of course alive, and were not souls merely, but
spirits also. Accordingly you read the word of God which was spoken to
Jeremiah, "Before I formed thee in the belly, I knew thee" [cf. Jer. 1:5]. Since
God forms us in the womb, He also breathes upon us, as he also did at the
first creation, when "the Lord God formed man, and breathed into him the
breath of life" [cf. Gen. 2:7]. Nor could God have known man in the womb,
except in his entire nature: "And before thou camest forth out of the womb, I
sanctified thee" [cf. Jer. 1:5]. Well, was it then a dead body at that early stage?
Certainly not. For "God is not the God of the dead, but of the living."[76]

27. Is the substance of both body and soul formed together at one and the
same time? Or does one of them precede the other in natural formation? We
indeed maintain that both are conceived, and formed, and perfectly simultaneously. . . . Now we allow that life begins with conception, because we contend
that the soul also begins from conception; life taking its commencement at the
same moment and place that the soul does. . . . For although we shall allow
that there are two kinds of seed—that of the body and that of the soul—we
still declare that they are inseparable, and therefore contemporaneous and
simultaneous in origin.[77]

37. Now the entire process of sowing, forming, and completing the human
embryo in the womb is no doubt regulated by some power, which ministers

75. *ANF* 3:468.
76. *ANF* 3:207.
77. *ANF* 3:207–8.

herein to the will of God, whatever may be the method which it is appointed to employ. . . . We, on our part, believe the angels to officiate herein for God. The embryo therefore becomes a human being in the womb from the moment that its form is completed. The law of Moses, indeed, punishes with due penalties the man who shall cause abortion, inasmuch as there exists already the rudiment of a human being, which has imputed to it even now the condition of life and death, since it is already liable to the issues of both, although, by living still in the mother, it for the most part shares its own state with the mother.[78]

On Modesty

In his use of Acts 15:28–29 (the Jerusalem Council's short list of prohibitions for gentile believers), Tertullian works with the Western textual reading and interpretation of the prohibition of blood: it means all taking of human blood (Bainton, "Early Church," 208). Tertullian argues that there are three unpardonable sins: idolatry, adultery, and the taking of a human life.

12. This is the first rule which the apostles, on the authority of the Holy Spirit, send out to those who were already beginning to be gathered to their side out of the nations: "It has seemed good," say they, "to the Holy Spirit and to us to cast upon you no ampler weight than that of those things from which it is necessary that abstinence be observed; from sacrifices, and from fornications, and from blood: by abstaining from which ye act rightly, the Holy Spirit carrying you" [cf. Acts 15:28–29]. Sufficient it is, that in this place withal there has been preserved to adultery and fornication the post of their own honor between idolatry and murder: for the prohibition upon "blood" we shall understand to be a prohibition much more upon human blood. Well, then, in what light do the apostles will those crimes to appear . . . which alone they prescribe as necessarily to be abstained from? Not that they permit others; but that these alone they put in the foremost rank, of course as not forgivable; they, who, for the heathens' sake, made the other burdens of the law forgivable. . . . But it is not lightly that the Holy Spirit has come to an agreement with us. . . . He has definitely enough refused pardon to those crimes the careful avoidance whereof he selectively enjoined. . . . Hence it is that there is no restoration of peace granted by the churches to "idolatry" or to "blood."[79]

78. *ANF* 3:217–18.
79. *ANF* 4:85–86.

The Crown

In 211, Emperor Septimius Severus died and his two sons became co-Augusti. Tertullian refers to the response of a Christian soldier (and consequent martyrdom, likely in AD 211) at the accession "of our most excellent emperors," when the soldiers received the traditional monetary gift ("donative"). It is not certain where the event occurred, but many modern scholars think it was in Carthage in North Africa (Sider, ed., *Tertullian*, 117).

On such occasions, the soldiers wore a laurel crown. In ancient times, heroes were given crowns made from the aromatic leaves and flowers of the laurel tree or shrub. In this treatise, Tertullian shows the many idolatrous connections of crowns.

This treatise, which reveals Tertullian's strong opposition to Christians in the military, also proves that they were present. By Tertullian's own account, his hero was a soldier (who felt compelled to leave the army). More important, other Christian colleagues of this hero did not abandon military life and were unhappy with what they considered the rash action of this martyr ("alone brave among so many soldier-brethren"). There is nothing, however, in Tertullian's text that suggests (as Harnack argues in *Militia Christi*, 83) that the Christian who threw off his crown only wanted the same right not to wear the crown that soldiers who worshiped Mithras enjoyed.

1. Very lately it happened thus: while the bounty of our most excellent emperors was dispensed in the camp, the soldiers, laurel-crowned, were approaching. One of them, more a soldier of God, more steadfast than the rest of his brethren, who had imagined that they could serve two masters, his head alone uncovered, the useless crown in his hand—already even by that peculiarity known to everyone as a Christian—was nobly conspicuous. Accordingly, all began to mark him out, jeering him at a distance, gnashing on him near at hand. The murmur is wafted to the tribune, for the person had already stepped out of his line. The tribune at once puts the question to him, "Why are you so different in your attire?" He declared that he had no liberty to wear the crown with the rest. Being urgently asked for his reasons, he answered, "I am a Christian." O soldier! boasting thyself in God. Then the case was considered and voted on; the matter was remitted to a higher tribunal; the offender was conducted to the prefects. At once he put away the heavy [military] cloak, and his disburdening commenced. He loosed from his foot the military shoe, beginning to stand upon holy ground. He gave up the sword, which was not necessary either for the protection of our Lord. From his hand likewise dropped the laurel crown. And now, purple-clad with the hope of his own blood, shod with the preparation of the gospel, girt with the sharper word of God, completely equipped in the apostles' armor, and crowned more worthily with the white crown of martyrdom, he awaits in prison the largess of Christ. Thereafter adverse judgments began to be passed upon his conduct—whether on the part of Christians I do not know, for those of the heathen are not different—as if he were headstrong and rash, and too eager to die, because, in being taken to task about a mere matter of dress, he brought trouble on the bearers of the Name,—he, forsooth, alone brave among so many soldier-brethren, he alone a Christian. It is plain that as they have rejected the prophecies of the Holy Spirit, they are also purposing the refusal of martyrdom. So they murmur that a peace so good and long is endangered for them. Nor do I doubt that some are already turning their back on the Scriptures, are making ready their luggage, are equipped for flight from city to city; for that is all of the gospel they care to remember. I know, too, their pastors are lions in peace, deer in the fight. As to the questions asked for extorting confessions from us, we shall teach elsewhere. Now, as they put forth also the objection, "But where are we forbidden to be crowned," I shall take this point up, as more suitable to be treated of here, being the essence, in fact, of the present contention. So that, on the one hand, the inquirers who are ignorant, but anxious, may be instructed; and on the other, those may be refuted who try to vindicate the sin, especially the laurel-crowned Christians themselves, to whom it is merely a question of debate, as if it might be regarded as either no trespass at all, or at least a doubtful one, because it may be made the subject of investigation. That is neither sinless nor doubtful, I shall now, however, show.[80]

2. I affirm that not one of the faithful has ever worn a crown upon his head, except at a time of trial. That is the case with all, from the catechumens to confessors and martyrs, or (as the case may be) deniers. Consider, then, whence the custom about which we are now chiefly inquiring got its authority. But when the question is raised why it is observed, it is meanwhile evident that it is observed. Therefore that can neither be regarded as no offense, or an uncertain one, which is perpetrated against a practice which is capable of defense, on the ground even of its repute and is sufficiently ratified by the support of general acceptance.[81]

> In chapters 3–4, Tertullian continues his argument against wearing a laurel crown on the basis of tradition. In chapters 5–6, he argues for the same conclusion on the basis of nature ("It is as much against nature to long after a flower with the head, as it is to crave food with the ear"). In chapter 7, he delves into the origins of the practice of wearing laurel crowns, arguing from pagan literature that this practice started with the pagan gods: "How foreign to us we should judge the custom of the crowned head, introduced as it was by, and thereafter constantly managed for the honor of, those whom the world has

80. *ANF* 3:93.
81. *ANF* 3:93–94.

believed to be gods." Chapter 8 responds to the objection that Christians (even Christ) use many things the pagans say were invented by their gods. In chapter 9, he argues that no figure in Jewish or Christian history ever wore a laurel crown. And in chapter 10, he seeks to show that the laurel crown originated with pagan gods and is now tightly wrapped up with pagan worship: "This attire belongs to idols, both from the history of its origin, and from its use by false religion." Since Christians are commanded to "flee idolatry," they must not wear the laurel crown. Then, at the end of chapter 10, he says he will turn to "the special grounds for wearing crowns."

There is disagreement on the meaning of the second sentence in chapter 11 (cited below in full). What is the "merely accidental"? As their additions to the text show, Helgeland et al. claim that military life itself is the "merely accidental": "What sense is there in discussing the merely accidental [i.e., military life], when that on which it rests [the idolatrous crown] is to be condemned?" (*Military*, 24). This interpretation fits with Helgeland's argument that Tertullian's primary objection to Christians in the military is not the issue of killing but the widespread idolatry in military life (cf. also Helgeland, "Roman Army," 738–44). But Helgeland's reading of the second sentence is almost certainly wrong. Tertullian scholar Robert D. Sider says of this text: "The 'crown' worn at certain times by soldiers is a secondary issue, a concomitant of the primary issue, military service."[82] In the third to last sentence of chapter 11, Tertullian prepares to end this section on the fact that military life itself is wrong for Christians and return to the argument about wearing the crown and he says that he will not comment more on this ("the primary aspect of the question" but rather return to "the secondary question"—i.e., the crown in chaps. 12–13).

11. To begin with the real ground of the military crown, I think we must first inquire whether warfare is proper at all for Christians. What sense is there in discussing the merely accidental, when that on which it rests is to be condemned? Do we believe it lawful for a human oath[83] to be superadded to one divine, for a man to come under promise to another master after Christ, and to abjure father, mother, and all nearest kinsfolk, whom even the law has commanded us to honor and love next to God Himself, to whom the gospel, too, holding them only of less account than Christ, has in like manner rendered honor? Shall it be held lawful to make an occupation of the sword, when the Lord proclaims that he who uses the sword shall perish by the sword [cf. Matt. 26:52]? And shall the son of peace take part in the battle when it does not become him even to sue at law? And shall he apply the chain, and the prison, and the torture, and the punishment, who is not the avenger even of his own

82. Personal correspondence, March 11, 2010.
83. A reference to the oath of unconditional allegiance (*sacramentum*) sworn to the emperor by Roman soldiers.

wrongs? Shall he, forsooth, either keep watch-service for others more than for Christ, or shall he do it on the Lord's day, when he does not even do it for Christ Himself? And shall he keep guard before the temples which he has renounced? And shall he take a meal where the apostle has forbidden him? And shall he diligently protect by night those whom in the day-time he has put to flight by his exorcisms, leaning and resting on the spear the while with which Christ's side was pierced? Shall he carry a flag, too, hostile to Christ? And shall he ask a watchword from the emperor who has already received one from God?[84] Shall he be disturbed in death by the trumpet of the trumpeter, who expects to be aroused by the angel's trump? And shall the Christian be burned according to camp rule, when he was not permitted to burn incense to an idol, when to him Christ remitted the punishment of fire? Then how many other offenses there are involved in the performances of camp offices, which we must hold to involve a transgression of God's law, you may see by a slight survey. The very carrying of the name over from the camp of light to the camp of darkness is a violation of it. Of course, if faith comes later, and finds any preoccupied with military service, their case is different, as in the instance of those whom John used to receive for baptism, and of those most faithful centurions, I mean the centurion whom Christ approves, and the centurion whom Peter instructs; yet, at the same time, when a man has become a believer, and faith has been sealed, there must be either an immediate abandonment of it, which has been the course with many; or all sorts of quibbling will have to be resorted to in order to avoid offending God, and that is not allowed even outside of military service; or, last of all, for God the fate must be endured which a citizen-faith[85] has been no less ready to accept. Neither does military service hold out escape from punishment of sins, or exemption from martyrdom. Nowhere does the Christian change his character. There is one gospel, and the same Jesus, who will one day deny everyone who denies, and acknowledge everyone who acknowledges God,—who will save, too, the life which has been lost for His sake; but, on the other hand, destroy that which for gain has been saved to His dishonor. With Him the faithful citizen is a soldier, just as the faithful soldier is a citizen. A state of faith admits no plea of necessity; they are under no necessity to sin, whose one necessity is, that they do not sin. For if one is pressed to the offering of sacrifice and the sheer denial of Christ by the necessity of torture or of punishment, yet discipline does not connive even at that necessity; because there is a higher necessity to dread denying and to undergo martyrdom, than to escape from suffering, and to render the homage required. In fact, an excuse of this sort overturns the entire essence of our sacrament, removing even the obstacle to voluntary

84. Tertullian may be referring to either the military watchword received from the commanding officer or the tattoo received by a military recruit. On the other hand, he may mean the creed as the Christian's watchword and/or the sign of the cross given at baptism (Sider, *Tertullian*, 129n50).

85. I.e., the faith of a Christian who is not a soldier.

sins; for it will be possible also to maintain that inclination is a necessity, as involving in it, forsooth, a sort of compulsion. I have, in fact, disposed of this very allegation of necessity with reference to the pleas by which crowns connected with official position are vindicated, in support of which it is in common use, since for this very reason offices must be either refused, that we may not fall into acts of sin, or martyrdoms endured that we may get quit of offices. Touching this primary aspect of the question, as to the unlawfulness even of a military life itself, I shall not add more, that the secondary question may be restored to its place. Indeed, if, putting my strength to the question, I banish from us the military life, I should now to no purpose issue a challenge on the matter of the military crown. Suppose, then, that the military service is lawful, as far as the plea for the crown is concerned.[86]

13. We have recounted, as I think, all the various causes of the wearing of the crown, and there is not one which has any place with us. All are foreign to us, unholy, unlawful, having been abjured already once for all in the solemn declaration of the sacrament. For they were of the pomp of the devil and his angels, offices of the world, honors, festivals, popularity huntings, false vows, exhibitions of human servility, empty praises, base glories, and in them all idolatry, even in respect of the origin of the crowns alone, with which they are all wreathed.[87]

Exhortation to Chastity

12. Are you to dissolve the conception by aid of drugs? I think to us it is no more lawful to hurt a child in process of birth, than one already born.[88]

On Flight in Persecution

In this treatise, Tertullian denounces Christians for fleeing in time of persecution. In chapter 8, Tertullian notes that Christ not only did not flee persecution but found "fault with Peter's sword." In the following section, he condemns Christians who pay bribes to tax collectors to avoid persecution. But Tertullian does not mean that Christians are doing all these evil things. "Free soldiers" are soldiers released from regular duty to do administrative work.

13. But of what will not cowardice convince people? As if Scripture both allowed them to flee, and commanded them to buy off! Finally, it is not enough

86. *ANF* 3:99–100.
87. *ANF* 3:102.
88. *ANF* 4:57.

if one or another is so rescued. Whole Churches have imposed tribute *en masse* on themselves. I know not whether it is matter for grief or shame when, among hucksters, and pickpockets, and bath-thieves, and gamesters, and pimps, Christians too are included as taxpayers in the lists of free soldiers and spies.[89]

To Scapula

This very short piece was probably written late in Tertullian's life.

1. Our religion commands us to love even our enemies, and to pray for those who persecute us, aiming at a perfection all its own, and seeking in its disciples something of a higher type than the commonplace goodness of the world. For all love those who love them; it is peculiar to Christians alone to love those that hate them.[90]

Minucius Felix
(probably late second to early third century)

Apart from his one extant work, *Octavius*, we know very little about Minucius Felix. He probably grew up in North Africa in a pagan home, received an excellent education, especially in rhetoric, and became a lawyer in Rome. At some point he converted to Christianity.

Octavius is the first Latin dialogue written to defend Christianity. The setting is Rome and the seaport Ostia. Minucius Felix refutes the typical charges against Christians. In chapter 30, quoted here, he responds to the charge that Christian rites of initiation include the slaughter of a baby. Minucius responds that unlike Romans, Christians even reject abortion, which he calls *parricidium*, the Roman legal word for intentional killing of a close relative. A little later he says Christians reject all homicide and cannot even watch a human person being killed.

The date is uncertain. Scholars agree that either Tertullian (in *The Apology*) used *Octavius* or the reverse, but there is no consensus on which was written first. Scholars date this work anywhere between about AD 161 and 210. See

89. *ANF* 4:124–25.
90. *ANF* 3:105.

Arbesmann, Daly, and Quain, *Tertullian*, 313–19; Glover and Rendall, *Minucius Felix*, 304–13; Holmes, "Octavius," 185–89; Gorman, *Abortion*, 58–59.

Octavius

30. And now I should wish to meet him who says or believes that we are initiated by the slaughter and blood of an infant. Think you that it can be possible for so tender, so little a body to receive those fatal wounds; for anyone to shed, pour forth, and drain that new blood of a babe scarcely come into existence? No one can believe this, except one who can dare to do it. And I see that you at one time expose your begotten children to wild beasts and to birds; at another, that you crush them when strangled with a miserable kind of death. There are some women who, by drinking medical preparations, extinguish the source of the future human being in their very bowels, and thus commit a parricide before they bring forth. And these things assuredly come down from the teaching of your gods. For Saturn did not expose his children, but devoured them. . . . The Roman sacrificers buried living a Greek man and a Greek woman . . . and to this day Jupiter Latiaris is worshiped by them with murder. . . . They also are not unlike to him who devours the wild beasts from the arena, besmeared and stained with blood, or fattened with the limbs or entrails of men. To us it is not lawful either to see or to hear of human slaughter; and so much do we shrink from human blood, that we do not use blood even of eatable animals in our food.[91]

Didascalia apostolorum (early third century)

Probably composed in northern Syria around AD 230, the lengthy church order *Didascalia apostolorum* has little on our topic except for a clear prohibition of abortion. In one section, however, the text instructs bishops and deacons to refuse gifts for the widows in their care if the gifts are given by a wide variety of wicked people. The list includes "soldiers who act lawlessly" and "Roman officials, who are defiled with wars and have shed innocent blood without trial." But there is no indication from the text whether Christians may be soldiers or kill. For introductory material, see Connolly, *Didascalia Apostolorum*, xxvi–xci; Bradshaw, *Christian Worship*, 78–80; Vööbus, *Didascalia*; and *Oxford Dictionary*, 482.

91. *ANF* 4:191–92.

3. You shall not kill a child through destruction [i.e., abortion], nor after he is born shall you kill him.[92]

18. For they receive, forsooth, to administer for the nourishment of orphans and widows, from rich persons who keep men shut up in prison, or ill-treat their slaves . . . or from forgers . . . or from dishonest tax-gatherers . . . or from soldiers who act lawlessly; or from murderers; or from spies who procure condemnations; or from any Roman officials, who are defiled with wars and have shed innocent blood without trial.[93]

Julius Africanus (c. AD 180–250)

Julius Africanus was born in Jerusalem, and spent time in Edessa and elsewhere in the East before he came to Rome. We do not know when he became a Christian, but he corresponded with Origen and included Jesus's death and resurrection in his widely read *History of the World* (only small fragments are extant), where he argues that Christianity is superior to pagan religion. He played a major role in a new public library at Rome and was at least somewhat prominent at the court of Emperor Alexander Severus (222–35). He dedicated his encyclopedic work called *Kestoi* (*Embroidered Girdles*) to the emperor (*Oxford Dictionary*, 918). Johnson (*Peace*, 29) says Julius Africanus was a Roman general, but there is no evidence he was ever even a soldier, much less a general (Vieillefond, "Cestes," 18).

What makes Julius Africanus so puzzling is that his *Kestoi* is a totally secular book, "devoid of distinctively Christian content" (Adler, "Africanus," 520). It has numerous references to classical authors and pagan deities, but no reference to the Bible, Jewish or Christian writings. He discusses magical things that most early Christian writers denounced. His prescriptions on abortion, love charms, horse racing, and gladiatorial contests were vigorously condemned by other early Christian writers (Thee, *Africanus*, 453, 465).

Especially important for our purposes is the fact that in his *Kestoi*, he claimed to be an expert on "just about everything having to do with the conduct of war" (Adler, "Africanus," 539). Most of the twenty-four books of his *Kestoi* have been lost, but we do have a substantial section of book 7 devoted to warfare (Vieillefond, "Cestes"). It includes advice on how to poison the enemy. This book claims to offer expert knowledge and advice on a vast array of military

92. Vööbus, *Didascalia*, 1:32.
93. Connolly, *Didascalia Apostolorum*, 158.

topics: military equipment; dealing with horses; using Euclid's geometry to measure rivers and walls; combating elephants; destroying the fields and trees of enemies; military maneuvers; treating wounds; and so on.

What does this mean for our understanding of Christian thinking about warfare in the early third century? Harnack calls Julius Africanus a "distinguished Christian teacher" and says, "So Christianity already possessed a military writer at the beginning of the third century" (*Militia*, 88). Helgeland, on the other hand, who seeks to cite all credible evidence that some Christians before Constantine accepted warfare, virtually ignores Julius Africanus, calling him "an enigmatic Christian author" ("Roman Army," 773).

Most modern scholars see a near total divide between the totally secular *Kestoi* and his explicitly Christian writings. The editor and translator of the extant portion of *Kestoi* speaks of Africanus's writings falling into "two almost contradictory groups": the Christian works and the secular ones (Vieillefond, "Cestes," 23). In a 2004 article in the *Journal of Theological Studies*, William Adler describes the *Kestoi* as "a curious work devoid of distinctively Christian content and unlike any other writing surviving from the early church" ("Africanus," 520). Adler calls Africanus a "fringe character in the church of his own day. . . . Africanus held no church office, formed no sect, had no school, taught no students, attracted no following" (Adler, "Africanus," 547).

It seems fair to conclude that Africanus's discussion of warfare in *Kestoi* should not be considered relevant in any significant way in our analysis of what the early church thought and taught about warfare, killing, or abortion. But to convey a flavor of his comments on warfare, I include a few sections from *Kestoi* 7.

1. On military equipment.

Among all the areas of knowledge, that of war is especially valuable. I have often asked myself what determined the outcome of military battles and why the Greeks have been conquered by the Romans, the Persians by the Greeks, and never on the other hand the Persians by the Romans. . . . Upon reflection, I have noticed that the reason is not found in superior strategy . . . ; rather the reason lies in the system of weapons and the type of military equipment.

2. On the destruction of the enemy.

Thus one must not only attack adversaries with an open battle; it is also necessary to combat enemies with a crowd of ruses, even the most secret.

[He describes how to prepare a mysterious potion that will cause the plague. One should mix it with food.] One then gives it to the enemy in any way that you can . . . [e.g.,] while simulating a precipitous retreat and abandoning, in the face of the attack, one's camp filled with this kind of food. This does not produce death the next day. The one who has tasted it does not perish immediately. It is a plague which works by surprise and affects those who have not

eaten the bread. It expands while acquiring companions. Its attack expands to the family, the town, the army, the nation.[94]

Origen (c. AD 185–254)

Origen was one of the most important, and certainly one of the most prolific, Christian authors before the time of Constantine. Born to a devout Christian family in Alexandria, the young Origen was immersed in both Greek culture and the Bible. When Origen was only eighteen, the bishop named him master of the famous catechetical school in Alexandria. Later, he studied Hebrew and deepened his knowledge of Greek philosophy, especially neo-Platonism. His friendship with Ambrosius, who paid more than a dozen people to write out and recopy Origen's flood of writings, enabled Origen to become one of the best known Christian thinkers of the day.

In about 231, Origen moved to Caesarea where he lived and taught for more than twenty years. In 249, he was imprisoned and tortured. He survived, but his weakened body gave out in 254, his seventieth year.

Origen's extant writings are voluminous. Brief passages in Origen's *Homilies on Joshua*; *On the Principles*; *Commentary on John* (written between 231 and 242); *Commentary on Matthew*; and *Commentary on 1 Corinthians* have some bearing on our topic. Unfortunately, his commentary on Matthew 5:38–48 is lost. For our purposes, the only major work is his famous *Against Celsus*, written near the end of his life (probably about 246–248), at the suggestion of his friend Ambrosius. We know almost nothing about Celsus except that many years earlier (probably about 177–80), a fairly well-informed pagan by this name had written a sharp, detailed attack on Christianity. Our only source of Celsus's ideas is the many quotations in Origen's critique. Among Celsus's arguments is the charge that if all Romans followed the Christian example of rejecting public office and military service, the Roman Empire would collapse.

We know from other sources that there were at least a few Christians in the Roman army by the last couple decades of the second century. But Celsus clearly thinks that the normal Christian practice is to reject military service. So, apparently, does Origen in the middle of the third century. The easiest way for Origen to respond to Celsus's argument would have been to say that Christians should and do serve in the imperial armies. But Origen says neither. Instead, he argues that God would protect the Roman Empire if everyone became a

94. Vieillefond, "Cestes," 104, 110, 112, 116, 118.

Christian and refused to kill. It is hard to understand how Origen could argue as he does if everyone knew that substantial numbers of Christians served as Roman soldiers.

Some modern scholars have argued that Origen did "not oppose war, properly undertaken" (Helgeland, "Roman Army," 749; see also the authors cited in Cadoux, *War*, 138–39). It is true that Origen says those who kill a tyrant do well (1.1); that in earlier time it was necessary to go to war to defend one's country (2.30); that the "former economy" used violence (4.9); that the bees offer a model to fight wars justly "if ever there arise a necessity for them" (4.82); that under an earlier "constitution," the Jews would have been destroyed if they had not gone to war (7.26). He also chided Celsus for belittling those who built cities and governments and went to war on behalf of their countries (4.83).

But several circumstances make it highly doubtful that Origen thought Christians should ever fight wars. In almost every instance where he speaks positively about wars, he explicitly refers to non-Christians (2.30; 4.9; 7.26). In no place does he say Christians should fight wars. Origen frequently refers to an earlier time ("economy" or "constitution") when wars were fought and contrasts that to the present time when Jesus's followers are peaceful and love their enemies (2.30; 4.9; 5.33; 7.26). Finally, he frequently says Christians love their enemies, do not take vengeance, and do not go to war (2.30; 3.8; 5.33; 7.26; 8.35; 8.73). He even declares that if all the Romans become Christians, they "will not war at all" (8.70). Christ forbade the killing of anyone (3.7).

It is surprising therefore to have Brennecke ("Kriegsdienst," 199) suggest that "the question whether one can be a soldier as a Christian is not really discussed." Origen clearly says "we do not fight under him [the emperor]" (*Against Celsus* 8.73).

Origen's primary reasons for opposing Christian participation in war are that Christians do not take vengeance on their enemies, but seek to love their enemies (2.30; 3.8; 8.35) and follow Christ's teaching (5.33; 7.26). Only twice does he mention the problem of idolatry in connection with our topic (8.65 and *Commentary on 1 Corinthians*). Thus to say that Origen's "objection to Christian enlistment was religious, not ethical; he was primarily opposed to Christians pledging loyalty to the emperor" (Helgeland, "Roman Army," 750; see others cited in Cadoux, *War*, 141), simply does not fit the data. Christians, just like the pagan Roman priests who are excused from the army, must be free of shedding blood (8.73).

For further information on Origen, see *ANF* 4:223–34; Chadwick, *Origen*, ix–xxxii; Tripolitis, *Origen*; Crouzel, *Origen*; and the extensive bibliography in Barkley, *Origen*, ix–xviii and 3–25.

On the Principles

In book 4 of *On the Principles* (written early in his life), Origen develops at length his understanding of how to properly interpret the Scriptures. He distinguishes between a literal and a spiritual understanding and illustrates his allegorical interpretation of many passages. In chapter 18, he says that a literal interpretation of Matthew 5:39 ("If anyone slaps you on the right cheek, turn to them the other cheek also") makes no literal sense because "everyone who strikes . . . smites the left cheek with his right hand." Origen apparently did not realize that in Jesus's day a blow on the right cheek meant that a superior had used an insulting (backhanded) slap of his right hand on an inferior (Stassen and Gushee, *Kingdom Ethics*, 138–39). But to say that this text shows that "Origen's order of priorities placed allegorical method higher than his feelings about war since even the command to turn the other cheek does not escape allegorization" (Helgeland, "Roman Army," 748–49) is to read into Origen's words what is simply not said. Repeatedly, Origen demonstrates a literal understanding of Jesus's command in Matthew 5 to love one's enemies (*Against Celsus* 2.30; 3.8; 7.26; 8.35). This text illustrates Origen's method of biblical interpretation, but it says nothing about his thinking on war.

4.18. And if we go to the Gospel and institute a similar examination, what would be more irrational than to take literally the injunction, "Salute no one by the way" [cf. Luke 10:4], which simple persons think the Savior enjoined on the apostles? The command, moreover, that the right cheek should be smitten [cf. Matt. 5:39], is most incredible, since everyone who strikes, unless he happen to have some bodily defect, smites the *left* cheek with his *right* hand. And it is impossible to take literally, the statement in the Gospel about the "offending" of the right eye. For, to grant the possibility of one being "offended" by the sense of sight, how, when there are two eyes that see, should the blame be laid upon the right eye? And who is there that, condemning himself for having looked upon a woman to lust after her, would rationally transfer the blame to the right eye alone, and throw *it* away?[95]

Homilies on Joshua

This excerpt illustrates Origen's allegorical exegesis by which he gives a spiritual meaning to a literal passage describing wars in Joshua.

Homily 15. Unless those physical wars bore the figure of spiritual wars, I do not think the books of Jewish history would ever have been handed down by

95. *ANF* 4:367.

the apostles to the disciples of Christ, who came to teach peace, so that they could be read in the churches. For what good was that description of wars to those to whom Jesus says, "My peace I give to you; my peace I leave to you" [John 14:27], and to whom it is commanded and said through the Apostle, "Not avenging your own selves" [Rom. 12:19], and, "Rather, you receive injury," and, "You suffer offense" [cf. 1 Cor. 6:7]? In short, knowing that now we do not have to wage physical wars, but that the struggles of the soul have to be exerted against spiritual adversaries, the Apostle, just as a military leader, gives an order to the soldiers of Christ, saying, "Put on the armor of God, so that you may be able to stand firm against the cunning devices of the Devil" [Eph. 6:11]. And in order for us to have examples of these spiritual wars from deeds of old, he wanted those narratives of exploits to be recited to us in church.[96]

Commentary on Matthew

Matt. 26:52. Soon Jesus said to him who had used the sword and cut off the right ear of that servant, "put up your sword into its place"—not "take away your sword"; there is therefore a place for a sword from which it is not lawful for anyone to take it who does not wish to perish, especially by the sword. For Jesus wishes his disciples to be "pacific," that putting down this warlike sword they should take up another pacific sword, which Scriptures call "the sword of the spirit." In a similar way he says, "all who take the sword shall perish by the sword," that is, all who are not pacific but inciters of wars, shall perish in that very war which they stir up. . . . But taking simply what He says, "those who take the sword shall perish by the sword," we should beware lest because of warfare or the vindication of our rights or for any occasion we should take out the sword, for no such occasion is allowed by this evangelical teaching, which commands us to fulfill what is written, "with those who hated me I was pacific." If therefore with those that hate peace we must be pacific, we must use the sword against no-one.[97]

Commentary on 1 Corinthians

The following statement relates to 1 Corinthians 9:11. Here Origen mocks Christian soldiers who think it is permissible to participate in idolatrous

96. Bruce, *Homilies on Joshua*, 138.

97. Quoted in Windass, "War," 240. The original is in Migne, *Patrologiae Graecae* 13:1751. Caspary also refers to a small fragment of Origen related to this text where Origen says, "One must accept those who lead the soldier's life" (*Origen*, 92), suggesting that Origen means it is permissible for a Christian to be in the army if he does not kill.

practices. Windass ("War," 240) says this is the only place he has found in which Origen connects military service with the problem of idolatry. Actually, Origen also mentions this in *Against Celsus* 8.65.

There are also some idolaters in our midst . . . [who] put forward the view that idolatry is something [in itself] indifferent. This sin [error] is met with most frequently in the armed forces. "Necessity leaves me no choice; the army demands this. I risk my neck if I don't offer sacrifice or vest in white and sprinkle on the incense according to the prescriptions of the army of the world"; and in spite of this, such a man calls himself a Christian![98]

Against Celsus

Origen argues here that it is legitimate to break unjust ("Scythian") laws. He concludes that it is legitimate both for citizens (presumably non-Christians) to kill a tyrant and for Christians to disobey unjust Roman laws, but he does not say Christians should kill tyrants.

1.1. The first point which Celsus brings forward, in his desire to throw discredit upon Christianity, is that the Christians entered into secret associations with each other contrary to law, saying that "of associations some are public, and that these are in accordance with the laws; others, again, secret, and maintained in violation of the laws." And his wish is to bring into disrepute what are termed the "love-feasts" of the Christians, as if they had their origin in the common danger, and were more binding than any other oaths. Since, then, he babbles about the public law, alleging that the associations of the Christians are in violation of it, we have to reply, that if a man were placed among Scythians, whose laws were unholy, and having no opportunity of escape, were compelled to live among them, such an one would with good reason, for the sake of the law of truth, which the Scythians would regard as wickedness, enter into associations contrary to their laws, with those likeminded with himself; so, if truth is to decide, the laws of the heathens which relate to images, and an atheistical polytheism, are "Scythian" laws, or more impious than these, if there be any such. It is not irrational, then, to form associations in opposition to existing laws, if done for the sake of truth. For as those persons would do well who should enter into a secret association in order to put to death a tyrant who had seized upon the liberties of a state, so Christians also, when tyrannized over by him who is called the devil, and by falsehood, form leagues contrary to the laws of the devil, against his power, and for the safety of those

98. Quoted in Windass, "War," 240. See also Claude Jenkins, "Origen on 1 Corinthians," *JTS* 9 (1907–8): 366–69.

others whom they may succeed in persuading to revolt from a government which is, as it were, "Scythian," and despotic.[99]

> Below Origen responds to Celsus's charge that Jesus did not "make himself visible."

2.30. We would say in reply, that so He did; for righteousness has arisen in His days, and there is abundance of peace, which took its commencement at His birth, God preparing the nations for His teaching, that they might be under one prince, the king of the Romans, and that it might not, owing to the lack of union among the nations, caused by the existence of many kingdoms, be more difficult for the apostles of Jesus to accomplish the task enjoined upon them by their Master, when He said, "Go and teach all nations." Moreover it is certain that Jesus was born in the reign of Augustus, who, so to speak, fused together into one monarchy the many populations of the earth. Now the existence of many kingdoms would have been a hindrance to the spread of the doctrine of Jesus throughout the entire world; not only for the reasons mentioned, but also on account of the necessity of men everywhere engaging in war, and fighting on behalf of their native country, which was the case before the times of Augustus, and in periods still more remote, when necessity arose, as when the Peloponnesians and Athenians warred against each other, and other nations in like manner. How, then, was it possible for the Gospel doctrine of peace, which does not permit people to take vengeance even upon enemies, to prevail throughout the world, unless at the advent of Jesus a milder spirit had been everywhere introduced into the conduct of things?[100]

3.7. Neither Celsus nor they who think with him are able to point out any act on the part of Christians which savors of rebellion. And yet, if a revolt had led to the formation of the Christian commonwealth, so that it derived its existence in this way from that of the Jews, who were permitted to take up arms in defense of the members of their families, and to slay their enemies, the Christian Lawgiver would not have altogether forbidden the putting of people to death; and yet He nowhere teaches that it is right for His own disciples to offer violence to anyone, however wicked. For He did not deem it in keeping with such laws as His, which were derived from a divine source, to allow the killing of any individual whatever. Nor would the Christians, had they owed their origin to a rebellion, have adopted laws of so exceedingly mild a character as not to allow them, when it was their fate to be slain as sheep, on any occasion to resist their persecutors.[101]

99. *ANF* 4:397.

100. *ANF* 4:443–44.

101. *ANF* 4:467. Contrary to Charles (*Between Pacifism and Jihad,* 36), there is nothing in this chapter about Christian soldiers.

3.8. But with regard to the Christians, because they were taught not to avenge themselves upon their enemies (and have thus observed the laws of a mild and philanthropic character); and because they would not, although able, have made war even if they had received authority to do so,—they have obtained this reward from God, that He has always warred in their behalf, and on certain occasions has restrained those who rose up against them and desired to destroy them.[102]

4.9. There came, then, although Celsus may not wish to admit it, after the numerous prophets who were reformers of the well-known Israel, the Christ, the Reformer of the whole world, who did not need to employ against people whips, and chains, and tortures, as was the case under the former economy.[103]

> In 4.82–83, Origen rejects Celsus's alleged argument that there is little difference between bees and ants on the one hand and persons on the other. Both groups have a sovereign, construct cities, and wage wars. Origen acknowledges some parallels but insists that the differences between rational persons and irrational bees and ants make the comparison silly.
>
> If we had only this statement from Origen, it would be reasonable to conclude that Origen "did not oppose war properly undertaken" (Helgeland, "Roman Army," 749). But we must compare the rather general statements here with his many explicit statements that Christians do not go to war.

4.82. Perhaps also the so-called wars among the bees convey instruction as to the manner in which wars, if ever there arise a necessity for them, should be waged in a just and orderly way among men. But the bees have no cities or suburbs. . . . Nor ought we to compare the proceedings taken by the bees against the drones with the judgments and punishments inflicted on the idle and wicked in cities.[104]

4.83. After Celsus has finished speaking of the bees, in order to depreciate (as far as he can) the cities, and constitutions, and governments, and sovereignties not only of us Christians, but of all humanity, as well as the wars which men undertake on behalf of their native countries, he proceeds, by way of digression, to pass a eulogy upon the ants, in order that, while praising them, he may compare the measures which people take to secure their subsistence with those adopted by these insects, and so evince his contempt for the forethought which makes provision for winter, as being nothing higher than the irrational providence of the ants, as he regards it.[105]

102. *ANF* 4:467–68.
103. *ANF* 4:500.
104. *ANF* 4:533–34.
105. *ANF* 4:534.

The exact meaning of "wordy swords," below, seems to be unclear to translators, but the subsequent reference to actual warfare is clear.

5.33. And to those who inquire of us whence we come or who is our founder, we reply that we are come agreeably to the counsels of Jesus, to "cut down our hostile and insolent 'wordy' swords into ploughshares, and to convert into pruning hooks the spears formerly employed in war." For we no longer take up "sword against nation," nor do we "learn war anymore," having become children of peace, for the sake of Jesus, who is our leader, instead of those whom our fathers followed, among whom we were "strangers to the covenant," and having received a law, for which we give thanks to Him that rescued us from the error (of our ways). . . . Our Superintendent, then, and Teacher, having come forth from the Jews, regulates the whole world by the word of His teaching.[106]

7.18–20, 22

In these chapters, Origen uses his exegetical method of figurative, allegorical interpretation (which was to become very influential for more than a millennium) to respond to Celsus's pointed question: How can you reconcile Old Testament commands to kill enemies with Jesus's peaceful teaching?

18. Celsus adds: "Will they not besides make this reflection? If the prophets of the God of the Jews foretold that he who should come into the world would be the Son of this same God, how could he command them through Moses to gather wealth, to extend their dominion, to fill the earth, to put their enemies of every age to the sword, to destroy them utterly, which indeed he himself did—as Moses says—threatening them, moreover, that if they did not obey his commands, he would treat them as his avowed enemies; whilst, on the other hand, his Son, the man of Nazareth, promulgated laws quite opposed to these, declaring that no one can come to the Father who loves power, or riches, or glory; that people ought not to be more careful in providing food than the ravens; that they were to be less concerned about their raiment than the lilies; that to him who has given them one blow, they should offer to receive another? Whether is it Moses or Jesus who teaches falsely? Did the Father, when he sent Jesus, forget the commands which he had given Moses? Or did he change his mind, condemn his own laws, and send forth a messenger with counter instructions?" Celsus, with all his boasts of universal knowledge has here fallen into the most vulgar of errors, in supposing that in the law and the prophets there is not a meaning deeper than that afforded by a literal rendering of the text.[107]

106. *ANF* 4:558.
107. *ANF* 4:617–18.

19. As to the promise made to the Jews that they should slay their enemies, it may be answered that anyone who examines carefully into the meaning of this passage will find himself unable to interpret it literally. It is sufficient at present to refer to the manner in which in the Psalms the just man is represented as saying, among other things, "Every morning will I destroy the wicked of the land; that I may cut off all workers of iniquity from the city of Jehovah" [Ps. 101:8]. Judge, then, from the words and spirit of the speaker, whether it is conceivable that, after having in the preceding part of the Psalm, as anyone may read for himself, uttered the noblest thoughts and purposes, he should in the sequel, according to the literal rendering of his words, say that in the morning and at no other period of the day, he would destroy all sinners from the earth, and leave none of them alive.[108]

20. We hold, then, that the law has a twofold sense—the one literal, the other spiritual—as has been shown by some before us. Of the first or literal sense it is said, not only by us, but by God, speaking in one of the prophets, that "the statutes are not good, and the judgments not good"; whereas, taken in a spiritual sense, the same prophet makes God say that "His statutes are good, His judgments are good." Yet the prophet is not saying things which are evidently contradictory of each other. Paul, in like manner, says that "the letter killeth, and the spirit giveth life," meaning by "the letter" the literal sense, and by "the spirit" the spiritual sense of Scripture.[109]

22. If I must now explain how the just man "slays his enemies," and prevails everywhere, it is to be observed that, when he says, "Every morning will I destroy the wicked of the land, that I may cut off all workers of iniquity from the city of Jehovah," by "the land" he means the flesh whose lusts are at enmity with God; and by "the city of Jehovah" he designates his own soul, in which was the temple of God, containing the true idea and conception of God, which makes it to be admired by all who look upon it. As soon, then, as the rays of the Sun of righteousness shine into his soul, feeling strengthened and invigorated by their influence, he sets himself to destroy all the lusts of the flesh, which are called "the wicked of the land," and drives out of that city of the Lord which is in his soul all thoughts which work iniquity, and all suggestions which are opposed to the truth. And in this way also the just give up to destruction all their enemies, which are their vices, so that they do not spare even the children, that is, the early beginnings and promptings of evil. In this sense also we understand the language of Psalm 137: "O daughter of Babylon, who art to be destroyed; happy shall he be that rewardeth thee as thou hast served us: happy shall he be that taketh and dasheth thy little ones

108. *ANF* 4:618.
109. *ANF* 4:618–19.

against the stones." For "the little ones" of Babylon (which signifies confusion) are those troublesome sinful thoughts which arise in the soul and he who subdues them by striking, as it were, their heads against the firm and solid strength of reason and truth, is the man who "dasheth the little ones against the stones"; and he is therefore truly blessed. God may therefore have commanded people to destroy all their vices utterly, even at their birth, without having enjoined anything contrary to the teaching of Christ; and He may Himself have destroyed before the eyes of those who were "Jews inwardly" all the offspring of evil as His enemies. And, in like manner, those who disobey the law and word of God may well be compared to His enemies led astray by sin; and they may well be said to suffer the same fate as they deserve who have proved traitors to the truth of God.[110]

> Below Origen seems to assume that the state must fight external enemies and use capital punishment, but Christians dare not do either.

7.26. However, if we must refer briefly to the difference between the constitution which was given to the Jews of old by Moses, and that which the Christians, under the direction of Christ's teaching, wish now to establish, we would observe that it must be impossible for the legislation of Moses, taken literally, to harmonize with the calling of the Gentiles, and with their subjection to the Roman government; and on the other hand, it would be impossible for the Jews to preserve their civil economy unchanged, supposing that they should embrace the Gospel. For Christians could not slay their enemies, or condemn to be burned or stoned, as Moses commands, those who had broken the law, and were therefore condemned as deserving of these punishments; since the Jews themselves, however desirous of carrying out their law, are not able to inflict these punishments. But in the case of the ancient Jews, who had a land and a form of government of their own, to take from them the right of making war upon their enemies, of fighting for their country, of putting to death or otherwise punishing adulterers, murderers, or others who were guilty of similar crimes, would be to subject them to sudden and utter destruction whenever the enemy fell upon them; for their very laws would in that case restrain them, and prevent them from resisting the enemy. And that same providence which of old gave the law, and has now given the Gospel of Jesus Christ, not wishing the Jewish state to continue longer, has destroyed their city and their temple: it has abolished the worship which was offered to God in that temple by the sacrifice of victims, and other ceremonies which He had prescribed. And as it has destroyed these things, not wishing that they should longer continue, in like manner it has extended day by day the Christian religion, so that it is now preached everywhere with boldness, and that in spite of the numerous obstacles

110. *ANF* 4:619–20.

which oppose the spread of Christ's teaching in the world. But since it was the purpose of God that the Gentiles should receive the benefits of Christ's teaching, all the devices of people against Christians have been brought to naught; for the more that kings, and rulers, and peoples have persecuted them everywhere, the more have they increased in number and grown in strength.[111]

7.58–59, 61

All of chapter 58 is a quote from Celsus who in turn includes a lengthy quotation from Plato's *Crito* to illustrate his argument that Jesus's teaching to reject avenging oneself and instead to turn the other cheek was taught earlier and better by Plato. In chapters 59 and 61, Origen responds that the similar teaching in Plato does not undermine the truth of Jesus's teaching.

58. "They have also," says he, "a precept to this effect, that we ought not to avenge ourselves on one who injures us, or, as he expresses it, 'Whosoever shall strike thee on the one cheek, turn to him the other also.' This is an ancient saying, which had been admirably expressed long before, and which they have only reported in a coarser way. For Plato introduces Socrates conversing with Crito as follows: 'Must we never do injustice to any?' 'Certainly not.' 'And since we must never do injustice, must we not return injustice for an injustice that has been done to us, as most people think?' 'It seems to me that we should not.' 'But tell me, Crito, may we do evil to any one or not?' 'Certainly not, O Socrates.' 'Well, is it just, as is commonly said, for one who has suffered wrong to do wrong in return, or is it unjust?' 'It is unjust. Yes; for to do harm to a man is the same as to do him injustice.' 'You speak truly. We must then not do injustice in return for injustice, nor must we do evil to anyone, whatever evil we may have suffered from him.' Thus Plato speaks; and he adds, 'Consider, then, whether you are at one with me, and whether, starting from this principle, we may not come to the conclusion that it is never right to do injustice, even in return for an injustice which has been received; or whether, on the other hand, you differ from me, and do not admit the principle from which we started. That has always been my opinion, and is so still.' Such are the sentiments of Plato, and indeed they were held by divine men before this time. But let this suffice as one example of the way in which this and other truths have been borrowed and corrupted. Anyone who wishes can easily by searching find more of them."[112]

59. When Celsus here or elsewhere finds himself unable to dispute the truth of what we say, but avers that the same things were said by the Greeks, our answer is, that if the doctrine be sound, and the effect of it good, whether it

111. *ANF* 4:621.
112. *ANF* 4:634.

was made known to the Greeks by Plato or any of the wise men of Greece, or whether it was delivered to the Jews by Moses or any of the prophets, or whether it was given to the Christians in the recorded teaching of Jesus Christ, or in the instructions of His apostles, that does not affect the value of the truth communicated. It is no objection to the principles of Jews or Christians, that the same things were also said by the Greeks, especially if it be proved that the writings of the Jews are older than those of the Greeks. And further, we are not to imagine that a truth adorned with the graces of Grecian speech is necessarily better than the same when expressed in the more humble and unpretending language used by Jews and Christians.[113]

61. From these remarks it is evident, that when Jesus said "coarsely," as Celsus terms it, "To him who shall strike thee on the one cheek, turn the other also; and if anyone be minded to sue thee at the law, and take away thy coat, let him have thy cloak also," He expressed Himself in such a way as to make the precept have more practical effect than the words of Plato in the *Crito*; for the latter is so far from being intelligible to ordinary persons, that even those have a difficulty in understanding him, who have been brought up in schools of learning, and have been initiated into the famous philosophy of Greece. It may also be observed, that the precept enjoining patience under injuries is in no way corrupted or degraded by the plain and simple language which our Lord employs.[114]

Below Origen rejects a statement by Celsus that rulers inflict great injury on those who insult them. Before citing Jesus's command to love one's enemies, Origen refers to the cases of two non-Christian rulers who acted in a similar way.

8.35. When Lycurgus had had his eye put out by a man, he got the offender into his power; but instead of taking revenge upon him, he ceased not to use all his arts of persuasion until he induced him to become a philosopher. And Zeno, on the occasion of someone saying, "Let me perish rather than not have my revenge on you," answered him, "But rather let me perish if I do not make a friend of you." And I am not yet speaking of those whose characters have been formed by the teaching of Jesus, and who have heard the words, "Love your enemies, and pray for them which despitefully use you, that ye may be the children of your Father which is in heaven; for He maketh His sun to rise on the evil and on the good, and sendeth rain on the just and on the unjust."[115]

113. Ibid.
114. *ANF* 4:635.
115. *ANF* 4:652.

> Origen responds here to Celsus's argument that if Christians are not willing to participate in society, they should not marry or even continue to live, but rather "depart hence with all speed."

8.55. To this we reply, that there appears to us to be no good reason for our leaving this world, except when piety and virtue require it; as when, for example, those who are set as judges, and think that they have power over our lives, place before us the alternative either to live in violence of the commands of Jesus, or to die if we continue obedient to them. But God has allowed us to marry, because all are not fit for the higher, that is, the perfectly pure life; and God would have us to bring up all our children, and not to destroy any of the offspring given us by His providence.[116]

8.65–75

> Chapters 65–75 represent one extended refutation of Celsus's charge that if everyone rejected military service and public office the way Christians do, then the empire would fall to barbarians. Celsus is apparently aware of Christians who reply that God would protect them and therefore argues that God did not protect the Jews (chap. 69). But Origen insists that if all the Romans became Christians, they would not go to war at all and God would protect them (chap. 70).

65. Moreover, we are to despise ingratiating ourselves with kings or any other persons, not only if their favor is to be won by murders, licentiousness, or deeds of cruelty, but even if it involves impiety towards God, or any servile expressions of flattery and obsequiousness, which thing are unworthy of brave and high-principled persons, who aim at joining with their other virtues that highest of virtues, patience and fortitude. But whilst we do nothing which is contrary to the law and word of God, we are not so mad as to stir up against us the wrath of kings and princes, which will bring upon us sufferings and tortures, or even death. For we read: "Let every soul be subject unto the higher powers. For there is no power but of God: the powers that be are ordained of God. Whosoever therefore resisteth the power, resisteth the ordinance of God" [Rom. 13:1–2]. . . . We will, however, never swear by "the fortune of the king," nor by ought else that is considered equivalent to God. For if the word "fortune" is nothing but an expression for the uncertain course of events, as some say, although they seem not to be agreed, we do not swear by that as God which has no existence, as though it did really exist and was able to do something, lest we should bind ourselves by an oath to things which have no existence. If, on the other hand (as is thought by others, who say that to swear by the fortune of the king of the Romans is to swear by his demon), what is

---

116. *ANF* 4:660–61.

called the fortune of the king is in the power of demons, then in that case we must die sooner than swear by a wicked and treacherous demon.[117]

68. Celsus goes on to say: "We must not disobey the ancient writer, who said long ago, 'Let one be king, whom the son of crafty Saturn appointed'; . . . For if all were to do the same as you, there would be nothing to prevent his being left in utter solitude and desertion, and the affairs of the earth would fall into the hands of the wildest and most lawless barbarians; and then there would no longer remain among people any of the glory of your religion or of the true wisdom." . . . [Origen replies:] Kings are not appointed by that son of Saturn, who, according to Grecian fable, hurled his father from his throne, and sent him down to Tartarus (whatever interpretation may be given to this allegory), but by God, who governs all things, and who wisely arranges whatever belongs to the appointment of kings. . . . In these circumstances the king will not "be left in utter solitude and desertion," neither will "the affairs of the world fall into the hands of the most impious and wild barbarians." For if, in the words of Celsus, "they do as I do," then it is evident that even the barbarians, when they yield obedience to the word of God, will become most obedient to the law, and most humane; and every form of worship will be destroyed except the religion of Christ, which will alone prevail. And indeed it will one day triumph, as its principles take possession of the minds of people more and more each day.[118]

69. Celsus, then, as if not observing that he was saying anything inconsistent with the words he had just used, "if all were to do the same as you," adds: "You surely do not say that if the Romans were, in compliance with your wish, to neglect their customary duties to gods and men, and were to worship the Most High, or whatever you please to call him, that he will come down and fight for them, so that they shall need no other help than his. For this same God, as yourselves say, promised of old this and much more to those who served him [i.e., the Jews], and see in what way he has helped them and you! They, in place of being masters of the whole world, are left with not so much as a patch of ground or a home; and as for you, if any of you transgresses even in secret, he is sought out and punished with death." As the question stated is, "What would happen if the Romans were persuaded to adopt the principles of the Christians, to despise the duties paid to the recognized gods and to men, and to worship the Most High?" this is my answer to the question. We say that "if two" of us "shall agree on earth as touching anything that they shall ask, it shall be done for them of the Father" of the just, "which is in heaven" [cf. Matt. 18:19]; for God rejoices in the agreement of rational beings, and

117. *ANF* 4:664.
118. *ANF* 4:665–66.

turns away from discord. And what are we to expect, if not only a very few agree, as at present, but the whole of the empire of Rome? For they will pray to the Word, who of old said to the Hebrews, when they were pursued by the Egyptians, "The LORD shall fight for you, and you shall hold your peace" [cf. Exod. 14:14]; and if they all unite in prayer with one accord, they will be able to put to flight far more enemies than those who were discomfited by the prayer of Moses when he cried to the Lord, and of those who prayed with him. Now, if what God promised to those who keep His law has not come to pass, the reason of its non-fulfillment is not to be ascribed to the unfaithfulness of God. But He had made the fulfillment of His promises to depend on certain conditions,—namely, that they should observe and live according to His law; and if the Jews have not a plot of ground nor a habitation left to them, although they had received these conditional promises, the entire blame is to be laid upon their crimes, and especially upon their guilt in the treatment of Jesus.[119]

70. But if all the Romans, according to the supposition of Celsus, embrace the Christian faith, they will, when they pray, overcome their enemies; or rather, they will not war at all, being guarded by that divine power which promised to save five entire cities for the sake of fifty just persons. For people of God are assuredly the salt of the earth: they preserve the order of the world; and society is held together as long as the salt is uncorrupted: for "if the salt have lost its savor, it is neither fit for the land nor for the dunghill; but it shall be cast out, and trodden under foot. He that hath ears, let him hear" [cf. Luke 14:34–35] the meaning of these words. When God gives to the tempter permission to persecute us, then we suffer persecution; and when God wishes us to be free from suffering, even in the midst of a world that hates us, we enjoy a wonderful peace, trusting in the protection of Him who said, "Be of good cheer, I have overcome the world" [cf. John 16:33]. And truly He has overcome the world. Wherefore the world prevails only so long as it is the pleasure of Him who received from the Father power to overcome the world; and from His victory we take courage. Should He even wish us again to contend and struggle for our religion, let the enemy come against us, and we will say to them, "I can do all things, through Christ Jesus our Lord, which strengtheneth me" [cf. Phil. 4:13]. For of "two sparrows which are sold for a farthing," as the Scripture says, "not one of them falls on the ground without our Father in heaven" [cf. Matt. 10:29–30]. And so completely does the Divine Providence embrace all things, that not even the hairs of our head fail to be numbered by Him.[120]

Leithart begins his comments on the following passage by saying that Origen's arguments "were often linked with conceptions of pollution" (*Constantine*,

119. *ANF* 4:666.
120. Ibid.

268). But this passage makes it quite clear that Christians, just like the pagan priests, should "keep their hands free from blood." The problem is killing people, not pagan rituals.

73. In the next place, Celsus urges us "to help the king with all our might, and to labor with him in the maintenance of justice, to fight for him; and if he requires it, to fight under him, or lead an army along with him." To this our answer is, that we do, when occasion requires, give help to kings, and that, so to say, a divine help, "putting on the whole armor of God." And this we do in obedience to the injunction of the apostle, "I exhort, therefore, that first of all, supplications, prayers, intercessions, and giving of thanks, be made for all people; for kings, and for all that are in authority" [cf. 1 Tim. 2:1–2]; and the more anyone excels in piety, the more effective help does he render to kings, even more than is given by soldiers, who go forth to fight and slay as many of the enemy as they can. And to those enemies of our faith who require us to bear arms for the commonwealth, and to slay people, we can reply: "Do not those who are priests at certain shrines, and those who attend on certain gods, as you account them, keep their hands free from blood, that they may with hands unstained and free from human blood offer the appointed sacrifices to your gods; and even when war is upon you, you never enlist the priests in the army. If that, then, is a laudable custom, how much more so, that while others are engaged in battle, these too should engage as the priests and ministers of God, keeping their hands pure, and wrestling in prayers to God on behalf of those who are fighting in a righteous cause, and for the king who reigns righteously, that whatever is opposed to those who act righteously may be destroyed!" And as we by our prayers vanquish all demons who stir up war, and lead to the violation of oaths, and disturb the peace, we in this way are much more helpful to the kings than those who go into the field to fight for them. And we do take our part in public affairs, when along with righteous prayers we join self-denying exercises and meditations, which teach us to despise pleasures, and not to be led away by them. And none fight better for the king than we do. We do not indeed fight under him, although he require it; but we fight on his behalf, forming a special army—an army of piety—by offering our prayers to God.

74. And if Celsus would have us to lead armies in defense of our country, let him know that we do this too, and that not for the purpose of being seen by people, or of vainglory. For "in secret," and in our own hearts, there are prayers which ascend as from priests in behalf of our fellow-citizens. And Christians are benefactors of their country more than others. For they train up citizens, and inculcate piety to the Supreme Being.

75. Celsus also urges us to "take office in the government of the country, if that is required for the maintenance of the laws and the support of religion." But we recognize in each state the existence of another national organization founded by the Word of God, and we exhort those who are mighty in word and of blameless life to rule over churches. Those who are ambitious of ruling we reject; but we constrain those who, through excess of modesty, are not easily induced to take a public charge in the church of God. And those who rule over us well are under the constraining influence of the great King, whom we believe to be the Son of God, God the Word. And if those who govern in the church, and are called rulers of the divine nation (that is, the church) rule well, they rule in accordance with the divine commands, and never suffer themselves to be led astray by worldly policy. And it is not for the purpose of escaping public duties that Christians decline public offices, but that they may reserve themselves for a diviner and more necessary service in the church of God—for the salvation of people. And this service is at once necessary and right.[121]

Commentary on John

20.290. For the fact that no one at all is a son of God from the beginning is clear from Paul's statement in which he also includes himself, "We were by nature children of wrath" [Eph. 2:3]. It is also clear from the statement, "But I say to you, Love your enemies and pray for those who persecute you, that you may become sons of your Father who is in heaven" [Matt. 5:44–45].

20.292. And if the only way one becomes a son of the Father who is in heaven is by loving one's enemies and praying for those who persecute one, it is clear that no one hears the words of God because he is of God by nature, but because he has received power to become a child of God and has made proper use of this power, and because he has loved his enemies and prayed for those who abuse him, and has become a son of the Father who is in heaven.[122]

Cyprian (c. AD 202–58)

Born into a wealthy pagan family in Carthage, Cyprian received an excellent classical education and became a teacher of rhetoric. Only much later in

---

121. *ANF* 4:667–68.
122. Heine, *Origen*, 266. See the similar passages in secs. 141–48 (236–37) and 106–7 (228–29).

life did he embrace Christianity. Soon after his baptism (probably at Easter, 246) he became a priest and, about two years later, he was elected bishop of Carthage.

Very quickly, Cyprian was forced to deal with the first empire-wide active persecution of Christians, initiated by Emperor Decius in 249–50. Cyprian went into hiding, but many of his flock abandoned the faith. After Decius's death in 251, persecution declined and Cyprian was able to return to Carthage where many of the lapsed Christians sought to return to the church. Much of the rest of his life (including many of his treatises and letters) was dedicated to the problems resulting from the return of those who had abandoned their faith during persecution. In 257, persecution resumed, this time even more severe, and Cyprian was beheaded in September 258.

I have included selections from five treatises and several letters. *To Donatus* was written soon after Cyprian's conversion. *Testimonies against the Jews* was written about 248–49 and *To Demetrian* (a bitter enemy of Christians) in 252. Cyprian wrote *On the Good of Patience* in 256 as he struggled with how to deal with lapsed Christians and those baptized by heretics. *To Fortunatus* was written (perhaps 257) to encourage a friend facing the possibility of martyrdom. The letters, written throughout his life as a Christian, have different numbers in *ANF* and more recent collections. I use the numbers in *ANF* with the numbers of more recent collections in brackets.

There is very little in Cyprian about war. Once he referred to Christians in the army (Letter 33 [39]). But he also says that manslaughter is a mortal sin (*On the Good of Patience* 14), and that Christians may not kill (Letter 55 [58])—not even guilty persons (Letter 56 [60]). He states that Christians must love their enemies (*Testimonies against the Jews* 3.49) and leave vengeance to God (ibid., 3.106). And in *To Donatus*, he deplores the killing of persons in both war and gladiatorial contests (chaps. 6–7). In *On the Good of Patience*, he quotes all of Matthew 5:43–48 (cf. also *Pontius's Life of Cyprian* 9).

Military imagery is very common in Cyprian's work (see Letters 8 [10], 24 [28], and 25 [31]). Swift (*Military*) says Cyprian's profound use of military metaphors should caution us against considering him a pacifist. Harnack has argued that the widespread use of military imagery prepared the way for the church's embrace of holy war in the fourth century (*Militia Christi*, 60–63). But there is no evidence here that Cyprian's use of military imagery in any way qualified his statements that Christians should not kill.

For further information, see Deferrari, *Cyprian*, v-xii and the introduction to each treatise; Clarke, *Letters of St. Cyprian*, I–IV (both the introduction to each volume and the massive notes on each letter); Brent, *St. Cyprian*, *Letters*, 11–44; Deferrari, *Biographies*, 3–32; Bobertz, *Cyprian*; and Walker, *St. Cyprian*.

To Donatus

Shortly after his baptism at Easter 246, Cyprian wrote to his friend about how his new faith had transformed his thought and action. In chapters 6–7, Cyprian condemns the bloody violence of both war and also the popular public spectacles where gladiators fought and killed (and were killed by) each other and wild beasts.

6. But in order that the characteristics of the divine munificence may shine forth . . . I shall reveal the darkness of a hidden world. For a little consider that you are being transported to the loftiest peak of a high mountain, that from this you are viewing the appearance of things that lie below you and with your eyes directed in different directions you yourself free from earthly contacts gaze upon the turmoils of the world. Presently you also will have pity on the world, and taking account of yourself and with more gratitude to God you will rejoice with greater joy that you have escaped from it. Observe the roads blocked by robbers, the seas beset by pirates, wars spread everywhere with the bloody horrors of camps. The world is soaked with mutual blood, and when individuals commit homicide, it is a crime; it is called a virtue when it is done in the name of the state. Impunity is acquired for crimes not by reason of innocence but by the magnitude of the cruelty.

7. Now if you turn your eyes and face toward the cities themselves, you will find a multitude sadder than any solitude. A gladiatorial combat is being prepared that blood may delight the lust of cruel eyes. The body is filled up with stronger foods, and the robust mass of flesh grows fat with bulging muscles, so that fattened for punishment it may perish more dearly. Man is killed for the pleasure of man, and to be able to kill is a skill, is an employment, is an art. Crime is not only committed but is taught. What can be called more inhuman, what more repulsive? It is a training that one may be able to kill, and that he kills is a glory. . . . And at such impious and terrible spectacles they do not realize that with their eyes they are parricides.[123]

Testimonies against the Jews

3.49. That even our enemies must be loved. In the Gospel according to Luke: "If you love those who love you, what thanks have you? For even sinners love those who love them" [Luke 6:32]. Also according to Matthew: "Love your enemies, and pray for those who persecute you, that you may be the children of your Father who is in heaven, who maketh His sun to rise upon the good

123. Deferrari, *Cyprian,* 12–13.

and the evil, and giveth rain upon the righteous and the unrighteous" [Matt. 5:44–45].[124]

3.106. That when a wrong is received, patience is to be maintained, and vengeance to be left to God. Say not, I will avenge me of mine enemy; but wait for the Lord, that He may be thy help [cf. Lev. 19:18]. Also elsewhere: "To me belongeth vengeance; I will repay, saith the Lord" [cf. Deut. 32:35]. Also in Zephaniah: "Wait on me, saith the Lord, in the day of my rising again to witness; because my judgment is to the congregations of the Gentiles, that I may take kings, and pour out upon them my anger" [cf. Zeph. 3:8].[125]

On the Dress of Virgins

11. God willed iron to be for the culture of the earth, but not on that account must murders be committed.[126]

To Demetrian

16. Cease to hurt the servants of God and of Christ with your persecutions, since when they are injured the divine vengeance defends them.

17. For this reason it is that none of us, when he is apprehended, makes resistance, nor avenges himself against your unrighteous violence, although our people are numerous and plentiful. Our certainty of a vengeance to follow makes us patient.[127]

> Cyprian says Christians pray for the warding off of enemies (of Rome). But that is not the same as praying "for the success of the imperial armies in warding off enemies" (Swift, *Military*, 48–49).

20. There flourishes with us the strength of hope and the firmness of faith. Among these very ruins of a decaying world our soul is lifted up, and our courage unshaken. . . . Although the vine should fail, and the olive deceive, and the field parched with grass dying with drought should wither, what is that to Christians? . . . And yet we always ask for the repulse of enemies, and for obtaining showers, and either for the removal or the moderating of

124. *ANF* 5:546.
125. *ANF* 5:555.
126. *ANF* 5:433.
127. *ANF* 5:462.

adversity; and we pour forth our prayers, and propitiating and appeasing God, we entreat constantly and urgently, day and night, for your peace and salvation.[128]

On the Good of Patience

> There is nothing in this passage to support Helgeland's argument that Cyprian's concern here (specifically his insistence that the hand that takes the Eucharist dare not be "sullied by the blood-stained sword") was "based on the Old Testament concept of ritual purity rather than on an injunction against killing based on moral considerations" ("Roman Army," 753). Cyprian's concern is clearly with immoral behavior: adultery, fraud, and killing persons.

14. But patience, beloved, not only keeps watch over what is good, but it also repels what is evil. In harmony with the Holy Spirit, and associated with what is heavenly and divine, it struggles with the defense of its strength against the deeds of the flesh and the body, wherewith the soul is assaulted and taken. Let us look briefly into a few things out of many, that from a few the rest also may be understood. Adultery, fraud, manslaughter, are mortal crimes. Let patience be strong and steadfast in the heart; and neither is the sanctified body and temple of God polluted by adultery, nor is the innocence dedicated to righteousness stained with the contagion of fraud; nor, after the Eucharist is carried in it, is the hand sullied by the blood-stained sword.[129]

16. What beyond;—that you should not swear or curse; that you should not seek again your goods when taken from you; that, when you receive a blow, you should give your other cheek to the smiter; that you should forgive a brother who sins against you, not only seven times, but seventy times seven times, but, moreover, all his sins altogether; that you should love your enemies; that you should offer prayer for your adversaries and persecutors? Can you accomplish these things unless you maintain the steadfastness of patience and endurance? And this we see done in the case of Stephen, who, when he was slain by the Jews with violence and stoning, did not ask for vengeance for himself, but for pardon for his murderers.[130]

128. *ANF* 5:463.
129. *ANF* 5:488. (Note: At this period in Carthage, the priest placed the consecrated bread in the hands of the communicant.)
130. Ibid.

The Letters of Cyprian

Letter 8 [10]. Cyprian to the martyrs and confessors in Christ our Lord and in God the Father, everlasting salvation. . . . The combat has increased, and the glory of the combatants has increased also. Nor were you kept back from the struggle by fear of tortures, but by the very tortures themselves you were more and more stimulated to the conflict; bravely and firmly you have returned with ready devotion, to contend in the extremest contest. Of you I find that some are already crowned, while some are even now within reach of the crown of victory; but all whom the danger has shut up in a glorious company are animated to carry on the struggle with an equal and common warmth of virtue, as it behoves the soldiers of Christ in the divine camp: that no allurements may deceive the incorruptible steadfastness of your faith, no threats terrify you, no sufferings or tortures overcome you. . . . The examination by torture waxing severer, continued for a long time to this result, not to overthrow the steadfast faith, but to send the people of God more quickly to the Lord. The multitude of those who were present saw with admiration the heavenly contest,—the contest of God, the spiritual contest, the battle of Christ,—saw that His servants stood with free voice, with unyielding mind, with divine virtue—bare, indeed, of weapons of this world, but believing and armed with the weapons of faith. The tortured stood more brave than the torturers; and the limbs, beaten and torn as they were, overcame the hooks that bent and tore them. . . . Oh, what a spectacle was that to the Lord,—how sublime, how great, how acceptable to the eyes of God is the allegiance and devotion of His soldiers! . . . In the heavenly camp both peace and war have their own flowers, with which the soldier of Christ may be crowned for glory.[131]

Letter 24 [28]. For you, who have become chiefs and leaders in the battle of our day, have set forward the standard of celestial warfare; you have made a beginning of the spiritual contest which God has purposed to be now waged by your valor; you, with unshaken strength and unyielding firmness, have broken the first onset of the rising war. Thence have arisen happy openings of the fight; thence have begun good auspices of victory. It happened that here martyrdoms were consummated by tortures.[132]

Letter 25 [31]. As a good captain, [the Lord] will at length bring forth His soldiers, whom He has hitherto trained and proved in the camp of our prison, to the field of the battle set before them. May He hold forth to us the divine arms, those weapons that know not how to be conquered,—the breastplate of righteousness, which is never accustomed to be broken,—the shield of faith,

---

131. *ANF* 5:287–89.
132. *ANF* 5:302 (letter 28 in Clarke, *Letters of St. Cyprian*, 2:23).

which cannot be pierced through,—the helmet of salvation, which cannot be shattered,—and the sword of the Spirit, which has never been wont to be injured.[133]

> In the following letter (probably written in February 251), Cyprian explains his appointment of Celerinus to a position in the church. Celerinus had been tried (perhaps before Emperor Decius) and tortured, but then released. Cyprian notes that Celerinus's persecution aligns with his family's tradition: his grandmother and two uncles were martyrs (Clarke, *Letters of St. Cyprian*, 2:186–92). The passage below suggests that Celerinus's uncles were once soldiers, and Clarke says this provides "casual evidence for Christians willing to adopt the profession of soldiers" (191). Actually, the text does not say the uncles became soldiers after becoming Christians. In fact, the text does not even say that they were Christians during the time when they were soldiers. It only says they were once soldiers but refused to reject Christ and were martyred.

Letter 33 [39]. Nor is that kind of title to glories in the case of Celerinus, our beloved, an unfamiliar and novel thing. He is advancing in the footsteps of his kindred; he rivals his parents and relations in equal honors of divine condescension. His grandmother, Celerina, was some time since crowned with martyrdom. Moreover, his paternal and maternal uncles, Laurentius and Egnatius, who themselves also were once warring in worldly armies, but were true and spiritual soldiers of God, casting down the devil by the confession of Christ, merited palms and crowns from the Lord by their illustrious passion.[134]

Letter 55 [58]. Nor let anyone, beloved, when he beholds our people driven away and scattered by the fear of persecution, be disturbed at not seeing the community gathered together, nor hearing the bishops preaching. All are not able to be there together, who may not kill but who must be killed.[135]

Letter 56 [60]. But when beaten back as well by the faith as by the vigor of the combined army, he perceived that the soldiers of Christ are now watching, and stand sober and armed for the battle; that they cannot be conquered, but that they can die; and that by this very fact they are invincible, because they do not fear death; that they do not in turn assail their assailants, since it is not lawful for the innocent even to kill the guilty; but that they readily deliver up both their lives and their blood; that since such malice and cruelty rages in the world, they may the more quickly withdraw from the evil and cruel. What a glorious spectacle was that under the eyes of God! What a joy of His

133. *ANF* 5:304 (letter 31 in Clarke, *Letters of St. Cyprian*, 2:36).
134. *ANF* 5:313 (letter 39 in Clarke, *Letters of St. Cyprian*, 2:55).
135. *ANF* 5:348 (letter 58 in Clarke, *Letters of St. Cyprian*, 3:62).

Church in the sight of Christ, that not single soldiers, but the whole camp, at once went forth to the battle which the enemy had tried to begin![136]

To Fortunatus

13. Who, then, does not with all his powers labor to attain to such a glory that he may become the friend of God, that he may at once rejoice with Christ, that after the earthly tortures and punishments he may receive divine rewards? If to soldiers of this world it is glorious to return in triumph to their country when the foe is vanquished, how much more excellent and greater is the glory when the devil is overcome, to return in triumph to paradise, and to bring back victorious trophies to that place whence Adam was ejected as a sinner.[137]

Gregory Thaumaturgus (mid-third century AD)

In the middle decades of the third century, Gothic tribes from beyond the Danube conducted a number of raids into Roman territory. After one raid (about AD 255–60) into Pontus (northeast Turkey today), a neighboring bishop asked Gregory, bishop of Neocaesarea (modern Niksar) for advice on how to respond to Roman Christians who had committed evil actions during the invasion. The extant version of Gregory's letter reflects the fact that it became part of the canon law of the Eastern church, but the basic content was probably written before AD 260.

Canon 7 vigorously condemns Christians from Pontus who joined the Gothic invaders and helped kill those of their own country. They must not be allowed to be "Hearers" in Christian worship. It is not clear from the text whether Gregory views their evil to be the killing of fellow citizens of Pontus, or whether he views killing in itself as wrong. Gregory says nothing about whether Christians from Pontus were actively engaged in fighting the Gothic invaders. For further information, see Heather and Matthews, *Goths*, 1–11.

6. Concerning those who forcibly detain captives (who have escaped) from the barbarians. Something quite unbelievable has been reported to us as having

---

136. *ANF* 5:351 (letter 60 in Clarke, *Letters of St. Cyprian*, 3:90). In spite of Cyprian's statement here that it is not lawful for Christians to kill even the guilty and his similar statement in letter 55, Clarke argues that letter 33 shows Cyprian is not a pacifist (3:230n18, 268n7).

137. *ANF* 5:506. Why Swift thinks this passage "is hard to reconcile with trenchant pacifism" (*Military*, 49) is unclear.

happened in your country, which can only be the work of faithless, impious men who do not so much as know the name of the Lord; and this is that men have reached such a point of cruelty and inhumanity as to detain forcibly some captives who have escaped from the barbarians. Send men out into the countryside [i.e., as a commission of inquiry], lest divine thunderbolts descend upon those who perpetuate such wickedness!

7. Concerning those who have been enrolled among the numbers of the barbarians, and have performed outrageous acts against those of their own race. As for those who have been enrolled among the barbarians and followed after them as prisoners, forgetting that they were men of Pontus, and Christians, and have become so thoroughly barbarized as even to put to death men of their own race by the gibbet or noose, and to point out roads and houses to the barbarians, who were ignorant of them; you must debar them even from the ranks of Hearers, until a common decision is reached about them by the assembly of saints, with the guidance of the Holy Spirit.[138]

Dionysius of Alexandria (c. AD 200–265)

Born into a wealthy, pagan family in Alexandria, Dionysius became a Christian fairly early in life. After serving as head of the famous Christian school in Alexandria, he became bishop of Alexandria and served during a time of great persecution. All of his many writings are lost, except for extensive quotations in the famous histories of Eusebius of Caesarea (c. 260–340).

Included here is a short selection of a letter (quoted in Eusebius, *Ecclesiastical History* 7.11) written during the reign of Emperor Valerian (253–60), who vigorously persecuted the church. Dionysius's list of the many Christian martyrs of that time indicates that Christians were in the Roman army.

But it would be a superfluous task for me to mention by name our (martyr) friends, who are numerous and at the same time unknown to you. Only understand that they include men and women, both young men and old, both maidens and aged matrons, both soldiers and private citizens,—every class and every age, of whom some have suffered by stripes and fire, and some by the sword, and have won the victory and received their crowns.[139]

138. Heather and Matthews, *Goths*, 8–9. Their translation is from the text in *PG* 10:1020–48.
139. *ANF* 6:96.

Archelaus (late third century AD)

Very little about Bishop Archelaus is certain. We have a somewhat unreliable version of a likely Syriac original of a disputation that the bishop held with a Manichean heretic somewhere in Mesopotamia, probably about 277. *ANF* publishes the document under the title *The Acts of the Disputation with the Heresiarch Manes*.

The account begins with the story of a large number of Christians who were taken captive at night by ferocious soldiers while the Christians were celebrating an annual religious festival in the countryside. Those who survived were ransomed by Marcellus, a very wealthy Christian. Surprised by Marcellus's generosity and spirit, some of the soldiers became Christians and abandoned military service. It is not clear how reliable the detailed story is, but the document shows that, toward the end of the third century, the author thought that at least some soldiers abandoned the army when they became Christians.

The Acts of the Disputation with the Heresiarch Manes

1. On a certain occasion, when a large body of captives were offered to the bishop Archelaus by the soldiers who held the camp in that place, their numbers being some seven thousand seven hundred, he was harassed with the keenest anxiety on account of the large sum of money which was demanded by the soldiers as the price of the prisoners' deliverance. . . . He at length listened to Marcellus, and explained to him the importance and difficulty of the case. And when . . . Marcellus heard his narration, without the least delay he went into his house, and provided the price demanded for the prisoners, according to the value set upon them by those who had led them captive; and unlocking the treasures of his goods, he at once distributed the gifts of piety among the soldiers . . . so that they seemed to be presents rather than purchase-money. And those soldiers were filled with wonder and admiration at the grandeur of the man's piety and munificence, and were struck with amazement, and felt the force of this example of pity; so that very many of them were added to the faith of our Lord Jesus Christ, and threw off the belt of military service, while others withdrew to their camp, taking scarcely a fourth part of the ransom.

Following is the account of the capture of the Christians.

2. Accordingly at that hour a multitude of soldiers suddenly surrounded us, supposing us, as I judge, to have lodged ourselves in ambush there, and to be persons with full experience and skill in fighting battles; and without making any exact inquiry into the cause of our gathering there, they threatened us with war, not in word, but at once by the sword. And though we were people who had never learned to do injury to anyone, they wounded us pitilessly with their missiles, and thrust us through with their spears, and cut our throats with their swords.[140]

Adamantius, *Dialogue on the True Faith* (probably late third or early fourth century AD)

This dialogue between a Catholic Christian (Adamantius) and gnostic Christians was written by an unknown author.

Dating the work is complicated. A majority of scholars date it between 270 and 313.[141] Hort dated it in the time of Constantine.[142] Others are less precise.[143]

Since this dialogue quotes substantially from Methodius's *On Free Will* (written sometime between 270 and 290), the earliest date would be 270. Whether it was written before Constantine's legalization of Christianity in 313 depends on complicated textual arguments. Twice, the text talks about the persecution of Christians. After a gnostic spokesperson says "We [Christians] have been frequently persecuted and are hated" (Pretty, *Adamantius*, 63), Adamantius says: "But now the king worships God" (Pretty, *Adamantius*, 64)—a fairly clear reference to Constantine. But there is strong reason to believe this is a later "correction" of an earlier Greek text because we have a Latin translation of this passage that assumes the persecution is still in the present (Pretty, *Adamantius*, 64). That would mean the original work was written before 313.[144]

But there is a second reference to the attitude of kings and rulers to Christ and Christians. And in this case, both the Greek text and the Latin text speak of acceptance of Christ and Christians rather than persecution: "Kings and all rulers listen to the bishops."[145] That would seem to suggest a date after 313 although it could conceivably come from the period of relative peace for

140. *ANF* 6:179–80.

141. Pretty, *Adamantius*, xvii, 16–17; Harnack, *Altchristlichen Literatur*, 150–51.

142. F. J. A. Hort, "Adamantius," in William Smith and Henry Wace, eds., *A Dictionary of Christian Biography* (London: John Murray, 1877), 1:39.

143. *Oxford Dictionary* dates it in the early fourth century (16) and Johannes Quasten says it "did not appear before the year AD 300" (*Patrology* 2:147).

144. Others argue this in addition to Pretty and Harnack. See those cited in P. Mordaunt Barnard in a review in the *Journal of Theological Studies* 2 (1901): 617–18, and especially W. H. van de Sande Bakhuyzen, ed., *Der Dialog des Adamantius* (Leipzig: J. C. Hinrichs, 1901).

145. Greek text is from Pretty, *Adamantius*, 190. Harnack argues that the Greek text in the second passage is also a later insertion—toward the end of Constantine's reign (*Altchristlichen*

the church in the late decades of the third century before Diocletian's intense persecution.

At present, it is not possible to be certain of the date of this dialogue. (Obviously, if it was written during the reign of Constantine, it is irrelevant for our discussion.) I am inclined to think that the weight of our limited evidence is at least modestly on the side of a date before 313. Therefore I include it.

Central to the first section quoted here is Adamantius's attempt to refute the gnostic claim that because the Gospels and Epistles contain things that differ from the Old Testament, therefore there must be two (or three) gods. He rejects the gnostic view that the father of Jesus Christ is not the creator God, and argues that the teaching of Jesus is consistent with the Old Testament.

This is an important passage for our purposes since the author clearly says, "It is right to wage a just war against those who go to war unjustly." He also says God ordained capital punishment for murderers through Moses. But what the author means to say about whether Christians should sometimes kill is less clear.

It is quite obvious that the author's most basic concern is to refute the gnostic view that the Old Testament contradicts the gospel and therefore there are two gods. He rejects all claims of contradictions arguing, for example, that the law also contains the gospel teaching on love for enemies.

At the same time, the author also embraces what one might call "progressive revelation." God's word was more simple when humanity was young. Later, God's teaching in the gospel was different "as the world progressed from its beginning, through the middle period to its perfected state." He also says that whereas the law's "eye for an eye" prevented strife through fear, the gospel prevents strife through persuasion and gentleness.

Also clear is the author's insistence that God combines love and justice. God rightly punishes wicked people. He even speaks of God's eternal punishment as deserved, arguing that in some sense God is applying the principle of "an eye for an eye." The author states that the gospel "recognizes the right of retaliation and the slaying of evil men," but all his examples refer to the eschatological judgment and God's punishment of the wicked. Clearly God rightly "kills" wicked people.[146]

Nowhere, however, does he say that Christians should kill people. Immediately after saying it is right to wage just war, he goes on to say it is right to preach peace without arms and then quotes the messianic prophecy of Isaiah

---

Literatur, 151), but that ignores the fact that the Latin translation (allegedly made from an earlier, pre-Constantinian Greek text) also describes acceptance, not persecution of Christians.

146. G. W. Trompf, the editor of the series in which Pretty's edition appears, says, "The main demonstration of a non-pacifistic Christ, mind you, is basically eschatological: Christ is coming again as a judge who will forcibly separate the righteous from the wicked. . . . Thus with the Adamantius Dialogue we find that the pacifistic temperament in the Church just before Diocletian's great persecution, is still holding; but there is a slight hint that the physical punishment of evildoers by a Christianized polity could be legitimate" (Pretty, *Adamantius,* xix–xx).

that the law will go out from Jerusalem, swords will be turned into ploughshares, and "they shall never again learn to make war" (Isa. 2:4).

Given his understanding of progressive revelation, it is quite possible that the author intends to argue (as did Origen) that God allowed killing in the Old Testament but now forbids it in the time of the gospel in the "maturity" of the world. That is a very plausible interpretation of this text, but it is not as clearly and explicitly argued here as it is in Origen.

The second selection (4.9–10) includes a statement indicating that desiring the death of someone who has committed adultery is not a crime. It is not clear, however, whether the author intends to say that capital punishment is legitimate for Christians. The text certainly does not say that explicitly. The author's primary concern is to make a basic philosophical point that rejects the gnostic idea that evil comes from a second God. The text is not focused on what is or is not ethical conduct for Christians. At the same time, the text does not forbid capital punishment by Christians, and what it means for our question of whether the early church believed Christians should participate in capital punishment is simply not clear.

In this excerpt, "Ad." is Adamantius the Catholic, "Meg." is Megethius the gnostic, "Eutr." is Eutropus, the allegedly neutral adjudicator of the debate, and "Dr." is Droserius, another gnostic voice.

1.9

Ad.: Prove that there are three Principles, and then proceed as you wish.

Meg.: I maintain that the Demiurge framed one set of laws, and that Christ made another set opposed to him.

Ad.: Because you suppose that there are different and opposing laws, you therefore conclude that there is first one and then another God?

Meg.: Most certainly! No one ever contradicted or opposed himself in the way that the Gospel opposes the Law. . . .

Ad.: It is indeed not unseemly to quote an example borrowed from earthly life in order to make what is said in the Scriptures clearer: the position resembles that of a woman who has just given birth to a child. She does not at first give him adult food, but nourishes him with milk, and afterwards uses richer and stronger food. The Apostle Paul, too, recognizes that the human beings' codes of law are provided according to their advancement. Thus he says, "I gave you milk to drink, not solid food, for you could not yet take it—nor indeed can you now, for you still have the fleshly nature" [1 Cor. 3:2–3]. God acted in the same way; He made codes of law for humankind in harmony with their development; some for Adam, as a babe; some for Noah; some for Abraham. Others were given through Moses, and yet others through the Gospel, according as the world progressed from its beginning through the middle period to its perfected state. In this way He reserved what is mature for the time of the world's maturity. However, lest you should think that I am guilty of confused reasoning, I will prove that the same God has framed laws of both kinds: He commanded Abraham to kill his son; after this He gave a law through Moses that men must not kill, but that he who has committed murder shall be killed in return. Because now the same God upholds killing and its opposite, do you claim that there are two Gods, opposed to one another?

Eutr.: Does the same God give a command to kill, and then not to kill?

Ad.: The very same. Moreover, He will be found to have done so not only in this instance, but also in very many instances. For example, He gave laws for sacrifices and whole burnt-offerings to be made to Him, and then for them not to be made. Let Megethius answer this: is He who commanded Isaac to be slaughtered and Who required sacrifices to be made one God, while He who forbad killing and the offering of sacrifices, another God?

1.10

Meg.: The God of the Jews and the Demiurge are one and the same, but *our* God is not His son.

Ad.: What proof do you offer that Christ is not the son of the Demiurge?

Meg.: Christ destroyed the works of the Demiurge, and I will prove that He destroyed them.

Ad.: Show that He destroyed them.

Meg.: The Creator God commanded Moses when he was leaving the land of Egypt. "Be ready; gird your loins; put shoes on your feet; have your staffs in your hands and your knapsacks on you; carry away gold, silver and all the other things from the Egyptians" [cf. Exod. 12:11; 3:22]. But our good Lord, when he was sending His disciples in to the world, said, "Neither shoes on your feet, nor knapsack, not two tunics, nor gold in your belts" [cf. Matt. 10:9]. See how clearly the good Lord is opposed to the teachings of the Creator God!

Ad.: Even if the matter he brought forward were contrary to the precept of the Gospels, it would be shown to emanate from one and the same God. However, I maintain that it is not contrary, but that the circumstances are different: in the one instance, some were sent from Jerusalem by Christ, commissioned to preach peace [cf. Acts 10:36]; in the other certain people were driven out of Egypt in war by their own servants.[147] These

---

147. The reference here is unclear. Pretty, *Adamantius*, 54n64 refers to Gen. 9:25–26, but that seems unlikely.

It is more likely that the author refers to the Israelites' exodus from Egypt. Robert D. Sider points out that the difficult Latin text probably means that pillaging the Egyptians was a kind of act of war, but it was justified because the Egyptians had mistreated their Hebrew servants (personal correspondence, August 5, 2011). I think the most likely interpretation is that Adamantius's

servants, since they had chosen war, had necessarily to be destroyed by war; even the Gospel recognizes the right of retaliation and the slaying of evil men. Thus it says, "The lord of that evil servant will come on a day when he knows not, and in an hour when he is not expecting, and will cut him in two and will assign him a place among the unbelieving" [cf Luke 12:46]. Hence it is right to wage a just war against those who go to war unjustly. In the same way it was right that those who preached peace should preach it without arms. Moreover, Isaiah the prophet said, "How pleasant are the feet of those who preach peace!" [Isa. 52:7]. There had also been a time designated in the prophet when arms would have to be broken up. He said, "A law shall come out of Sion, and a word of the Lord from Jerusalem, and He shall judge between nations, and convict many people, and they shall break up their swords for ploughs, and their spears for sickles; and nation shall never take sword against nation, and they shall never again learn to make war" [Isa. 2:3–4].

Eutr.: This is not a discrepancy, since it has been shown that even Christ retaliated against evil men, when He said that the evil slave was to be separated [cf. Matt. 25:28–30].

1.11

Meg.: The prophet of the God of creation, when war came upon the people, went up to the top of the mountain and stretched out his hands to God so that he might destroy many in the battle [cf. Exod. 17:8ff.]. Yet our Lord, because He is good, stretched out *His* hands, not to destroy, but to save men. So where is the similarity? One, by stretching out his hands, destroys, the Other saves.

Ad.: It may, perhaps, be necessary to make close examination of the stretching out of the hands of both Moses and Christ. If there be a resemblance, all should be well; if however, there be no resemblance, this must be demonstrated, for Moses, by stretching out his hands, saved the people faithful to God, but destroyed their opponents, and Christ's action did the same. If indeed Christ's outstretched hands had saved everybody— believers and unbelievers; murderers and adulterers—then you would seem to have made a point, but if those who believed in Him were saved,

---

gnostic opponent Megethius has just said that the creator God's sanctioning of the pillaging of the Egyptians contradicts Jesus's teaching. Adamantius rejects the charge by arguing that (1) since the Egyptians had mistreated the Hebrews (a kind of act of war), therefore pillaging the Egyptians (also a kind of act of war) was justified ("it is right to wage a just war against those who go to war unjustly"); and (2) Luke 12:46 shows that God rightly punishes evildoers at the final judgment. But Adamantius insists that the circumstances between the Hebrews leaving Egypt and the time of Christians are different. The apostles were sent out from Jerusalem preaching peace without arms. Then he quotes the messianic prophecy from Isa. 2:3–4 about beating swords into ploughshares. It is unlikely therefore that Adamantius means that Christians should wage "just war."

while those who disbelieved perished (like Amalek), where is the contradiction? Christ stretched out His hands, and afterwards the temple and city of the unbelievers were destroyed, while the people were scattered and perished. So the stretching out of the hands of both Moses and Christ has the same effect—Moses's action becoming a prefiguration of Christ's. Both saved the believers, and both destroyed the unbelievers.

1.12

Meg.: The Lord brought to view in the Law says, "You shall love him who loves you and you shall hate your enemy" [cf. Lev. 19:18]. But *our* Lord, because He is good, says "Love your enemies, and pray for those who persecute you" [cf. Matt. 5:44].

Ad.: If it lay only in the Gospel, you spoke well; but suppose we find it commanded in the Law also? . . . But take the case of Moses, when the people advanced to kill him, and the glory of the Lord overshadowed him. It was Divine justice that those who had advanced should be destroyed like enemies. According to the record, the destruction fell, and the people would have perished had not Moses, ignoring their hatred, besought God on behalf of his enemies. He said, "Aaron, take the censer in your hand, and go to meet the destroyer" [cf. Num.16:46]. Hearing this, Aaron met him, and the destruction abated. Again, there was David, who, when he was pursued by Saul, found an opportunity to destroy him, but did not do so. On the contrary, he offered a prayer for him [cf. 1 Sam. 24 and 26]. Once more there is Jeremiah, who, though he was cast into a pit by his enemies, bore no malice, but actually prayed for them [cf. Jer. 38:6ff]. Now, it says in the Gospel writing, "Depart from Me, you who work lawlessness into the outer darkness! there will be weeping and gnashing of teeth" [Matt. 7:23], so you see that the Gospel agrees with the Law.

1.13

Meg.: The prophet of the God of Creation, so that he might destroy more of the enemy, stopped the sun from setting until he should finish slaying those who were fighting against the people [cf. Josh. 10:12–14]. But the Lord, because He is good, says, "Let not the sun go down upon your anger" [cf. Eph. 4:26].

Ad.: So far as those are concerned who wrongly brought war upon their masters, it has been shown that their destruction was just; consequently Christ also gave orders that one who had lived a bad life should be cast "into the outer darkness! There it will be weeping and gnashing of teeth" [cf. Matt. 8:12; 13:42, 50]. With respect to the statement, "Let not the sun go down upon your anger," this teaching is found operating in the Law, not only in command but also action. There it stands written that

Aaron and his sister Miriam angered Moses by their deeds [cf. Num. 12:1ff.]. The result was that Miriam contracted leprosy through the anger. When asked by Aaron, Moses did not await the setting of the sun, but immediately besought God to heal his sister. You see, then, that provision was made even in the Law to prevent the sun from going down upon anger. . . . It has become clear, then, that the teaching "Let not the sun go down upon your anger," is found in both the Law and the Gospel. . . .

1.14

Meg.: I will prove that the Gospel is opposed to the Law. . . .

Ad.: If you claim that He is not good because he has instituted divergent laws, observe that even Christ does not differ from Him in any way, for like the Creator God, He enacts divergent laws. He says, "Love your enemies," and afterwards tells the enemies of the Faith, "Depart into the outer darkness!" [cf. Matt. 5:44]. How could He love the enemies whom He sent into the outer darkness? What sort of love would this be?

1.15

Meg.: It says in the Law, "Eye for eye and tooth for tooth," but the Lord, because He is good, says in the Gospel, "If anyone should slap you on the cheek, turn the other one to him" [cf. Matt. 5:39].

Ad.: The legal requirements have been laid down in a most satisfactory and convenient manner. The first injunction, found in the Law, was a precautionary measure, given to prevent someone from attempting to deprive another of his eye, and to put a stop to the spirit of revenge. Now, as in the Law, fear prevented strife, so also in the Gospel, in the same manner, retaliation and resentment, brought about by a paltry blow, were checked by means of submission and persuasion. So both fear and gentleness are fitted to bring peace. One man stopped fighting because of fear, while the other clung to peace through gentleness. If you claim that reprisals have been spoken of only in the Law, take note of what the Gospel says, "The measure you give will be the measure you get" [cf. Matt. 7:2]. Perceive still more clearly from the same Gospel how every one is rewarded in the measure that he has done this—as it were, *eye for eye*—when He says, "Whoever shall deny Me before men—him I also will deny before My Father in heaven" [cf. Matt. 10:33]. It has been shown, then, through both the Law and the Gospel, that what each one has done to his brother—this he will receive back.

1.16

Ad.: It has been clearly demonstrated, then, that the prophets and Christ own one and the same God. If He is one, and, as you say, He is known to be good only, without being just, why does He command Judas, wickedly unjust, to be justly cast into the sea? I think that the punishment of sinners belongs to the nature of a just God, and not to One who is "good" after your fashion. A God who is merely good, and not at the same time just, ought not to punish anyone, but if He *does* punish, He will at the same time be just.[148]

4.9

Dr.: All that the Law forbade, I call evil, such as murder, adultery, theft, immorality, and whatever the Law forbids.

Ad.: All these things are of an "accidental" nature. Murder is not substance, nor again is adultery, nor are any of the similar evils. . . . Man is held to be "evil" because of what he does, and not because of what he is in substance. We said that a human is called evil from things that are "accidental" to his or her substance.

4.10

Dr.: You claimed that evil is in conduct, and not in substance; but evil proves to have existence through substance. Please, then, explain more fully how evil is in conduct, and not in substance.

Ad.: I affirm that at first there is nothing naturally bad; but that it is called bad according to the manner of its use. The term "adultery" refers to the union of man and woman. Now, if a man should have union with his wife for the procreation of children and the continuation of the race, such union is good; but if he forsakes and insults the lawful marriage by illicit union, he is guilty of a great wrong. The union itself is the same, but the circumstances of its use are not. The same thing can be said of unchastity in general. Sexual union, then, considered apart from the circumstances of its use, is not evil. It becomes evil only when a wrongful use is apparent. I point out that it is the same with murder. Should a man desire the death of someone caught in adultery, demanding the punishment of his shameless act, he does no crime.[149] Yet, if a man kills someone who has done nothing illegal, on a mere pretext, or for the purpose of removing his household property—that is, his money or goods—he does wrong. The act is the same in both cases, but the circumstances of the act make the difference.[150]

---

148. Pretty, *Adamantius*, 49–59.

149. This whole paragraph by Adamantius, including the statement on the legitimacy of desiring the death of an adulterer, is a quotation from Methodius's *On Free Will*, probably written between 270 and 290. (On Methodius, see Patterson, *Methodius*, and the literature cited there.) For a French translation of the Slavonic, see A. Vaillant, "Le de autexusio de Méthode D'Olympe, Version slave," in *Patrologia Orientalis* 22 (Paris: Firmin-Didot et Cie, 1930), 790.

150. Pretty, *Adamantius*, 137–39.

Arnobius of Sicca (d.c. AD 330)

We know very little about Arnobius, except that he wrote *Against the Pagans* sometime before 311 and probably during the reign of Emperor Diocletian (284–304). A recent scholarly study of Arnobius concludes that the book was written between late 302 and mid-305—during the Diocletian persecution (Simmons, *Arnobius*, 47–93). Arnobius probably lived and taught rhetoric for a time in the town of Sicca, which was about one hundred miles southwest of Carthage in North Africa. He became a Christian later in life, and as a layperson and recent convert without a full understanding of his new faith, he wrote this vigorous attack on pagan Roman religion.

One of his central concerns was to refute the charges that more recent natural disasters and military attacks on the Roman Empire happened because the rise of Christian faith caused a loss of belief in the traditional Roman gods. His response is to declare that if everyone would follow Jesus's teaching against killing others, there would be universal peace.

Helgeland suggests that "Arnobius's distaste for war is part of a theological criticism of Roman religion" ("Roman Army," 757). That is not inaccurate, but it is also clear that in one of his most explicit condemnations of war, his stated reason is that Christ taught that his followers should not shed human blood.

See further McCracken, *Arnobius*, 1:2–18; and Simmons, *Arnobius*.

Against the Pagans

1.6. Although you allege that those wars which you speak of were excited through hatred of our religion, it would not be difficult to prove, that after the name of Christ was heard in the world, not only were they not increased, but they were even in great measure diminished by the restraining of furious passions. For since we, a numerous band of people as we are, have learned from His teaching and His laws that evil ought not to be repaid with evil, that it is better to suffer wrong than to inflict it, that we should rather shed our own blood than stain our hands and our conscience with that of another, an ungrateful world is now for a long period enjoying a benefit from Christ, inasmuch as by His means the rage of savage ferocity has been softened, and has begun to withhold hostile hands from the blood of a fellow-creature. But if all without exception, who feel that they are people not in form of body but in power of reason, would lend an ear for a little to His salutary and peaceful rules, and would not, in the pride and arrogance of enlightenment, trust to their own senses rather than to His admonitions, the whole world, having turned the use of iron into more peaceful occupations, would now be living in the most placid tranquility, and would unite in blessed harmony, maintaining the sanctity of treaties.[151]

1.63. Do you then see that if He [Christ] had determined that none should do Him violence, He should have striven to the utmost to repel His enemies, even by directing His power against them? Could not He, then, who had restored their sight to the blind, make His enemies blind if it were necessary? Was it hard or troublesome for Him to make them weak, who had given strength to the feeble? Did He who bade the lame walk, not know how to take from them all power to move their limbs, by making their sinews stiff? Would it have been difficult for Him who drew the dead from their tombs to inflict death on whom He would? But because reason required that those things which had been foreordained should be done here also in the world itself, and in no other fashion than was done, He, with gentleness passing understanding and belief, regarding as but childish trifles the wrongs which people did Him, submitted to the violence of savage and most hardened soldiers. Nor did He think it worthwhile to take account of what their daring had aimed at, if He only showed to His disciples what they were in duty bound to look for from Him. . . . The Master and Teacher directed His laws and ordinances that they might find their end in fitting duties. Did he not destroy the arrogance of the proud? Did He not quench the fires of lust? Did He not check the craving of greed? Did He not wrest the weapons from their hands, and rend from them all the sources of every form of corruption? To conclude, was He not Himself gentle, peaceful, easily approached, friendly when addressed? Did He not, grieving at people's miseries, pitying with His unexampled benevolence all in any wise afflicted with troubles and bodily ills, bring them back and restore them to soundness?

1.64. What, then, constrains you, what excites you to revile, to rail at, to hate implacably Him whom no one can accuse of any crime?[152]

2.1. Did He ever, in claiming for Himself power as king, fill the whole world with bands of the fiercest soldiers; and of nations at peace from the beginning, did He destroy and put an end to some, and compel others to submit to His yoke and serve Him?[153]

3.26. My opponent says that Mars has power over wars; whether to quell those which are raging, or to revive them when interrupted, and kindle them in time of peace. For if he calms the madness of war, why do wars rage every

151. *ANF* 6:415.
152. *ANF* 6:431–32.
153. *ANF* 6:433.

day? But if he is their author, we shall then say that the god, to satisfy his own inclination, involves the whole world in strife; sows the seeds of discord and variance between far-distant peoples; gathers so many thousand men from different quarters, and speedily heaps up the field with dead bodies; makes the streams flow with blood, sweeps away the most firmly-founded empires, lays cities in the dust, robs the free of their liberty, and makes them slaves; rejoices in civil strife, in the bloody death of brothers who die in conflict, and, in fine, in the dire, murderous contest of children with their fathers.[154]

4.36. For why, indeed, have our writings deserved to be given to the flames? Our meetings to be cruelly broken up, in which prayer is made to the Supreme God, peace and pardon are asked for all in authority, for soldiers, rulers, friends, enemies, for those still in life, and those freed from the bondage of the flesh; in which all that is said is such as to make people humane, gentle, modest, virtuous, chaste, generous in dealing with their substance, and inseparably united by the bonds of kinship with all on whom the sun shines.

4.37. But this is the state of the case, that as you are exceedingly strong in war and in military power, you think you excel in knowledge of the truth also, and are pious before the gods, whose might you have been the first to besmirch with foul imaginings.[155]

Lactantius (c. AD 250–325)

Born in North Africa and a student of Arnobius of Sicca, Lactantius became one of the most famous teachers of rhetoric of his time. In fact, so widespread was his fame that he was appointed (sometime in the late 290s) to an official chair of Latin rhetoric in Nicomedia, Bithynia (now Turkey), where the emperor Diocletian lived.

Sometime in his later middle years, Lactantius became a Christian, probably before he moved to the city of the imperial court. Unfortunately for him, Diocletian decided in the winter of 302–3 to launch a massive, widespread persecution of Christians. At Diocletian's court, Lactantius encountered two prominent anti-Christian pagans, an unnamed philosopher and Hierocles,

154. *ANF* 6:471.
155. *ANF* 6:488. In the last sentence of chap. 36, I follow the textual reading and translation of McCracken, *Arnobius*, 1:407.

governor of Bithynia, who played a prominent role in persuading Diocletian to launch the Great Persecution.

Lactantius responded with the famous book *The Divine Institutes*—a brilliant defense of Christianity written in superb Ciceronian Latin. It was the first systematic presentation of the Christian faith in Latin. He probably started writing the book about 304 and completed the first draft before the persecution ended in 311. (The two dedications to Constantine were probably written later.) Drawing on his vast knowledge of classical thought, he argued that Christian faith and practice are vastly superior to their Greco-Roman counterparts.

Most of the relevant texts for our purposes come from books 5 and 7 of *The Divine Institutes*. In book 5, where he deals with justice, Lactantius argues that in order to do justice, one must have two things: true piety (pietas), which comes only through knowing the true God in Jesus Christ; and fairness (aequitas), which involves living Christ's teaching on loving one's neighbor. Consequently, when he speaks of justice and the just person, he is referring to the behavior of Christians.

A few years after the Great Persecution started, Lactantius moved to the West where he soon enjoyed the protection of Constantine (one of the contenders for the emperorship). By about 310, he was the tutor of Constantine's son Crispus. In 313, Constantine and Licinius agreed to end the persecution of Christians and proclaim religious freedom for all. Lactantius continued to write in the dramatically new situation until his death in about 325.

Lactantius is especially interesting because we have the Divine Institutes written in the midst of the Great Persecution as well as later writings penned in a time of freedom for Christians. In *The Divine Institutes*, all killing is wrong: infanticide, gladiatorial contests, capital punishment, and war. He explicitly argues that a just person dare not be engaged in military service (6.20).

After the persecution, however, Lactantius's views seem to change somewhat. In *On the Death of the Persecutors* (c. AD 313–15), he celebrates the military victories of Constantine and his allies (chaps. 44–48). In *On the Anger of God* (c. AD 316), he defends rather than condemns capital punishment (chap. 17). And in *Epitome of the Divine Institutes* (his abbreviation of the earlier work) written about 320 or later, he condemns infanticide, suicide, capital punishment, and attendance at gladiatorial contests, but omits warfare (chaps. 63–64). (It is interesting that here in the *Epitome* he seems to condemn the imposition of capital punishment although in *On Anger* he defends it.)

For further introductory material, see Bowen and Garnsey, *Lactantius*, 1–54; and McDonald, *Lactantius*, 3–14.

The Divine Institutes

1.18. What is the case of our own countrymen? Are they more wise? For they despise valor in an athlete, because it produces no injury; but in the case of a king, because it occasions widely spread disasters, they so admire it as to imagine that brave and warlike generals are admitted to the assembly of the gods, and that there is no other way to immortality than to lead armies, to lay waste the territory of others, to destroy cities, to overthrow towns, to put to death or enslave free peoples. Truly the greater number of people they have cast down, plundered, and slain, so much the more noble and distinguished do they think themselves; and ensnared by the show of empty glory, they give to their crimes the name of virtue. I would rather that they should make to themselves gods from the slaughter of wild beasts, than approve of an immorality so stained with blood. If anyone has slain a single person, he is regarded as contaminated and wicked, nor do they think it lawful for him to be admitted to this earthly abode of the gods. But he who has slaughtered countless thousands of people, has inundated plains with blood, and infected rivers, is not only admitted into the temple, but even into heaven. In Ennius, Africanus thus speaks: "If it is permitted anyone to ascend to the regions of the gods above, the greatest gate of heaven is open to me alone." Because, in truth, he extinguished and destroyed a great part of the human race. Oh how great the darkness in which you were involved, O Africanus, or rather O poet, in that you imagined the ascent to heaven to be open to people through slaughters and bloodshed! And Cicero also assented to this delusion. . . . I indeed cannot determine whether I should think it a subject of grief or of ridicule, when I see grave and learned, and, as they appear to themselves, wise people, involved in such miserable waves of errors. If this is the virtue which renders us immortal, I for my part should prefer to die, rather than to be the cause of destruction to as many as possible. If immortality can be obtained in no other way than by bloodshed, what will be the result if all shall agree to live in harmony? And this may undoubtedly be realized, if people would cast aside their pernicious and impious madness, and live in innocence and justice. Shall no one, then, be worthy of heaven? Shall virtue perish, because it will not be permitted that people rage against other people?[156]

3.18. For no one saw that which is most true, that the soul is both created and does not die, because they were ignorant why that came to pass, or what was the nature of humanity. Many therefore of them, because they suspected that the soul is immortal, laid violent hands upon themselves, as though they were about to depart to heaven. Thus it was with Cleanthes and Chrysippus, with Zeno, and Empedocles. . . . Nothing can be more wicked than this. For if a homicide is guilty because he is a destroyer of a person, he who puts himself to death is under the same guilt, because he puts to death a person. Yea, that crime may be considered to be greater, the punishment of which belongs to God alone. For as we did not come into this life of our own accord; so, on the

156. *ANF* 7:31.

other hand, we can only withdraw from this habitation of the body which has
been appointed for us to keep, by the command of Him who placed us in this
body that we may inhabit it, until He orders us to depart from it; and if any
violence is offered to us, we must endure it with equanimity, since the death
of an innocent person cannot be unavenged, and since we have a great Judge
who alone always has the power of taking vengeance in His hands.

All these philosophers, therefore, were homicides; and Cato himself, the
chief of Roman wisdom, who, before he put himself to death, is said to have
read through the treatise of Plato which he wrote on the immortality of the
soul, and was led by the authority of the philosopher to the commission of
this great crime.[157]

5.8. But if God only were worshiped, there would not be dissensions and wars,
since people would know that they are the children of one God; and, therefore, among those who were connected by the sacred and inviolable bond of
divine relationship, there would be no plotting, inasmuch as they would know
what kind of punishments God prepared for the destroyers of souls, who sees
through secret crimes, and even the very thoughts themselves. There would be
no fraud or plundering. . . . There would not, therefore, as I have said, be these
evils on the earth, if there were by common consent a general observance of
the law of God, if those things were done by all which our people alone perform. How happy and how golden would be the condition of human affairs,
if throughout the world gentleness, and piety, and peace, and innocence, and
equity, and temperance and faith, took up their abode! In short, there would
be no need of so many and varying laws to rule people, since the law of God
alone would be sufficient for perfect innocence; nor would there be any need
of prisons, or the swords of rulers or the terror of punishments, since the
wholesomeness of the divine precepts infused into the breasts of people would
of itself instruct them to works of justice.[158]

In the following chapter, Lactantius argues that the pagans, who call the
Christians impious and unjust, are really the impious people. Almost as an aside,
he notes that Christians "keep away from human blood" (see further 6.20).

5.9. For they call impious those who are certainly pious and who keep away
from human blood.[159]

5.10. What then, or where, or of what character is piety? Truly it is among those
who are ignorant of wars, who maintain concord with all, who are friendly

157. *ANF* 7:88–89.
158. *ANF* 7:143.
159. McDonald, *Lactantius*, 349.

even to their enemies, who love all people as brothers and sisters, who know how to restrain their anger, and to soothe every passion of the mind with calm government. . . . Nor is it difficult to show why the worshipers of the gods cannot be good and just. For how shall they abstain from the shedding of blood who worship bloodthirsty deities, Mars and Bellona?[160]

> In chapter 17, Lactantius presents the ideas of a Roman writer, Carneades, who argued that it would often be foolish to act justly. Among his examples were: (1) a shipwrecked man who comes upon a weaker person floating on a plank; if he acts unjustly and pushes the other person off the plank, he survives, but if he acts justly, he dies; (2) a soldier fleeing from a conquering army who comes upon a wounded soldier fleeing on a horse; if he acts unjustly and pushes the other person off the horse, he escapes, but if he acts justly, he perishes.

5.18. The just man, he [Carneades] says, if he does not take away from the wounded man his horse, and from the shipwrecked man his plank, in order that he may preserve his own life, is foolish. First of all, I deny that it can in anyway happen that a person who is truly just should be in circumstances of this kind; for the just person is neither at enmity with any human being, nor desires anything at all which is the property of another. For why should he take a voyage or what should he seek from another land, when his own is sufficient for him? Or why should he carry on war, and mix himself with the passions of others, when his mind is engaged in perpetual peace with others? Will the person be delighted with foreign merchandise or with human blood, who does not know how to seek gain, who is satisfied with his mode of living, and considers it unlawful not only himself to commit murder, but to be present with those who do it, and to behold it![161] But, I omit these things, since it is possible that a person may be compelled even against his will to undergo these things.[162] . . . He is not a fool who does not even spare himself to prevent injury to another, which is an evil. And this, indeed, reason and the truth itself dictate. For we see that in all animals, because they are destitute of wisdom, nature is the provider of supplies for itself. Therefore they injure others that they may profit themselves, for they do not understand that committing an injury is evil. But a person who has the knowledge of good and evil, abstains

---

160. *ANF* 7:146.

161. In this sentence, I follow the translation of Bowen and Garnsey, *Lactantius*, 314–15, and McDonald, *Lactantius*, 370.

162. Helgeland says that in this passage Lactantius "admitted that there was a necessity for some killing, recognizing that a man may be compelled against his will to go to war" ("Roman Army," 758). Lactantius's words do not explicitly exclude Helgeland's interpretation, but they certainly do not demand it. What "these things" refers to is not entirely clear, and elsewhere Lactantius says explicitly that the just person cannot engage in warfare or homicide of any kind (7.20).

from committing an injury even to his own damage, which an animal without reason is unable to do; and on this account innocence is reckoned among the chief virtues of persons. Now by these things it appears that he is the wisest person who prefers to perish rather than to commit an injury, that he may preserve that sense of duty by which he is distinguished from the dumb creation. . . . A wise person never gives himself to the pursuit of gain, because he despises these earthly advantages: nor does he allow anyone to be deceived, because it is the duty of a good person to correct the errors of people, and to bring them back to the right way.[163]

5.23. Since, therefore, he does injury to none, nor desires the property of others, and does not even defend his own if it is taken from him by violence, since he knows how even to bear with moderation an injury inflicted upon him, because he is endued with virtue; it is necessary that the just man should be subject to the unjust, and that the wise should be insulted by the foolish, that the one may sin because he is unjust and the other may have virtue in himself because he is just.[164]

> The following passage illustrates Lactantius's frequent use of military imagery to describe the Christian life.

6.4. In the whole of this life, because God has provided an adversary for us, that we might be able to acquire virtue, present gratification must be laid aside, lest the enemy should overpower us. We must be on the watch, must post guards, must undertake military expeditions, must shed our blood to the uttermost; in short, we must patiently submit to all things which are unpleasant and grievous, and the more readily because God our commander has appointed for us eternal rewards for our labors. And since in this earthly warfare people expend so much labor to acquire for themselves those things which may perish in the same manner as that in which they were acquired, assuredly no labor ought to be refused by us, by which that is gained which can in no way be lost.[165]

6.5. It is a virtue to restrain anger, to control desire, to curb lust; for this is to flee from vice. For almost all things which are done unjustly and dishonestly arise from these affections. For if the force of this emotion which is called anger be blunted, all the evil contentions of people will be lulled to rest; no one will plot, no one will rush forth to injure another. Also, if desire be restrained, no one will use violence by land or by sea, no one will lead an army to carry off and lay waste the property of others.[166]

---

163. *ANF* 7:153–54. This item is in chap. 17 in Bowen and Garnsey, *Lactantius*, 314–15.
164. *ANF* 7:160. This is in chap. 22 in Bowen and Garnsey, *Lactantius*, 327.
165. *ANF* 7:166.
166. *ANF* 7:167.

6.6. For how can a person be just who injures, who hates, who despoils, who puts to death? And they who strive to be serviceable to their country do all these things: for they are ignorant of what this being serviceable is, who think nothing useful, nothing advantageous, but that which can be held by the hand. . . .

Whoever, then, has gained for his country these goods—as they themselves call them—that is, who by the overthrow of cities and the destruction of nations has filled the treasury with money, has taken lands and enriched his countrymen—he is extolled with praises to heaven: in him there is said to be the greatest and perfect virtue. And this is the error not only of the people who are ignorant, but also of philosophers.[167]

> Below Lactantius mocks Rome's idea of a just war. He argues that faith in the true God is the only source of justice. Lacking that, the Romans defined self-interest as justice. The *fetiales* mentioned here were priestly ambassadors who declared war.

6.9. For why is it that there are different and various laws amongst all people, but that each nation has enacted for itself that which it deemed useful for its own affairs? But how greatly utility differs from justice the Roman people themselves teach, who, by proclaiming war through the fetiales, and by inflicting injuries according to legal forms, by always desiring and carrying off the property of others, have gained for themselves the possession of the whole world.[168]

6.18. Cicero says in those same books respecting Offices: "But if anyone should wish to unravel this indistinct conception of his soul, let him at once teach himself that he is a good person who profits those whom he can, and injures no one unless provoked by injury."

Oh how he marred a simple and true sentence by the addition of a few words! For what need was there of adding these words, "unless provoked by injury"? that he might append vice as a most disgraceful tail to a good person, and might represent him as without patience, which is the greatest of all the virtues. He said that a good person would inflict injuries if he were provoked: now he must necessarily lose the name of a good person from this very circumstance, if he shall inflict injury. For it is not less the part of a bad person to return an injury than to inflict it. For from what source do contests, from what source do fightings and contentions, arise among people, except that impatience opposed to injustice often excites great tempests? But if you meet injustice with patience, than which virtue nothing can be found more

167. *ANF* 7:169.
168. *ANF* 7:171.

true, nothing more worthy of a person, it will immediately be extinguished, as though you should pour water upon a fire.[169]

Below Lactantius condemns the popular Roman gladiatorial contests where gladiators fought and killed each other.

6.20. I ask now whether they can be just and pious, who, when they see men placed under the stroke of death, and entreating mercy, not only suffer them to be put to death, but also demand it, and give cruel and inhuman votes for their death, not being satisfied with wounds nor contented with bloodshed. Moreover, they order them, even though wounded and prostrate, to be attacked again, and their corpses to be torn apart with blows, that no one may delude them by a pretended death. They are even angry with the combatants, unless one of the two is quickly slain; and as though they thirsted for human blood, they hate delays. They demand that other and fresh combatants should be given to them, that they may satisfy their eyes as soon as possible. Being imbued with this practice, they have lost their humanity. Therefore they do not spare even the innocent, but practice upon all that which they have learned in the slaughter of the wicked. It is not therefore appropriate that those who strive to keep to the path of justice should be companions and sharers in this public homicide. For when God forbids us to kill, He not only prohibits us from open violence, which is not even allowed by the public laws, but He warns us against the commission of those things which are esteemed lawful among people. Thus it will be neither lawful for a just man to engage in military service,[170] since his military service is justice itself, nor to accuse anyone of a capital charge, because it makes no difference whether you put a person to death by word, or rather by the sword, since it is the act of putting to death itself which is prohibited. Therefore, with regard to this precept of God, there ought to be no exception at all but that it is always unlawful to put to death a person, whom God willed to be a sacred creature.

Therefore let no one imagine that even this is allowed, to strangle newly-born children, which is the greatest impiety; for God breathes into their souls for life, and not for death. But people, that there may be no crime with which they may not pollute their hands, deprive souls as yet innocent and simple of the light which they themselves have not given. Can anyone, indeed, expect that they would abstain from the blood of others who do not abstain even from their own? They are without any controversy wicked and unjust. What

---

169. *ANF* 7:184.

170. The Latin is "Ita neque militare iusto licebit, cuius militia est ipsa iustitia" (Ingremeau, *Lactance*, 318). Ingremeau's translation: "Le juste ne pourra pas servir dans l'armée" (319). Bowen and Garnsey translate this as "A just man may not be a soldier" (*Lactantius*, 375). McDonald translates this as "Neither will it be permitted a just man . . . to enter military service" (*Lactantius*, 452). Swift: "to serve in the army" (*Military*, 62).

are they whom a false piety compels to expose their children? Can they be considered innocent who expose their own offspring as a prey to dogs, and as far as it depends upon themselves, kill them in a more cruel manner than if they had strangled them? Who can doubt that he is impious who gives occasion for the pity of others? For, although that which he has wished should befall the child—namely, that it should be brought up—he has certainly consigned his own offspring either to servitude or to the brothel. But who does not understand, who is ignorant what things may happen, or are accustomed to happen [to infants who are abandoned], in the case of each sex, even through error? For this is shown by the example of Oedipus alone, confused with twofold guilt. It is therefore as wicked to expose as it is to kill. But truly parricides complain of the scantiness of their means, and allege that they have not enough for bringing up more children; as though, in truth, their means were in the power of those who possess them, or God did not daily make the rich poor, and the poor rich. Wherefore, if anyone on account of poverty shall be unable to bring up children, it is better to abstain from intercourse with one's wife than with wicked hands to mar the work of God.

If, then, it is not permitted to commit homicide in any way, it is not allowed us to be present at all, lest any bloodshed should stain the conscience, since that blood is offered for the gratification of the people.[171]

On the Death of the Persecutors

This chapter reports that Christians (this text does not say whether they are soldiers) at the court of Emperor Diocletian made the sign of the cross ("the immortal sign") while pagans examined entrails to predict the future. When repeated attempts failed, the Christians were blamed. Diocletian then commanded everyone in the palace and soldiers elsewhere to sacrifice to the Roman gods. Harnack (*Militia Christi*, 94–95) speculates that "for a long time" Christian soldiers had been participating in pagan sacrificial rites while making the sign of the cross. But this text does not say whether the Christians at the court included Christian soldiers, nor does it provide any evidence about how widespread or longstanding was the practice of Christians making the sign of the cross at pagan rituals.

10. Diocletian, as being of a timorous disposition, was a searcher into futurity, and during his abode in the East he began to slay victims, that from their livers he might obtain a prognostic of events; and while he sacrificed, some

---

171. *ANF* 7:186–87. In light of this explicit statement that all killing is wrong and that military service is forbidden, it is very puzzling when Helgeland says that in this treatise, Lactantius "gives no indication what his attitude to Christian enlistment might be" ("Roman Army," 758)!

attendants of his, who were Christians, stood by and they put the *immortal sign* on their foreheads. At this the demons were chased away and the holy rites interrupted. The soothsayers trembled, unable to investigate the wonted marks on the entrails of the victims. They frequently repeated the sacrifices, as if the former had been unpropitious; but the victims, slain from time to time, afforded no tokens for divination. At length Tages, the chief of the soothsayers, either from guess or from his own observation, said, "There are profane persons here, who obstruct the rites." Then Diocletian, in furious passion, ordered not only all who were assisting at the holy ceremonies, but also all who resided within the palace, to sacrifice, and, in case of their refusal, to be scourged. And further, by letters to the commanding officers, he enjoined that all soldiers should be forced to the like impiety, under pain of being dismissed from the service.[172]

> Below, Emperor Diocletian's son-in-law Galerius tries to persuade Diocletian to order massive persecution of Christians, but Diocletian initially refuses. It is clear that there are Christians in the army.

11. Diocletian and Galerius held councils together. . . . The old man long opposed the fury of Galerius, and showed how pernicious it would be to raise disturbances throughout the world and to shed so much blood; that the Christians were accustomed with eagerness to meet death; and that it would be enough for him to exclude persons of that religion from the court and the army.[173]

44. And now a civil war broke out between Constantine and Maxentius. . . . Constantine, with steady courage and a mind prepared for every event, led his whole forces to the neighborhood of Rome, and encamped them opposite to the Milvian bridge. . . .

Constantine was directed in a dream to cause the heavenly sign to be delineated on the shields of his soldiers, and so to proceed to battle. He did as he had been commanded, and he marked on their shields the letter X, with a perpendicular line drawn through it and turned round thus at the top being the cipher of Christ. Having this sign, his troops stood to arms. The enemies advanced. . . .

This destructive war being ended, Constantine was acknowledged as emperor, with great rejoicings, by the senate and people of Rome.[174]

> In the east, two powerful generals, Licinius and Daia, were battling to be emperor. Licinius was in partnership with Constantine.

172. *ANF* 7:305.
173. Ibid.
174. *ANF* 7:318.

46. The armies thus approaching each other, seemed on the eve of a battle. Then Daia made this vow to Jupiter, that if he obtained victory he would extinguish and utterly efface the name of the Christians. And on the following night an angel of the Lord seemed to stand before Licinius while he was asleep, admonishing him to arise immediately, and with his whole army to put up a prayer to the Supreme God, and assuring him that by so doing he should obtain victory. Licinius fancied that, hearing this, he arose, and that his monitor, who was nigh him, directed how he should pray, and in what words. Awaking from sleep, he sent for one of his secretaries, and dictated these words exactly as he had heard them:—

"Supreme God, we beseech Thee; Holy God, we beseech Thee; unto Thee we commend all right; unto Thee we commend our safety; unto Thee we commend our empire. By Thee we live, by Thee we are victorious and happy. Supreme Holy God, hear our prayers; to Thee we stretch forth our arms. Hear, Holy Supreme God."

Many copies were made of these words, and distributed amongst the principal commanders, who were to teach them to the soldiers under their charge. At this all men took fresh courage, in the confidence that victory had been announced to them from heaven. . . . Accounts came that Daia was in motion; the soldiers of Licinius armed themselves, and advanced. A barren and open plain, called Campus Serenus, lay between the two armies. They were now in sight of one another. The soldiers of Licinius placed their shields on the ground, took off their helmets, and, following the example of their leaders, stretched forth their hands towards heaven. Then the emperor uttered the prayer, and they all repeated it after him. The host, doomed to speedy destruction, heard the murmur of the prayers of their adversaries.

47. So the two armies drew nigh; the trumpets gave the signal; the military ensigns advanced; the troops of Licinius charged. But the enemies, panic-struck, could neither draw their swords nor yet throw their javelins. . . . The Supreme God did so place their necks under the sword of their foes, that they seemed to have entered the field, not as combatants, but as men devoted to death.

48. Not many days after the victory, Licinius, having received part of the soldiers of Daia into his service, and properly distributed them, transported his army into Bithynia, and having made his entry into Nicomedia, he returned thanks to God, through whose aid he had overcome; and on the ides of June, while he and Constantine were consuls for the third time, he commanded the following edict for the restoration of the Church, directed to the president of the province, to be promulgated:—

"When we, Constantine and Licinius, emperors, had an interview at Milan, and conferred together with respect to the good and security of the commonweal, it seemed to us that, amongst those things that are profitable to humanity in general, the reverence paid to the Divinity merited our first and chief attention, and that it was proper that the Christians and all others should have liberty to follow that mode of religion which to each of them appeared best; so that God, who is seated in heaven, might be benign and propitious to us, and to everyone under our government."[175]

52. Let us therefore with exultation celebrate the triumphs of God, and oftentimes with praises make mention of His victory.[176]

On the Anger of God

17. But if God carries on the care of the world, it follows that He cares for the life of people, and takes notice of the acts of individuals, and He earnestly desires that they should be wise and good. This is the will of God, this the divine law; and he who follows and observes this is beloved by God. It is necessary that He should be moved with anger against the person who has broken or despised this eternal and divine law. If, he [Epicurus] says, God does harm to anyone, therefore he is not good. They are deceived [Lactantius replies] by no slight error who defame all censure, whether human or divine, with the name of bitterness and malice, thinking that he ought to be called injurious who visits the injurious with punishment. But if this is so, it follows that we have injurious laws, which enact punishment for offenders, and injurious judges who inflict capital punishments on those convicted of crime. But if the law is just which awards the transgressor his due, and if the judge is called upright and good when he punishes crimes,—for he guards the safety of good people who punishes the evil,—it follows that God, when He opposes the evil, is not injurious; but he himself is injurious who either injures an innocent person, or spares an injurious person that he may injure many. . . .

For it cannot fail to be, that he who is just and good is displeased with things which are bad, and that he who is displeased with evil is moved when he sees it practiced. Therefore we arise to take vengeance, not because we have been injured, but that discipline may be preserved, morals may be corrected, and licentiousness be suppressed. This is just anger; and as it is necessary in a person for the correction of wickedness, so manifestly is it necessary in God, from whom an example comes to people. For as we ought to restrain those who are subject to our power, so also ought God to restrain the offences of all.[177]

175. *ANF* 7:319–20.
176. *ANF* 7:322.
177. *ANF* 7:273–74.

Epitome of the Divine Institutes

63. What is so dreadful, what so foul, as the slaughter of a person? Therefore our life is protected by the most severe laws; therefore wars are detestable. Yet custom finds how a person may commit homicide without war, and without laws; and this is a pleasure to him, that he has avenged guilt. But if to be present at homicide implies a consciousness of guilt, and the spectator is involved in the same guilt as the perpetrator, then in these slaughters of gladiators, he who is a spectator is no less sprinkled with blood than he who sheds it; nor can he be free from the guilt of bloodshed who wished it to be poured out, or appear not to have slain, who both favored the slayer and asked a reward for him.

64. It is an old precept not to kill, which ought not to be taken in this light, as though we are commanded to abstain only from homicide, which is punished even by public laws. But by the intervention of this command, it will not be permitted us to apply peril of death by word, nor to put to death or expose an infant, nor to condemn one's self by a voluntary death.[178]

178. *ANF* 7:249.

Part 2

Church Orders
and Synods

Apostolic Tradition (probably early third century)

Almost everything about the *Apostolic Tradition* is disputed. It was originally written in Greek, but only translations have survived. The exact wording of the original is uncertain. Some modern scholars believe the document was written by one church leader in the late second or early third century in Rome; many others think the document is a collection from several sources. Even the geographical location of the original document is debated, with a few scholars (e.g., Cerrato, *Hippolytus*) arguing for a setting in Asia Minor.

The vast majority of modern scholars, however, have concluded that the *Apostolic Tradition* comes from the early third century, is the earliest of several church orders, and that the later ones use considerable material from this document. All of them outline rites and customs of the Christian church. Dix and Chadwick think the *Apostolic Tradition* reflects the actual practice of the Roman church about 180 and argue that the text comes from the first half of the third century (*Apostolic Tradition*, xxxvii–xxxviii, xl). The latest edition of *The Oxford Dictionary of the Christian Church* essentially agrees with this conclusion (92). After massive scholarly examination, Allen Brent concludes that at least two authors lie behind the *Apostolic Tradition* but that the document clearly should be dated in the early third century in Rome (Brent, *Hippolytus*, 195, 303, and elsewhere).

For our purposes, the authorship does not matter as much as the date. What is important is that the bulk of modern scholarship believes the document comes from the later second or first part of the third century and reflects the rites and practices of the church at that time—and perhaps even earlier. The authors of the authoritative scholarly edition used here believe the core document (which includes all of the material used here) goes back to the mid-second century (Bradshaw et al., *Apostolic Tradition*, 14). And the document itself claims to be outlining "the tradition which has remained up to now" (chap. 1). Since (a) the original Greek of the *Apostolic Tradition* was translated into Arabic, Ethiopic, Latin, and a Coptic dialect and (b) several later church orders incorporated substantial material from it, we can conclude at the very least that this document enjoyed fairly wide circulation and influence. It is probably one of the best sources for the thinking of many Christians in the later second and earlier third centuries on the topics it discusses.

The first part of the *Apostolic Tradition* deals with the installation of bishops, presbyters, deacons, and other church leaders, including widows and virgins. Chapter 15 begins a new section on how to deal with "those who are newcomers to hearing the word." Church leaders must carefully examine why these people "are seeking the faith" and want to be taught the Christian faith. These church leaders are to examine the "activities they [catechumens] must give up" and the church must reject as catechumens those engaged in unacceptable activities—pimps, prostitutes, gladiators, anyone who has "the power of the sword"—unless they agree to abandon those unacceptable activities. Normally, those who are accepted for teaching continue as catechumens for three years (chaps. 17–19), after which they receive baptism (chaps. 20–21). See Bradshaw et al., *Apostolic Tradition*, 96–135.

Chapter 16 clearly states that a soldier must be told not to kill and that if he is given that command, he must refuse. Nor may he take the military oath. Anyone "who has the power of the sword" must abandon that role or be rejected for teaching. In these cases, the document is providing directions for those who wish to become catechumens. But it also states that those who are already catechumens or believers (i.e., baptized) who volunteer for the army must be rejected "because they distance themselves from God." In light of this, it is puzzling that Helgeland, Daly, and Burns say that this document has "no reference whatever to a prohibition of killing in combat" (Helgeland et al., *Military*, 36). This seems to be a direct contradiction of the text. The document shows that people who are in the army or serve as public officials responsible for capital punishment are being attracted to Christianity and are coming to the church for instruction. Interestingly, the situation described here seems somewhat similar to that implied by Tertullian, who acknowledges that there are Christians in the military (*On Idolatry* 19; *The Crown* 1).

The church's response to those who are ordinary soldiers is not that they must leave the army immediately. Rather, they must not take the military oath (which involved idolatry as Tertullian points out) and they dare not kill. It is important to remember that at this time, many Roman soldiers served in settings where they never fought any battles (Watson, *Roman Soldier*, 31; see also below, p. 191). If they are commanded to kill, they must disobey the order if they want to be catechumens. This document does not tell us whether such people managed to stay in the army and keep the prohibitions (no killing, no military oath). Since soldiers normally took the military oath three times per year, remaining in the army would, at least, have been very complicated. Higher officials who have "the power of the sword" (i.e., have the authority to order or carry out capital punishment) must abandon that position if they want to become catechumens. Equally clearly, no one who is already a catechumen or already baptized dare choose to enlist in the army. This text shows, in the words of Louis Swift, that the church "was still throwing all its weight behind efforts to discourage Christians from having anything to do with the service" (*Military Service*, 47).

Not surprisingly, later church orders (that date after the time of Emperor Constantine) used substantial parts of the *Apostolic Tradition* but modify the statements about public office and the military (see the next section).

The original Greek of the *Apostolic Tradition* is not extant, but we have the text of several translations including the Sahidic (a Coptic dialect), Arabic, Ethiopic, and Latin. Bradshaw et al., *Apostolic Tradition*, gives an English translation of these four translations in parallel columns. I use the English translation of the Arabic and note the two places where there is a noteworthy variation from the other translations.

For further information, see especially Bradshaw et al., *Apostolic Tradition*; Baldovin, "Apostolic Tradition"; Brent, *Hippolytus*; Cerrato, *Hippolytus*; Dix and Chadwick, *Apostolic Tradition*; and the vast literature cited in these places.

15. Concerning new people who are beginning to enter the faith and the activities they must give up. Those who are newcomers to hearing the Word, let them be taken first to the teachers before all the people come in, and be asked the reason why they are seeking the faith.

16. Concerning the activities and what should be the correct behavior after [certain] activities and the activities that should be followed by those who come for catechesis. . . . One who is a gladiator or teaches gladiators or swordsmanship or military skills or weapons training should stop or be excluded. . . . A soldier in the sovereign's army[1] should not kill, or if he is ordered to kill, he should refuse.[2] If he stops, so be it; otherwise he should be excluded.

Concerning those who wear red[3] or believers who become soldiers or astrologers or magicians or such like: let them be excluded. One who has the power of the sword or the head of a city and wears red, let him stop or be excluded. A catechumen or a believer, if they want to be soldiers, let them be excluded because they distance themselves from God.[4]

---

1. The Sahidic translation says "a soldier who has authority."
2. The Sahidic translation includes a prohibition against swearing (i.e., the military oath). That may imply (although it is not stated explicitly) that idolatry was part of the problem. What is stated explicitly is that Christians are not to kill. The text does not support Helgeland's implication that idolatry was the main problem ("Roman Army," 752).
3. I.e., the purple worn by prominent public officials.
4. Bradshaw et al., *Apostolic Tradition*, 82, 88, 90.

Three Later Church Orders

There are other church orders that incorporate considerable material from the *Apostolic Tradition*: book 8 of *Apostolic Constitutions*; *The Canons of Hippolytus*; and *The Testament of the Lord* (*Testamentum Domini*).

Apostolic Constitutions was probably written in Syria about 375–380. *The Canons of Hippolytus* (extant only in Arabic) is largely a derivative of the *Apostolic Tradition* and was not written by Hippolytus. The original Greek (now lost) may date from as early as 336–340 and have been compiled in Egypt, but the present text is no older than the late fourth century. *The Testament of the Lord* (which also includes a great deal of the *Apostolic Tradition*) is generally thought to come from the fifth century.

All three of these church orders are from at least a few decades after Constantine had ended the persecution of Christians (two of them are from six or more decades after). And the first two significantly modify the *Apostolic Tradition*'s clear condemnation of killing and prohibition of catechumens or baptized Christians joining the military.

The *Apostolic Constitutions* says nothing about soldiers not killing or Christians not joining the military. Soldiers are simply told to do no injustice and to be content with their wages.

Interestingly *The Canons of Hippolytus*, even though being written, at the earliest, two decades after Constantine effectively embraced Christianity, still maintain much of the rigor of the *Apostolic Tradition*. Neither the soldier nor the official with authority for capital punishment dare kill. The document first says that a Christian dare not become a soldier and then provides an exception: if "compelled by a chief bearing a sword." Shedding someone's blood is a sin that precludes immediate partaking of the Eucharist, but a person guilty of that sin may receive the Eucharist after extensive repentance.

The latest document, *The Testament of the Lord*, still insists that a soldier or an official dare not kill, and anyone who wishes to be baptized must abandon the military. A catechumen or baptized person dare not become a soldier.

It is hardly surprising that church orders that date from a time when large numbers of Christians served in the armies of Christian emperors modify somewhat the strict prohibitions of the *Apostolic Tradition*. What is more surprising, perhaps, is that even at this date they retain so much of the earlier teaching.

For an introduction to these documents, see Bradshaw et al., *Apostolic Tradition*, 9–11; Bradshaw, *Canons of Hippolytus*. The volume by Bradshaw et al. conveniently prints translations of all three of these church orders (along with the major versions of the *Apostolic Tradition*) in parallel columns that enable easy comparison.

Apostolic Constitutions

8. Let a soldier who comes be taught to do no injustice or to extort money, but to be content with his given wages. Let the one who objects be rejected.[5]

The Canons of Hippolytus

13. Whoever has received the authority to kill, or else a soldier, they are not to kill in any case, even if they receive the order to kill. They are not to pronounce a bad word. Those who have received an honor are not to wear wreaths on their heads. Whosoever is raised to the authority of a prefect or the magistracy and does not put on the righteousness of the gospel is to be excluded from the flock and the bishop is not to pray with him.

14. A Christian must not become a soldier, unless he is compelled by a chief bearing the sword. He is not to burden himself with the sin of blood. But if he has shed blood, he is not to partake of the mysteries, unless he is purified by a punishment, tears, and wailing. He is not to come forward deceitfully but in the fear of God.[6]

The Testament of the Lord

If anyone be a soldier or in authority, let him be taught not to oppress or to kill or to rob, or to be angry or to rage and afflict anyone. But let those rations suffice him that are given to him. But if they wish to be baptized in the Lord, let them cease from military service or from the [post of] authority, and if not let them not be received.

Let a catechumen or a believer of the people, if he desires to be a soldier, either cease from his intention, or if not let him be rejected. For he has despised God by his thought, and leaving the things of the Spirit, he has perfected himself in the flesh, and has treated the faith with contempt.[7]

5. Bradshaw et al., *Apostolic Tradition*, 89.
6. Ibid., 91.
7. Ibid.

Synod of Arles (AD 314)

By AD 313, Emperor Constantine controlled the Western part of the Roman Empire. The famous decision at Milan (313) granted religious freedom and restored property confiscated from Christians.

In 314, Constantine summoned Christian leaders from across the West to the Synod of Arles. For our purposes, canon 3 is of special interest: "Concerning those who throw down their arms in time of peace, we have decreed that they should be kept from communion" (Helgeland, "Roman Army," 805).

Scholars have puzzled over and debated the meaning of this canon. Would it not be in a time of war rather than in a time of peace that soldiers would want to escape the army? Some have speculated that the text should be corrected to read "in time of war." But scholars as diverse as Harnack (*Militia Christi*, 100) and Bainton (*War and Peace*, 81) insist that there is no valid reason for modifying the text.

I find it at least plausible, indeed probably illuminating, to read this canon in light of the Church Orders. The *Apostolic Tradition* (early third century), as mentioned earlier, was translated into a number of languages and then incorporated with modifications into several later church orders. It is fair to assume, therefore, that the *Apostolic Tradition* enjoyed fairly wide circulation and influence.

The *Apostolic Tradition* says explicitly that soldiers who come for catechetical training must be told that they dare not kill. It does not say they must leave the army if they want to receive teaching for baptism, but they dare not kill. If that view was widespread in the third-century church, then canon 3 of the Synod of Arles stands in significant continuity with this earlier teaching. The *Apostolic Tradition* also said that soldiers who became catechumens dare not take the (pagan) military oath, but Constantine would probably have made changes that would have removed that problem.

Constantine obviously did not want to lose Christian soldiers. On my interpretation, the Synod of Arles supports his interests in a way that is in substantial (although not complete) continuity with the earlier tradition. During peacetime, when a soldier would not normally need to kill, Christian soldiers not only may, but must stay in the army. But canon 3 does not forbid leaving the army in time of war, when killing would be unavoidable.

The interesting case of St. Martin of Tours fits this understanding. During the reign of Constantine, Martin became a Christian while in the army and he remained there for two years, wearing his sword. But when an actual battle became imminent, he refused to use his sword—although he volunteered to stand unarmed in the army's front line (Dörries, *Constantine*, 112–13).

If my interpretation is correct, canon 3, then, illustrates how the church sought both to adapt to the dramatically new situation under Emperor Constantine and also to maintain continuity with earlier teaching.

3. Concerning those who throw down their arms in time of peace, we have decreed that they should be kept from communion.

Part 3

Miscellaneous Items

The Infancy Gospel of Thomas

In addition to the books eventually accepted by the church as part of the canonical New Testament, a large number of apocryphal gospels and other writings appeared in the early centuries. Some attributed fantastic miracles to the boy Jesus; many promoted various heresies, such as gnosticism. Mainstream Christian writers like Irenaeus (*Against Heresies* 1.20; *ANF* 1:345) and Eusebius (*Ecclesiastical History* 3.25) denounced them, and they never received widespread acceptance in the church. But the fact that they were written and circulated in Christian circles indicates that some Christians found them interesting and considered the actions of Jesus depicted in the writings acceptable.

Of special interest here is *The Infancy Gospel of Thomas*. In this writing, the boy Jesus curses someone who bumps into him (the person dies); blinds children; and curses a teacher who strikes him (the teacher dies). How, if at all, is this material relevant to our understanding of the early church's thinking on killing?

Thanks to a recent dissertation, we now know a little more about *The Infancy Gospel of Thomas*, although much remains unclear (Chartrand-Burke, "Infancy Gospel"). It has nothing to do with the *Gospel of Thomas* (Helgeland, "Roman Army," 763–64, seems to equate the two). A majority of scholars think it appeared in the second century (Chartrand-Burke, "Infancy Gospel," 267). Our earliest manuscript is from the eleventh century (279), but there are a number of versions in many languages (247). By the end of the fourth century, it was known in Cyprus, Egypt, and Italy. The numerous translations suggest, according to Hennecke-Schneemelcher (*Apocrypha*, 1:392) that it "enjoyed a wide popularity."

It is difficult to know whether the description of Jesus in this narrative should modify in any way the picture we have developed from the other writers we have surveyed. Robert Daly says (without citing evidence!), "The evidence from the popular apocryphal gospels, for example, suggests that violence was not at all strange to the thinking and feeling of the popular masses of early Christians" (Daly, "Military Force," 180). In fact, an extensive search in the vast apocryphal Christian literature dating before the time of Constantine has located no other statements or narratives of this kind. *The Gospel of Pseudo-Matthew* also contains three stories of the young Jesus doing violence (chaps. 28–29, 38; *ANF* 8:378, 381), but *The Gospel of Pseudo-Matthew* was completed in the eighth or ninth century (Elliott, *Apocryphal NT*, 86). An Arabic infancy gospel from the fifth or sixth century also contains some of these violent stories (ibid., 100–104). Helgeland also suggests, on the basis of very weak evidence,[1] that this narrative reflects the thinking of significant numbers of Christians, although he acknowledges that the Fathers "would have disagreed unanimously with the view of Jesus's youth communicated in the Apocryphal Gospels and its implications for Christian ethics" ("Roman Army," 764).

Several things are clear. Prominent Christians denounced apocryphal writings like *The Infancy Gospel of Thomas*. It never appears on any extant list of early Christian writings considered authoritative by any group of Christians. And it depicts Jesus doing things that contradict the picture of Jesus that we see in both the canonical Gospels and the writings of the Fathers.

3:2. Seeing what had happened, Jesus said to him: "Your fruit (shall be) without root and your shoot dried up like a branch carried out by a strong wind."
   3. And immediately that child withered.

4:1. While he was going from there with his father Joseph, someone running bumped into his shoulder. And Jesus said to him: "Cursed be your ruling faculty." And immediately he died. And at once the people, seeing that he died, cried out and said: "Whence was this boy begotten that his word becomes deed?"

5:1. And Joseph said to Jesus: "Why do you say such things? They suffer and hate us." And the boy said to Joseph: "Wise words are known to you. Whence your words came, you are not ignorant; they were told of a five-year-old. And, unable to raise those (children) up, these people too shall receive their punishment." And immediately the ones accusing him were blinded.
   2. And Joseph took hold of his ear and pulled hard.

13:1. And Joseph seeing his way of thinking and sensible mind was unwilling for him to be unacquainted with letters. And he handed him over to another teacher. And the teacher, writing for him the alphabet, would say: "Say, alpha."

1. Helgeland cites Eusebius (*Ecclesiastical History* 3.25), but in the passage Helgeland cites, Eusebius is referring to the *Gospel of Thomas*, not *The Infancy Gospel of Thomas*. Helgeland also refers to Irenaeus (*Against Heresies* 1.20), but in the passage he refers to, Irenaeus says nothing about Jesus doing any violence (although he does refer to Jesus's exchange with his teacher about the letters of the alphabet).

2. But the boy said: "First you say to me what is the beta and I will tell you what is the alpha." And the teacher became irritated and hit him. And Jesus cursed him and the teacher fell and died.[2]

Paul of Samosata

Roland Bainton has described Paul of Samosata as "the first Christian bishop to hold the post of civil magistrate and to employ a bodyguard" ("Early Church," 194). What does his story tell us about Christians and the military?

Paul was the bishop of Antioch (now Antakya in southern Turkey near Syria) from about AD 261 to 268. Our primary source is Eusebius (*Ecclesiastical History* 7.29–30), who tells us Paul had a bodyguard, preferred to be called a ducenarius, and was deposed as a heretic.

A ducenarius was a highly paid official in a Roman province who would likely have had a bodyguard. Paul probably did hold this government position (Norris, "Paul," 60–65), although some scholars disagree (Millar, "Paul," 13).

Paul was accused of christological heresy (denying the deity of Christ) at two synods: first in 264 and then in the winter of 268/269 when he was deposed.

Eusebius quotes at length from the letter sent, among other places, to the bishops of Rome and Alexandria. This letter says that Paul was deposed for his heresy, but it also describes at length his unusual, immoral behavior: he acquired vast wealth through extortion and bribery; he was proud and haughty; and he traveled with "blooming and beautiful" women. The end of the letter indicates that they would have acted against Paul because of his unethical behavior had not his theological heresy already excluded him from the body of Christ.

It is surely the case that the behavior of Paul of Samosata is not representative of accepted Christian thought and behavior in the late third century. For more information on Paul of Samosata, see Millar, "Paul"; Norris, "Paul"; and the bibliography in the *Oxford Dictionary*, 1250–52.

7.30. After other things they describe as follows the manner of life which he led: "Whereas he has departed from the rule of faith, and has turned aside after base and spurious teachings, it is not necessary,—since he is without,—that we should pass judgment upon his practices: as for instance in that although formerly destitute and poor, and having received no wealth from his fathers, nor made anything by trade or business, he now possesses abundant wealth

2. Chartrand-Burke, "Infancy Gospel," 226–28, 239; there is also a translation of several versions in *ANF* 8:395–404.

through his iniquities and sacrilegious acts, and through those things which he extorts from the brethren, depriving the injured of their rights and promising to assist them for reward, yet deceiving them, and plundering those who in their trouble are ready to give that they may obtain reconciliation with their oppressors, 'supposing that gain is godliness';—or in that he is haughty, and is puffed up, and assumes worldly dignities, preferring to be called ducenarius rather than bishop; and struts in the market-places, reading letters and reciting them as he walks in public, attended by a body-guard, with a multitude preceding and following him, so that the faith is envied and hated on account of his pride and haughtiness of heart;—or in that he practices chicanery in ecclesiastical assemblies, contrives to glorify himself, and deceive with appearances, and astonish the minds of the simple, preparing for himself a tribunal and lofty throne,—not like a disciple of Christ,—and possessing a 'secretum,'—like the rulers of the world,—and so calling it. . . . To anticipate something of what we shall presently write, he is unwilling to acknowledge that the Son of God has come down from heaven. And this is not a mere assertion, but it is abundantly proved from the records which we have sent you; and not least where he says 'Jesus Christ is from below.' . . . For how can he reprove or admonish another not to be too familiar with women,—lest he fall, as it is written,—when he has himself sent one away already, and now has two with him, blooming and beautiful, and takes them with him wherever he goes, and at the same time lives in luxury and surfeiting? Because of these things all mourn and lament by themselves; but they so fear his tyranny and power, that they dare not accuse him. But as we have said, while one might call the man to account for this conduct, if he held the Catholic doctrine and was numbered with us, since he has scorned the mystery and struts about in the abominable heresy of Artemas (for why should we not mention his father?), we think it unnecessary to demand of him an explanation of these things."

Afterwards, at the close of the epistle, they add these words:

"Therefore we have been compelled to excommunicate him, since he sets himself against God, and refuses to obey; and to appoint in his place another bishop for the Catholic Church."[3]

The Acts of Xanthippe and Polyxena

This writing is a religious novel full of incredulous tales of numerous miracles (*ANF* 9:205–17).

3. *NPNF*[2] 1:314–15.

In chapter 25, the endangered Christian virgin, Polyxena, is rescued from an evil man. But he gathers eight thousand men to recover her by force. The tiny band of Christians to whom she has been entrusted for protection use the sign of the cross to defend themselves and kill five thousand of the attackers! In chapter 39, in another incident, Polyxena is protected by Christian men "prepared for the battle." They vanquish all evil attackers.

The date of the composition of this novel is not certain. Our earliest manuscripts date from the eleventh century and the first known reference to it seems to be in the tenth century. But three modern scholars date the novel in the third century.[4] If it does come from the third century, then this novel is evidence that at least a few Christians in the third century thought it proper to kill five thousand pagans using the cross.

It is far more likely, however, that the novel originates well after the time of Constantine. Max Bonnet has argued that the text contains nine words that only acquired the meaning they have in this novel in the fourth and fifth centuries.[5] In the most thorough study of the date and composition of this novel that has been undertaken thus far, Eric Junod argued (in a lengthy article published in 1989) that this novel appeared in the late fourth or early fifth century.[6] In her 2003 doctoral dissertation on this novel, Jill Gorman accepts Junod's dating (Gorman, "Xanthippe and Polyxena," 7–12). If indeed this dating of the novel is correct, then this novel has no relevance for our study of pre-Constantinian Christian thought about killing.[7]

4. M. R. James, *Apocrypha Anecdota 1* (Cambridge: Cambridge University Press, 1893), 43–85; E. N. Bennett, "James' Apocrypha Anecdota," *Classical Review* 8 (1894): 101–3; Stevan Davies, *The Revolt of the Widows: The Social World of the Apocryphal Acts* (Carbondale: Southern Illinois University Press, 1980), 10.

5. Max Bonnet, "Sur les Actes de Xanthippe et Polyxene," *Classical Review* 8 (1894): 336–41.

6. Eric Junod, "Vie et conduite des saintes femmes Xanthippe, Polyxene, et Rebecca," in *Oecumenica et Patristica: Festschrift für Wilhelm Schneemelcher zum 75*, ed. Damaskinos Papandreou et al. (Stuttgart: Kohlamner, 1989), 83–105, esp. 90–91.

7. Helgeland, who argues that popular apocryphal Christian writings affirming killing circulated rather widely in the third century ("Roman Army," 763–64), does not even mention this novel.

Part 4

Other Evidence of Christian Soldiers before Constantine

"The Thundering Legion"

In approximately AD 173, Marcus Aurelius Antoninus, Roman emperor from 161–80, and his troops experienced a "miraculous" victory over a vastly larger army of German invaders near the Danube River.[1] Much about the incident is uncertain. But credible Christian and Roman sources tell of an unexpected rainstorm and thunderstorm that saved the exhausted, thirst-stricken, vastly outnumbered Roman army. We have even discovered a column erected in Rome sometime after AD 176 that depicts the miraculous weather. An unexpected victory, aided by astonishing weather, must have occurred.

Whereas the Roman sources attribute the miracle to pagan gods, almost all Christian writers say the miracle was the result of the prayers of Christian soldiers in the emperor's army. Two of these Christian sources (Tertullian and Apollinarius) are dated within twenty-five years of the event. Both these Christian authors say the Christian soldiers were from the Twelfth Legion (*Legio XII Fulminata*), normally stationed at Melitene in Armenia (central Turkey today). We know from epigraphical evidence that parts of this legion were in the Danube region at this time. We also know that there were Christians in the area of the legion's home base. Also significant is the fact that Apollinarius was bishop at this time, in an area not too far from the legion's home base. It is highly likely, therefore, that there were Christian soldiers present at this important battle. That means that by the latter part of the second century there were some Christians serving in the Roman army. Whether they were already Christians when they enlisted, or became Christians while in the army, these sources do not tell us.

Nor do any of the sources related to this event tell us how many Christians were in the army. Writing at approximately the same time as this event (c. 177–80), the Roman writer Celsus attacks Christians for refusing to serve in the army and thus endangering the empire. If Celsus is right, there were probably very few Christians in the Roman army at this time. But we simply lack the hard evidence to say how many there were. What is clear, beyond any

1. See Helgeland's careful, extensive analysis of the relevant data in "Roman Army," 766–73.

reasonable doubt, is that there were some Christians in the Roman army by the late second century.[2]

We need to be cautious, however, about concluding that the presence of Christians in the Twelfth Legion "created no apparent scandal" (Swift, *Military*, 37) and means that Christians had no objections to military service. Even less warranted is speculation that the Christian fathers and even grandfathers of the Christian soldiers in the Twelfth Legion in AD 173 were soldiers (Johnson, *Peace*, 46). It is true that, in the two passages where Tertullian refers to Christians in the army (Tertullian's central concern is to argue that good emperors did not persecute Christians, who in fact are good citizens), he does not condemn Christians engaged in bloody battle. But elsewhere, Tertullian vigorously condemns all killing and opposes Christian enlistment in the army. That there were Christians in the army is clear, but the incident of "The Thundering Legion" does not warrant the conclusion that by the late second century, large numbers of Christians considered killing, or service in the army, legitimate.

Tertullian's Statements

Our earliest extant references to this incident by Christian writers come from Tertullian. In his first writing (*Apology*, AD 197), he argues that only bad Roman emperors, not those who were wise and just, have persecuted Christians. As evidence, Tertullian cites the letters of Marcus Aurelius, which, Tertullian claims, witness to a miraculous rain caused by the prayers of Christian soldiers. But, as Lightfoot points out (*Apostolic Fathers*, 473), the language Tertullian uses "shows that he had no direct or personal knowledge" of any letter the emperor wrote about this incident. In *To Scapula* (probably his last writing, about September 212 [Barnes, *Tertullian*, 55]), where he also pleads for acceptance of Christians, he again alludes briefly to the surprising rain provided by the prayers of Christian soldiers.

Apology 5. Such as these have always been our persecutors,—men unjust, impious, base, of whom even you yourselves have no good to say. . . . But among so many princes from that time to the present day, with anything of divine and human wisdom in them, point out a single persecutor of the Christian name. So far from that, we, on the contrary, bring before you one who was their protector, as you will see by examining the letters of Marcus Aurelius, that most grave of emperors, in which he bears his testimony that Germanic drought was removed by the rains obtained through the prayers of

2. For this whole incident, in addition to Helgeland, "Roman Army," 766–73, see Harnack, "Quellen," 835–82; Swift, *Military*, 38–40; Harnack, *Militia Christi*, 74; and the extensive discussion in Lightfoot, *Apostolic Fathers*, 465–76.

the Christians who chanced to be fighting under him. And as he did not by public law remove from Christians their legal disabilities, yet in another way he put them openly aside, even adding a sentence of condemnation, and that of greater severity, against their accusers.[3]

To Scapula 4. Marcus Aurelius also, in his expedition to Germany, by the prayers his Christian soldiers offered to God, got rain in that well-known thirst.[4]

Eusebius's Account

In book 5 of *Ecclesiastical History*, probably first published before AD 300, Eusebius includes a fairly extensive version of this incident. Especially interesting is his comment that both pagan and Christian writers have talked about the story. Eusebius quotes Tertullian, understanding Tertullian to say that he knew of letters from the emperor Marcus Aurelius to the Roman senate describing the incident. Especially interesting is Eusebius's reference to Apollinarius, a Christian bishop who lived in the latter part of the second century. He wrote a *Defense of the Faith* (now lost) that was probably presented to Marcus Aurelius about AD 172 (*Oxford Dictionary*, 86). Eusebius does not say where in Apollinarius he found the reference to the incident, but some assume it was in his now lost *Defense of the Faith* (Lightfoot, *Apostolic Fathers*, 476). Obviously, if that is correct, then the date of that work must be after the date of the "miraculous" event. We do know that *Defense of the Faith* was presented to Emperor Marcus Aurelius, who died in 180. Therefore, Apollinarius's comments (if they were in *Defense of the Faith*) provide a very early witness that dates only several years, at the latest, after these events. In fact, Harnack ("Regenwunder," 837) dates *Defense of the Faith* to 174 or 175, and therefore concludes that Apollinarius's reference was written only one to two years after the event. Very soon after the event, then, it is highly probable that Christians believed that Christian soldiers had produced this great military victory. It is interesting that the only specific information that Eusebius attributes to Apollinarius is wrong. Apollinarius allegedly said that the Twelfth Legion received the name "Thundering" because of this event (see Lightfoot [*Apostolic Fathers*, 475] who suggests that Eusebius misunderstood Apollinarius at this point), but we know from inscriptions that the legion received its name at least one hundred years earlier (Helgeland, "Roman Army," 771).

Ecclesiastical History 5.5. It is reported that Marcus Aurelius Caesar, brother of Antoninus, being about to engage in battle with the Germans and Sarmatians,

3. *ANF* 3:22.
4. *ANF* 3:107.

was in great trouble on account of his army suffering from thirst. But the soldiers of the so-called Melitene legion, through the faith which has given strength from that time to the present, when they were drawn up before the enemy, kneeled on the ground, as is our custom in prayer, and engaged in supplications to God. This was indeed a strange sight to the enemy, but it is reported that a stranger thing immediately followed. The lightning drove the enemy to flight and destruction, but a shower refreshed the army of those who had called on God, all of whom had been on the point of perishing with thirst.

This story is related by non-Christian writers who have been pleased to treat the times referred to, and it has also been recorded by our own people. By those historians who were strangers to the faith, the marvel is mentioned, but it is not acknowledged as an answer to our prayers. But by our own people, as friends of the truth, the occurrence is related in a simple and artless manner. Among these is Apollinarius, who says that from that time the legion through whose prayers the wonder took place received from the emperor a title appropriate to the event, being called in the language of the Romans the Thundering Legion. Tertullian is a trustworthy witness of these things. In *Apology for the Faith*, which he addressed to the Roman Senate, and which work we have already mentioned, he confirms the history with greater and stronger proofs. He writes that there are still extant letters of the most intelligent Emperor Marcus in which he testifies that his army, being on the point of perishing with thirst in Germany, was saved by the prayers of the Christians. And he says also that this emperor threatened death to those who brought accusation against us. He adds further:

"What kind of laws are those which impious, unjust, and cruel persons use against us alone? which Vespasian, though he had conquered the Jews, did not regard; which Trajan partially annulled, forbidding Christians to be sought after; which neither Adrian, though inquisitive in all matters, nor he who was called Pius sanctioned." . . .[5]

The Spurious Letter of Marcus Aurelius

Scholars agree that this letter is a forgery dating, at the earliest, from the early fourth century. Adolf Harnack has shown that this forged letter was inspired in part by the so-called "edict of toleration" in 313 (Harnack, "Quellen," 865). Helgeland points out that it is inconceivable that Marcus Aurelius could have sent such a letter, because it contradicts other things he said and did about Christians ("Roman Army," 769; see also Lightfoot, *Apostolic Fathers*, 469–76). So this letter provides no reliable historical information about this incident. Interestingly, at some point, the forgery was added to the end of Justin Martyr's

5. *NPNF*[2] 1:219–20.

> *First Apology.* It is also intriguing that this fourth-century Christian forgery says that preparing weapons and arms is "hateful" to Christians because of "the God they bear about in their conscience."

The Emperor Caesar Marcus Aurelius Antoninus, Germanicus, Parthicus, Sarmaticus, to the People of Rome, and to the sacred Senate greeting: I explained to you my grand design, and what advantages I gained on the confines of Germany, with much labour and suffering, in consequence of the circumstance that I was surrounded by the enemy; I myself being shut up in Carnuntum by seventy-four cohorts, nine miles off. And the enemy being at hand, the scouts pointed out to us, and our general Pompeianus showed us that there was close on us a mass of a mixed multitude of 977,000 men, which indeed we saw; and I was shut up by this vast host, having with me only a battalion composed of the first, tenth, double and marine legions. Having then examined my own position, and my host, with respect to the vast mass of barbarians and of the enemy, I quickly betook myself to prayer to the gods of my country. But being disregarded by them, I summoned those who among us go by the name of Christians. And having made inquiry, I discovered a great number and vast host of them, and raged against them, which was by no means becoming; for afterwards I learned their power. Wherefore they began the battle, not by preparing weapons, nor arms, nor bugles; for such preparation is hateful to them, on account of the God they bear about in their conscience. Therefore it is probable that those whom we suppose to be atheists, have God as their ruling power entrenched in their conscience. For having cast themselves on the ground, they prayed not only for me, but also for the whole army as it stood, that they might be delivered from the present thirst and famine. For during five days we had got no water, because there was none; for we were in the heart of Germany, and in the enemy's territory. And simultaneously with their casting themselves on the ground, and praying to God (a God of whom I am ignorant), water poured from heaven, upon us most refreshingly cool, but upon the enemies of Rome a withering hail. And immediately we recognised the presence of God following on the prayer—a God unconquerable and indestructible. Founding upon this, then, let us pardon such as are Christians, lest they pray for and obtain such a weapon against ourselves. And I counsel that no such person be accused on the ground of his being a Christian. But if any one be found laying to the charge of a Christian that he is a Christian, I desire that it be made manifest that he who is accused as a Christian, and acknowledges that he is one, is accused of nothing else than only this, that he is a Christian; but that he who arraigns him be burned alive. And I further desire, that he who is entrusted with the government of the province shall not compel the Christian, who confesses and certifies such a matter, to retract; neither shall he commit him. And I desire that these things be confirmed by a decree of the Senate. And I command this my edict to be published in the

Forum of Trajan, in order that it may be read. The prefect Vitrasius Pollio will see that it be transmitted to all the provinces round about, and that no one who wishes to make use of or to possess it be hindered from obtaining a copy from the document I now publish.[6]

Dio's Roman History

> Cassius Dio Cocceianus was born about AD 160 into a prominent family in Bithynia (part of present-day Turkey). He came to Rome about 180, occupied several important positions, and became a friend of the emperor. From approximately 200–222, he worked on his most famous publication, *Roman History*. Since he was in Rome for some years less than a decade after the famous rainstorm, his report merits careful attention.
>
> Interestingly, Dio attributes the "miraculous" rain to an Egyptian magician and the god Mercury and says nothing about Christian prayers or Christian soldiers. In the eleventh century, a Christian copyist inserted an interpolation, explaining that Dio probably purposefully ignored the fact that the rain happened because of the prayers of Christian soldiers.

72. So Marcus subdued the Marcomani and the Iazyges after many hard struggles and dangers. A great war against the people called the Quadi also fell to his lot and it was his good fortune to win an unexpected victory, or rather it was vouchsafed him by Heaven. For when the Romans were in peril in the course of the battle, the divine power saved them in a most unexpected manner. The Quadi had surrounded them at a spot favourable for their purpose and the Romans were fighting valiantly with their shields locked together; then the barbarians ceased fighting, expecting to capture them easily as the result of the heat and their thirst. So they posted guards all about and hemmed them in to prevent their getting water anywhere; for the barbarians were far superior in numbers. The Romans, accordingly, were in a terrible plight from fatigue, wounds, the heat of the sun, and thirst, and so could neither fight nor retreat, but were standing in the line and at their several posts, scorched by the heat, when suddenly many clouds gathered and a mighty rain, not without divine interposition, burst upon them. Indeed, there is a story to the effect that Arnuphis, an Egyptian magician, who was a companion of Marcus, had invoked by means of enchantments various deities and in particular Mercury, the god of the air, and by this means attracted the rain.

[This is what Dio says about the matter, but he is apparently in error, whether intentionally or otherwise; and yet I am inclined to believe his error was chiefly intentional. . . . Marcus had a division of soldiers (the Romans call a division

6. *ANF* 1:187.

a legion) from Melitene; and these people are all worshipers of Christ. Now it is stated that in this battle, when Marcus found himself at a loss what to do in the circumstances and feared for his whole army, the prefect approached him and told him that those who are called Christians can accomplish anything whatever by their prayers and that in the army there chanced to be a whole division of this sect. Marcus on hearing this appealed to them to pray to their God; and when they had prayed, their God immediately gave ear and smote the enemy with a thunderbolt and comforted the Romans with a shower of rain. . . .

Dio goes on to say that] when the rain poured down, at first all turned their faces upwards and received the water in their mouths; then some held out their shields and some their helmets to catch it, and they not only took deep draughts themselves but also gave their horses to drink. And when the barbarians now charged upon them, they drank and fought at the same time; and some, becoming wounded, actually gulped down the blood that flowed into their helmets, along with the water. So intent, indeed, were most of them on drinking that they would have suffered severely from the enemy's onset, had not a violent hail-storm and numerous thunderbolts fallen upon the ranks of the foe. Thus in one and the same place one might have beheld water and fire descending from the sky simultaneously; so that while those on the one side were being consumed by fire and dying; and while the fire, on the one hand, did not touch the Romans, but, if it fell anywhere among them, was immediately extinguished, the shower, on the other hand, did the barbarians no good, but, like so much oil, actually fed the flames that were consuming them, and they had to search for water even while being drenched with rain. Some wounded themselves in order to quench the fire with their blood, and others rushed over to the side of the Romans, convinced that they alone had the saving water; in any case Marcus took pity on them. He was now saluted imperator by the soldiers, for the seventh time; and although he was not wont to accept any such honour before the senate voted it, nevertheless this time he took it as a gift from Heaven, and he sent a despatch to the senate.[7]

Historia Augusta

This set of biographies of the emperors comes from the hands of six different authors. Some may have been written as early as 293 and others as late as 324. The biography of Marcus Antoninus has only one sentence on the famous rain, which this author attributes to the prayers of Marcus (Magie, *Historiae Augustae*, 1:xi).[8]

7. Cary, *Dio's Roman History*, 9:27–33.
8. For other references to this incident by Roman historians, see Lightfoot, *Apostolic Fathers*, 472.

24. By his prayers he summoned a thunderbolt from heaven against a war-engine of the enemy, and successfully besought rain for his men when they were suffering from thirst.[9]

Emperor Marcus Aurelius's Column

The final evidence about this rainstorm is a column of the emperor erected soon after AD 176.[10] One scene depicts rain flowing from the hands of the god Jupiter Pluvius. Two scenes before this, there is a depiction of a lightning bolt destroying an enemy siege tower. The emperor is shown on bended knee praying and the column credits the lightning bolt to his prayer (Helgeland, "Roman Army," 769).

A Third-Century Christian
Prayer Hall Near a Military Camp

Recent archaeological work at the site of the Roman Sixth Legion Ferrata's camp at Megiddo (about fifteen kilometers southwest of Nazareth) has discovered a third-century Christian prayer hall very close to the camp. The prayer hall was one room within a larger building (probably owned by the Roman army) where Roman soldiers, perhaps centurions, lived. A mosaic on the floor of the prayer hall has largely survived. Various archaeological evidence suggest a date of about AD 230 for the mosaic.

One inscription on the mosaic shows that a centurion who is a "brother" paid for the mosaic. Another inscription on the mosaic indicates it was a Christian prayer hall with a table to celebrate the Eucharist. We can be certain only of one Christian centurion here, but it is likely that the Christians worshiping in this prayer chapel, in a building owned by the Roman army, and located very close to the legion's camp, included more than one Christian soldier. See Tepper and DiSegni, *Prayer Hall*, 5–54. I include two inscriptions from the floor's mosaic.

"Gaianus, also called Porphyrius, centurion, our brother, has made the pavement at his own expense as an act of liberality. Brutius has carved out the work."

9. Magie, *Historiae Augustae*, 1:193.
10. See Giovanni Becatti, *Colonna di Marco Aurelio* (Milan: Domus, 1957), plates 9–12, and the discussion by Helgeland, "Roman Army," 769.

"The god-loving Akeptous [a woman] has offered the table to God Jesus Christ as a memorial."[11]

Epitaphs

Epitaphs of Christian Soldiers

Inscriptions on the tombstones of Christian soldiers provide solid evidence of Christians in the Roman army. But the number of such epitaphs that are clearly pre-Constantinian and clearly indicate that the soldier was a Christian is very small. In his *Christian Attitudes toward War and Peace* (69), Roland Bainton noted that an earlier scholar, Leclercq, had drawn up a list of 176 such epitaphs, but Bainton pointed out that only six belong unmistakably to the time before Constantine. Helgeland accepted these six from Bainton and added one more (nos. 12, 21, 22, 24, 29, 46, and 47 printed in Leclercq's article, "Militarisme" in Cabrol's *Dictionnaire d'Archéologie Chrétienne* [1933], 2:1107–81 [hereafter cited as *DACh*]). Helgeland also suggested seven other epitaphs printed in the journal *L'année epigraphique* (*AE*) over a number of years (49 [1936]; 144 [1937]; 138 [1938]; 171 [1939]; 43, 246 [1946]; 257 [1950]; Helgeland, "Roman Army," 791).

But there are several problems with both sets. First the six (Bainton) or seven (Helgeland) from Leclercq. Neither Bainton nor Helgeland tell us why they say these inscriptions are pre-Constantinian. The text of 29 has the date of 201. Information provided by Leclercq indicates a pre-Constantinian date for 12 and 21. But I can locate no evidence that shows that 22, 24, 46, and 47 are pre-Constantine. Leclercq, however, dates 47 in the late second century and Hornus (*Lawful*, 119n8) accepts that date and notes that this epitaph comes from the Christian cemetery of Priscilla in Rome; therefore we can count this as evidence of a Christian soldier in the late second century. The text of 12, 21, and 29 all clearly speak of a soldier. Since 21 and 29 are from Christian cemeteries in Rome, we can be fairly sure these two and probably 47 represent pre-Constantine Christian soldiers.[12]

There are similar problems with the seven epitaphs identified by Helgeland and printed in the *L'année epigraphique*. I cannot find any indication of the

---

11. Tepper and DiSegni, *Prayer Hall*, 34, 36.
12. The situation for no. 12, found at Besancon, is less clear. I have found no clear evidence identifying this location as a Christian burial ground, and the text contains no indication that the soldiers were Christians. Hornus, *Lawful*, 121n19 assumes the mother was a Christian.

date for 49, 144, 246, and 257, and 138 clearly has the date of AD 582. That leaves just two. 171 has a clear third-century date (about 246–49), and the imagery on the sarcophagus that bears the inscription suggests this Praetorian soldier was a Christian (Hornus, *Lawful*, 119, 280n9). The notes to 43 suggest this epitaph refers to a third-century Christian soldier. So we have from Helgeland's second list perhaps two more epitaphs of pre-Constantine Christian soldiers.

Hornus provides two more epitaphs of Christian soldiers: one of Aurelius Posidonius, a former soldier buried in the tomb of a Christian family in Thrace,[13] and one of Aurelius Manos, buried in Phrygia in the late third or very early fourth century.[14]

There are three other epitaphs that very likely refer to pre-Constantine Christian soldiers. The epitaph of Marcus Julius Eugenius indicates that he was a Christian soldier during the intense persecution in the East in about 310. He somehow managed to escape and soon became a bishop in Laodicea. William Ramsay also included an epitaph of the Aurelii brothers, which he says refers to Christian soldiers and comes from the mid-third century (likewise Hornus, *Lawful*, 119). This epitaph is from Phrygia, now western Turkey. We also have an epitaph of the Christian Aurelius Gaius, who was probably forced out of the army, after a long military career, in about 303 (Tepper and DiSegni, *Prayer Hall*, 51–52). It is also possible, but not certain, that Prosenes (d. 217) was a Christian soldier.

Hornus (*Lawful*, 121) also identified four inscriptions that he believed were prepared by soldiers for Christian members of their families (12 below is an example).

That means there are perhaps eleven epitaphs that fairly clearly speak of Christian soldiers before the time of Constantine and perhaps four others prepared by soldiers for Christian family members. It is of course quite possible that there were others that have been lost, but speculation in the absence of evidence is inappropriate. All we can say for sure is that we do have a very few epitaphs that prove that there were at least a few Christian soldiers before Constantine.

I have chosen to provide translations of all the seven inscriptions from Leclercq cited by Bainton and Helgeland and the seven from *L'année epigraphique* cited by Helgeland even though most of them do not clearly speak of pre-Constantinian Christian soldiers. The epitaphs of Eugenius, the Aurelii brothers, and Prosenes are also included. I am most grateful to professor Owen Ewald for all these translations.

A new, exhaustive study of this topic would be very useful.

---

13. See Jeanne and Louis Robert, "Bulletin épigraphique," *Revue des études grecques* 75 (1962): 175; Robert, *Noms indigènes*, 364–65n5; Hornus, *Lawful*, 119, 281n10.

14. See Hornus, *Lawful*, 119–20, 281n13; Robert, *Noms indigènes*, 361–65. Robert shows that Manos was an equestrian archer who served in the military of the governor of Phrygia in the last decade of the third century.

Inscriptions from Leclercq's "Militarisme" in DACh

12. Marius Vitalis, spouse of Virginia, legionary centurion, and Marius Nicidianus, her son, quaestor, made this tomb for his mother, carried from far away and interred here, and she has lived thirty-six years while blameless in the sight of her husband, with rare quarreling, and she was content with her husband alone.

21. For Caelius Placidius, who re-enlisted in the army. Placida his daughter and Peculius his freedman made this for the sweetest patron.

22. To the gods and to the shades. Ulpia Emerita set up this inscription for her son Valerius Emeritus, who re-enlisted in the army and who deserved this inscription well.

24. This burial was arranged for Julius Lea, seven days before the Kalends of August (July 26). Antoninus, *beneficiarius*, made this monument in peace for her, who deserved it well.

29. To the gods and to the shades. Cossutius, spouse of Eutyche Aurelia, made this monument for his Roman spouse, dearest and sweetest, with whom he lived twenty-eight years, member of the Second Parthian Severan Legion, in the consulship of Favianus and Mucius (AD 201), 3 days before the Ides of April (April 10th).

46. Five months, twelve days and for Aurelia Barbara . . . who lived twenty-six years, nine months and [?] days . . . Aurelius Barbas, veteran of the army of our Emperors, prefect of the Tenth Cohort [and centurion?], made this tomb for his dearest, who well deserved it.

47. To Publius Marcellus, a Roman knight, veteran of the army of our two Emperors.

Inscriptions from L'année epigraphique

49 [1936]. Here lies Theodora, slave of God, (spouse) of Antiagrucius the centurion.

144 [1937]. In memory of Leontianus the soldier from the unit of the Alecutti.

138 [1938]. Here lies Solomon of great memory, who became count of the Circitorians, great *domesticus* [military staff assistant] and vicar of Thrace, and died in the month of November 7, in the first *indictio* [fifteen-year period], while Flavius Tiberius Mauricius was in his first year as our Emperor [AD 582].

171 [1939]. Aelius Martinus, of the first Praetorian Cohort made this monument both for Statia Moschianes his wife and for Statia Martina, their daughter. Aelius Verinus, who re-enlisted during the reign of the Augusti (Sep. Sev & Caracalla) made this monument for his brother and well-deserving relatives.

43 [1946]. In memory, for Flavius Ursacius from the unit "Fighters in Front" from the school of the Bracati.

246 [1946]. From the shop of the Parapatosi, by the vow of Felix Ilis.

257 [1950]. Marcus Caecilius Caeno paid his vow with a willing spirit to Jupiter Assaecus.

Epitaph of Prosenes

It is not entirely clear that this epitaph refers to a Christian soldier. Prosenes, a prominent official at the imperial court died in AD 217. Prosenes's freedman Ampelius added an inscription on Prosenes's sarcophagus after he (Ampelius) returned from military campaigns. Some have thought that the phrase "welcomed to God" (*receptus ad Deum*) suggests that Prosenes was a Christian (see Marucchi, *Epigraphy*, 225) but that is not a necessary conclusion. Cadoux says the freedman was a Christian (*War*, 236) but nothing in the text says that. See also Cadoux, *Early Church*, 392, 421. Hornus, *Lawful*, 120, also includes this among the epitaphs of Christian soldiers.

Prosenes, welcomed to God on the fifth day before the Nones of April (April 1st), at Saurus in Campania, when Praesens and Extricatus were consuls, the latter for the second time [AD 217]. His freedman Ampelius wrote this inscription as he returned into the City (Rome) from his campaigns.[15]

Epitaph of Aurelius Posidonius

Aurelius Pyrrhus, Taurus, [names missing], his wife, and Aurelia Chryseis, wife of Proclus, prepared this dedication in the cemetery from their own funds for Aurelius Posidonius, the veteran soldier, for the sake of memory. This man's

---

15. Latin text in Cadoux, *War*, 236n4, and Marucchi, *Epigraphy*, 225.

tomb is not to be sold, and please do not inter another. But if someone dares, he will pay 33 denarii to the sacred treasurer and as much again to the city.[16]

Epitaph of Aurelius Manos

Aurelius Niceros the Second prepared the hero-shrine for himself and his wife and his children, and I made my own shrine. Here has lain Aurelius Manos, soldier, cavalryman, archer, and bearer of the dragon-standard on the staff of the most outstanding general Castorius Constans. And whoever else cares for this tomb, you are with God in his view.[17]

Epitaph of the Aurelii Brothers

The Aurelii, Gaius and Menophilus, from the armies, sons of Aurelius Asclas Faustus and Aurelia Domna, daughter of Irenaeus, prepared in common the tomb and the urn buried below it with its enclosure for themselves and their wives Messalina, daughter of Papas, and Basilo, daughter of Euxenus. So no other person may bury or place an alien corpse or urn, only our legitimate children may do so. But if anyone will do the opposite, it will be for him contrary to God, and he will be liable to the Imperial treasury for a long time. A copy of this inscription was filed in the records office.[18]

Epitaph of Marcus Julius Eugenius

During the first decade of the fourth century, Eugenius served in the military in the Roman province of Pisidia (south central Turkey today).[19] Since both he and his father-in-law were senators, Eugenius would have begun his military career as a centurion. It was probably about 310 that Maximin (one of the two Roman emperors in the East)[20] issued an order that everyone in the

16. Georgius Mihailov, ed., *Inscriptiones Graecae in Bulgaria repertae* (Sofia: Academiae Litterarum Bulgaricae, 1961), 3:80 (no. 1007).

17. Robert, *Noms indigènes*, 361.

18. Ramsay, *Phrygia*, 2:717. It is not clear why Ramsay implies that the Aurelii brothers are Christians.

19. There is some debate about his exact role since the key Greek word *strateuō* can mean both serve in the civil service or be a soldier (Helgeland, "Roman Army," 793). But it is probable that he was a soldier. Another extant epigraph that probably also refers to him, after he became a bishop, speaks of his "spiritual belt"—probably an allusion to the military belt he previously wore as a soldier (Calder, "Bishop," 49).

20. In theory, at this time, a tetrarchy (two Augusti and two Caesars) ruled the Roman Empire, but there was much confusion and many competing claims.

army must sacrifice to the Roman gods and not be allowed to leave the army. Eugenius suffered severe persecution, but somehow managed to get out of the army and soon became a bishop in Laodicea where he served the church for twenty-five years. Clearly his former military career did not prevent him from being chosen as a bishop. Perhaps the torture he received for his refusal to offer pagan sacrifices made a difference. (See further Calder, "Bishop," 42–59; and Helgeland, "Roman Army," 792–93.)

Marcus Julius Eugenius, son of Cyrillus Celer of Kouessos, a member of the (Laodicean) senate, having served (as an officer) in the *officium* of the governor of Pisidia and having married Flavia Julia Flaviana, daughter of Gaius (Julius) Nestorianus, a man of (Roman) senatorial rank; and having served with distinction; and when a command had meanwhile gone forth in the time of Maximinus that Christians should offer sacrifice and not quit the service, having endured very many tortures under Diogenes governor (of Pisidia) and having contrived to quit the service, maintaining the faith of the Christians; and having spent a short time in the city of the Laodiceans; and having been made bishop by the will of Almighty God; and having administered the episcopate for 25 full years with great distinction; and having rebuilt from its foundations the entire church and all the adornment around it, consisting of stoai and tetrastoa and paintings and mosaics and fountain and outer gateway; and having furnished it with all the construction in masonry and, in a word, with everything; and being about to leave the life of this world; I made for myself a plinth and a sarcophagus on which I caused the above to be engraved, for the distinction of the church and of my family.[21]

Epitaph of the Wife of the Centurion Aurelius Gaius

Aurelius Gaius provides a long list of his military service after enlistment in many places including Germany, Syria, Arabia, and Egypt. He was probably dismissed from the army after Diocletian's edict of 303 and returned to his home in Pessinus (central Turkey). Gaius and his daughter prepared this epitaph for the tomb of his son and wife. The reference to the resurrection indicates that he was a Christian although there is no indication of when he became a Christian. (See Tepper and DiSegni, *Prayer Hall*, 51–52.)

Aurelius Gaius Jr., who enlisted in the First Legion Italica stationed in Moesia [Bulgaria], was selected [to serve] in the Eighth Legion Augusta stationed in Germany, then in the Iovia Scythica in the provinces of Scythia [Dobruja in eastern Romania] and Pannonia [Hungary]; served as a tyro, apprentice

---

21. Translation in Calder, "Epigraphy," 45.

calvaryman, then lancer, aide-de-camp of a centurion triarius, aide-de-camp of a centurion ordinatus, aide-de-camp of a centurion princeps, then aide-de-camp in the mobile forces of the emperor with the First Legion Iovia Scythica; toured the provinces of Asia, Caria, [—], Lydia, Lycaonia, Cilicia, [—Pho] enice, Syria, Arabia, Palestine, Egypt, Alexandria, India (Ethiopia?), [—], Mesopotamia, Cappadocia, [—], Galatia, Bithynia, Thracia, Moesia, Karpia [eastern Hungary], [—], Sarmatia [Ukraine] four times, Viminacium [Kosto-lac near Belgrade], the land of the Goths twice, Germany [the land north of the Danube, Czekoslovakia], [—] Dardania [western Macedonia] Dalmatia, Pannonia, [—], Gallia, Spain, Mauritania [Morocco and Algeria]; then was promoted, and after having suffered many hardships he came home to his native Pessinus [Sivrihisar in central Turkey], taking up his residence in the village of Kotiaion. [Together with his daughter] Macedonia he set up this stele on the tomb of Juli [his son (or Juliana his daughter)] and Areskusa his most sweet wife, at his own expense, for the sake of memory, until the resur-rection. Farewell to all![22]

Military Martyrs

From a number of different sources, it is clear that the number of Christians in the Roman army increased significantly in the latter half of the third century. Since pagan worship, especially sacrifice to the emperor, was an important part of army life, it is not entirely clear how these Christian soldiers managed their dual loyalties. Perhaps Tertullian's comment (*On Idolatry* 19) that the rank and file soldier did not need to sacrifice helps to explain the situation. As the story of Marinus (see p. 152) shows, however, the army would not tolerate soldiers (especially prospective centurions) who publicly declared their refusal to sacrifice to the emperor. In a sense, there may have existed a kind of unwrit-ten "don't ask, don't tell" policy. When Christians publicly defied army rules and rejected pagan worship (e.g., Maximilian and Marcellus below), they were executed. Those who remained silent survived.

This situation seems to have continued up until 299. For the first fourteen years of his reign (284–305), Emperor Diocletian largely tolerated Christianity. The number of Christians was expanding rapidly and they gradually occupied a greater number of important positions in society and government. Our sources show that there were also increasing numbers of Christians in the army.

22. *L'Année épigraphique* 777 (1981); translation from Tepper and Di Segni, *Prayer Hall*, 51–52.

Things changed in 299 when Diocletian ordered all soldiers to sacrifice to the Roman gods. Those who refused were forced to leave the army. Then, on February 23, 303, Diocletian's "First Edict" ordered the destruction of Christian churches and the burning of their scriptures. The "Fourth Edict" (Spring 304) commanded everyone in the Roman Empire to sacrifice to the Roman gods (see Simmons, *Arnobius*, 32–46). Many Christians—including a number of Christian soldiers—were martyred.

Martyrdom of Marinus (c. AD 260)

Marinus was probably a soldier in the Legio X Fretensis that was stationed in Palestine during this period. Bishop Theotecnus was a personal friend of Eusebius who provides this account in 7.15 of his *Ecclesiastical History*. The account does not tell us how long Marinus had been a Christian, but the fact that other soldiers knew he was a Christian indicates that he had been a Christian for at least a little while. For some background and the Greek text, see Musurillo, *Martyrs*, xxxvi, 240–43.

7.15. At this time, when the peace of the churches had been everywhere restored, Marinus in Cæsarea in Palestine, who was honored for his military deeds, and illustrious by virtue of family and wealth, was beheaded for his testimony to Christ, on the following account. The vine-branch is a certain mark of honor among the Romans, and those who obtain it become, they say, centurions. A place being vacated, the order of succession called Marinus to this position. But when he was about to receive the honor, another person came before the tribunal and claimed that it was not legal, according to the ancient laws, for him to receive the Roman dignity, as he was a Christian and did not sacrifice to the emperors; but that the office belonged rather to him. Thereupon the judge, whose name was Achæus, being disturbed, first asked what opinion Marinus held. And when he perceived that he continually confessed himself a Christian, he gave him three hours for reflection. When he came out from the tribunal, Theotecnus, the bishop there, took him aside and conversed with him, and taking his hand led him into the church. And standing with him within, in the sanctuary, he raised his cloak a little, and pointed to the sword that hung by his side; and at the same time he placed before him the Scripture of the divine Gospels, and told him to choose which of the two he wished. And without hesitation he reached forth his right hand, and took the divine Scripture. "Hold fast then," says Theotecnus to him, "hold fast to God, and strengthened by him may you obtain what you have chosen, and go in peace." Immediately on his return the herald cried out calling him to the tribunal, for the appointed time was already completed. And standing before the tribunal, and manifesting greater zeal for the faith, immediately, as he was, he was led away and finished his course by death.[23]

The Acts of Maximilian (AD 295)

Maximilian's father, Victor (who clearly was a Christian), was a *temonarius*, an official in charge of the *temo*, which was a tax to support the outfitting of military recruits, but there is no clear evidence that Victor was a soldier (contra Harnack, *Militia Christi*, 97). On March 12, 295, Victor brought his twenty-one-year-old son to the proconsul Dion at Tebessa to be enlisted as a soldier. But Maximilian refused. Although he is very explicit that he cannot join the army because he is a Christian, the account never tells us why Maximilian thinks his Christian faith requires him to refuse. (Brock, it seems to me, goes beyond the evidence in his argument that Maximilian's concern was opposition to killing ["St. Maximilian," 195–209].) When the proconsul tries to persuade the young man by noting that Christians are serving in the military bodyguard of the emperor, Maximilian simply says that they must answer for themselves. This story shows both that at the end of the third century some Christians were in the military and that others considered it impossible to be a soldier and a Christian. That the church buried Maximilian next to Cyprian, the famous bishop and martyr, suggests that there was strong support for his action in the North African church. (See further Musurillo, *Martyrs*, xxxvii, 244–49.)

On the twelfth day of March at Tebessa, in the consulship of Tuscus and Anullinus, Fabius Victor was summoned to the forum together with Maximilian; Pompeianus was permitted to act as their advocate.

The advocate spoke: "Fabius Victor, agent in charge of the recruiting tax, is present for his hearing along with Valerian Quintianus, imperial representative, and Victor's son Maximilian, an excellent recruit. Seeing that Maximilian has good recommendations, I request that he be measured."

The proconsul Dion said: "What is your name?"

Maximilian replied: "But why do you wish to know my name? I cannot serve because I am a Christian."

The proconsul Dion said: "Get him ready."

While he was being made ready, Maximilian replied: "I cannot serve. I cannot commit a sin. I am a Christian."

"Let him be measured," said the proconsul Dion.

23. *NPNF*[2] 1:303. Brennecke says that Bishop Theotecnus makes no objection to the military career of his church member ("Kriegsdienst," 199). That is true, but it would be equally accurate to say the bishop makes no defense of Marinus's military career. The text simply describes the event without any indication of what the bishop thought about Christians in the military.

After he was measured, one of the staff said: "He is five foot ten."

Dion said to his staff: "Let him be given the military seal."

Still resisting, Maximilian replied: "I will not do it! I cannot serve!"

"Serve, or you will die," said Dion.

"I shall not serve," said Maximilian. "You may cut off my head, I will not serve this world, but only my God."

The proconsul Dion said: "Who has turned your head?"

"My own soul," said Maximilian, "and the one who has called me."

Dion said to Victor, the boy's father: "Speak to your son."

Victor said: "He is aware and can take his own counsel on what is best for him."

Dion said to Maximilian: "Agree to serve and receive the military seal."

"I will not accept the seal," he replied. "I already have the seal of Christ who is my God."

Dion addressed his staff: "Let him be given the seal."

Maximilian resisted and said: "I will not accept the seal of this world; and, if you give it to me, I shall break it, for it is worthless. I am a Christian. I cannot wear a piece of lead around my neck after I have received the saving sign of Jesus Christ my Lord, the son of the living God. You do not know him; yet he suffered for our salvation; God delivered him up for our sins. He is the one whom all we Christians serve: we follow him as the prince of life and the author of salvation."

"You must serve," said Dion, "and accept the seal—otherwise you will die miserably."

"I shall not perish," said Maximilian. "My name is already before my Lord. I may not serve."

Dion said: "Have regard for your youth: serve. This is what a young man should do."

"My service is for the Lord," Maximilian replied. "I cannot serve the world. I have already told you: I am a Christian."

The proconsul Dion said: "In the sacred bodyguard of our lords Diocletian and Maximian, Constantius and Maximus, there are soldiers who are Christian, and they serve."

Maximilian replied: "They know what is best for them. But I am a Christian and I cannot do wrong."

"What wrong do they commit," said Dion, "who serve in the army?"

Maximilian replied: "Why, you know what they do."

The proconsul Dion said: "Serve. If you despise the military service you will perish miserably."

Maximilian replied: "I shall not perish, and if I depart from this world, my soul lives with Christ my Lord."

"Strike out his name!" said Dion. And when his name had been struck out, Dion said: "Because you have refused military service out of disloyalty, you will receive a suitable sentence as an example to the others." Then he read the following decision from a tablet: "Whereas Maximilian has disloyally refused the military oath, he is sentenced to die by the sword."

"Thank God!" said Maximilian.

He had lived in this world twenty-one years, three months, and eighteen days. And when he was led to the spot, he said: "My dearest brothers, hasten with all eagerness, with as much courage as you can, that it may be given to you to see the Lord, and that he may reward you with a similar crown."

Then with a joyous countenance he turned and said to his father: "Give this executioner my new clothes which you prepared for my military service. Then I shall receive you with my division of a hundred, and we shall glory with the Lord together."

Soon afterwards he died. A woman named Pompeiana obtained his body from the magistrate and, after placing it in her own chamber, later brought it to Carthage. There she buried it at the foot of a hill near the governor's palace next to the body of the martyr Cyprian. Thirteen days later the woman herself passed away and was buried in the same spot. But Victor, the boy's father, returned to his home in great joy, giving thanks to God that he had sent ahead such a gift to the Lord, since he himself was soon to follow.

Thanks be to God! Amen.[24]

The Acts of Marcellus (probably AD 298)

In North Africa in the city of Tingis (in Morocco today) a Christian centurion named Marcellus publicly threw away his military belt (thus renouncing his military oath) at a public festival celebrating the joint birthday of the emperors Diocletian and Maximian. Harnack says the legion was normally based at Alexandria (*Militia Christi*, 98). The text makes it quite clear that Marcellus objected to the idolatry in the army: he threw down his military belt in front of the legion's standards, which Roman soldiers revered with religious awe; and he explicitly denounced the Roman gods.

This story comes to us in divergent texts and scholars do not embrace one definitive text. I use the one that Musurillo (*Martyrs*, xxxvii–xxxix) considers most reliable.

In the city of Tingis, while Fortunatus was governor, it was the celebration of the emperor's birthday. At length, when everyone was dining at the banquet table, a centurion named Marcellus rejected these pagan festivities, and after throwing down his soldier's belt in front of the legionary standards which were there at the time, he bore witness in a loud voice: "I am a soldier of Jesus Christ,

24. Musurillo, *Martyrs*, 245–49.

the eternal king. From now I cease to serve your emperors and I despise the worship of your gods of wood and stone, for they are deaf and dumb images."

Now the soldiers that heard this were amazed, and arresting him, they threw him into prison and went to report the affair to the governor Fortunatus. When he had heard the story he ordered Marcellus to be kept in prison. After the banquet was over, he ordered Marcellus to be brought into his council chamber. When the centurion Marcellus was brought in, the prefect Anastasius Fortunatus spoke to him as follows: "What was your intention in violating military discipline by taking off your belt and throwing it down with your staff?"

"On 21 July," Marcellus replied, "while you were celebrating the emperor's feast day, I declared clearly and publicly before the standards of this legion that I was a Christian, and said that I could not serve under this military oath, but only for Christ Jesus, the son of God the Father almighty."

The prefect Fortunatus said: "I cannot conceal your rash act. And so I must report this to the emperors and to Caesar; and you will be handed over to my lord Aurelius Agricolanus. . . ."

On 30 October, at Tingis, when Marcellus of the rank of centurion was brought into court, one of the court secretaries announced: "The prefect Fortunatus has referred the case of the centurion Marcellus to your jurisdiction. There is a letter from him here, which I shall read with your permission."

Agricolanus said: "Have it read.". . .

After the letter was read, Agricolanus said: "Did you say the things that are recorded in the prefect's report?"

"Yes, I did," answered Marcellus.

"You held the military rank of centurion, first class?" asked Agricolanus.

"Yes," said Marcellus.

"What madness possessed you," asked Agricolanus, "to throw down the symbols of your military oath and to say the things that you did?"

Marcellus replied: "No madness possesses those who fear the Lord."

"Then you did say all of those things," asked Agricolanus, "that are set down in the prefect's report?"

"Yes, I said them," answered Marcellus.

Agricolanus said: "You threw down your weapons?"

Marcellus replied: "Yes, I did. For it is not fitting that a Christian, who fights for Christ his Lord, should fight for the armies of this world."

Agricolanus said: "What Marcellus has done merits punishment according to military rules. And so, whereas Marcellus, who held the rank of centurion, first class, has confessed that he has disgraced himself by publicly renouncing his military oath, and has further used expressions completely lacking in control as are recorded in the report of the prefect, I hereby sentence him to death by the sword."[25]

25. Ibid., 251–55.

The Martyrdom of Julius the Veteran (AD 304)

Diocletian's fourth edict (January or February 304) ordered death to Christians who would not sacrifice to the pagan gods. Julius may have died in Durostorum in Lower Moesia (a city in the Danube in modern Bulgaria). See further Musurillo, *Martyrs*, xxxix, 260–65.

Julius says that he has been a soldier for twenty-seven years, fought in seven military campaigns, and was inferior to no one in battle. He even reenlisted. Furthermore, he explicitly notes that he has been a Christian for his entire military career. It would appear that Julius does not view fighting as a soldier as incompatible with his Christian faith. But at the trial, Julius says that during all those twenty-seven years in the Roman army, he made a mistake (*errare*) and served foolishly. One would like to have further explanation. Does he mean that he now sees that as a Christian he should not have killed people as the *Apostolic Tradition* and Christian writers teach (see Arner, *Pro-Life*, 89–90)? Or does he only mean that his faithful service as a soldier is not being respected and rewarded by Rome and therefore his appropriate military career was a foolish mistake? Our text does not provide a clear answer.

In the time of persecution, when the glorious ordeals which the Christians faced looked to merit the eternal promises, Julius was arrested by the prefect's staff soldiers and he was brought before the prefect Maximus.

"Who is this?" asked Maximus.

One of the staff replied: "This is a Christian who will not obey the laws."

"What is your name?" asked the prefect.

"Julius," was the reply.

"Well, what say you, Julius?" asked the prefect. "Are these allegations true?"

"Yes, they are," said Julius. "I am indeed a Christian. I do not deny that I am precisely what I am."

"You are surely aware," said the prefect, "of the emperors' edicts which order you to offer sacrifice to the gods?"

"I am aware of them," answered Julius. "But I am a Christian and I cannot do what you want; for I must not lose sight of my living and true God."

The prefect Maximus said: "What is so serious about offering some incense and going away?"

Julius replied: "I cannot despise the divine commandments or appear unfaithful to my God. In all the twenty-seven years in which I made the mistake, so it appears, to serve foolishly in the army, I was never brought before a magistrate either as a criminal or a trouble-maker. I went on seven military campaigns, and never hid behind anyone nor was I the inferior of any man in battle. My chief never found me at fault. And now do you suppose that I, who was always found to be faithful in the past, should now be unfaithful to higher orders?"

"What military service did you have?" asked Maximus the prefect.

"I was in the army," answered Julius, "and when I had served my term I reenlisted as a veteran. All of this time I worshiped in fear the God who made heaven and earth [cf. Acts 4:24], and even to this day I show him my service."

"Julius," said Maximus the prefect, "I see that you are a wise and serious person. You shall receive a generous bonus if you will take my advice and sacrifice to the gods."

"I will not do what you wish," answered Julius, "lest I incur an eternal penalty."

"If you think it a sin," answered the prefect Maximus, "let me take the blame. I am the one who is forcing you, so that you may not give the impression of having consented voluntarily. Afterwards you can go home in peace, you will pick up your ten-year bonus, and no one will ever trouble you again."

"This is the money of Satan, and neither it nor your crafty talk can deprive me of the eternal light. I cannot deny God. So, deliver sentence against me as a Christian."

Maximus said: "If you do not respect the imperial decrees and offer sacrifice, I am going to cut your head off.". . .

"Listen to me and offer the sacrifice," said Maximus, "lest I put you to death as I promised."

"I have chosen death for now," said Julius, "that I might live with the saints forever."

The prefect Maximus then delivered the sentence as follows: "Whereas Julius has refused to obey the imperial edicts, he is sentenced to death.". . .

There was a man named Isichius, a soldier who was a Christian, who was also being kept in prison. He said to the holy martyr: "Julius, I beg you, fulfill your promise in joy. Take the crown which the Lord has promised to give to those who believe in him, and remember me, for I too will follow you. . . ."

Julius then kissed Isichius. "Hasten, my brother, and follow me," he said. "He whom you greeted will hear your last requests."

Then he took the blindfold and bound his eyes, bent his neck, and said: "Lord Jesus Christ, I suffer this for your name. I beg you, deign to receive my spirit together with your holy martyrs."

And so the Devil's servant struck the blessed martyr with a sword and brought his life to an end. . . .[26]

Final Note

In addition, there is a story about the martyrdom of the soldier Dasius about 304, but Musurillo doubts that this later account is reliable (*Martyrs*, xl–xli).

26. Ibid., 261–65.

There is also an account of about forty martyrs that may (scholars are very unsure of its reliability) come from about 320. It says nothing about them being soldiers, but later writers refer to them as soldiers and one modern scholar concludes that they were all soldiers (see Musurillo, *Martyrs*, xlix, lviii).

Eusebius's *Ecclesiastical History*

Longtime bishop of Caesarea Eusebius (AD 260–339) was a prolific writer and the founder of church history. His *Ecclesiastical History* provides our most extensive source for the history of the early church. Books 1–7, probably first published before 300, trace church history up to 284. The selection from 6.42 is a quotation from Dionysius, bishop of Alexandria, describing the terrible persecution under Emperor Decius in 250–251. Clearly, there were Christian soldiers in Alexandria at this time.

Book 8 describes the great persecution that began in 303, and finally ended in 311. It is clear from the brief selections here from book 8 that by the beginning of the fourth century, there were significant numbers of Christians both in the Roman army and in important governmental offices.

For Eusebius and his *Ecclesiastical History*, see Maier, *Eusebius*, 9–20, and the bibliography on 385–88.

The following excerpt (from Bishop Dionysius) describes a scene before a Roman judge who is torturing and killing Christians.

Brennecke ("Kriegsdienst," 199) says that this text indicates that for Dionysius, bishop of Alexandria, Christian soldiers "pose no theological problem," but that is to read his own assumptions into the text. The text says absolutely nothing about what Dionysius thought about the appropriateness of Christian soldiers. It merely shows that they existed, and that Dionysius approved of their courage in confessing Christ.

6.42. A band of soldiers, Ammon and Zeno and Ptolemy and Ingenes, and with them an old man, Theophilus, were standing close together before the tribunal. And as a certain person who was being tried as a Christian, seemed inclined to deny, they standing by gnashed their teeth, and made signs with their faces and stretched out their hands, and gestured with their bodies. And when the attention of all was turned to them, before any one else could seize them, they rushed up to the tribunal saying that they were Christian, so that the governor and his council were affrighted. And those who were on trial appeared most courageous in prospect of their sufferings, while their judges trembled. And they went exultingly from the tribunal rejoicing in their testimony; God himself having caused them to triumph gloriously.[27]

8.1. This persecution began with the brethren in the army.[28]

8.4. He did not wage war against all of us at once, but made trial at first only of those in the army. For he supposed that the others could be taken easily if he should first attack and subdue these. Thereupon many of the soldiers were seen most cheerfully embracing private life, so that they might not deny their piety toward the Creator of the universe. For when the commander, whoever he was, began to persecute the soldiers, separating into tribes and purging those who were enrolled in the army, giving them the choice either by obeying to receive the honor which belonged to them, or on the other hand to be deprived of it if they disobeyed the command, a great many soldiers of Christ's kingdom without hesitation, instantly preferred the confession of him to the seeming glory and prosperity which they were enjoying. And one and another of them occasionally received in exchange, for their pious constancy not only the loss of position, but death.[29]

8.9. *[One of the martyrs was Philoromus.]* . . . These indeed were wonderful; but yet more wonderful were those who, being distinguished for wealth, noble birth, and honor, and for learning and philosophy, held everything secondary to the true religion and to faith in our Savior and Lord Jesus Christ. Such an one was Philoromus, who held a high office under the imperial government at Alexandria, and who administered justice every day, attended by a military guard corresponding to his rank and Roman dignity.[30]

8.11. A small town of Phrygia, inhabited solely by Christians, was completely surrounded by soldiers while the men were in it. Throwing fire into it, they consumed them with the women and children while they were calling upon Christ. This they did because all the inhabitants of the city, and the curator himself, and the governor, with all who held office, and the entire populace, confessed themselves Christians, and would not in the least obey those who commanded them to worship idols.[31]

In April 311, the edict of Galerius temporarily ended the severe persecution in the East. But Galerius died very soon thereafter and Emperor Maximin quickly promoted renewed persecution in the East. In June 312, Maximin

27. *NPNF*[2] 1:285.
28. *NPNF*[2] 1:323.
29. *NPNF*[2] 1:326.
30. *NPNF*[2] 1:330.
31. *NPNF*[2] 1:331–32.

issued decrees urging vigorous persecution. In chapter 9, Eusebius describes a series of disasters that followed: famine, widespread illness, and war with the Armenians who "were also Christians." Clearly Christian Armenians fought in 312 to protect themselves against a persecuting emperor.

9.8. In addition to this the tyrant was compelled to go to war with the Armenians, who had been from ancient times friends and allies of the Romans. As they were also Christians and zealous in their piety toward the Deity, the enemy of God had attempted to compel them to sacrifice to idols and demons, and had thus made friends foes, and allies enemies. All these things suddenly took place at one and the same time, and refuted the tyrant's empty vaunt against the Deity. For he had boasted that, because of his zeal for idols and his hostility against us, neither famine nor pestilence nor war had happened in his time. These things, therefore, coming upon him at once and together, furnished a prelude also of his own destruction. He himself with his forces was defeated in the war with the Armenians, and the rest of the inhabitants of the cities under him were terribly afflicted with famine and pestilence.[32]

An Early Christian Kingdom?

In the first book (probably published before AD 300) of his *Ecclesiastical History*, Eusebius included a letter allegedly sent to Jesus by King Abgar of Edessa (in southeastern Turkey near the Syrian border today). He also quoted Jesus's alleged response and said one of Jesus's seventy disciples was sent to King Abgar, who became a Christian (1.13). Obviously, if a king converted to Christianity in the mid-first century, that would suggest that such a kingdom probably also had Christian soldiers in the first century.

All modern scholars, of course, consider Eusebius's account about Jesus's contemporary King Abgar to be pure legend. But some modern scholars do think that King Abgar the Great of Osrhoene (capitol at Edessa) did become a Christian about AD 200 (Bainton, "Early Church," 194), making his kingdom the "world's first Christian Kingdom" (Jenkins, *Lost History*, 54).

Recent scholarship, however, indicates that this is highly unlikely. The Christian author Julius Africanus lived at Edessa at this time and knew the royal family. He called King Abgar a "holy man" but never said he was a Christian (Segal, *Edessa*, 70). None of the royal coins from Edessa contain any hint of Christianity. "The evidence of Abgar VIII's conversion . . . proves to be extremely

32. *NPNF*[2] 1:362.

flimsy" (Brock, "Syriac Christianity," 227). Similarly, Millar says, "There is thus no good evidence that the kings of Edessa were ever Christian" (*Roman Near East*, 476–77). After reviewing the evidence, Ross reached the same conclusion: "There is, then, no compelling reason to believe that royal Edessa was ever 'officially' Christian, or even that Christians were in the majority there before the fourth century" (*Roman Edessa*, 135).[33]

In his *Ecclesiastical History*, Eusebius tells us that during the time of Maximin's persecution in 312–13, Maximin waged a war against the Armenians (living in what today is northeast Turkey). Eusebius says "they were Christians" and Maximin was worn out by the Armenian war (9.8.2, 4). It is clear that Christian Armenians took up arms in 312 to defend themselves against a persecuting emperor. Scholars believe King Trdat of Armenia converted to Christianity sometime around 311–13 (Thomson, "Mission," 30–32).[34] That there was a Christian king with many Christians in his army by the early fourth century is clear. This simply adds to the evidence from many sources that, by the fourth century, more and more Christians were engaged in military service.

33. A somewhat parallel situation involves Philip the Arabian, who was emperor from 244–49. Eusebius says he was a Christian (*Church History* 6.34; NPNF² 1:278) and Crouzel (*Origen*, 3–4) agrees. But most modern historians reject this; see *Oxford Dictionary*, 1284.

34. Arpee, *Armenian Christianity*, 15, dates it a little earlier, to AD 301. See also the discussion in Nersessian, *Treasures of the Ark*, 19–20.

Afterword

What does all this data tell us about the thinking of the early church on abortion, capital punishment, military service, and war?

Previous Answers

On the last issue—war and military service—Christian writers over the last century have taken two basic positions. Some have argued that Christians before Constantine were largely pacifist. A second group of scholars describes the relevant evidence as "small, divided, and ambiguous,"[1] suggesting that the evidence permits only an ambiguous answer to our question.

The Pacifist View

A number of scholars—one thinks especially of Roland Bainton, C. J. Cadoux, and John Howard Yoder—have argued that the early church in the first three centuries was predominantly opposed to Christian participation in war. Bainton says: "The age of persecution down to the time [of] Constantine was the age of pacifism to the degree that during this period, no Christian author to our knowledge approved of Christian participation in battle."[2] Bainton and Cadoux clearly acknowledge that beginning in the later second century, there were at least a few Christians who served in the Roman army and that their numbers increased in the third century. Although sources do not allow an accurate assessment of the number of Christian soldiers, they probably represented a reasonably small number.[3]

---

1. Leithart, *Constantine*, 278.
2. Bainton, *War and Peace*, 66.
3. Every author would likely summarize the data with slight differences, but others who would substantially agree with Bainton would include Guy Hershberger, Jean-Michel Hornus, Ronald G. Musto, and Rob Arner.

The "Small, Divided, and Ambiguous" View

Among the many who have argued this position in the last fifty years, John Helgeland has probably written the most extensive, detailed scholarly analysis. His rejection of the pacifist answer is pointed:

> There is practically no evidence from the Fathers which would support the argument that the early church denied enlistment on the ground that killing and war were opposed to the Christian ethic. The pacifist argument is an artificial construct bringing together passages, torn from their context, and arranged in a way no Father ever could have done; no unequivocal statement to support that argument can be found, and certainly not one of any length such as a paragraph three or four sentences long.[4]

These authors argue that there are only a small number of relevant texts.[5] They find a diversity of views even among these texts,[6] and even some support of the "just war" concept, at least in Origen.[7] Some speculate that vigorous opponents of Christian participation in the army like Tertullian and Origen may have been a small articulate minority that did not represent the majority of Christians.[8]

Furthermore, these authors argue that certainly by the late second century there were substantial numbers of Christians in the Roman army, and their numbers expanded greatly in the course of the third century. The fact that there is no record of controversy when Constantine used a Christian symbol on his army's standards and ended persecution, and that the Christian world embraced him and celebrated his military victories, suggests that large numbers of Christians before Constantine did not oppose military service.[9]

Finally, those writers that did oppose Christian participation in the army did so primarily because of the way army life was immersed in pagan religion, not because of some principled ethical opposition to killing.[10] Or, as Johnson argues, it was because of an intense eschatology, which expected the imminent return of Christ, and therefore placed little value on Christian concern for societal order.[11]

---

4. Helgeland, "Roman Army," 764–65. See also his "Christians," 156.

5. Leithart, *Constantine*, 270; Lee, *Pacifism*, 67.

6. Leithart, *Constantine*, 259; Charles, *Between Pacifism and Jihad*, 37; Johnson, *Peace*, 19.

7. Daly, "Military Force," 179; Caspary, *Origen*, 127–32; Leithart, *Constantine*, 268.

8. Leithart, *Constantine*, 259, 261. Cf. Oliver and Joan O'Donovan's comment: "There is no reason to think Tertullian idiosyncratic for the second and third centuries" (*Political Thought*, 3).

9. Johnson, *Peace*, 14–15; Leithart, *Constantine*, 272.

10. Helgeland, "Roman Army," 744, 765.

11. Johnson, *Peace*, 12–17, 42.

A New Consensus?

Roman Catholic theologian David Hunter and Mennonite ethicist Alan Kreider have more recently summarized what they consider to be a new consensus in modern scholarship:

1. Idolatry: The most vigorous opponents (e.g., Tertullian and Origen) of Christian military service grounded their opposition at least as much on the pervasive idolatry in military life as on opposition to killing.
2. Division: From at least the end of the second century, there was a "divergence in Christian opinion and practice,"[12] and Christian support for participation in the army grew throughout the third century.
3. Continuity: "The efforts of [post-Constantinian] Christians to justify participation in warfare for a 'just' cause (most notably that of Augustine) stand in fundamental continuity with at least one strand of pre-Constantinian tradition."[13]
4. Regional Variation: Christian attitudes and practices differed in different regions of the empire. Christian opposition to military participation was strongest in the heart of the empire and weakest on the borders.[14]

My own view is that some—but not all—of this alleged consensus is correct. The following sections present my attempt to summarize what I consider to be the most historically warranted conclusions about the thinking and practice of the pre-Constantinian church on killing, war, and military participation. But before I take up that very complex question, however, I will begin with the (relatively!) noncontroversial areas of the early church's views on abortion and capital punishment.

Abortion

Eight different authors in eleven different writings mention abortion.[15] In every instance, the writing unequivocally rejects abortion. The blunt condemnation of the *Didache* is typical: "You shall not murder a child by abortion."[16]

12. Hunter, "Decade of Research," 93.
13. Ibid., 417.
14. Kreider, "Church Orders," 417.
15. *Didache* 2; *Epistle of Barnabas* 19; *Apocalypse of Peter* 8; Athenagoras, *Plea* 35; Clement of Alexandria, *Educator* 2.10 and *Prophetic Eclogues* 48–50; Tertullian, *Apology* 9, *Soul* 26–27, 37, and *Chastity* 12; Minucius Felix, *Octavius* 30; *Didascalia apostolorum* 3.
16. *Didache* 2.

In two cases no reason is given for the condemnation.[17] But all the others condemn abortion either because the unborn child has a soul from the moment of conception, or because abortion is killing and Christians do not do that.

Both Clement of Alexandria[18] and Tertullian[19] say that the unborn child has a soul from the moment of conception. Tertullian supports his argument that the embryo in the womb is a truly human life known and treasured by God by referring to the fact that John the Baptist leaped in Elizabeth's womb when Mary arrived[20] and that in Jeremiah 1:5, God says he sanctified Jeremiah while he was in his mother's womb. Athenagoras adds that the fetus in the womb is a "created being and therefore an object of God's care."[21]

By far the most common reason (mentioned at least six times) for opposing abortion is that abortion is killing a human being, and that is wrong. The *Apocalypse of Peter* describes excruciating punishment suffered in hell by parents "because they forsook the commandment of God and killed their children."[22] Athenagoras refutes the rumor that Christians are cannibals by arguing that Christians consistently oppose killing, indeed they do not even watch killing by attending gladiatorial games. In that context he says that women "who use drugs to bring on abortion commit murder."[23]

In a similar way, Tertullian condemns abortion because all murder is wrong: "In our case, murder being once for all forbidden, we may not destroy even the fetus in the womb."[24] Minucius Felix condemns abortion as parricide, insisting that for Christians "it is not lawful either to see or to hear of human slaughter"—much less do it.[25]

Capital Punishment

The pre-Constantinian references to capital punishment are less frequent. Four different writers say that Christians must not participate in capital punishment.[26] In two other texts, however, there is one sentence that says that

17. *Epistle of Barnabas* 19; Tertullian, *Chastity* 12.
18. *Prophetic Eclogues* 50.
19. *Soul* 27.
20. Luke 1:41–45.
21. *Plea* 35.
22. *Apocalypse* 8.
23. *Plea* 35.
24. *Apology* 9.
25. *Octavius* 30.
26. Tertullian, *Idolatry* 17, 19; Origen, *Against Celsus* 7.26; Lactantius, *Institutes* 7.20; *Apostolic Tradition* 16. There is also one sentence in Adamantius, *Dialogue on the True Faith* 4.10 on capital punishment, but it is not clear what the author means to say about Christian engagement in capital punishment.

desiring the death of an adulterer is not a crime.[27] In both instances, this one sentence serves to illustrate a philosophical point. There is no clear indication of whether Christians should or should not participate in capital punishment in such a case.

In his treatise *On Idolatry*, Tertullian asks whether a Christian can be a government official. He responds by listing a large number of activities, including pagan sacrifices, which such a person must avoid. One of these includes "sitting in judgment on anyone's life"[28]—that is, a Christian dare not participate in ordering capital punishment. Two chapters later, Tertullian asks whether a Christian can serve in the military even at a low rank, where "there is no necessity for taking part in [pagan] sacrifices or capital punishment."[29] Tertullian clearly means to say that a Christian dare not participate in either pagan worship or capital punishment.

In his response to Celsus, Origen distinguishes sharply between the "constitution" given to the Jews by Moses and that given to Christians by Christ. Under Moses's law, the Jews could kill enemies and use capital punishment. But Christ's gospel is different: Christians cannot "slay their enemies or condemn to be burned or stoned."[30] Christians must not use capital punishment.

In his *Divine Institutes*, written very early before he joined Constantine, Lactantius vigorously rejects Christian participation in all killing, including capital punishment. (When he speaks of "justice" and a "just man," he means the ethical behavior that Christian faith demands.)

> Thus it will be neither lawful for a just man to engage in military service . . . nor to accuse anyone of a capital charge, because it makes no difference whether you put a person to death by word or rather by sword, since it is the act of putting to death itself which is prohibited. Therefore with regard to this precept of God, there ought to be no exception at all but that it is always unlawful to put to death a person whom God willed to be a sacred creature.[31]

A Christian dare not even charge someone with an offense that could result in capital punishment, much less actually carry out such a sentence.[32]

Finally we have the *Apostolic Tradition* (probably late second or early third century). It explicitly says that if a prominent government official, one who

27. Adamantius, *Dialogue on the True Faith* 4.10. Adamantius quotes this sentence from Methodius, *On Free Will* (see 100n149 above).

28. *Idolatry* 17.

29. Ibid., 19.

30. Origen, *Against Celsus* 7.26.

31. Lactantius, *Institutes* 6.20.

32. Interestingly, Lactantius mentions capital punishment twice in the period after he has joined Constantine. In *Anger* (316), he clearly argues that capital punishment is not just permissible but desirable to preserve order. But in his *Epitome* (an abbreviation of his *Divine Institutes*), written in AD 320 or later, he again condemns capital punishment (*Epitome* 64).

"wears red" and has the power to order capital punishment, seeks catechetical training to be baptized as a Christian, he must abandon his government position: "One who has the power of the sword or the head of a city and wears red, let him stop or be excluded."[33]

The extant pre-Constantinian Christian comments on capital punishment that clearly refer to what Christians should or should not do, all say that Christians must not participate in capital punishment; it involves killing a person and Christians do not do that.

Killing, War, and Military Service

Here we enter contested territory.

It is certainly true that the relevant texts are somewhat limited and brief. Except for Tertullian's *Crown*, there is no full treatise devoted to our topic. We could wish to have much more data—longer writings on the topic, more inscriptions, and so on—but having far less primary data than the modern historian would like is a problem for all of Greco-Roman and early Christian history. We must carefully assess the data we do have and refuse to fill in gaps with unwarranted speculation.

I will summarize the extant data under nine headings: (1) Killing is wrong; (2) Jesus's teaching on loving enemies; (3) Christ fulfills Isaiah's messianic prophecies of peace; (4) Explicit rejection of military service; (5) The reasons for rejecting Christian participation in the military; (6) Implied prohibition of Christian participation in the military; (7) Use of military language; (8) Some ambiguous texts; and (9) Evidence of Christian soldiers before Constantine.

KILLING IS WRONG

Nine different Christian writers in sixteen different treatises say that killing is wrong.[34] No extant Christian writing before Constantine argues that there is any circumstance under which a Christian may kill.[35]

Athenagoras (d. about 180) seeks to refute the charge that Christians eat human flesh by insisting that Christians constantly reject killing people in all areas. They oppose abortion, infanticide, and gladiatorial contests (they even

33. *Apostolic Tradition* 16.

34. Athenagoras, *Plea* 35; Tertullian, *Spectacles* 2, *Patience* 3, *Modesty* 12; Minucius Felix, *Octavius* 30; Origen, *Matthew*, *Celsus* 3.7, 8.73; Cyprian, *Donatus* 6, 7, *Patience* 14, and letters 55 and 56; Archelaus, *Disputation* 2; Arnobius of Sicca, *Pagans* 1.6, 2.1; Lactantius, *Divine Institutes* 1.18; 3.18; 5.8–10, 18; 6.6, 20; *Apostolic Tradition* 16.

35. The only exception is the bizarre apocryphal *Infancy Gospel of Thomas* 3:3; 4:1; 13:2, where the boy Jesus kills people who annoy him. See pp. 129–30 for a discussion of why this writing is largely irrelevant for our purposes.

refuse to watch them). "How then, when we do not even look on [gladiatorial contests], lest we should contract guilt and pollution can we put people to death?"[36]

Tertullian (d. 225) similarly denounces gladiatorial contests insisting that God "puts his prohibition on every sort of man-killing."[37] Jesus, in rebuking Peter's use of the sword at his arrest, "cursed for ever after the works of the sword."[38] The prohibition against shedding human blood is so important that violation of this command cannot be forgiven.[39] Minucius Felix (d. approx. 200) insists that "to us it is not lawful either to see or to hear of human slaughter." In fact, "so much do we shrink from human blood, that we do not use blood even of eatable animals in our food."[40]

Origen (d. 254) unequivocally insists that under no circumstances should Christians kill. In his commentary on Matthew 26:52, he warns Christians "lest because of warfare or the vindication of our rights or for any occasion we should take out the sword, for no such occasion is allowed by this evangelical teaching. . . .We must use the sword against no one." In response to Celsus, he insists that unlike Moses, the Christian lawgiver, Jesus, completely forbid putting people to death. Christ "nowhere teaches that it is right for his own disciples to offer violence to anyone, however wicked. For he did not deem it in keeping with the laws such as His . . . to allow killing of any individual whatever."[41]

Cyprian (d. 258) insists that manslaughter is a "mortal crime." The hand that carries the Eucharist dare not be "sullied by the blood-stained sword."[42] Writing at a time of widespread persecution and considerable martyrdom, Cyprian the bishop refers to his flock as those "who may not kill, but who must be killed."[43] Even though mercilessly persecuted, the Christians "do not in turn assail their assailants, since it is not lawful for the innocent even to kill the guilty."[44]

In the late third century, Archelaus describes a scene where a large number of Christians engaged in a religious festival were suddenly surrounded by hostile soldiers. He states: "Though we were people who had never learned to do injury to anyone, they wounded us pitilessly."[45]

Arnobius of Sicca wrote *Against the Pagans*, probably sometime between 302 and 305, to reject the charge that recent natural disasters and military

36. *Plea* 35.
37. *Spectacles* 2.
38. *Patience* 3.
39. *Modesty* 12.
40. *Octavius* 30.
41. *Against Celsus* 3.7.
42. *Patience* 14.
43. Letter 55.
44. Letter 56.
45. *Disputation* 2.

attacks on the Roman Empire were the fault of Christians. He points out that Christians have learned from Christ that "it is better to suffer wrong than to inflict it, that we should rather shed our own blood than stain our hands and our consciences with that of another." If all would follow Christ's "peaceful rules," the whole world would live in peace.[46]

No one is more clear and explicit about the fact that Christians oppose all killing than Lactantius. In *The Divine Institutes*, written in the first decade of the fourth century in the midst of the severe Diocletian persecution, Lactantius discusses the topic at six different places in four books of his great defense of Christian faith.[47]

Christians "keep away from human blood."[48] They are "ignorant of wars," friendly even to their enemies.[49] They do not carry on war or commit murders or even watch killings. In fact, they prefer "to perish rather than commit an injury."[50] When they are treated violently they respond peacefully, knowing that they have a "great Judge who alone always has the power of taking vengeance in his hands."[51] Lactantius asserts that Cicero is wrong to argue that a great person could justly inflict injury on another if he were first injured.[52] Christians do not put people to death, not even themselves.[53] Suicide is wrong because one "puts to death a person."[54]

If everyone became a Christian—"if those things were done by all which our people alone perform"—there would be no need for prisons, swords of rulers, or punishments. "There would not be dissentions and wars."[55]

In chapter 20 of book 6, Lactantius condemns every kind of killing of human beings. Abortion, infanticide, exposure of newborn children, gladiatorial contests, capital punishment, and warfare are all wrong. Christians are not even to attend the gladiatorial contests where the crowds thirst for human blood. "It is not therefore appropriate that those who strive to keep to the path of justice [i.e., Christians] should be companions and sharers in this public homicide. For when God forbids us to kill, He not only prohibits us from open violence, which is not even allowed by the public laws, but he warns us against the commission of those things which are esteemed lawful among people. Thus it will be neither lawful for a just man to engage in military service . . . nor to accuse anyone of a capital charge, because it makes no difference whether you put a person to death by word or rather by sword,

46. *Pagans* 1.6.
47. *Divine Institutes* 1.18; 3.18; 5.8–10, 18; 6.6, 20.
48. *Divine Institutes* 5.9.
49. *Divine Institutes* 5.10.
50. *Divine Institutes* 5.18.
51. *Divine Institutes* 3.18.
52. *Divine Institutes* 6.18.
53. *Divine Institutes* 6.6.
54. *Divine Institutes* 3.18.
55. *Divine Institutes* 5.8.

since it is the act of putting to death itself which is prohibited. Therefore, with regard to this precept of God, there ought to be no exception at all but that it is always unlawful to put to death a person who God willed to be a sacred creature." Finally, after discussion of abortion and infanticide, he concludes: "It is not permitted to commit homicide in any way." [56]

Finally, we have the pre-Constantinian church order, the *Apostolic Tradition*. Many types of people who seek preparation for baptism must be told to stop certain activities if they wish to be catechumens. People who are gladiators, or teach "gladiators or swordsmanship or military skills or weapons training should stop or be excluded" from preparation for baptism.

The teaching on soldiers who become interested in Christian faith and want to move toward baptism is interesting. This church order does not demand that they instantly abandon the army. Rather, they must be told that they dare not kill. If they agree, they may enter catechetical training. But if they are unwilling to refuse to kill, they must be excluded. "A soldier in the sovereign's army should not kill, or if he is ordered to kill, he should refuse. If he stops, so be it; otherwise he should be excluded." [57]

On the other hand, someone who is already a catechumen or baptized Christian dare not join the army. "A catechumen or a believer, if they want to be soldiers, let them be excluded because they distance themselves from God." [58]

The early church's writings on every kind of killing of human beings is quite clear. From our earliest extant writings on the topic until just a few years before Constantine, writers insist unanimously that Christians must not kill.

JESUS'S TEACHING ON LOVING ENEMIES

Matthew 5:38–48 is probably the most frequently cited biblical text in the writings collected here. At least ten different writers in at least twenty-eight different places cite or refer to this biblical passage and note that Christians love their enemies and turn the other cheek. [59] Occasionally they explicitly link this passage to a rejection of killing and war, but in most instances they do not. In at least nine cases, however, they link the passage to some statement

56. *Divine Institutes* 6.20. In his later writings, after Lactantius joins Constantine, he does approve of warfare (*Death of the Persecutors* 44, 46–48, 52).

57. *Apostolic Tradition* 16.

58. *Apostolic Tradition* 16. Interestingly, this pre-Constantinian teaching on soldiers carried over to some extent in post-Constantinian church orders (*Canons of Hippolytus* 13–14; *Testament of the Lord*).

59. *Didache* 1:2; *Second Clement* 13; Justin Martyr, *First Apology* 14–16, *Trypho* 85, 96; Irenaeus, *Against Heresies* 2.32; 3.18; 4.13; Athenagoras, *Plea* 1, 11; Clement of Alexandria, *Educator* 3.12, *Exhortation* 10, *Miscellanies* 4.8; Tertullian, *Apology* 31, 37, *Spectacles* 16, *Patience* 6, 8, *Marcion* 4.16, *Scapula* 1; Origen, *Celsus* 7.58–61; 8.35, *Commentary on John*; Cyprian, *Jews* 3.49, *Patience* 16; Lactantius, *Divine Institutes* 5.10.

about Christians being peaceable, ignorant of war, opposed to attacking others, and so on. From the earliest post-New Testament writing to the last pre-Constantinian writing, our authors cite Jesus's call to love our enemies.[60]

The *Didache*, the earliest post–New Testament writing, partially cites and partially summarizes Matthew 5:38–48 in its first chapter. The Christian way of life involves praying for enemies, turning the other cheek, and not committing murder (1, 2). *Second Clement* notes that, although they should love their enemies, Christians sometimes fail to do so (13).

Justin Martyr (d. 167) says that people who formerly hated and destroyed one another have become Christians and now pray for their enemies and live peacefully together.[61] Because of Christ's teaching, those who have become Christians have "changed their violent and tyrannical disposition."[62] In his *Dialogue with Trypho*, he again cites Jesus's call to love enemies[63] and later states, "We who were [formerly] filled with war and mutual slaughter and every wickedness have each through the whole earth changed our warlike weapons—our swords into ploughshares and our spears into implements of tillage."[64] Similarly, Irenaeus (d. 202) briefly alludes to turning the other cheek in a section claiming that the coming of the gospel resulted in swords being changed into ploughshares and people becoming "unaccustomed to fighting."[65]

Athenagoras (d. c. 180) confidently compares the practice of ordinary uneducated Christians with learned scholars. Scholars have not managed to love their enemies, but among the Christians, "uneducated persons and artisans and old women" follow Jesus's teaching to love their enemies.[66]

Clement of Alexandria (d. 215) cites Matthew 5:39–40 and then adds that "we do not train our women like amazons to manliness in war since we wish the men even to be peaceable."[67]

In one place, Tertullian (d. 225) notes that Christians are to love their enemies and then goes on to say both that Christians have penetrated every area of Roman life, including the military camps, and also that they consider it better "to be slain than to slay."[68] If we had only this text from Tertullian, we could plausibly conclude that he sees no contradiction between Jesus's com-

---

60. See Ferguson's discussion of the way love of enemies was central to Christian moral catechesis in the second century ("Love of Enemies," 81). See also Arner's argument that patience, rooted in an understanding of Matt. 5:38–48, was central to the ethic of the early church (*Pro-Life*, 98–105).

61. *First Apology* 14.

62. *First Apology* 16.

63. *Trypho* 85, 96.

64. *Trypho* 110.

65. *Against Heresies* 2.32.

66. *Plea* 1, 11.

67. *Miscellanies* 4.8.

68. *Apology* 37.

mand to love enemies and participation in the Roman army. But in *Spectacles*, written at the same time (197, early in his Christian life), Tertullian cites the command to love enemies[69] and also says God "puts his prohibition on every sort of man-killing."[70]

It is interesting, however, that in spite of Tertullian's very strong views against Christians using the sword or joining the army, he hardly ever connects those views with Jesus's command to love enemies, which he often cites elsewhere. So too Origen (d. 254), who refers to Jesus's command to love enemies at least four times but never connects it to his strongly held views that Christians dare not kill. Nor does Cyprian (d. 258) make that connection in his two references to Jesus's teaching about enemies. In his *Divine Institutes*, Lactantius once alludes to being friendly to enemies in a passage where he says Christians are ignorant of wars.[71] But even he does not use Jesus's command to love enemies in his more extensive, uncompromising statements against killing and war. It seems surprising that in the more than two dozen references to loving enemies, only Justin Martyr, Clement of Alexandria, and (very briefly) Irenaeus and Lactantius draw any explicit connection between loving enemies and war. On the other hand, neither is there any hint in all these passages that killing and war are compatible with loving enemies.

CHRIST FULFILLS ISAIAH'S MESSIANIC PROPHECIES OF PEACE

The messianic prophecies of a coming time of peace (Isa. 2:2–4 [cf. Mic. 4:1–4] and Isa. 11:6–9) are quoted somewhat frequently—at least eight times by five different authors.[72] Isaiah 2:4 seems especially important: "They will beat their swords into ploughshares and their spears into pruning hooks. Nation will not take up sword against nation, nor will they train for war anymore." With one exception, every Christian writer who cites these prophecies also explicitly concludes that Christ fulfilled them and that therefore Christians do not engage in war.

Justin Martyr (d. 167) quotes Isaiah 2:3–4 and then argues that there is proof that this prophecy has been fulfilled. Twelve "illiterate" men went out from Jerusalem proclaiming that they were sent by Christ to teach the word of God. The result? "We who formerly used to murder one another do not only now refrain from making war upon our enemies, but also that we may not lie or deceive our examiners, willingly die confessing Christ."[73] Similarly, in his

69. *Spectacles* 16.
70. *Spectacles* 2.
71. *Divine Institutes* 1, 10.
72. Justin Martyr, *First Apology* 39, *Trypho* 110; Irenaeus, *Apostolic Preaching* 61, *Against Heresies* 4.34; Tertullian, *Jews* 3, *Marcion* 21; Origen, *Celsus* 5.33; Adamantius, *Dialogue on the True Faith*, 1.10.
73. *First Apology* 39.

Dialogue with Trypho, Justin Martyr quotes Micah 4:1–7 and then proceeds to argue that this prophecy has been fulfilled in the work of Christ and the apostles. Again the evidence for this claim is the transformation of Christians: "We who were filled with war and mutual slaughter and every wickedness have each through the whole earth changed our warlike weapons—our swords into ploughshares and our spears into implements of tillage."[74]

Irenaeus (d. 202) advances the same argument. After stating that the new covenant in Christ brings peace, he quotes Isaiah 2:3–4. The preaching of the apostles, he claims, has "caused such a change in the state of things, that these nations did form the swords and war-lances into ploughshares . . . that is instruments for peaceful purposes and they are now unaccustomed to fighting, but when smitten offer also the other cheek."[75] Irenaeus does not mean that all nations have abandoned war; he means Christians have abandoned their swords and now are unaccustomed to fighting.

In *Apostolic Preaching*, Irenaeus advances the same argument using Isaiah 11:6–7. People from different nations "who at an earlier time had become brutal and beast-like because of selfish pride, till some of them took on the likeness of wolves and lions, ravaging the weaker, and waged war on their like" now gather together peacefully like lambs. Their "wild and untamed nature" has been changed through Christ.[76]

Tertullian (d. 225) makes the same argument. He quotes and comments on Isaiah 2:3–4, pointing out that the text refers to the Christians who have been called out of the nations. "For the practice of the old law was to avenge itself by the vengeance of the sword . . . but the new law's practice was to point to clemency and to convert to tranquility the pristine ferocity of 'swords' and 'lances' and to remodel the pristine execution of 'war' upon the rivals and foes of the law into the peaceful actions of 'ploughing' and 'tilling' the land."[77] Similarly, in *Against Marcion*, he again quotes Isaiah 2:2–3 to argue that Christians exchange "injurious minds and hostile tongues and all kinds of evil" for "pursuits of moderation and peace. Christ is promised not as powerful in war, but pursuing peace."[78]

Finally, Origen clearly alludes to Isaiah 2:3–4 without quoting it at length. Christians "convert into pruning hooks the spears formerly employed in war. For we no longer take up 'sword against nation' nor do we 'learn war anymore,' having become children of peace for the sake of Jesus."[79]

In all but one instance where they quote these messianic prophecies from Isaiah, our writers say that Christians have abandoned war. Formerly, before

74. *Trypho* 110.
75. *Against Heresies* 4.34.
76. *Apostolic Preaching* 61.
77. *Jews* 3.
78. *Against Marcion* 3.21.
79. *Celsus* 5.33.

becoming Christians, they were engaged in warfare but now, taught by Christ, they do not train for or engage in war.

It is also important to note that the reason given in these texts for the fact that Christians do not train for or engage in war is not any connection with idolatry or eschatological hope for the imminent return of Christ. It is simply that Christ, who fulfilled the messianic prophecies, taught Christians to live this way.

EXPLICIT REJECTION OF MILITARY SERVICE

Tertullian (d. 225) is the first Christian writer who we know explicitly rejected the idea of Christian service in the military. Earlier, Justin Martyr and Irenaeus, quoting Isaiah 2, said that Christians do not go to war. That would seem to imply that Christians should not join the military, but they do not say that explicitly. Tertullian does.

In his *On Idolatry*, Tertullian asks "whether a believer may turn himself into military service" even if he would be a lower level soldier "to whom there is no necessity for taking part in sacrifices or capital punishment." His discussion shows that there were Christians in Tertullian's day that did argue for such participation. But Tertullian answers with a firm no.[80]

What are his reasons? It is clear from this treatise and others that Tertullian believes that military life is deeply enmeshed in idolatrous practices. But here he argues that a Christian dare not enlist even if he could avoid idolatry. It is impossible to serve two masters; one cannot take the military oath of absolute allegiance to the emperor and maintain one's unconditional loyalty to Christ. Furthermore, Christ "unbelted every soldier." "How will a Christian man war, nay how will he serve even in peace without a sword, which the Lord has taken away? For albeit . . . a centurion had believed; still the Lord afterward, in disarming Peter, unbelted every soldier."[81] In this treatise Tertullian clearly gives reasons other than idolatry for his rejection of military service.

Tertullian's *The Crown* is the only pre-Constantinian treatise devoted entirely to Christians and the military. It is very clear from his extensive discussion of the idolatrous practices of military life that Tertullian opposes Christian participation in the military in part because of idolatry. But chapter eleven again includes other reasons. Here, after many chapters on idolatry (which he calls the "secondary" question) he raises what he terms the "primary" issue: "The unlawfulness even of a military life itself." Again the reasons for his position include the impossibility of serving two masters. He also mentions neglect of family. Furthermore, Christ said those who use the sword will perish by the sword. How can "the son of peace take part in the battle when it does

80. *Idolatry* 19.
81. Ibid.

not become him even to sue at law?" Idolatry is clearly not Tertullian's only reason for rejecting the idea of Christian military service.

In about 246–248, Origen wrote a lengthy rebuttal to a lost attack on Christianity (written about seventy years earlier) by Celsus, a learned Roman writer. Celsus charged that if all the Romans did as the Christians do, refusing public office and military service, the Roman empire would collapse. In his response, Origen says, "We no longer take up 'sword against nation' nor do we 'learn war anymore' having become children of peace for the sake of Jesus."[82] If Origen had thought either that many Christians currently served in the Roman army or that they should, he would obviously have simply corrected Celsus's misinformed views. Instead, Origen simply accepts Celsus's view of Christian behavior and explains why it is for the best.

"If all the Romans, according to the supposition of Celsus, embrace the Christian faith, they will not war at all, being guarded by that divine power."[83] "Celsus urges us to help the king with all our might and to labor with him in the maintenance of justice, to fight for him; and if he requires it, to fight under him or lead an army along with him."[84] Origen responds by saying that Christians pray for the king. That is more effective help than that of soldiers who fight for him. "To those enemies of our faith who require us to bear arms for the commonwealth and to slay people," Origen replies that even the Romans permit their pagan priests to "keep their hands from blood."[85] By their prayers, the Christians "do not indeed fight under him, although he require it; but we fight on his behalf, forming a special army—an army of piety—by offering our prayers to God."[86] Origen is clearly implying that Christians do not and should not serve in the Roman army.[87]

In the first few years of the fourth century, Lactantius unequivocally rejects killing of every kind, and indicates that this also means it is wrong for Christians to serve in the military. "When God forbids us to kill . . . he warns us against the commission of those things which are esteemed lawful among people. Thus it will be neither lawful for a just man to engage in military service . . . nor to accuse anyone of a capital charge . . . since it is the act of putting to death itself which is prohibited."[88] Christians should not join the military, because all killing is wrong.

---

82. *Celsus* 5.33.
83. *Celsus* 8.70.
84. *Celsus* 8.73.
85. In light of this and other statements by Origen, it is puzzling that Helgeland claims that Origen's objection to Christians in the military "never claimed as their basis the likelihood that Christians would be forced to kill other people in combat" ("Christians," 156).
86. *Celsus* 8.73.
87. See pp. 185–88 below for a discussion of the fact that at least a few Christians were in the army at this time.
88. *Divine Institutes* 6.20.

Finally, we have the *Apostolic Tradition*'s explicit statement that catechumens and believers must not enter military service. "A catechumen or a believer, if they want to be soldiers, let them be excluded because they distance themselves from God."[89] Here, the reason for the prohibition is general. But in the same section, the text says that if a soldier becomes interested in Christian teaching, he must be told not to kill. Similarly, a government official with the power of capital punishment must also stop or be rejected. Since the concern in these cases is the evil of killing, it is reasonable to assume this is the primary reason for the *Apostolic Tradition*'s prohibition against Christians choosing to enlist in the military.

THE REASONS FOR REJECTING CHRISTIAN PARTICIPATION IN THE MILITARY

Why do these writers reject Christian participation in the military? The reasons are several. Tertullian certainly believes that the pervasive presence of idolatry in military life is a very strong reason for avoiding it, but he also cites other reasons including the fact that Christ "unbelted every soldier." In Origen's long response to Celsus with regard to Christians in the military, only once does he mention idolatry. He also mentions it in his commentary on 1 Corinthians. But the primary reasons Origen opposes Christian participation in war are that Christians reject vengeance and love their enemies,[90] and follow Christ's teaching.[91] Just like the pagan Roman priests who are excused from the army, Christians must be free of shedding blood.[92] It simply does not fit the data to say that Origen's "objection to Christian enlistment was religious, not ethical; he was primarily opposed to pledging loyalty to the emperor."[93]

Lactantius is very clear. It is precisely because Lactantius believes that all killing is prohibited by God that he opposes participation in the military.[94] And this is likely also the decisive reason in the case of the prohibition in the *Apostolic Tradition*.

Our authors cite both idolatry and Christian ethical demands to love enemies and not kill as their reasons for opposing Christian participation in the military. But the latter, not the former, is the more frequently cited reason.[95]

89. *Apostolic Tradition* 16.
90. *Celsus* 2.30; 3.8; 8.35.
91. *Celsus* 5.33; 8.26.
92. *Celsus* 8.73.
93. Helgeland, "Roman Army," 750.
94. *Divine Institutes* 6.20.
95. Brennecke's claim that the question of military service for Christians in the Roman Empire was much more a matter of cult (i.e., idolatry) than the ethics of killing ("Kriegsdienst," 180) is inconsistent with the evidence.

James Johnson has argued that a changing view of eschatology dramatically affected the early church's view of war. He argues that the first-century Christians may have avoided military service, but the reason was not opposition to war but belief that the things of the world did not matter because Christ would return very soon. As the world continued, Christian eschatology changed; Christians became more accepting of warfare.[96] If Johnson intends his argument to apply only to the first one hundred years of post-apostolic Christianity, then his argument is sheer speculation. We have no writings explicitly on Christian engagement in warfare from this period. For the next two centuries, as Bainton has pointed out, "No Christian author ever overtly assigns the 'shortening of the times' as a reason for objection to participation in warfare."[97] Nothing in our texts supports this argument.[98] Origen certainly did not advocate the kind of radical eschatology Johnson describes, although he did oppose Christian killing and participation in the military. As Brock points out, Johnson's theory does not fit Origen.[99] Nor does it fit Lactantius.

Pre-Constantinian Christian writers opposed Christian participation in the military both on ethical grounds (they dare not kill) and religious grounds (they must avoid idolatry). But the first reason is mentioned more often than the second.

Implied Prohibition of Christian Participation in the Military

Justin Martyr (d. 167) claims that whereas formerly they were filled with war, now those who have become Christians have abandoned weapons of war. This he says has happened "through the whole earth." "We who were filled with war and mutual slaughter and every wickedness have each through the whole earth changed our warlike weapons—our swords into ploughshares and our spears into implements of tillage."[100] That certainly sounds as if Justin Martyr thinks Christians do not and should not serve in the military. Furthermore, since in this treatise Justin Martyr is writing to persuade Jews to become Christians, he could not have made this argument if non-participation in the military were not the widespread practice of Christians at the time.

In three places, Clement of Alexandria (d. 215) says that Christians do not use the musical instruments associated with war. He notes that many pagans

96. Johnson, *War* 12–17, 42.

97. Bainton, "Early Church," 201.

98. Swift also clearly rejects this view: "Not only do we have no text which gives this hope as a reason for refusing to serve, but those Christian writers who most vehemently opposed the idea of Christian soldiers were not invariably expecting or hoping for an immediate Parousia" ("War," 865).

99. Brock, *Pacifism*, 12.

100. *Trypho* 110.

use various musical instruments (trumpet, timbrel, flute, etc.) to arouse them to war. Christians on the other hand use "the one instrument of peace, the Word alone." "We no longer employ the ancient psaltery and trumpet and timbrel and flute, which those expert in war, despisers of the fear of God, were wont to make use of."[101] Clement repeats the same thing almost word for word in *Educator* 2.4. Similarly, later he notes: "The loud trumpet, when sounded, collects the soldiers, and proclaims war. And shall not Christ, breathing a strain of peace to the ends of the earth, gather together his own soldiers of peace? Well, by his blood and by the word, he has gathered the bloodless host of peace."[102]

Clement also says that Christians do not train for war. "For it is not in war but in peace that we are trained. War needs preparation and luxury craves abundance, but peace and love, simple and quiet sisters, require no arms."[103] He also says that Christians, unlike others, gather together "an unarmed, an unwarlike, a bloodless, a passionless, a stainless host . . . people adorned with love."[104] And in still another place, he notes: "We do not train our women like amazons to manliness in war since we wish men even to be peaceable."[105] These statements do not explicitly say Christians should not join the military, but they imply that it was not common practice for them to do so.[106]

Origen (d. 254) argues that the widespread peace initiated by Augustus was important for the spread of the gospel. Earlier, it seemed necessary for men everywhere to wage wars on behalf of their country. "How then was it possible for the Gospel doctrine of peace, which does not permit people to take vengeance even upon enemies to prevail throughout the world, unless at the advent of Jesus a milder spirit had been everywhere introduced?"[107] Origen clearly means to say that Christians do not fight wars.

Lactantius mocks the Roman view that the successful military general should be honored, even admitted to the abode of the gods. "He who has slaughtered countless thousands of people, has inundated plains with blood and infected rivers is not only admitted into the temple, but even into heaven."

101. *Exhortation* 4.
102. *Educator* 1.11.
103. *Educator* 1.12.
104. *Rich Man* 34.
105. *Miscellanies* 4.8.
106. For a discussion of one text that several modern scholars say shows that Clement accepted military service for Christians, see my argument that they have misinterpreted the text (see pp. 34–35 above on *Exhortation* 10). On the other hand, there is one passage (*Miscellanies* 4.14) that probably indicates that in Clement's thinking being in the military did not preclude one from being a Christian. Most of Clement's statements suggest that he thinks Christians do not train for the military and are an unarmed people who do not shed blood. But he probably thought—perhaps in a way similar to the *Apostolic Tradition*—that a Christian could be in the military if he did not kill.
107. *Celsus* 2.30.

He blames this absurdity on the warlike gods the Romans worship.[108] Christians, on the other hand, reject all killing and refuse to participate in warfare. If everyone worshiped the true God, "there would not be dissensions and wars."[109]

The texts cited in this section do not explicitly say that Christians should not join the military. If these were the only texts we had, it would not be entirely clear what they tell us about their authors' views on joining the military. But in light of all the other statements we have previously examined, it seems quite likely that we should add them to the list of passages that speak against Christians joining the military.

USE OF MILITARY LANGUAGE

Some scholars have argued that the frequent use of military language by the writers cited here raises questions about whether they really opposed war.[110] Harnack has claimed that the military language changed the thinking of the early Christians, leading eventually to the embrace of holy war in the later fourth century.[111]

I have only included a sampling of the many places where pre-Constantinian Christian writers employ military imagery, but this usage was not at all uncommon.[112]

One of our earliest post-canonical documents, *First Clement* (c. 80–100), uses vivid military imagery. "With all zeal, then, brethren, let us serve as good soldiers and his [Christ's] irreproachable command. Let us remember the discipline, obedience and submission that our government troops exhibit when they carry out orders."[113]

In the midst of a severe persecution in the middle of the third century, Cyprian, bishop of Carthage, wrote a series of powerful letters to encourage people. Cyprian uses a great deal of military imagery to describe the struggle. The Church is a diverse camp full of brave soldiers "bare, indeed, of weapons of this world, but believing and armed with the weapons of faith."[114] The "soldiers of Christ . . . stand sober and armed for the battle."[115]

Half a century later, in the midst of the terrible Diocletian persecution, Lactantius often uses military metaphors to describe the Christian response.

108. *Divine Institutes* 1.18; 5.10.
109. *Divine Institutes* 5.8.
110. Swift, *Military*, 33.
111. Harnack, *Militia Christi*, 32, 63.
112. In addition to Swift and Harnack, see Helgeland et al., *Military*, 18–19; and Cadoux, *War*, 161–70.
113. *First Clement* 37.
114. Letter 8.
115. Letter 56.

"We must be on the watch, must post guards, must undertake military expeditions" in obedience to "God our commander."[116]

In his discussion of *First Clement*'s use of military language, Swift acknowledges that the text "does not endorse Christian participation in war [but] one would nonetheless have difficulty in reconciling it with a pacifist stance. The fact that the author is not at all embarrassed by such imagery very likely indicates that the problem of Christians serving in the army was not an issue for him."[117] In the case of *First Clement*, the text contains no explicit statements to refute Swift (although it also contains nothing to support his speculation). But other statements by Cyprian and Lactantius, who use military language just as freely as *First Clement* does, clearly show that their use of military language in no way means they endorse actual warfare. Right in the middle of a passage using military language, Cyprian says the soldiers of Christ "do not in turn assail their assailants since it is not lawful for the innocent even to kill the guilty."[118] In the *Divine Institutes*, Lactantius definitely supports a pacifist stance, yet he often uses military language to speak of Christians. His usage of military language in no way modifies his explicit opposition to all kinds of killing and his rejection of Christian participation in the military. Nowhere in the pre-Constantinian writers have I found any indication that the use of military language led to any weakening of opposition to killing and participation in the military.

SOME AMBIGUOUS TEXTS

In *Against Heresies*, Irenaeus (d. 202) quotes from Romans 13:1–4 (government does not bear the sword in vain) and argues that God acted to restrain humanity's furious evil by ordaining government to promote some degree of justice "through dread of the sword."[119] Clearly Irenaeus thought the Roman government's use of the sword to preserve order was a positive thing.

But does that mean he thought Christians should use the sword? Absolutely nothing in Irenaeus suggests that. In other places he says that Christians must love their enemies and not strike back when others strike them.[120] He points out that the law of Christ (fulfilling Isaiah's prophecy) has produced Christian people who have turned their swords into ploughshares and are "now unaccustomed to fighting." When smitten, they turn the other cheek;[121] formerly brutal wagers of war "no sooner believed [in Christ] than they were

116. *Divine Institutes* 6.4.
117. Swift, *Military*, 33.
118. Letter 56.
119. *Against Heresies* 5.24.
120. *Against Heresies* 2.32.
121. *Against Heresies* 4.34.

changed."[122] Irenaeus apparently approves of the Roman government's use of the sword to preserve order, but he also clearly says that Christians do not use the sword.

Johnson has argued that in Clement of Alexandria (d. 215), we see the beginnings of the Just War tradition.[123] And Helgeland has said that Clement considered military service acceptable for Christians.[124] How strong is the evidence?

In *Educator*, Clement says going barefoot for a man is appropriate "except when he is on military service."[125] But nothing in the text says that Christians may legitimately be in the military. At the most, it shows that he knew of Christians in the military.

In the next chapter, he condemns soldiers who like to be "decked with gold."[126] But again, nothing in the text says these are Christian soldiers, much less that Christian service in the army is acceptable.

In another place, Clement cites John the Baptist's command to soldiers to be content with their wages without further comment.[127] Nothing in this text says anything about whether Clement thinks it is permissible for a Christian to be a soldier. A little later in the same chapter, he cites Jesus's command to love our enemies and turn the other cheek but he does not comment on what that means about Christian participation in the military.

In *Miscellanies*, Clement cites Deuteronomy 20:5–7 and refers to the "human law" that allows a newly married man to be free of military service for a year, and a little later in the same chapter, he refers to Deuteronomy 20:10, which stipulates that a walled city may not be attacked and considered an enemy until a herald has invited the city to surrender. But nothing in either section says anything about whether or not Christians may serve in the military.

Finally, a number of scholars have claimed that Clement's comments in *Exhortation to the Greeks* 10 indicate that he accepts military service for a Christian.[128] But, as I show in the introduction to that passage, Clement actually says that if a soldier becomes a Christian, then he must follow the teaching of Christ.[129]

If we only had these comments from Clement, we might properly conclude that he thinks that it is acceptable for Christians to serve in the army (although that would be an argument from silence, since none of the above texts clearly assert that). But we have other statements from Clement that rather clearly

122. *Apostolic Preaching* 61.
123. Johnson, *Peace*, 20–22.
124. Helgeland, "Christians," 154.
125. *Educator* 2.12.
126. *Educator* 2.13.
127. *Educator* 3.12.
128. See pp. 34–35 above.
129. See pp. 34–35 above.

point in the opposite direction. He says that Christians employ the "one in-strument of peace" (the Word) rather than the trumpets of war.[130] Christ gathers his "bloodless host," his "soldiers of peace," rather than blowing the trumpet that collects "soldiers and proclaims war."[131] Twice he cites Jesus's command to turn the other cheek.[132] He notes that not only do Christians not train women to be warriors but also "wish the men even to be peaceable,"[133] and he quotes Jesus's call to love enemies.[134]

It is true that there is relatively little material on our topic in Clement, but an argument from silence proves nothing on either side of the debate. Noth-ing in Clement says Christians dare kill. Nothing endorses or encourages Christians joining the military. And a number of texts talk about Christians turning the other cheek, being peaceable, and not training for war. He does seem to be aware of soldiers becoming Christians, but his advice (parallel to the *Apostolic Tradition*) is that such people must obey the commands of Christ, their commander.

In *On the Resurrection of the Dead*, Tertullian (d. 225) contrasts the sword "drunk with the blood of the brigand's victims" with the sword "which has received honorable stains in war, and has been thus engaged in a better man-slaughter." Such a sword "will secure its own praise by consecration."[135] Swift is probably right to say that this passage demonstrates that Tertullian can distinguish "between murder and killing in war."[136] But it says nothing about whether Christians should use the sword. That Tertullian insisted vigorously that they should not do so is explicit in many passages. Christ "cursed, for the time to come the works of the sword."[137] "By disarming Peter, [Christ] unbelted every soldier."[138] And in *The Crown*, he argues strongly against Christians serving in the military.

Some modern scholars have argued that Origen did "not oppose war, prop-erly undertaken."[139] It is true that Origen says those do well who kill a tyrant;[140] that in earlier times it was necessary to go to war to defend one's country;[141] that the "former economy" used violence;[142] that the bees offer a model to

---

130. *Exhortation* 4.
131. *Exhortation* 11.
132. *Educator* 2.12, and *Miscellanies* 4.8.
133. *Miscellanies* 4.8.
134. *Miscellanies* 4.14, and *Educator* 3.12.
135. *Resurrection* 16.
136. Swift, *Military*, 40.
137. *Patience* 4.
138. *On Idolatry* 19.
139. Helgeland, "Roman Army," 749; see also the authors cited in Cadoux, *War*, 138–39. See Hunter's critique of such arguments in "Decade of Research," 88.
140. *Celsus* 1.1.
141. *Celsus* 2.30.
142. *Celsus* 4.9.

fight wars justly "if ever there arise a necessity for them";[143] that under an earlier "constitution," the Jews would have been destroyed if they had not gone to war.[144] He also chides Celsus for belittling those who built cities and governments and went to war on behalf of their countries.[145]

But several circumstances make it highly doubtful that Origen thought Christians should fight in wars. In almost every instance where he speaks positively about wars, he explicitly refers to non-Christians.[146] In no place does he say Christians should fight. Origen frequently refers to an earlier time ("economy" or "constitution") when wars were fought and contrasts that to the present time when Jesus's followers love their enemies and do not go to war.[147] Finally, he frequently says Christians love their enemies, do not take vengeance, and do not go to war.[148] He even declares that if all the Romans became Christians, they "will not war at all."[149] Christ forbade the killing of anyone.[150]

It is true that Origen says that Christians, in obedience to Paul's command to pray for one's rulers, wrestle "in prayers to God on behalf of those who are fighting in a righteous cause, and for the king who reigns righteously." He can even say that "none fight better for the king than we do." But he immediately adds: "We do not indeed fight under him, although he require it; but we fight on his behalf, forming a special army—an army of piety—by offering our prayers to God."[151] Origen clearly appreciates the peace that Rome brings and thinks that Rome sometimes fights just wars,[152] but he is equally clear that Christians do not and should not engage in such warfare. If everyone became Christian, there would be no wars.[153]

Finally, there is the one sentence without further elaboration in Adamantius, *Dialogue on the True Faith,* that "it is right to wage a just war against those who go to war unjustly" (1.10). But as I showed earlier, there is nothing in this text that says Christians ought to fight wars.

The texts we have examined in this section show that Irenaeus and Origen appreciated the relative peace that Roman military power brought, and that

143. *Celsus* 4.82.
144. *Celsus* 7.26.
145. *Celsus* 4.83.
146. *Celsus* 2.30; 4.9; 7.26.
147. *Celsus* 2.30; 4.9; 5.33; 7.26.
148. *Celsus* 2.30; 3.8; 5.33; 8.26; 8.35; 8.73.
149. *Celsus* 8.70.
150. *Celsus* 3.7.
151. *Celsus* 8.73.
152. See also *Celsus* 2.30.
153. Caspary (*Origen,* 129) is probably right that Origen's understanding of the old and new dispensations helps us understand Origen here. Under the old dispensation, the Jews rightly fought wars. But in the new dispensation, Christians refuse to fight, obeying Christ's command to love their enemies. It is legitimate for Roman rulers to fight just wars until all become Christians.

Tertullian distinguishes between murder and killing in war, but none of these texts say that it is right for Christians to join the military and kill. In fact, they say that Christians must not kill and, sometimes, suggest they should not join the military. There is not nearly as much ambiguity in these texts as some scholars allege. To say that we see here the beginnings of the Just War tradition is to build a huge argument on very weak evidence.

Just War Christians may argue that it is problematic to both give thanks for the *Pax Romana* made possible by the Roman army and say that Christians dare not join that army. But that seems to be precisely what Origen and other early Christians thought. To argue that their gratitude for the *Pax Romana* constitutes the beginnings of the Just War tradition seems unjustified when the same early Christian authors explicitly reject the core argument of the Just War tradition (i.e., that *Christians* must sometimes reluctantly go to war for the sake of peace). At most, one can say that later Christians, like St. Augustine, when faced with the same question of the value of the *Pax Romana*, came to a fundamentally different conclusion than Origen.

EVIDENCE OF CHRISTIAN SOLDIERS BEFORE CONSTANTINE

Alongside the teaching of the pre-Constantinian Christian authors, we must place the evidence of Christians in the army. Here our evidence is very spotty; we cannot arrive at anything like a precise number. But from at least AD 173, we have clear evidence that at least a few Christians served in the Roman army.

The earliest evidence relates to "The Thundering Legion." Both pagan and Christian sources (plus an inscription in Rome) speak of a miraculous victory of a small Roman army. That several Christian sources, including two fairly close to the events, attribute the victory to the prayers of Christian soldiers in The Thundering Legion make it highly likely that there were at least a few Christian soldiers present.[154] Unfortunately, to try to specify how many would be sheer speculation.

Clement of Alexandria (d. 215) has a very brief comment ("Has knowledge taken hold of you while engaged in military service?") that shows that he was aware of soldiers coming to faith in Christ.[155]

Tertullian (d. 225) who sharply condemns Christian participation in the Roman army is nevertheless aware of the existence of Christian soldiers. In his *Apology* (written in 197), Tertullian seeks to refute the charges that Christians are dangerous enemies of Rome: "We sail with you, and fight with you."[156] A bit earlier, he claims: "We are but of yesterday, and we have filled every place among you—cities, islands, fortresses, towns, market, palace,

154. See pp. 137–44 above.
155. *Exhortation* 10; *Educator* 2.12; and *Miscellanies* 4.14 may suggest the same.
156. *Apology* 42.

senate, forum."[157] Obviously Tertullian's rhetoric and enthusiasm has led to exaggeration, but there is no doubt that Tertullian knew of some Christians in the army (again, we cannot know how many).

That is equally clear in his treatise on *The Crown*.[158] Tertullian begins the book with the story of a Christian soldier who threw off his laurel crown during a military procession and was executed. Nor was he the only Christian soldier present. Tertullian indicates that fellow Christian soldiers resented this action, fearing it would promote more widespread persecution. Tertullian disagrees: "He [the martyr] alone brave among so many soldier-brethren, he alone a Christian."[159] Apparently there were more than a few Christian soldiers in this military unit.

In his lengthy *Against Celsus* (written c. 246–248) Origen responds to Celsus's charge that if all Romans imitated the Christian rejection of military service, the empire would collapse. Origen's response is not to say that Celsus is misinformed because Christians *do* join the military. Rather, he repeatedly argues that Christians should not and *do not* go to war.[160]

But in one place, he does indicate that he knows of Christians in the military. In his commentary on 1 Corinthians, he mocks those confused Christians who think they can be Christians and also sprinkle a little incense on pagan altars. This confusion, he notes, "is met with most frequently in the armed forces." Origen clearly knows of Christians in the army who somehow try to justify their participation in idolatrous practices.

Again, we have no clear indication of numbers, but we do know that Celsus had attacked Christians for not serving in the army. If Origen knew that large numbers of Christians were soldiers, then the most obvious answer to Celsus would have been simply to correct Celsus's misinformation. Instead, Origen says Christians do not serve in the army and explains why. It is significant that in the middle of the third century a very widely read Christian author could claim that Christians do not serve in the Roman army. Obviously, some did, and Origen knew that. But his general response to Celsus makes little sense unless their numbers were relatively small.

Sometime between 253 and 260, Dionysus of Alexandria writes a letter about the current persecution of Christians. Among the martyrs, he says, are "both soldiers and private citizens."[161] At about the same time, a Christian soldier named Marinus—a person "honored for his military deeds"—was martyred in Palestine. The account does not tell us how long he had been a Christian.[162]

157. *Apology* 37.
158. *Crown* 1.11.
159. In chap. 11, Tertullian again speaks of Christians in the army.
160. *Celsus* 3.8; 5.33; 7.26; 8.73.
161. See p. 91 above.
162. See pp. 152–53 above.

From the last decade of the third century, we have the stories of two martyrs: one who refused to join the army and the other a centurion. In 295 in North Africa, a young military recruit named Maximillian refused to join the army. In an effort to persuade him to change his mind, the proconsul pointed out that the sacred bodyguards of the two emperors and caesars all had Christian soldiers, but Maximillian remained adamant and was martyred. The fact that he was quickly buried right next to the grave of Cyprian, the famous martyred bishop of Carthage, suggests that the North African church was not displeased with Maximillian's refusal to join the army.

Three years later in Tingis (modern Morocco) a Christian soldier named Marcellus rejected his military oath because he was unwilling to continue to participate in pagan practices. The fact that he was a centurion indicates that he had been a soldier for some time. He also died a martyr.

In early 304, Emperor Diocletian issued his fourth edict on the persecution of Christians. Those who refuse to sacrifice to the pagan gods must die. Later that year, Julius the Veteran was arrested (probably in a city on the Danube in modern Bulgaria) for refusing to offer sacrifice. Idolatry is clearly the problem. At his trial, Julius reports that he had served in the army for twenty-seven years, had reenlisted, and had fought boldly in seven military campaigns. "Nor was I the inferior of any man in battle," he reports. Julius also says that he had been a Christian for all of this time in the army, so he may very well have been a Christian when he first enlisted. Just before Julius is executed, he talks with another Christian soldier who is in prison. Nowhere in this account is there any suggestion that Julius's military career was an embarrassment to the church.[163]

It is quite clear from Eusebius's *Ecclesiastical History* that by the early fourth century, there were substantial numbers of Christians in the Roman army. He reports that Diocletian began the terrible persecution of 303–311 in the army.[164] Initially, Christian soldiers had a choice: stay in the army and sacrifice or leave the army at great financial loss. "Many of the soldiers," Eusebius says, chose to leave. "A great many soldiers of Christ's kingdom" promptly left the army and some were martyred.[165]

After a brief lull in persecution in the East, Emperor Maximin Daia renewed persecution of Christians in the Eastern part of the empire in 312. Eusebius reports that famine, plague, and military defeat followed. Maximin attacked the Armenians (living in northeastern modern Turkey) who he says "were also Christians." But, Eusebius reports, Maximin "was defeated in the war with the Armenians."[166] Apparently large numbers of Armenians were Christians by 312 and they were a central part of the successful Armenian army.

163. Eusebius, *Ecclesiastical History* 8.
164. *Ecclesiastical History* 8.1.
165. *Ecclesiastical History* 8.4.
166. *Ecclesiastical History* 9.8.

We do not have any real indication of the number of Christians in Constantine's army in the West. Nor do we know how accurate is Eusebius's (or Lactantius's somewhat different) account of Constantine's alleged sighting (or dream) of the sign of the cross just before his decisive victory at the Milvian Bridge outside of Rome in 312. But after 312, Constantine used Christian symbols on his military insignia,[167] and in 313, the two emperors of West and East, Constantine and Licinius, met at Milan and jointly signed letters declaring religious freedom throughout the empire.[168] Christians were probably only 10–15 percent of the population of the empire at this point, but it is highly unlikely that Constantine would have placed Christian symbols on his military insignia if there had not been at least a substantial number of Christians in his army.

Overall, the references to Christian soldiers indicate that they were present in many places from Rome east. There is one reference each for Thrace and Bulgaria and two for North Africa. Rome has three references. The largest number of instances refers to Christian soldiers in the east: five in present-day Turkey, three in Alexandria in Egypt, and two in Palestine. It is also interesting that the earliest evidence (the "Thundering Legion") and (probably) the instance of the largest group of Christian soldiers (the Armenian Christians who defeated one of the emperors in 312) both come from present-day Turkey. The paucity of our sources permits only very cautious generalization. But it would seem that before Constantine, Christian soldiers were more common in the area that stretched from modern Turkey through Palestine to Egypt.[169]

167. See Leithart, *Constantine*, 64–79, and the literature cited there.

168. Ibid., 99.

169. A careful analysis of both the time of references to Christian soldiers and also to the geographical location of these soldiers adds a little to our understanding. The small number of our sources, however, compels us to be cautious about sweeping generalizations.

From the second century, we have four references: (1) there were at least a few Christian soldiers in the "Thundering Legion" in about AD 173, when it fought along the Danube, although this legion was normally based in Melitene in Armenia, now Turkey (above, pp. 137–44); (2) an inscription (Leclercq, *L'Année épigraphique*, no. 47) that is thought to be from Rome in the late second century (above, p. 145); (3) another inscription from Rome (Leclercq, *L'Année épigraphique*, no. 29) dated 201 (above, p. 145); (4) and Tertullian's *Apology* (written in Carthage in North Africa in about 197), which says there are Christians in the Roman army (above, pp. 45–46). Thus we have a total of four certain references by 201—two from Rome, and one each from North Africa and present-day Turkey.

From the first half of the third century, we have at least four references to Christian soldiers: (1) one inscription (no. 171, location uncertain) from about AD 246–49 (above, pp. 146, 148); (2) a Christian prayer hall frequented by at least one Christian centurion in Palestine in about 230 (above, pp. 144–45); (3) Tertullian's story in *The Crown* (c. 211) about a Christian soldier who upset other Christian soldiers by refusing to participate in pagan rituals and was martyred (probably at Carthage in North Africa; above, pp. 58–59); (4) in his commentary on 1 Corinthians (written in Alexandria or Palestine sometime in the first half of the third century), Origen mocks Christians who think they may participate in idolatrous practices—an attitude, he notes, "met most frequently in the armed forces" (above, pp. 70–71). That makes at least four references

But we simply do not know how many Christians were in the Roman army in the year 173 or 250 or 312. That there were at least a very few in 173 is clear. That a significant Roman pagan (Celsus) writing about the same time thought there were either very few or none is also quite certain. That Origen, perhaps the most widely read Christian of his day, could simply accept Celsus's generalization about AD 250 is also important, especially since Origen is living in the East, where we have the largest number of references to Christian soldiers before Constantine.

Equally certain, however, are the growing indications in the third century, especially in the last decade of the third century and the first decade of the fourth, that there were substantial numbers of Christians in the Roman army. Cadoux's argument that Diocletian would hardly have launched his intense persecution of Christians if a large portion of his soldiers were Christians has a ring of plausibility.[170] But so does the argument that Constantine would

---

to Christian soldiers in the first half of the third century—one from North Africa, one from Palestine, one from either Egypt or Palestine, and one of uncertain location.

One other early-third-century document is relevant. The church order *The Apostolic Tradition* (perhaps from Rome) describes soldiers who come to the church exploring the possibility of baptism. But they are told they must refuse orders to kill (above, pp. 119–21)!

There are at least three references to Christian soldiers early in the second half of the third century: (1) a letter (c. 253–60) from Dionysius, bishop of Alexandria (quoted in Eusebius's *Ecclesiastical History*), which refers to many martyrs in Alexandria, including Christian soldiers (above, p. 91); (2) Marinus, a Christian soldier who was martyred in Palestine in about 260 (above, p. 152–53); and (3) an inscription from Phrygia (part of Turkey today) from the mid-third century that refers to the Aurelii brothers, who were Christian soldiers (above, p. 149). All three of these are from the east: Egypt, Palestine and present-day Turkey.

Toward the end of the third century and in the first decade of the fourth century, there are many indications of increasing numbers of Christian soldiers: (1) the soldier Marcellus was martyred for his Christian faith in about 298 in Tingis (Morocco today), but his legion was normally based at Alexandria (above, pp. 155–56); (2) Julian the Veteran was martyred in about 304 in present day Bulgaria (above, pp. 157–58); (3) in about 295, when the young Maximilian refused military service, the Roman proconsul tries to persuade him to join by arguing that there were Christian soldiers in the military bodyguard of the emperors (above, pp. 153–55); (4) an inscription of Aurelius Manos refers to a Christian soldier in Phrygia (part of Turkey) in the late third or early fourth century (above, p. 149); (5) Marcus Julius Eugenius was a Christian soldier serving in Pisidia (south-central Turkey today) in the early fourth century until he had to escape in 310 (above, pp. 149–50); (6) the Christian Aurelius Gaius was forced out of the military in 303 after a long military career (above, pp. 150–51); (7) Aurelius Posidonius was probably a Christian soldier in Thrace (above, pp. 146, 148–49); (8) three other inscriptions, one of which is from Rome (nos. 12, 21, and 43 in Leclercq, *L'Année épigraphique* are probably all from the third century, and no. 21 is from Rome; see above, pp. 145, 147); (9) Eusebius tells us that the great persecution that began in 303 started with Christians in the army (above, p. 160); (10) in 312, the anti-Christian emperor in the east provoked war with the Armenians (central Turkey today)—who Eusebius says were Christians—and the Armenians won (above, pp. 160–61). Of the known locations in this last period, there are three instances of Christian soldiers in present-day Turkey, and one each in Alexandria, Bulgaria, Rome, and Thrace.

170. Cadoux, *War*, 243.

not have done what he did in 312 if there had not been significant numbers of Christians in his army. Our available data do not permit us to be specific, but there were certainly substantial numbers of Christian soldiers before Constantine and Licinius declared religious toleration in 313.

Conclusions

Several things are clear, others less so.

First, up until the time of Constantine, there is not a single Christian writer known to us who says that it is legitimate for Christians to kill or join the military.[171]

Second, there is a substantial number of passages written over a period of many years that explicitly say that Christians must not and/or do not kill or join the military. Nine different Christian writers in sixteen different treatises explicitly say that killing is wrong. Four writers in five treatises clearly argue that Christians do not and should not join the military. In addition, four writers in eight different works strongly imply that Christians should not join the military. At least eight times, five different authors apply the messianic prophecy about swords being beaten into ploughshares (Isa. 2:4) to Christ and his teaching. Ten different authors in at least twenty-eight different places cite or allude to Jesus's teaching to love enemies and, in at least nine of these places, they connect that teaching to some statement about Christians being peaceful, ignorant of war, opposed to attacking others, and so forth. All of this represents a considerable body of evidence.

To argue, as Helgeland does, that there is practically no evidence from the Fathers that would support the argument that the early church denied enlistment on the ground that killing and war were opposed to the Christian ethic[172] seems to ignore the evidence.

It is true that there is only one full treatise (Tertullian's *Crown*) on the topic, but the data is not miniscule. There are many statements by a number of authors that condemn killing and/or joining the military.[173]

To argue, as does Leithart, that Origen and Tertullian represented "a small articulate minority"[174] or to suggest, as does Daly, that "pacifism may not even

---

171. The only conceivable exceptions are (1) the violent actions of the young Jesus in the apocryphal *Infancy Gospel of Thomas*, which no Christian writer cited as authoritative; (2) Julianus Africanus's *Cestes*, which is secular; and (3) Adamantius, *Dialogue on the True Faith*. There is no argument in any of these that it is legitimate for Christians to kill or join the army.

172. Helgeland, "Roman Army," 764–65.

173. Origen devotes most of chaps. 65–75 (esp. chaps. 68–70, 73) of book 8 to refuting Celsus's charge that if everyone rejected military service and public office the way Christians do, the empire would collapse. Lactantius also argues in a fairly extended section (*Divine Institutes* 6.20) that killing of every kind, including in warfare, is wrong.

174. *Constantine*, 259; similarly Lebreton and Zeiller, *Primitive Church*, 1156–58.

have been known among Christian laymen"[175] is not only sheer speculation, but also runs counter to the evidence that we do have.

Third, the rejection of killing is comprehensive. These authors condemn, as Origen says, "killing of any individual whatever,"[176] or as Tertullian puts it, "every sort of man-killing."[177] This comprehensive rejection of killing includes abortion, capital punishment, gladiatorial contests (even watching them), infanticide, and warfare. After condemning all these forms of killing, Lactantius concludes: "It is not permitted to commit homicide in any way."[178]

Fourth, it is simply not accurate to say that the primary reason that these authors reject military service for Christians is the problem of idolatry in the army. Idolatry is the issue that Tertullian discusses the most; although he also gives other reasons including Christ's "unbelting every soldier." Origen mentions idolatry twice, but his primary emphasis is on the fact that Christ taught love for enemies and rejection of vengeance, and that Christians should not shed human blood. In both Lactantius and the *Apostolic Tradition*, it is clear that the reason for the prohibition is that Christians must not kill. Opposition to killing human beings, not fear of idolatry, is the more frequently given reason for rejection of Christian military service. And there is no evidence in the texts that eschatological expectation of Christ's near return had any bearing on these writers' views on participation in the military.

Fifth, there is very little basis in the texts for describing the early Christian view as "divided and ambiguous." There are no authors who argue that killing or joining the military is permissible for Christians. On these questions, every writer who mentions the subject takes essentially the same position. Some pre-Constantinian Christian writers say more about these topics than others. Some do not discuss them at all. But to conclude from this relative silence or paucity of surviving texts that other writers disagreed with the extant texts would be sheer speculation. The texts we have do not reflect any substantial disagreement.

Sixth, there is little basis for the suggestion that these pre-Constantinian texts provide the beginnings of an Augustinian, Just War argument.[179] It is true that many of these authors appreciated the widespread peace provided by Roman rule. Origen recognizes that capital punishment and war were allowed under the "former economy" that applied to the nation of Israel. He even says that the bees provide a model of how to fight wars justly "if ever there arose

175. Daly, "Military Force," 180. Payne and Payne's summary of the thinking of the early church (*Just Defense*, 75–88) is also inaccurate.

176. *Celsus* 3.7.

177. *Spectacles* 2.

178. *Divine Institutes* 6.20.

179. If Adamantius had expanded on the one sentence on just war in *Dialogue on the True Faith* and argued that Christians could engage in it, that treatise would be an exception. But there is no such statement.

a necessity for them." But Origen is very clear and explicit that the new law taught by Christ explicitly forbids killing and warfare for Christians. There is no hint whatsoever in Origen of the core idea of the Just War tradition that Christians must reluctantly take up the sword to preserve justice and peace. As Hunter points out, "The whole point of Origen's discussion is to insist that Christians may not participate in warfare, *even for a just cause.*"[180]

Seventh, the evidence clearly shows that there were at least a few Christians in the Roman army by the late second century and early third. In the mid-third century, Origen mocks and condemns the way some Christian soldiers justify throwing a little incense on pagan altars.[181] By the late third century and the first decade of the fourth century there are clearly substantial numbers of Christians serving as soldiers.

This fact is the only substantive basis in our data for saying that the pre-Constantinian church was divided in its views on military service. The writers are not divided in their stated views, but a growing number of Christians do serve and justify their action. In *Idolatry* (c. 203–206), Tertullian briefly cites some of the arguments that Christian soldiers are using to justify their military service.[182]

In the *Apostolic Tradition* (probably late second or early third century) and several other places, we catch a glimpse of one probable way that the presence of Christians in the army developed. The *Apostolic Tradition* clearly condemns baptized Christians joining the military. But it also deals with the fact that some soldiers are becoming interested in Christianity. It does not demand that they abandon the army before they receive catechetical training, but they must agree not to kill. In *The Crown* (c. 211) Tertullian notes that "if faith comes later, and finds any occupied with military service, their case is different."[183] Tertullian adds that many have promptly left the army, but he does not demand that, although he thinks that remaining a soldier will require "all sorts of quibbling."[184]

It helps us understand the *Apostolic Tradition*'s position to remember two things. First, it was very difficult and costly for a Roman soldier to leave the army before his term of service (typically, twenty-five years) was over. And second, many Roman soldiers in the first three centuries seldom or never fought in military campaigns. In *On Flight in Persecution*, 13, Tertullian refers to "free soldiers"—that is, soldiers released from regular duty to do administrative work. R. W. Davies wrote an article providing numerous examples from this

180. Hunter, "Decade of Research," 88 (Turner's italics). Turner says claims that the beginnings of the later Just War tradition are in Origen "do more to reveal the prejudices of the authors than they serve to illuminate Origen's own position" (ibid.).

181. *Commentary on I Corinthians.*

182. *Idolatry* 19.

183. *Crown* 11.

184. *Crown* 11. See also Clement of Alexandria above, pp. 34–35.

period where the Roman legions were employed in what was essentially police work.[185] Statements by two of the prominent historians of the Roman army underline this point. In a book published by Cornell University Press, G. R. Watson said that "once the soldier had been trained, he could look forward to a life which would be spent mainly in conditions of peace. . . . Many soldiers may never have been called upon to take part in a campaign."[186] And Ramsay MacMullen in a Harvard University Press book focused on the Roman army in the years 200–400, noted that "many a recruit need never have struck a blow in anger, outside of a tavern."[187] If that was the situation for large numbers of Roman soldiers, one can understand that it was quite plausible for Christians to say that soldiers who wish to become Christians may remain in the army if they agree never to kill.

That is not to say that no Christian soldiers actually fought in battle. Those in the "Thundering Legion" in 173 very probably did. Julius the Veteran (d. 304) clearly did. So did the large number of Armenian Christian soldiers who helped defeat the pagan emperor Maximin Daia in 312.

There is an obvious disconnect between the unanimous teaching of all extant Christian writers who state that killing is wrong, and the clear evidence that more and more Christians were in the army. Lactantius pens one of the most explicit, sweeping rejections of any type of killing by Christians, and he writes it in the first decade of the fourth century when the evidence is quite clear that substantial numbers of Christians are fighting in military battles. How to understand this disconnect is not clear.

Johnson and others have suggested that the lack of evidence for any significant controversy about the embrace of Constantine, the celebration of his military victories, and the large number of Christians in the Roman armies of the fourth century suggest that Christian opposition to killing and warfare had long since disappeared as the majority Christian viewpoint (if indeed it had ever been that).[188] Swift, however, does point to some evidence of fourth-century Christians struggling to reconcile their present context with earlier views.[189] Wrestling with Johnson's suggestion, however, would require careful examination of a vast literature beyond the scope of this book. (Johnson's thesis is worthy of careful, comprehensive study.)

---

185. Davies, "Police Work," 700. Helgeland, however, rightly points out that not all police work was nonviolent ("Roman Army," 793–95).

186. Watson, *Roman Soldier*, 143.

187. MacMullen, *Soldier*, v.

188. Johnson, *Peace*, 14–15. See also Leithart, *Constantine*, 272, and Helgeland, "Roman Army," 815–16.

189. Swift, *Military*, 93–101, 150–51. See also Musto, *Peace Tradition*, 42. Cf. the O'Donovans' comment that "fourth-century writers, however, found no moral difficulty with military service in war, unaware, apparently, of the gulf dividing their attitudes from earlier ones." In contrast, they note the substantial "conscientious anxiety which frequently surfaced in the fourth and fifth centuries about responsibility for capital punishment" (*Political Thought*, 3).

In reflecting on the disconnect between the unanimous teaching of Christian writers and the increasing number of Christians in the army, it is probably not irrelevant to note that, frequently over the course of Christian history, Christian laity have not lived what Christian leaders have taught. Today, vast numbers of Christians of all traditions ignore what Christian leaders say about divorce and materialism. It would hardly be surprising if that disconnect also occurred in the early centuries. In fact, we know that both Tertullian and Origen mocked what they considered the weak justification of Christian soldiers for what they were doing.[190]

The historian, of course, would welcome much more data than we have on the official teaching of the church. It would be exceedingly helpful if we could be reasonably certain how widely accepted was the teaching of the late second- and early third-century church order known as the *Apostolic Tradition*, which rejects killing and Christian enlistment in the army. We lack the necessary evidence to know with certainty if this work represents the official teaching and practice of many churches, or merely reflects the personal views of a few authors. There is certainly not adequate evidence to justify Harnack's sweeping speculation that "these instructions of the moralists were in no way followed in the third century."[191] The fact that it was translated into Arabic, Ethiopic, Latin, and Coptic is one measure of its somewhat widespread use and acceptance. So is the fact that another church order, probably compiled in Egypt perhaps around 336–340, uses large sections of the *Apostolic Tradition* (including the stipulation that soldiers may not kill and must refuse if they are commanded to do so).[192] We certainly do not have enough evidence to say that the *Apostolic Tradition* represents the official teaching of the third-century church. But the modest data we do have suggest that it reflects far more than the personal views of a few isolated thinkers.

What we can say with confidence is that every extant Christian statement on killing and war up until the time of Constantine says Christians must not kill, even in war.[193] That a growing number of Christians, especially in the late third and early fourth centuries, acted contrary to that teaching is

190. Tertullian, *Idolatry* 19; Origen, *Commentary on I Corinthians*.

191. Harnack, *Militia Christ*, 87.

192. Brock, "Eusebius and Syriac Christianity," 91.

193. I discovered J. Daryl Charles's essay, "Pacifists, Patriots, or Both? Second Thoughts on Pre-Constantinian Early-Christian Attitudes toward Soldiering and War" (*Logos* 13, no. 2 [Spring 2010]: 17–55) only after completing this book. The teaching of the early church is not nearly as ambiguous as he suggests. It is astonishing to have Charles argue that Origen pointed "out the fact of Christians' presence in the Roman army in response to the criticisms of the pagan philosopher Celsus" (30). In fact, Origen's response to Celsus was that if the Romans acted like Christians in rejecting war, then war would cease (see above, 79–83, esp. 81). To say that Lactantius does not "address Christians in the military per se" (35) flatly ignores Lactantius's explicit statement that "it will be neither lawful for a just man [a Christian] to engage in military service" (above, 110).

also clear. Whether in doing so they were following other Christian teachers and leaders who justified their conduct, we cannot say with certainty. But we have absolutely no evidence to support the suggestion that such teachers ever existed until the time of Constantine. Any claim that they did is sheer speculation.[194]

194. An example of such speculation is Brennecke's assertion that the bishops of the church, as pastoral leaders, saw no problem with Christians in the military ("Kriegsdienst," 200–201). He provides no clear evidence to support his argument. In two cases where he implies this conclusion, the text contains no such statement (see above, 153n23 and 159).

Bibliography

Adler, William. "Sextus Julius Africanus and the Roman Near East in the Third Century." *JTS* n.s. 55, no. 2 (2004): 520–50.

Arbesmann, Rudolph, Emily Joseph Daly, and Edwin A. Quain. *Tertullian: Apologetic Works and Minucius Felix: Octavius*. New York: Fathers of the Church, 1950.

———. *Tertullian: Disciplinary, Moral and Ascetical Works*. FC 40. New York: Fathers of the Church, 1959.

Arner, Rob. *Consistently Pro-Life: The Ethics of Bloodshed in Ancient Christianity*. Eugene, OR: Pickwick, 2010.

Arpee, Leon. *A History of Armenian Christianity: From the Beginning to Our Own Time*. New York: Armenian Missionary Association of America, 1946.

Bainton, Roland H. *Christian Attitudes toward War and Peace: A Historical Survey and Critical Re-Evaluation*. New York: Abingdon, 1960.

———. "The Early Church and War." *HTR* 39 (1946): 189–212.

Baldovin, John F. "Hippolytus and the Apostolic Tradition: Recent Research and Commentary." *TS* 64, no. 3 (2003): 520–42.

Barkley, Gary Wayne. *Origen: Homilies on Leviticus 1–16*. FC 83. Washington, DC: Catholic University of America Press, 1990.

Barnard, Leslie W. *Athenagoras: A Study in Second Century Christian Apologetic*. Paris: Beauchesne, 1972.

———, ed. and trans. *St. Justin Martyr: The First and Second Apologies*. ACW 56. New York: Paulist Press, 1997.

Barnes, Timothy David. *Tertullian: A Historical and Literary Study*. Rev. ed. Oxford: Clarendon, 1985.

Bethune-Baker, J. F. *The Influence of Christianity on War*. Cambridge: Macmillan and Bowes, 1888.

Bobertz, C. A. *Cyprian of Carthage as a Patron: A Social Historical Study of the Role of Bishop in the Ancient Christian Community of North Africa*. Ann Arbor: UMI, 1993.

Bowan, Anthony, and Peter Garnsey. *Lactantius: Divine Institutes*. TTH 40. Liverpool: Liverpool University Press, 2003.

Bowman, Alan K., Peter Garnsey, and Averil Cameron, eds. *The Crisis of Empire, A.D. 193–337*. Vol. 12, Cambridge Ancient History. 2nd ed. Cambridge: Cambridge University Press, 2005.

Bradshaw, Paul F., ed. *The Canons of Hippolytus*. Nottingham: Grove, 1987.

———. *The Search for the Origins of Christian Worship*. 2nd ed. New York: Oxford University Press, 2002.

Bradshaw, Paul F., Maxwell E. Johnson, and L. Edward Phillips. *The Apostolic Tradition: A Commentary*. Hermeneia. Minneapolis: Fortress, 2002.

Bremmer, Jan N., and Istvan Czachesz, eds. *The Apocalypse of Peter*. Leuven: Peeters, 2003.

Brennecke, Hanns Christof. "Kriegsdienst und Soldatenberuf für Christen und die Rolle des römischen Heeres für die Mission." In *Krieg und Christentum: Religiöse Gewalttheorien in der Kriegserfahrung des Westens*, edited by Andreas Holzem. Krieg in der Geschichte 50. Paderborn: Ferdinand Schöningh, 2009.

Brent, Allen. *Hippolytus and the Roman Church in the Third Century: Communities in Tension before the Emergence of a Monarch-Bishop*. Leiden: Brill, 1995.

———. *St. Cyprian of Carthage: On the Church, Select Treatises*. Crestwood, NY: St. Vladimir's Seminary Press, 2006.

———. *St. Cyprian of Carthage, Select Letters*. Crestwood, NY: St. Vladimir's Seminary Press, 2006.

Brock, Peter. "The Military Question in the Early Church: A Selected Bibliography of a Century's Scholarship (1888–1987)." Toronto, 1988.

———. *Pacifism in Europe to 1914*. Princeton: Princeton University Press, 1972.

———. "Why Did St. Maximilian Refuse to Serve the Roman Army?" *JEH* 45, no. 2 (1994): 195–209.

Brock, Sebastian. "Eusebius and Syriac Christianity." In *Eusebius, Christianity and Judaism*, edited by Harold W. Attridge and Gohei Hata. Detroit: Wayne State University Press, 1992.

Bruce, Barbara J., trans. *Origen: Homilies on Joshua*. Edited by Cynthia White. FC 105. Washington, DC: Catholic University of America Press, 2002.

Buell, Denise Kimber. "Producing Descent/Dissent: Clement of Alexandria's Use of Filial Metaphors as Intra-Christian Polemic." *HTR* 90 (1997): 89–104.

Butterworth, G. W., ed. and trans. *Clement of Alexandria: Exhortation to the Greeks; The Rich Man's Salvation; To the Newly Baptized*. LCL. 1919; repr., Cambridge, MA: Harvard University Press, 2003.

Cadoux, Cecil John. *The Early Church and the World*. Edinburgh: T&T Clark, 1925.

———. *The Early Christian Attitude to War*. 1919; repr., New York: Seabury, 1982.

Calder, W. M. "A Fourth-Century Lycaonian Bishop." *Exp.* 6 (1908): 385–408.

———. "Studies in Early Christian Epigraphy." *JRS* 10 (1920): 42–59.

Cary, Ernest, trans. *Dio's Roman History*. LCL. 9 vols. Cambridge, MA: Harvard University Press, 1914–27.

Caspary, Gerard E. *Politics and Exegesis: Origen and the Two Swords*. Berkeley: University of California Press, 1979.

Cerrato, J. A. *Hippolytus between East and West: The Commentaries and the Provenance of the Corpus*. Oxford: Oxford University Press, 2002.

Chadwick, Henry. *Early Christian Thought and the Classical Tradition: Studies on Justin, Clement, and Origen*. New York: Oxford University Press, 1966.

———. *Origen: Contra Celsum*. Cambridge: Cambridge University Press, 1953.

Charles, J. Daryl. *Between Pacifism and Jihad: Just War and Christian Tradition.* Downers Grove, IL: InterVarsity, 2005.

Chartrand-Burke, Tony. "The Infancy Gospel of Thomas: The Text, Its Origins and Its Transmission." PhD diss., University of Toronto, 2001.

Clarke, G. W. *The Letters of St. Cyprian.* 4 vols. ACW 43–44, 46–47. New York: Newman Press, 1984–9.

Connolly, R. Hugh. *Didascalia Apostolorum: The Syriac Version Translated and Accompanied by the Verona Latin Fragments.* London: Oxford University Press, 1929.

Crehan, Joseph Hugh, ed. and trans. *Athenagoras: Embassy for the Christians; The Resurrection of the Dead.* ACW 23. New York: Newman Press, 1955.

Cross, F. L., and E. A. Livingstone, eds. *The Oxford Dictionary of the Christian Church.* 3rd rev. ed. Oxford: Oxford University Press, 2005.

Crouzel, Henri. *Origen.* Translated by A. S. Worrall. San Francisco: Harper, 1989.

Daly, Robert J. "Military Force and the Christian Conscience in the Early Church: A Methodological Approach." *Proceedings of the Thirty-Seventh Annual Convention, The Catholic Theological Society of America* 37 (1982): 178–81.

————. "Military Service and Early Christianity: A Methodological Approach." *SP* 18, no. 1 (1985): 1–8.

Davies, R. W. "Police Work in Roman Times." *History Today*, October 1968, 700–707.

Deferrari, Roy J., ed. *Early Christian Biographies.* FC 15. New York: Fathers of the Church, 1952.

————, trans. and ed. *Saint Cyprian: Treatises.* FC 36. New York: Fathers of the Church, 1958.

Dix, Gregory, and Henry Chadwick. *The Treatise on the Apostolic Tradition of St. Hippolytus of Rome.* 1937; repr., London: Alban, 1992.

Donna, Rose Bernard, trans. *Saint Cyprian: Letters (1–81).* FC 51. Washington, DC: Catholic University of America Press, 1964.

Doran, Robert. *Stewards of the Poor: The Man of God, Rabbula, and Hiba in Fifth-Century Edessa.* CSS 208. Kalamazoo, MI: Cistercian Publications, 2006.

Dörries, Hermann. *Constantine the Great.* Translated by Roland H. Bainton. New York: Harper Torchbooks, 1972.

Dunn, Geoffrey D. *Tertullian.* New York: Routledge, 2004.

Ehrman, Bart D. *The Apostolic Fathers.* 2 vols. LCL 24–25. Cambridge, MA: Harvard University Press, 2003.

Elliott, J. K. *The Apocryphal New Testament: A Collection of Apocryphal Christian Literature in an English Translation.* Oxford: Clarendon, 1993.

Evans, Ernest, ed. and trans. *Tertullian Adversus Marcionem.* Oxford: Clarendon, 1972.

Falls, Thomas B., ed. *Writings of Saint Justin Martyr.* FC 6. New York: Christian Heritage, 1948.

Ferguson, Everett. "Love of Enemies and Nonretaliation in the Second Century." In *The Contentious Triangle: Church, State and University*, edited by Rodney L. Petersen and Calvin Augustine Pater, 81–96. SCES 51. Kirksville, MO: Truman State University Press, 1999.

Ferguson, John, ed. and trans. *Clement of Alexandria: Stromateis, Books One to Three.* FC 85. Washington, DC: Catholic University of America Press, 1991.

Frend, W. H. C. *Martyrdom and Persecution in the Early Church.* Oxford: Blackwell, 1965.

Friesen, John. "War and Peace in the Patristic Age." In *Essays on War and Peace: Bible and Early Church*, edited by Willard M. Swartley. Occasional Papers 9. Elkhart, IN: Institute of Mennonite Studies, 1986.

Gero, Stephen. "Miles Gloriosus: The Christian and Military Service According to Tertullian." *CH* 39 (1970): 285–98.

Glimm, Francis X., Joseph M. F. Marique, and Gerald G. Walsh, trans. *The Apostolic Fathers.* FC 1. Washington, DC: Catholic University of America Press, 1962.

Glover, T. R., and Gerald H. Rendall, trans. *Tertullian and Minucius Felix.* LCL. Cambridge, MA: Harvard University Press, 1931.

Goodspeed, Edgar J. *A History of Early Christian Literature.* Chicago: University of Chicago Press, 1966.

Gorman, Jill. "Reading and Theorizing Women's Sexualities: The Representation of Women in the Acts of Xanthippe and Polyxena." PhD diss., Temple University, 2003.

Gorman, Michael J. *Abortion and the Early Church: Christian, Jewish, and Pagan Attitudes in the Greco-Roman World.* Downers Grove, IL: InterVarsity, 1982.

Grant, Robert M. *The Apostolic Fathers: A New Translation and Commentary.* Vol. 1. New York: Thomas Nelson and Sons, 1964.

Harnack, Adolf. "Die Quellen der Berichte über das Regenwunder im Feldzuge Marc Aurel's gegen die Quaden." *Sitzungsberichte der Königlich Preussischen Akademie der Wissenschaften zu Berlin* 36 (1894): 835–82.

———. *Geschichte der altchristlichen Literatur bis Eusebius.* 2nd ed. Vol. 2.2. Leipzig: J. C. Hinrichs, 1958.

———. *Militia Christi: The Christian Religion and the Military in the First Three Centuries.* Translated by David M. Gracie. Philadelphia: Fortress, 1981.

Heather, Peter, and John Matthews. *The Goths in the Fourth Century.* TTH 11. Liverpool: Liverpool University Press, 1991.

Heine, Ronald E. *Origen: Commentary on the Gospel according to John, Books 13–32.* FC 89. Washington, DC: Catholic University of America Press, 1993.

Helgeland, John. "Christians and the Roman Army, A.D. 173–337." *CH* 43 (1974): 149–63, 200.

———. "Christians and the Roman Army from Marcus Aurelius to Constantine." ANRW 2.23.1 (1979): 724–834.

———. "The Early Church and War: The Sociology of Idolatry." In *Peace in a Nuclear Age: The Bishops' Pastoral Letters in Perspective.* Edited by Charles J. Reid Jr., 34–47. Washington, DC: Catholic University of America Press, 1986.

———. "Roman Army Religion." *Aufstieg und niedergang der römischen Welt* 2.16.1 (1978): 1470–1505.

Helgeland, John, Robert J. Daly, and J. Patout Burns. *Christians and the Military.* Philadelphia: Fortress, 1985.

Hennecke, Edgar. *New Testament Apocrypha.* Edited by Wilhelm Schneemelcher. Translated by R. M. Wilson. Philadelphia: Westminster, 1965.

Holmes, Dennis. "The Date of the Octavius." *AJP* 50, no. 2 (1929): 185–89.

Holmes, Michael W., ed. *The Apostolic Fathers: Greek Texts and English Translations.* Grand Rapids: Baker Academic, 2007.

Hornus, Jean-Michel. *It Is Not Lawful for Me to Fight: Early Christian Attitudes toward War, Violence, and the State.* Translated by Alan Kreider and Oliver Coburn. Rev. ed. Scottdale, PA: Herald, 1980.

Hunter, David G. "A Decade of Research on Early Christians and Military Service." *RSR* 18, no. 2 (1992): 87–94.

Ingremeau, Christiane. *Lactance: Institutions Divines.* SC 509. Paris: Cerf, 2007.

Jefford, Clayton N. *The Apostolic Fathers and the New Testament*. Peabody, MA: Hendrickson, 2006.

Jenkins, Philip. *The Lost History of Christianity*. San Francisco: HarperOne, 2008.

Johnson, James Turner. *The Quest for Peace: Three Moral Traditions in Western Culture and History*. Princeton: Princeton University Press, 1987.

Krieder, Alan. "Military Service in the Church Orders." *JRE* 31 (2003): 415–42.

Kyle, Donald G. *Spectacles of Death in Ancient Rome*. London: Routledge, 1998.

Lake, Kirsopp, trans. *The Apostolic Fathers*. 2 vols. LCL. Cambridge, MA: Harvard University Press, 1930–52.

———. *Eusebius: The Ecclesiastical History*. 2 vols. LCL. Cambridge, MA: Harvard University Press, 1926.

Lebreton, Jules, and Jacques Zeiller. *The History of the Primitive Church*. Vol. 4, *The Church in the 3rd Century*. New York: Macmillan, 1949.

Lee, Umphrey. *The Historic Church and Modern Pacifism*. Nashville: Abingdon, 1993.

Leithart, Peter J. *Defending Constantine: The Twilight of an Empire and the Dawn of Christendom*. Downers Grove, IL: IVP Academic, 2010.

Lightfoot, J. B. *The Apostolic Fathers: Part II, S. Ignatius, S. Polycarp*. London: Macmillan, 1885.

MacMullen, Ramsay. *Soldier and Civilian in the Later Roman Empire*. Cambridge, MA: Harvard University Press, 1963.

Magie, David. *The Scriptores Historiae Augustae*. 3 vols. LCL. Cambridge, MA: Harvard University Press, 1921–32.

Maier, Paul L. *Eusebius: The Church History*. Grand Rapids: Kregel, 1999.

Marucchi, Orazio. *Christian Epigraphy: An Elementary Treatise*. Chicago: Ares, 1974.

McCracken, George E., trans. *Arnobius of Sicca: The Case against the Pagans*. 2 vols. ACW 7–8. Westminster, MD: Newman Press, 1949.

McDonald, Mary Francis. *Lactantius: The Divine Institutes, Books I–VII*. FC 49. Washington, DC: Catholic University of America Press, 1964.

Merton, Thomas. *Clement of Alexandria: Selections from the Protreptikos*. Norfolk, CT: New Directions, 1962.

Millar, Fergus. "Paul of Samosata, Zenobia and Aurelian: The Church, Local Culture and Political Allegiances in Third-Century Syria." *JRS* 61 (1971): 1–17.

———. *The Roman Near East, 31 BC–AD 336*. Cambridge, MA: Harvard University Press, 1993.

Musto, Ronald G. *The Catholic Peace Tradition*. Maryknoll, NY: Orbis, 1986.

Musurillo, Herbert. *The Acts of the Christian Martyrs*. New York: Oxford University Press, 1972.

Nersessian, Vref. *Treasures of the Ark: 1700 Years of Armenian Christian Art*. Los Angeles: J. Paul Getty Museum, 2001.

Norris, Frederick W. "Paul of Samosata: Procurator Decenarius." *JTS* 35 (1984): 50–70.

O'Donovan, Oliver, and Joan Lockwood O'Donovan, eds. *From Irenaeus to Grotius: A Sourcebook in Christian Political Thought*. Grand Rapids: Eerdmans, 1999.

Oulton, John Ernest Leonard, and Henry Chadwick, eds. and trans. *Alexandrian Christianity: Selected Translations of Clement and Origen*. LCC 2. Philadelphia: Westminster, 1954.

Patterson, L. G. *Methodius of Olympus: Divine Sovereignty, Human Freedom, and Life in Christ*. Washington, DC: Catholic University of America Press, 1997.

Payne, Keith B., and Karl I. Payne. *A Just Defense: The Use of Force, Nuclear Weapons, and Our Conscience*. Portland: Multnomah, 1987.

Pretty, Robert A., and Garry W. Trompf, ed. and trans. *Adamantius: Dialogue on the True Faith in God.* Leuven: Peeters, 1997.

Ramsay, W. M. *The Cities and Bishoprics of Phrygia.* 2 vols. Oxford: Clarendon, 1895–97.

Rankin, David. *Athenagoras: Philosopher and Theologian.* Burlington, VT: Ashgate, 2009.

Robert, Louis. *Noms indigènes dans l'Asie-Mineure greco-romaine.* Paris: A. Maisonneuve, 1963.

Ross, Steven K. *Roman Edessa: Politics and Culture on the Eastern Fringes of the Roman Empire, 114–242 CE.* London: Routledge, 2001.

Ruyter, Knut Willem. "Pacifism and Military Service in the Early Church." CC 32, no. 1 (1982): 54–70.

Segal, J. B. *Edessa: "The Blessed City."* Oxford: Clarendon, 1970.

Sider, Robert D. *Ancient Rhetoric and the Art of Tertullian.* Oxford: Oxford University Press, 1971.

———, ed. *Christians and Pagans in the Roman Empire: The Witness of Tertullian.* FC 2. Washington, DC: Catholic University of America Press, 2001.

Simmons, Michael Bland. *Arnobius of Sicca: Religious Conflict and Competition in the Age of Diocletian.* Oxford: Clarendon, 1995.

Smith, Joseph P., ed. and trans. *St. Irenaeus: Proof of the Apostolic Preaching.* ACW 16. New York: Newman Press, 1952.

Stassen, Glen H., and David P. Gushee. *Kingdom Ethics: Following Jesus in Contemporary Context.* Downers Grove, IL: IVP Academic, 2003.

Stewart-Sykes, Alistair. *Hippolytus: On the Apostolic Tradition.* Crestwood, NY: St. Vladimir's Seminary Press, 2001.

Swartley, Willard M., ed. *Essays on War and Peace: Bible and Early Church.* Occasional Papers 9. Elkhart, IN: Institute of Mennonite Studies, 1986.

Swift, Louis J. *The Early Fathers on War and Military Service.* FC 19. Wilmington, DE: Michael Glazier, 1983.

———. "War and the Christian Conscience I: The Early Years." ANRW 2.23.1 (1979): 835–68.

Tepper, Yotam, and Leah DiSegni. *A Christian Prayer Hall of the Third Century CE at Kefar 'Othnay (Legio).* Jerusalem: Israeli Antiquities Authority, 2006.

Thee, Francis C. R. *Julius Africanus and the Early Christian View of Magic.* Tübingen: Mohr, 1984.

Thomson, Robert W. "Mission, Conversion and Christianization: The Armenian Example." HUS 12, nos. 2–3 (1988–89): 27–45.

Tripolitis, Antonia. *Origen: A Critical Reading.* New York: Peter Lang, 1985.

Unger, Dominic J., ed. and trans. *St. Irenaeus of Lyons: Against the Heresies.* ACW 55. New York: Paulist Press, 1978.

Vieillefond, Jean-René. *Les "Cestes" de Julius Africanus.* CEHCP 20. Paris: Didier, 1970.

Vööbus, Arthur. *The Didascalia apostolorum in Syriac.* 2 vols. Louvain: Secrétariat du Corpus SCO, 1979.

Walker, G. S. M. *The Churchmanship of St. Cyprian.* ESH 9. Richmond: John Knox, 1969.

Waszink, J. H., and J. C. M. van Winden. *Tertullianus: De Idololatria.* Leiden: Brill, 1987.

Watson, G. R. *The Roman Soldier.* Ithaca, NY: Cornell University Press, 1969.

Weigel, George. *Tranquilitas Ordinis: The Present Failure and Future Promise of American Catholic Thought on War and Peace.* Oxford: Oxford University Press, 1987.

Windass, G. S. "The Early Christian Attitude Toward War." ITQ 24, no. 3 (1962): 235–48.

Wood, Simon P., ed. and trans. *Clement of Alexandria: Christ the Educator.* FC 23. New York: Fathers of the Church, 1954.

Wright, Donald F. "War in a Church-Historical Perspective." EQ 57, no. 2 (1985): 133–61.

Scripture Index

Old Testament

Genesis

2:7 56
9:25–26 96n147

Exodus

3:22 96
12:11 96
14:14 81
17:8 97

Leviticus

19:18 86, 98

Numbers

12:1 99
16:46 98

Deuteronomy

20:5–7 39, 182
20:10 40, 182
23:7 39
32:35 54, 86

Joshua

10:12–14 98

1 Samuel

24 98
26 98

Psalms

45:2 52
45:3 52, 55
45:4 52
101:8 75
137 75

Proverbs

21:1 28

Isaiah

2 175
2:2–3 53
2:2–4 23, 173
2:3 27
2:3–4 25, 28, 46, 97, 97n147, 173
2:4 53, 95, 173
8:4 56
11:1–9 30n21
11:6–7 29
52:7 53, 97
53:7 48
66:5 53

Jeremiah

1:5 56, 166
38:6 98

Micah

4:1–4 23, 25, 173
4:1–7 23, 26
4:2 27
4:2–3 28

Zephaniah

3:8 86

Zechariah

7:10 54
8:17 54

New Testament

Matthew

4:9 28
5:21–48 28
5:22 24
5:38 30
5:38–48 172
5:39 48, 69, 99
5:39–40 40

5:39–48 19
5:40 38
5:43–48 84
5:44 24, 45n52, 98, 99
5:44–45 31, 40, 83, 86
6:34 36
7:2 99
7:23 98
8:12 98
10:9 96
10:29–30 81
10:33 99
13:42 98
13:50 98
18:19 80
22:17–21 24
22:21 38
25:28–30 97
26:52 60, 70
39–41 24

Luke

1:41–45 56, 166n20
3:14 38
6:31 55
6:32 85

6:35–36 26
9:51–56 47
10:4 69
12:46 97, 97n147
14:34–35 81
17:3–4 38
22:49–51 48

John

14:27 70
16:33 81
18:10–11 48

Acts

10:36 96
15:28–29 57

Romans

3:4 29
8:38–39 40
10:15 53
12:14 24
12:17 48
12:19 70
13:1 29

13:1–2 79
13:4 27

1 Corinthians

3:2–3 95
6:7 70
9:11 70

Ephesians

2:3 83
4:8 55
4:26 98
6:11 70
6:14–17 35, 52

Philippians

4:13 81

1 Timothy

2:1–2 82

Revelation

1:16 52

Index of Ancient Sources
and Early Christian Writings

New Testament Apocrypha and Pseudepigrapha

Acts of Xanthippe and Polyxena

25 133
39 133

Apocalypse of Peter

8 22, 165n15
9 166n22

Gospel of Pseudo-Matthew

28–29 130
38 130

Infancy Gospel of Thomas

3:2 130
3:3 168n35
4:1 130, 168n35
5:1 130
13:1 130
13:2 131, 168n35

Classical Works and Authors

1 Clement

37 21, 180n113

2 Clement

13 21, 171n59, 172

Adamantius

Dialogue on the True Faith

1.9 95–96
1.10 96–97, 173n72, 184
1.11 97–98
1.12 98
1.13 98–99
1.14 99
1.15 99
1.16 99–100
4.9 100
4.9–10 95
4.10 100, 166n26, 167n27

Archelaeus

Acts of the Disputation with the Heresiarch Manes

1 92
2 92–93, 168n34, 169n45

Arnobius of Sicca

Against the Pagans

1.6 101–2, 168n34, 170n46
1.63 102
1.64 102
2.1 102, 168n34

3.26 102–3
4.36 103
4.37 103

Athenagoras

A Plea for the Christians

1 30–31, 171n59, 172n66
11 30, 31, 171n59, 172n66
35 31–32, 165n15, 166n21,
   166n23, 168n34, 169n36

Cassius Dio

Roman History

72 142–43

Clement of Alexandria

The Educator

1.7 34, 36
1.8 34
1.11 179n102
1.12 36, 179n103
2.4 36–37
2.10 37, 165n15
2.12 33, 37, 182n125, 183n132
2.12–13 33
2.13 37–38, 182n126
3.3 38
3.12 33, 38, 171n59, 182n127,
   183n134

Exhortation to the Greeks

3 34
4 33, 179n101, 183n130
10 33, 35, 171n59, 179n106,
    182
11 33, 35–36, 183n130

Miscellanies

1.23 38–39
1.24 39
2.18 33, 39–40
4.8 33, 40, 171n59, 172n67,
    179n105, 183n132,
    183n133
4.14 33, 40, 179n106, 183n134

Prophetic Eclogues

48 41
48–50 165n15
49 41
50 41

*Who Is the Rich Man That
Shall Be Saved?*

34 41, 179n104

Cyprian

To Demetrian

16 86
17 86
20 86–87

To Donatus

6 85, 168n34
6–7 84
7 85, 168n34

On the Dress of Virgins

11 86

To Fortunatus

13 90

On the Good of Patience

14 84, 87, 168n34, 169n42
16 87, 171n59

Letters

8 [10] 84, 88, 180n114
24 [28] 84, 88
25 [31] 84, 88–89
33 [39] 84, 89, 90n136
55 [58] 84, 89, 168n34,
    169n43
56 [60] 84, 89–90, 168n34,
    169n44, 180n115, 181n118

*Testimonies against the
Jews*

3.49 84, 85–86, 171n59
3.106 86

Didache

1 19, 172
1:2 171n59
2 19, 165n15, 165n16, 172

Didascalia apostolorum

3 65, 165n15
18 65

Epistle of Barnabas

19 20, 165n15, 166n17

Eusebius

Ecclesiastical History

3.25 129, 130n1
5.5 139–40
6.34 162n33
6.42 159–60
7.11 91
7.15 152
7.29–30 131
8.1 160
8.4 160
8.9 160
8.11 160–61
9.8 161
9.8.2 162
9.8.4 162

Gregory Thaumaturgus

6 90–91
7 91

Historia Augusta

24 144

Homer

Iliad

2.872 38

Irenaeus

Against Heresies

1.20 129, 130n1
2.32 27–28, 171n59, 172n65,
    181n120
3.18 28n16, 171n59
4.13 28n16, 171n59
4.34 27, 28, 173n72, 174n75,
    181n121
4.36 27
5.24 27, 28–29, 181n119

*Proof of the Apostolic
Preaching*

59–61 30n21
61 29, 30n21, 173n72, 174n76,
    182n122
86–100 27
96 29–30

Julius Africanus

Kestoi

7 66–67

Justin Martyr

Dialogue with Trypho

85 24n8, 25, 171n59, 172n63
96 25–26, 171n59, 172n63
109 23
110 23, 26, 172n64, 173n72,
    174n74, 178n100

First Apology

14 172n61
14–16 171n59
14–17 24
14–20 23
16 172n62

30–53 23
39 173n72, 173n73

Second Apology
4 25

Lactantius

On the Anger of God
17 104, 114

On the Death of the Persecutors
10 111–12
11 112
44 112, 171n56
44–48 104
46 113
46–48 171n56
47 113
48 113–14
52 114, 171n56

Divine Institutes
1 173n71
1.18 104–5, 168n34, 170n47, 180n108
3.18 105–6, 168n34, 170n47, 170n51, 170n54
5 104
5.8 106, 170n55, 180n109
5.8–10 168n34, 170n47
5.9 106, 170n48
5.10 106–7, 170n49, 171n59, 180n108
5.17 107
5.18 107–8, 168n34, 170n47, 170n50
5.23 108
6.4 108, 181n116
6.5 108
6.6 109, 168n34, 170n47, 170n53
6.9 109
6.18 109–10, 170n52
6.20 104, 106, 110–11, 167n31, 168n34, 170n47, 171n56, 176n88, 177n94
7 104
7.20 107n162, 166n26
10 173n71

Epitome of the Divine Institutes
63 115
63–64 104
64 115, 167n32

Martyrdom of Marinus
7.15 152–53

Methodius

On Free Will
167n27

Minucius Felix

Octavius
30 63, 64, 165n15, 166n25, 168n34, 169n40

Origen

Against Celsus
1.1 68, 71, 183n140
2.30 68, 69, 72, 177n90, 179n107, 183n141, 184n146, 184n147, 184n148, 184n152
3.7 68, 72, 168n34, 169n41, 184n150
3.8 68, 69, 73, 177n90
4.9 68, 73, 183n142, 184n146, 184n148
4.82 68, 73, 184n143
4.83 68, 73–74, 184n145
5.33 68, 74, 173n72, 174n79, 176n82, 177n91, 184n147, 184n148
7.18 74
7.19 75
7.20 75
7.22 75–76
7.26 68, 69, 76–77, 166n26, 167n30, 184n144, 184n146, 184n147
7.58 77
7.58–61 171n59
7.59 77–78
7.61 78

8.26 177n91, 184n148
8.35 68, 69, 78–79, 171n59, 177n90, 184n148
8.55 79
8.65 68, 71, 79–80
8.68 80
8.69 80–81
8.70 68, 81–82, 176n83, 184n149
8.73 68, 82, 168n34, 176n84, 176n86, 177n92, 184n148, 184n151
8.74 82
8.75 83
61 77
65–75 79
69 79
70 79

Commentary on 1 Corinthians
9:11 70–71

Commentary on John
20.106–7 83n122
20.141–48 83n122
20.290 83
20.292 83

Commentary on Matthew
5:38–48 67
26:52 70

Homilies on Joshua
15 69–70

On the Principles
4.18 69

Pontius

Life of Cyprian
9 84

Tatian

Address to the Greeks
11 26

Tertullian

Against the Jews

3 46, 173n72, 174n77

Against Marcion

1.23 47n58
3.14 52
3.21 53, 174n78
3.22 53
4.16 53–55, 171n59
5.18 55–56
21 173n72

Apology

4 43
5 138–39
6 43
7 42n45
9 43–44, 165n15, 166n24
16 43–44
25 44–45
30 45
31 45, 45n52, 171n59
37 42, 45, 171n59, 172n68
42 42, 45–46
46 46

Crown

1 58–59, 120
2 59–60
3–4 59
5–6 59
7 59
9 60

10 60
11 60–62
12–13 60
13 62

Exhortation to Chastity

12 62, 165n15, 166n18

On Flight in Persecution

8 62
13 62–63

On Idolatry

17 49, 166n26, 167n28
18 49–50
19 43, 50–51, 120, 166n26,
    167n29, 175n80, 175n81,
    183n137

On Modesty

12 57, 168n34, 169n39

On Patience

3 47–48, 168n34, 169n38
4 183n137
6 48, 171n59
8 48, 171n59
10 48–49

On the Resurrection of the Dead

16 51–52, 183n135

To Scapula

1 63, 171n59
4 139

On the Soul

26 56
26–27 165n15
27 56, 166n19
35 47n58
37 56–57, 165n15

On the Spectacles

2 47, 168n34, 169n37, 173n70
16 47, 171n59, 173n69

Church Orders and Synods

Apostolic Constitutions

8 123

Apostolic Tradition

15 120, 121
16 120, 121, 166n26, 168n33,
    168n34, 171n57, 171n58,
    177n89

Canons of Hipploytus

13 123
13–14 171n58
14 123

Synod of Arles

3 125

Author Index

Adler, William, 65, 66
Arbesmann, Rudolph, 43, 45n53, 49n62, 64
Arner, Rob, 15n6, 157, 172n60
Arpee, Leon, 162n33

Bainton, Roland H., 13n2, 57, 124, 131, 145, 146, 161, 163n2, 178n97
Baldovin, John F., 121
Barkley, Gary Wayne, 68
Barnard, Leslie W., 23, 24, 32n24
Barnard, P. Mordaunt, 93n144
Barnes, Timothy David, 43, 138
Becatti, Giovanni, 144n10
Bethune-Baker, J. F., 43
Bobertz, C. A., 84
Bonnet, Max, 133
Bowan, Anthony, 104, 107n161, 108n163, 108n164, 110n170
Bradshaw, Paul F., 64, 119, 120, 121, 122
Bremmer, Jan N., 22
Brennecke, Hanns Christof, 68, 153n23, 159, 177n95, 195n194
Brent, Allen, 84, 119, 121
Brock, Peter, 13n1, 153, 162, 178, 194n192
Bruce, Barbara J., 70
Buell, Denise Kimber, 41n43
Burns, J. Patout, 21, 120

Cadoux, Cecil John, 13n2, 23, 68, 148, 189n170
Calder, W., 149n19, 150, 150n21
Cary, Ernest, 143n7
Caspary, Gerard E., 184n153
Cerrato, J., 121
Chadwick, Henry, 33, 68, 121
Charles, J. Daryl, 72

Chartrand-Burke, Tony, 129, 131n2
Clarke, G., 84, 88n132, 89, 90
Connolly, R., 64
Crehan, Joseph Hugh, 30, 32n24
Crouzel, Henri, 162n33
Czachesz, Istvan, 22

Daly, Emily Joseph, 43, 45n53, 49n62, 64
Daly, Robert J., 21, 120, 129, 164n7, 191n175
Davies, R. W., 193n185
Deferrari, Roy J., 84, 85n123
DiSegni, Leah, 144, 146, 150, 151n22
Dix, Gregory, 121
Dörries, Hermann, 124
Dunn, Geoffrey D., 43

Ehrman, Bart D., 21
Elliott, J., 130
Evans, Ernest, 43

Falls, Thomas B., 24
Ferguson, Everett, 33, 172n60

Garnsey, Peter, 104, 107n161, 108n163, 108n164, 110n170
Gero, Stephen, 43
Glimm, Francis X., 20
Glover, T. R., 64
Goodspeed, Edgar J., 27, 30
Gorman, Jill, 133
Gorman, Michael J., 15n6, 19, 30, 37n32, 41n43, 56, 64
Grant, Robert M., 19
Gushee, David P., 69

Heather, Peter, and John Matthews, 90, 91n138
Heine, Ronald E., 83n122
Helgeland, John, 13n2, 21, 33n25, 34, 42n45,
    44, 45n53, 50n65, 60, 66, 68, 69, 73, 87, 101,
    107n162, 111n171, 120, 121n2, 124, 130,
    137n1, 139, 144, 145, 146, 150, 164, 176n85,
    180n112, 182n124, 183n139, 190n172,
    193n188
Hennecke, Edgar, 21n5, 22, 22n7, 41n42, 129
Holmes, Dennis, 64
Holmes, Michael W., 19, 20n3, 21n5
Hornus, Jean-Michel, 146, 148
Hort, F. J. A., 93n142
Hunter, David G., 13n2, 165n12, 192n180

Ingremeau, Christiane, 110

James, M. R., 133
Jefford, Clayton N., 19
Jenkins, Claude, 71n98, 161
Johnson, James Turner, 33, 34, 138, 164n9, 178,
    182n123, 193n188
Johnson, Maxwell E., 119, 120, 121, 122
Junod, Eric, 133

Krieder, Alan, 165n14
Kyle, Donald G., 15n7, 47

Lebreton, Jules, 190n174
Leithart, Peter J., 81, 163n1, 164, 188n167,
    193n188
Lightfoot, J., 138n2, 139, 140, 143n8

MacMullen, Ramsay, 193n187
Magie, David, 143, 144
Maier, Paul L., 159
Marique, Joseph M. F., 20
Marucchi, Orazio, 148
McCracken, George E., 101, 103n155
McDonald, Mary Francis, 104, 106n159, 110n170
Merton, Thomas, 36n28
Migne, J.-P., 70n97
Mikhailov, Georgius, 149n16
Millar, Fergus, 131, 162
Musto, Ronald G., 193n189
Musurillo, Herbert, 152, 153, 155, 156n25, 157,
    158n26

Norris, Frederick W., 131

O'Donovan, Joan Lockwood, 164n8, 193n189
O'Donovan, Oliver, 164n8, 193n189
Oulton, John Ernest Leonard, 33

Patterson, L., 100n149
Payne, Karl I., 191n175
Payne, Keith B., 191n175
Phillips, L. Edward, 119, 120, 121, 122
Pretty, Robert A., 93, 93n145, 94n146, 96n147,
    100n148, 100n150

Quain, Edwin A., 43, 45n53, 49n62, 64

Ramsay, William, 146, 149n18
Rankin, David, 30
Rendall, Gerald H., 64
Robert, Jeanne, 146
Robert, Louis, 146, 149n17
Ross, Steven K., 162

Segal, J. B., 161
Sider, Robert D., 43, 58, 60
Simmons, Michael Bland, 101
Smith, Joseph P., 27, 29n20
Stassen, Glen H., 69
Swift, Louis J., 21, 24, 34, 43, 51, 84, 86,
    90n137, 121, 138, 138n2, 178n98, 180n110,
    181n117, 183n136, 193n189

Tepper, Yotam, 144, 146, 150, 151n22
Thee, Francis C., 65
Thomson, Robert W., 162
Tripolitis, Antonia, 68
Trompf, G. W., 94n146

Unger, Dominic J., 27

Vaillant, A., 100n149
van de Sande Bakhuyzen, W. H., 93n144
van Winden, J. C. M., 43, 51n68
von Harnack, Adolf, 13n2, 34, 58, 93n141,
    93n145, 111, 124, 138n2, 140, 153, 180n111,
    194n191
Vieillefond, Jean-René, 65, 66, 67n94
Vööbus, Arthur, 64

Walker, G. S. M., 84
Walsh, Gerald G., 20
Waszink, J. H., 43, 51n68
Watson, G. R., 120, 193n186
Weigel, George, 13n4
Windass, G. S., 70n97, 71
Wood, Simon P., 34, 38n35

Zeiller, Jacques, 190n174

Subject Index

Abgar of Edessa, 161
abortion
  Apocalypse of Peter on, 22, 166
  Apology on, 44
  Clement on, 33, 166
  Didache on, 19, 165
  Didascalia apostolorum on, 64–65
  Educator on, 37
  Epistle of Barnabas on, 20
  Exhortation to Chastity on, 62
  Octavius on, 63, 64
  Plea for the Christians on, 30, 32
  Prophetic Eclogues on, 41, 166
  On the Soul on, 56–57, 166
  summary view of, 165–66
  Tertullian on, 166
  See also infanticide
Acts of Marcellus, 155–56
Acts of Maximilian, 153–55
*Acts of the Disputation with the Heresiarch
    Manes*, 92–93, 168, 169
Acts of Xanthippe and Polyxena, 132–33
Adamantius, 93, 184
Address to the Greeks, 26
adultery
  Against Heresies on, 28
  Dialogue on the True Faith on, 95, 100
  Didache on, 19
  Exhortation to the Greeks on, 35
  On Modesty on, 57
Against Celsus, 68, 69, 71–83, 166–69, 171, 173,
    174, 176, 177, 179, 183, 184
Against Heresies, 27–29, 129, 130, 171–74, 181
Against Marcion, 47, 52–56, 171, 173, 174
Against the Jews, 46, 173, 174

Against the Pagans, 101–3, 168, 170
Alexander Severus, 65
Alexandria, 20, 30, 32, 67, 91
ambition, 26
Ambrosius, 67
anger
  Against Heresies on, 28
  On the Anger of God on, 104, 114
  Educator on, 38
  First Apology on, 24
  On Patience on, 48
Antioch, 131
Antoninus Pius, 23
Apocalypse of Peter, 22, 165, 166
Apollinarius, 137
Apology, 42–46, 138–39, 165, 166, 171, 172
Apostolic Constitutions, 123
Apostolic Tradition, 119–21, 120, 121, 166, 168,
    171, 177
Archelaus, 92
Arnobius of Sicca, 101, 169–70
atheism, 30–31
Athenagoras, 30, 172
Aurelii brothers, 149
Aurelius Manos, 149
Aurelius Posidonius, 148–49

blood, spilling
  Against Celsus on, 82
  Against the Pagans on, 101
  Divine Institutes on, 106–7, 111
  Educator on, 38
  On the Good of Patience on, 87
  On Modesty on, 57

Caesarea, 67
cannibalism
   Plea for the Christians on, 30, 31–32
Canons of Hipploytus, 123, 171
capital punishment
   Against Celsus on, 76–77, 167
   On the Anger of God on, 104, 114
   Apostolic Tradition on, 120, 121, 167–68
   Dialogue on the True Faith on, 94, 95
   Divine Institutes on, 167
   On Idolatry on, 50–51, 167
   summary view of, 166–68
Carthage, 42, 58
charity, law of, 27, 29–30, 46–47, 48, 54–55
cheek, turning the other
   Against Celsus on, 77–78
   Against Heresies on, 28
   Clement on, 33
   Didache on, 19
   Exhortation to the Greeks on, 35
   First Apology on, 24
   On Patience on, 48
   Plea for the Christians on, 31
   On the Principles on, 69
child-murder. *See* infanticide
Christianity
   Against Celsus on, 72–73
   Against the Jews on, 46
   Exhortation to the Greeks on, 32
Christian life
   Apology on, 42, 43–46
   Divine Institutes on, 104, 106–8
   Educator on, 32, 37–38
   On Flight in Persecution on, 62–63
   Miscellanies on, 32–33
Cicero, 109
Clement, 20
Clement of Alexandria, 32, 166, 172, 178–79,
   182–83, 185
Commentary on 1 Corinthians, 70–71
Commentary on John, 83
Commentary on Matthew, 67, 70
conception
   Prophetic Eclogues on, 41
   On the Soul on, 56–57
Constantine, 104, 112, 124
conversion, during military service, 34, 35
Corinth, 20
Crown, 58–62, 120
cursing, Jesus's, 129–31
Cyprian, 83–84, 169, 181

Decius, 84
Dialogue on the True Faith, 95–100, 166, 167,
   173, 184
Dialogue with Trypho, 23–26, 171–74, 178
Didache, 19, 165, 171, 172
Didascalia apostolorum, 65, 165
Dio (Cassius Dio Cocceianus), 142–43
Diocletian, 101, 103–4, 111–14
Dionysius of Alexandria, 91, 186
Divine Institutes, 104–11, 166–68, 170, 171,
   173, 176, 177, 180, 181

earthly rule, submission to. *See* government,
   submission to
Ecclesiastical History, 91, 129–31, 139–40, 152,
   159–62
Educator, The, 33, 34, 36–38, 165, 171, 179,
   182, 183
embryos
   Prophetic Eclogues on, 41
   On the Soul on, 56–57
enemies, loving your
   Against Celsus on, 68, 78–79
   Against Heresies on, 27–28, 172
   Against Marcion on, 53–55
   Apology on, 172
   Commentary on John on, 83
   Dialogue on the True Faith on, 98
   Dialogue with Trypho on, 23, 25–26, 172
   Didache on, 172
   Divine Institutes on, 173
   First Apology on, 24, 172
   Miscellanies on, 172
   On Patience on, 42, 48
   Plea for the Christians on, 30, 31
   To Scapula on, 63
   Second Clement on, 21
   On the Spectacles on, 47, 173
   summary view of, 171–73
   Testimonies Against the Jews on, 84, 85–86
Epistle of Barnabas, 20, 165, 166
Epitome of the Divine Institutes, 104, 115, 167
Eusebius of Caesarea, 27, 131, 139–40, 159–62,
   187
Exhortation to Chastity, 62, 165, 166
Exhortation to the Greeks, 33–36, 171, 179,
   182, 183
exodus from Israel, 96n147
exposure, child. *See* infanticide

false witness, bearing, 35
First Apology, 23, 24, 171–73
First Clement, 21, 180

forgiveness, 38
fornication, 26

gladiator contests
   Apostolic Tradition on, 120, 121
   Divine Institutes on, 110–11
   To Donatus on, 84, 85
   Plea for the Christians on, 30, 31–32
   On the Spectacles on, 47
gnosticism, 93–100
God
   gnostic debate on, 93–100
   as military commander, 20, 21, 34, 35
   as warrior, 52, 55–56
Gospel law, and Mosaic law, 74–76, 94–96, 99,
   169, 174
Gospel of Pseudo-Matthew, 130
government, submission to
   Against Celsus on, 71, 76–77
   Against Heresies on, 27, 28–29
   Educator on, 38
   Exhortation to the Greeks on, 34, 35
   First Apology on, 24
   On Idolatry on, 49–51
   See also military service, Christian
Greek gods, 34
Gregory Thaumaturgus, 90

hatred, 47
hell, 22
heretical beliefs
   Against Heresies on, 27–29
   Against Marcion on, 43
   Paul of Samosata, 131–32
   Historia Augusta, 143–44
   Homilies on Joshua, 69–70
hypocrisy, 21

idolatry
   Apology on, 44
   Commentary on 1 Corinthians on, 68, 70–71
   Crown on, 58–62
   On Idolatry on, 49–51, 192
   and military service, 43, 49–51, 165, 191
   On Modesty on, 57
Iliad, 38
incest, 30, 32
Infancy Gospel of Thomas, 129–31, 130, 131,
   168
infanticide
   Apocalypse of Peter on, 22
   Apology on, 44

Didache on, 19
Didascalia apostolorum on, 65
Educator on, 37
Epistle of Barnabas on, 20
Octavius on, 64
Plea for the Christians on, 30, 32
   See also abortion
infidelity, 22
Irenaeus, 27, 174, 181–82

Jesus
   as child in *Infancy Gospel of Thomas*, 129–31
   as instructor/teacher, 36
   letter of Abgar of Edessa to, 161
   visibility of, 72–73
   as warrior, 52
John the Baptist, 33
Julius Africanus, 65, 161
justice, 104, 106–10
Justin Martyr, 23, 26, 172, 173–74, 178
Just War tradition, 33, 182–83, 185, 191–92

Kestoi, 66–67
killing
   Against Celsus on, 82, 169
   Apology on, 42
   The Canons of Hippolytus on, 122, 123
   Dialogue on the True Faith on, 94
   Divine Institutes on, 104–6, 110–11, 170–71
   Exhortation to the Greeks on, 34, 35
   On the Good of Patience on, 87, 169
   Gregory Thaumaturgus on, 90–91
   Infancy Gospel of Thomas on, 129–31
   Letters of Cyprian on, 84, 88–90, 169
   Octavius on, 63, 64
   Plea for the Christians on, 30–32, 168–69
   Proof of the Apostolic Preaching on, 29–30
   On the Spectacles on, 47, 169
   summary view of, 168–71
   Synod of Arles on, 124–25

Lactantius, 103–4, 167, 170–71, 176, 177, 179–
   80, 180–81, 190–91
law, Mosaic, 34–35, 39, 74–76, 81, 95–96, 99,
   174
law, Roman, 23, 27, 44, 47, 63, 71, 157
law of charity, 27, 29–30, 46–47, 48, 54–55
leadership, 39
Letters of Cyprian, 84, 88–90, 168, 169, 180,
   181
Licinias, 104, 113–14
Life of Cyprian, 84

love
    Dialogue on the True Faith on, 94
    Miscellanies on, 39–40
    On Patience on, 48
    To Scapula on, 63
Lyons, 27

manliness, 39–40
manslaughter, 84
Marcus Aurelius Antoninus, 137–44
Marcus Julius Eugenius, 149–50
Martin of Tours, Saint, 124–25
Martyrdom of Julius the Veteran, 157–58, 187,
    193
Martyrdom of Marinus, 152–53, 152–53, 187
Mesopotamia, 26
Methodius, 93, 100n149
military imagery
    in Cyprian's works, 84, 88–89, 180
    in *Divine Institutes*, 108–9, 180–81
    in *First Clement*, 20, 21, 180, 181
    summary view of, 180–81
military service, Christian
    Against Celsus on, 67–68, 79–81, 176, 177,
        183–84, 186
    Against Heresies on, 181–82
    ambiguous texts on, 181–85
    Apology on, 42, 44, 138–39, 185–86
    Apostolic Constitutions on, 122, 123
    Apostolic Tradition on, 120, 121, 124, 177,
        191–92
    Archelaus on, 92–93
    The Canons of Hippolytus on, 122, 123
    Clement on, 33
    Crown on, 58–62, 175, 186, 192
    On the Death of the Persecutors on, 104,
        111–14
    Dialogue on the True Faith on, 184
    Dialogue with Trypho on, 178
    Dionysius of Alexandria on, 91
    Divine Institutes on, 104, 110–11, 176, 177,
        179–80
    Ecclesiastical History on, 139–40, 159–62, 187
    Educator on, 33, 37–38, 179, 182
    epitaphs and inscriptions on graves, 145–51
    Exhortation to the Greeks on, 33, 34, 35,
        178–79, 182–83
    Historia Augusta on, 143–44
    and idolatry, 43, 165
    On Idolatry on, 43, 49–51, 175
    Letters of Cyprian on, 84, 88–90
    military martyrs, 151–59
    Miscellanies on, 39, 40, 182

Origen on, 183–84
prayer hall near military camp, 144–45
pre-Constantine evidence of, 185–88
On the Resurrection of the Dead on, 51–52,
    183
Roman History on, 142–43
To Scapula on, 139
summary view of, 163–65, 175–80
Synod of Arles on, 124–25
Tertullian on, 43
The Testament of the Lord on, 122, 123
Twelfth Legion victory at Danube, 137–44
See also government, submission to
Minucius Felix, 63
Miscellanies, 33, 38–40, 171, 172, 179, 183
Montanism, 43
Mosaic law, 34–35, 39, 74–76, 81, 95–96, 99
Moses, 39
murder
    Against Heresies on, 28
    Didache on, 19
    On the Dress of Virgins on, 86
    First Apology on, 23, 24–25
    Octavius on, 63
    Plea for the Christians on, 30–32
    On the Spectacles on, 47

neighbor, loving your
    Against Heresies on, 28
    Didache on, 19
    Miscellanies on, 39–40
    Proof of the Apostolic Preaching on, 30

obedience
    Exhortation to the Greeks on, 35–36
    First Clement on, 21
Octavius, 64, 165, 166, 168, 169
On Flight in Persecution, 62–63
On Free Will, 167
On Idolatry, 43, 49–51, 120, 166, 167, 175, 183
On Modesty, 57, 168, 169
On Patience, 47–49, 168, 169, 171, 183
On the Anger of God, 104, 114
On the Death of the Persecutors, 104, 111–14,
    171
On the Dress of Virgins, 86
On the Good of Patience, 84, 87, 168, 169, 171
On the Principles, 69
On the Resurrection of the Dead, 51–52, 183
On the Soul, 47, 56–57, 165, 166
On the Spectacles, 47, 168, 169, 171, 173
Origen, 32, 65, 67–68, 167, 169, 173, 174, 176,
    179, 183–84, 186, 190–92

pacifism
  Against Celsus on, 74–76
  Against Heresies on, 27–29
  Against the Pagans on, 101–3
  Apology on, 42
  Clement on, 33
  Dialogue with Trypho on, 23, 25–26
  Educator on, 36–37
  Exhortation to the Greeks on, 33
  First Apology on, 23, 24–25
  Homilies on Joshua on, 69–70
  summary view of, 163–65
Pantaenus, 32
patience, 24
Paul of Samosata, 131–32
pedophilia, 35
persecution
  Against the Pagans on, 103
  To Demetrian on, 86
  On Flight in Persecution on, 62–63
pillaging, 96–97, 96n147
Plato, 23, 77
A Plea for the Christians, 30–32, 165, 166, 168, 169, 171, 172
poisoning, 66–67
Polycarp of Smyrna, 27
progressive revelation, 94, 95
Proof of the Apostolic Preaching, 27, 29–30, 173, 174, 182
prophecies of peace
  Against Celsus on, 174
  Against Heresies on, 28, 174
  Against the Jews on, 174
  Dialogue with Trypho on, 23, 25–26, 174
  First Apology on, 23, 24–25, 173
  Proof of the Apostolic Preaching on, 174
  summary view of, 173–75
Prophetic Eclogues, 41, 165
Prosenes, 148
public office
  Against Celsus on, 67–68, 83
  The Canons of Hippolytus on, 122, 123
  The Testament of the Lord on, 122, 123
punishment
  On the Anger of God on, 104, 114
  Apocalypse of Peter on, 22
  Dialogue on the True Faith on, 94, 100
  Prophetic Eclogues on, 41

repentance
  Against Heresies on, 28
  Second Clement on, 21

revenge
  Against Celsus on, 77–78
  Against Marcion on, 53–55
  Against the Jews on, 46
  Apology on, 45
  Dialogue on the True Faith on, 94, 99
  On Patience on, 48
  Proof of the Apostolic Preaching on, 30
  Testimonies Against the Jews on, 84, 85–86
Roman gods, 44–45
Roman History, 142–43
Roman History (Dio), 142–43
Rome and Roman law, 23, 27, 44, 47, 63, 71, 157

salvation, 35
Samaria, 23
scriptural interpretation, 69
Scythians, 71
Second Apology, 25
Second Clement, 21, 171, 172
Septimus Severus, 58
simplicity, in living, 36
soul, introduction of the
  Prophetic Eclogues on, 41
  On the Resurrection of the Dead on, 51–52
  On the Soul on, 56–57
stealing
  Exhortation to the Greeks on, 35
  Miscellanies on, 38–39
suicide, 25
Synod of Arles, 124–25

Tatian, 26
Tertullian, 42, 138–39, 166, 167, 169, 172–73, 174, 175, 177, 183, 185–86, 190–92
Testimonies against the Jews, 84–86, 171
To Demetrian, 86–87
To Donatus, 84, 85, 168
To Fortunatus, 90
To Scapula, 63, 139, 171
traitors, 90–91
Trajan, 47
Twelfth Legion victory at Danube, 137–44, 185
tyranny, 131–32

unity of Christian church, 20–21

violence
  Against Celsus on, 74–76
  On Patience on, 48
  See also blood, spilling

war
  in *Acts of Xanthippe and Polyxena*, 133
  Against Celsus on, 68, 73–76, 79–81
  Against Heresies on, 27–29
  Against Marcion on, 53
  Against the Jews on, 46
  Against the Pagans on, 101–3
  Apology on, 42
  Clement on, 33
  Commentary on Matthew on, 70
  To Demetrian on, 86–87
  Dialogue on the True Faith on, 94, 98–99
  Dialogue with Trypho on, 23, 25–26
  To Donatus on, 84, 85
  Exhortation to the Greeks on, 33
  First Clement on, 20–21
  Homilies on Joshua on, 69–70
  Kestoi on, 65–67
  Miscellanies on, 33
  Proof of the Apostolic Preaching on, 27, 29–30
  On the Resurrection of the Dead on, 51–52
  summary view of, 163–65, 168–71
way of life/way of death, 19
way of light/way of darkness, 20
Who Is the Rich Man That Shall Be Saved? 41,
  179